MW01104420

Abraham's People

A Kenyan Dynasty

BY JANE CLARE BARSBY

Abraham's People is based loosely on the story of the life of Abraham Lazarus Block and draws on a range of information to include his own memoirs, those of his sister, Lily Haller, and his grand-daughter, Ora Hirshfeld. The book also draws on the research and publications of Errol Trzebinski. In the interests of providing a historical biographical novel rather than a dry recitation of facts, considerable liberties have been taken with dates and characters (in particular that of Major Ringer, who actually left Kenya in 1910 and died in 1912). Footnotes indicate those instances where such liberties have been taken.

Abraham Lazarus Block, 1883-1965

III

Copyright © Jane Barsby

ISBN: 978-9966-065-29-2

The Author asserts the moral right to be identified as the author of this work.

Design and layout by MJS, Nairobi

Printed and bound in UK.

All rights reserved. No part of this publication may be reproduced, stored in a retrieval system, or transmitted, in any form or by any means, electronic, mechanical, photocopying, recording or otherwise, without the prior permission of the publishers and author.

ACKNOWLEDGEMENTS

My thanks to Jeremy Block, Ora Lesham, Ruth Rabb, Errol Trzebinski, Jonathan Barsby, Jonathan Block, Geraldine Dunford, Theo Hirshfeld, Shel Arensen, Stephen Mills, Brian Stutchbury, James Willson and Michael Tremlett.

UNDER HIS WINGS

O thou that dwellest in the covert of the Most High, and abidest in the shadow of the Almighty;
I will say of the Lord, who is my refuge and my fortress, my God, in whom I trust,
That He will deliver thee from the snare of the fowler, and from the noisome pestilence.
He will cover thee with His pinions, and under His wings shalt thou take refuge.

–Psalm 91, The Old Testatment

I T HAD BEEN RAINING AND the trees dripped on the mourners as they wound their way through the headstones in Nairobi's Jewish Cemetery. There were no pathways and the thick red mud caked their shoes. The sun had come out and it blazed down from a pale blue sky.

The ground steamed.

A gaping red hole lay in a patch of green grass; a pile of turf neatly stacked to one side; and planks had been laid to either side of the grave. The earth was red and the tree roots showed bone-white where the shovels had sliced through them.

The mourners formed a corridor, through which the coffin was carried; the family followed in its wake. The men wore yarmulkes; some of the women were veiled. There was complete silence as the procession made its way to the graveside; but a pair of ibis flew shrieking overhead, and the black kites keened.

The rabbi began to speak and the ancient words of the kaddish[1] floated up into the branches of the trees, through them, and away into the white ether beyond. The ebb and flow of Psalm 91 washed over the pale grey tombstones and through the black-clad figures. When all had been said, the coffin containing the mortal remains of Abraham Lazarus Block was lowered, straining on its heavy ropes, into the ground.

One by one the Block family stepped forward to shovel earth on to his coffin. It was the iron red earth of Africa and it was heavy and still wet; small stones rolled across the polished wood.

A woman stepped forward; she unpinned a small bunch of blue-green leaves from her lapel, and threw them down into the grave.

A boy stood with his father in the family group. He watched the woman and he tugged on his father's hand. The man bent to hear his whispered words.

'What did the lady throw into Grandpa's grave?'

'Rue. It's a herb,' said his father.

'Why?'

'Rue is the national flower of Lithuania,' said his father, 'your grandfather was born there.'

The man straightened and the boy fell into silence.

There were hundreds of mourners and it took time for each of them to approach the grave, pick up the shovel and empty it three times on to the coffin below.

The family remained still and silent throughout.

As they walked away, some of the mourners offered them the traditional words of comfort
'Hamakom y'nachem etkhem b'tokh sha'ar avelei tziyon viyrushalayim,' they said.
'The Omnipresent will comfort you among the mourners of Zion and Jerusalem.'
But the family, as was the custom, made no reply.

CHAPTER 1

THE LAST PAGANS OF EUROPE

There are stars whose light only reaches the earth long after they have fallen apart.
There are people whose remembrance gives light in this world, long after they have passed away.
This light shines in our darkest nights on the road we must follow.
—The Talmud

THE ANCIENT LAND OF LITHUANIA was spread like a counterpane across the cold plains of northern Europe. It rolled, majestic and innocent of all but the slightest hills, to the icy shores of the Baltic Sea. Of its total breadth almost one third was quilted by forests; and another third was spangled by lakes.

Towards the north of this land, the forests were dense and resin-scented; and their shadowy vaults were ranged by yellow-eyed wolves. Towards the south, the forests were dappled with oak, ash, rowan and holly; and their bright glades were roamed by fallow deer, elks, foxes and rootling boars.

Deep within the forests, where only the strongest shafts of light could penetrate the gloom, stood sacred groves of mighty oaks. And ancient springs bubbled with hallowed water, which seeped up from caverns far below. Amid these groves, the early Baltic tribes of the Latvians, the Prussians and the Lithuanians, paid homage to the pagan gods of earth, fire and water.

Beyond the forests, where the rolling plains met the icy shore, shards of bright amber blinked in the sand. Clear as liquid honey, it was all that remained of the resinous tears of an earlier forest, which had swathed the land some sixty-million-years before. Now, washed up by the waves, the sugar-brown amber crystals, some set deep with petrified flies, were as precious as Baltic gold; and the people sought them, treasured them, and traded with them.

The Lithuanian tribes people remained loyal to the gods of the greenwood groves for many thousands of years, but the Latvians and the Prussians did not. The Latvians moved east, the Prussians moved west, and both were conquered by the crusading monks of the order of the Teutonic Knights.

By the 10th century, all of the Baltic States had been converted to Christianity. And by the 12th century all of the Baltic people had been absorbed into the great power-troika of Russia, Prussia and Austria. All except for the Lithuanians, that is: and they, wild, wayward and insular, held true to their pagan rites for another three centuries.

But by that time the great medieval age had almost drawn to its close.

Many attempts were made to lure the Lithuanians and their rulers, the Grand Dukes, away from their pagan ways, but none of them succeeded until the year of 1377, when the Grand Duke Jogaila was offered the hand in marriage of Hedwig, the Polish Queen. He was also offered the Polish Crown and a glittering array of western alliances if he would but surrender his faith. This was temptation indeed; and Jogaila succumbed, but his people were not so easily bought.

Jogaila was forced to hack down the sacred groves and expel the virgins from the Temple of the Sacred Flame in Vilnius before his people understood that the time had finally come for them to shed their pagan ways. When this was done, Jogaila declared himself King of a united Poland and Lithuania, and the two nations remained twinned until the end of the 17th century, when both were engulfed by the Russian Empire.

Because Roman Catholicism had arrived so late in Lithuania, it had to fight hard to replace paganism in the hearts of the Lithuanians. Stubborn and superstitious, the people clung fast to the old ways; and even the land seemed to wrap itself ever closer in the folds of the forests where paganism had been born.

When the 18th century dawned, it found Lithuania still dark. It was a place of few towns and many villages, the latter flung like pebbles across plains sequin-studded by nearly four thousand lakes.

Some of the lakes were so great that strings of islands floated in their blue waters; and the islands were studded with white-towered castles and blue-domed churches. Other lakes were so small that they were little more than ponds, where teal, grebe and moorhens pottered.

Over the lakes flew skeins of grey geese, honking and rowdy. On their shores stood battalions of stock-still storks. But when the time for breeding arrived the storks would lift clumsily into the air and fly away to build raggedly untidy nests amid the tall chimney pots of the villages.

The villages straggled and rambled along deeply rutted lanes. The cottages were long and low; and they hunched against the elements. They had sharp-steepled porches to protect the people from the tumble of snow and the hurl of rain. Their windows were small with diamond panes that admitted only a glimmer of light from the milk-pale springs and the brief golden summers. The cottages were assaulted by the seasons until they became weathered and bone-grey. Their timbered walls were lime-tinged with lichen, and their crannies were plumped with emerald cushions of moss. They were topped by a tangle of thatch contained by carved wooden eaves painted in bright red and blue. But the thatch slumped and the paint faded and soon all the cottages had something of the air of fairytale dwellings. Though there was little of the fairytale about the lives of those who dwelled in them.

Of all these pebble-scattered villages there were some that stood apart. They were not conclusively cut off from the rest, and they were not completely embraced by them. These villages were known as *shtetls*[1], and they were the home of the Jews, some of whom had arrived in Lithuania as early as the 9th century. Little more than hamlets, the *shtetls* were often to be found at the crossroads, where they could be easily reached and swiftly left. Sometimes they would cling to the farthest fringes of the great country estates where the nobles could enjoy easy access to the coffers of the Jewish moneylenders, and gamble and pleasure away their ancestral lands into the patiently waiting Jewish hands.

This did not endear the Jews of Lithuania to her nobility; and the nobles clamoured to have them banished to the farthest reaches of the empire.

The place of banishment was called The Pale of Settlement.

CHAPTER 2

THE JEWISH PROBLEM

What is the Jew? What kind of unique creature is this whom all the rulers of all the nations of the world have disgraced and crushed and expelled and destroyed; persecuted, burned and drowned, and who, despite their anger and their fury, continues to live and to flourish.

The Jew is eternal. He is the embodiment of eternity.

–Leo Tolstoy (1828 -1910)

T HE PALE OF SETTLEMENT WAS a sweeping crescent of land, which had been scythed from the former lands of Lithuania, Ukraine, Poland, Latvia and Belarus. An entirely notional area, it was enclosed by a line drawn on a map by the plump and bejewelled hand of the Tsarina, Catherine 'The Great' in the year of 1791. The line once drawn, Catherine turned her hand to the task of barricading her Jewish subjects behind its invisible pale. Her reason, she said, was so that they could no longer exert an evil influence over her Christian subjects.

Life beyond the pale was hard. The land was poor and often half-frozen, the taxes were disproportionately heavy, and the Jewish children were not considered worthy of higher education. But this was how Catherine desired the life of her Jews to be in the land beyond the pale.

This was not how the lives of Eastern Europe's Jews had always been. When they had first arrived, in the 8th century, seeking solace from persecution in the Byzantine Empire, they had been welcomed. The rulers of the Baltic States had hoped that Jewish industry and business acumen might serve to enrich their nations and fill their own coffers with gold.

And so it had.

The rulers had invited more Jewish communities to settle on their lands until, by the 12th century, there were over sixty Jewish commercial centres flourishing in Lithuania alone. And the towns of Kovno and Vilnius had flowered into cradles of Jewish learning.

It was a golden age for Baltic Jewry but it did not last.

It was the very brilliance and industry of the Jews that brought about their downfall. They were gifted traders and wily financiers, and they became adept in acquiring mortgages on the lands of the nobles; and leases on the mills and the taverns of the peasants. This continued until the 14th century by which time great swathes of noble land lay in Jewish hands; and Jews ran most of Lithuania's taverns and mills.

This did not suit the Lithuanians who envied the Jews their cleverness and hated them for their insular self-sufficiency; and a brooding resentment began to simmer against them.

In 1495 a Lithuanian Grand Duke more grasping and self-serving than his ancestors came to power. Young, headstrong and greedy, Alexander Jagellon needed gold to fuel his ambitions; and the loyalty of his nobles to put them into action. But his coffers were empty and his nobles carped incessantly about their ensnarement to Jewish moneylenders.

Alexander's solution was simple: he expelled the Jews from Lithuania and seized their assets for himself. Then he tore up the mortgages that the Jews had held on the lands of his nobles. In this the Duke made a severe error. Deprived of Jewish wealth and bereft of Jewish industry, Lithuania languished. Alexander was forced to invite the Jews to return, to restore their wealth and to re-instate their mortgage rights. But by this time the damage had been done. The delicate weft and warp of Jewish-Christian coexistence had been ripped apart and it would not mend. Worse still, a precedent had been set for Jewish persecution with impunity. And, once unleashed, the genie could not be put back in the bottle.

In 1517, Martin Luther spoke out against the venality and corruption of the Roman Catholic Church, and the great Protestant Reformation swept through Western Europe until it lapped at the shores of the Baltic States.

In Lithuania, the Catholic priests waited for the anger of the people to descend upon them, as it had done elsewhere. But before the axe fell, the priests sought to deflect it by means of a scapegoat; and they chose the Jews. They denied the corruption of the Catholic Church and blamed the unrest in Europe on the venality of the Jews.

As a result, a new paragraph was added to the Lithuanian constitution. 'The Jews shall not wear costly clothing, nor gold chains,' it read, 'nor shall their wives wear gold or silver ornaments. The Jews shall not have silver mountings on their sabres and daggers; they shall be distinguished by characteristic clothes; they shall wear yellow caps, and their wives kerchiefs of yellow linen, in order that all may be enabled to distinguish Jews from Christians.'

From this point onwards, the persecution of the Jews worsened until, in 1795, Lithuania became part of the Russian Empire. And then it became much worse.

By 1804, the majority of Jews had been banned from living in Russia's villages and compelled to congregate in *shtetls*. They were not permitted to hold leases or mortgages and they could not trade in alcohol. By 1812 the Jews of Moscow had been expelled from the city and sent to work in factories termed 'special'. And in that same year the Russian Government coined a new phrase: The Jewish Problem.

Now it became fashionable in the higher echelons of the Russian Empire to declare one's hatred for the Jews. The intelligentsia held glamorous gatherings where the great names of the day argued how best the Jews might be expelled from the Empire forever.

In 1827, Tsar Nicholas I determined to solve his inherited Jewish Problem once and for all. His solution, like that of Duke Alexander Jagellon before him, was simple. Nicholas decreed that all Russia's Jews were to be pronounced either 'useful' or 'non-useful'. The useful, such as the merchants, craftsmen and agriculturalists, were to be allowed to continue to build the Russian economy. The non-useful, such as the many thousands of unskilled Jews, were to be conscripted into the Russian army.

And with them were to go all Jewish boys over the age of twelve.

As Lithuania's Jews reeled from the cruelty of this edict, they were offered a reprieve. The Tsar declared that if they agreed to work on the land as peasants, their sons would be spared.

Thousands of Jewish families flooded into the agricultural work camps set up to receive them. But it made no difference. In 1843, the Tsar expelled all the Jews from Kiev. Then he decreed that no Jewish settlements would be permitted beyond a 30-kilometer radius of Russia's borders.

CHAPTER 3

SAMUEL BLOCK

Energy is the basis of everything. Every Jew, no matter how insignificant, is engaged in some decisive and immediate pursuit of a goal… It is the most perpetual people of the earth…

–Johann Wolfgang von Goethe, German dramatist, novelist and poet (1749-1832)

I T WAS INTO THE FAMILY of a flax merchant by the name of Lazarus Block that a son named Samuel was born in 1849. The Merchant Block lived in a *shtetl* called Kirkel, which stood a few miles beyond the 13th century walls of the fortified town of Kovno[1].

Kovno stood on the banks of the Nemunas River and was girded by thick white walls now crumbling with age. Beyond the walls lay a patchwork of forest, pasture and orchards, and the town was ringed by a series of low-lying lakes known as sink holes, into which both cows and people regularly disappeared.

The Nemunas River was wide and its slow brown waters braided themselves around hundreds of tiny islets, some of which were little more than weed-wreathed sandbanks where flat-bottomed boats were upturned to dry. The streets of Kovno were so narrow that the housewives could shake hands with their neighbours while standing in their upper chambers; and they were cobbled with stones worn concave with age.

In the centre of the town was a square to which all the crooked streets eventually led. On one side of this square stood the squat towers of the Church of St Francis. On the other rose the tapering spires of the Cathedral of St Peter and St Paul. In the southernmost corner of the square stood the Baroque façade of the city hall, and beyond this lay the oldest, darkest, and most cramped part of the town; it was known as the Jewish Quarter.

The Jews of Kovno had arrived in the 13th century under the leadership of their Patriarch, Daniel of Troki, a scholar of such veneration and renown that Jews flocked from all over Europe to settle within the reach of his words. Kovno flowered into a centre of Jewish culture, and such was its commercial reach that Yiddish was the mother tongue; Russian the language of officialdom; Polish or Latvian, the language of border trade; and Hebrew the language of learning and faith.

In the hamlet of Kirkel life was pastoral and slow. The Block family was not wealthy but its cottage was more generously structured than many of its fellows. It was timbered with a thatched roof; and it was filled with heavy wooden benches, tables and dressers. In a corner of the kitchen stood a spinning wheel upon which the women of the house spun flax. Behind the cottage was a ramble of sheds in which animals were kept, dairy work done and meat smoked and cured. Beyond the outhouses lay the Merchant Block's fields. There was also a stand of forest where timber was felled and milled.

Like his brothers Samuel Block was reared as a farmer and a merchant. He grew up sturdy like his father; but from his mother he inherited his undeniable good looks. He had dark eyes set wide in an open face; he had a cleft chin, thick dark hair and an unusual brilliance of smile.

By the time Samuel had reached the age of twelve, his father had become concerned over the steady rise of antagonism towards the Jewish people. Reluctantly, the Merchant Block decided that the time had come to leave the exposure of the *shtetl* and to conceal his family amid the thousands of Jews already pressed into the Jewish Quarter of Kovno.

Wrenched from the rustic familiarity of the little *shtetl*, Samuel was forced to learn a new way of living. He clung to the labyrinthine streets of the Jewish Quarter, which became his sanctuary and his prison. Rarely venturing beyond its walls, he learned that it was not wise, possessed of an obviously Jewish face and Jewish tongue, to linger by the great Catholic cathedral, or to tarry too long in the square where the cameo-faced ladies swung by in their polished carriages; and where the gentlemen who rode alongside them might read insult into the most fleeting Jewish glance. He learned to keep his eyes downcast and his expression blank in the presence of Gentiles. And he learned to read the augurs of trouble.

Trouble crept like a rat into the Jewish Quarter; and if he cast his mind back, Samuel could rarely discern the point at which it stepped out of the gutters and into the street. But when that moment came there would be a taint of sweat in the air, and the rat of fear would dart and dive through the streets with its thick grey tail curling behind it.

Looks of stealthy cunning would creep across the faces of his father's clients. They would wipe their hands down their breeches after touching his father's hands. Later, legs astride and tankards hugged to their chests, they would mutter and prod at newspapers where tales would be told of honest townsfolk wronged by the venality of Jews.

Trouble broke at night when the denizens of the Jewish Quarter were locked behind their doors. There would be shouting and rushing, pounding and screaming. There would be the splintering of doorjambs, the wrenching of bolts, the crash of glass, and the pounding of feet as the Jews snatched up what they could and ran. Only later, when the fury of their neighbours had been spent, would they creep back to their homes with humility writ large upon their faces.

As Samuel grew beyond boyhood, the Russian Government gave a name to the trouble that the Jews feared. They called it a pogrom[2] and, with its brutish new name, the trouble grew darker. Where once there had been only hounding and looting now there came spilt blood and broken bones. Then from the ghettos of Minsk and Kiev crept spectral tales of rape, murder and infanticide.

The Jews of Kovno turned to their elders for succour, but received only the old story of the *Kehilat Kovno*. It was a 17th century fable, the tale of Rabbi Moshe Soloveichik, who had sued the burghers of Kovno for the damage done to him; and won his case. There had been a time when the recitation of the tale had bolstered community courage, but that time was gone. And now the people began to speak of escape from the cold cruelty of the Russian Empire into a life of hope far beyond its shores.

At the age of sixteen, his education complete, Samuel Block apprenticed himself to a cabinetmaker; he had decided that he needed to learn a trade in order that he might escape the toils of familial duty. He felt trapped within the walls of the tenement in the Jewish Quarter. He had read forbidden books about Jewish Enlightenment[3] and he wanted to explore the freedom it promised, but he could not do so under the narrow gaze of his family and community.

When he reached the end of his apprenticeship Samuel was twenty-years-old. And now his need to leave Kovno was more pressing than ever. Great changes had been wrought in Kovno as a result of the Emancipation of the Serfs[4]. Finally released from the bitterness of their feudal servitude, thousands of newly freed serfs had descended upon Russia's towns in search of work and shelter. In Kovno, where nearly half the population was Jewish, there was not enough work or shelter to go around and resentment against the Jews had swelled. Pogroms broke out all over the Empire, but now they were orchestrated and fuelled by the army.

In desperation and despair, thousands of Jewish families fled to Europe and America. Briefly, Samuel considered joining them; but the escape routes were treacherous and his savings were meagre. So he decided instead try his luck in the ancient town of Vilnius.

The Gates of Dawn, Vilnius 1897

St Anne's Church, Vilnius 1900

The streets of Vilnius, 1897

CHAPTER 4

VILNIUS

There is no success without hardship.
—Sophocles (496-406 BC)

IT TOOK SAMUEL TWO DAYS to reach Vilnius[1] and along the way his eyes were opened to the beauty of his homeland. He had never had cause to venture beyond Kovno before. But now he walked by sky-blue lakes and grey-gloomed forests, across pale golden plains and over purple-domed heathland. His horizons burst open before him; but nothing that he saw prepared him for the grandeur of Vilnius.

The closer Samuel drew to the walls of Vilnius, the more horses, carts and people joined him on the road. The forest of church spires grew thicker, and their crosses winked golden in the sun. There was only one point of entry to the town: through a pair of studded doors known as the Gates of Dawn and these, when he arrived, had been flung wide open; and a torrent of life jostled through them.

Beyond the Gates of Dawn stood a blackened tower with a great iron cross on its roof. Squatting beneath it, on the curbstones of the cobbles, was a line of elderly women. They were telling their rosaries; some rocking back and forth in religious transports. Samuel beckoned an urchin; he asked what the women were waiting for. The child squinted sideways up at Samuel as if unwilling to believe that anyone could not know the answer to this question. The women waited to enter the dark tower, he said. It housed an icon of the Virgin cast in black and gold. She granted miracles to all those who prayed at her feet.

High above the town, on a rounded hump of a hill, stood a square tower. It was known as Gediminas Tower and had been built by the 13th century warrior duke, Gediminas, after whom many a Lithuanian boy was named. Below the hill was a tangle of lanes, all of which led to the Great Square where a stone effigy of the Duke still reared on his warhorse. In the Square stood Vilnius Cathedral, which boasted a silver casket containing the bones of Saint Casimir. Lines of pilgrims waited in the square; and when their turn came, they approached the casket on their knees and pressed their lips to its silvered plinth.

Rendered suddenly awkward amid so many Catholic shrines, Samuel searched the crowds for a Jewish face and directions to the Jewish Quarter. He was sent beneath the dark portals of the Baslian Gate and beyond it into the maze of the Old Town. Here, high on a corner, hung a painted sign. It read Jew Street. Beyond it stretched a darkened muddle of streets where the tottering houses leaned close enough to touch; Samuel felt safe.

Samuel spent two years in the Old Town of Vilnius and, during that time, he built himself a business. He became inured to the closeness of streets ever tainted by the stench of tanners, fullers and butchers. He worked alongside weavers, dyers and glass blowers; he grew accustomed to the cries of the blood-letters and the teeth-pullers. He nodded to the moneylenders, who stood on their doorsteps, their hands clasped behind their backs, and their white stockinged feet rocking gently to and fro in their red leather slippers.

Samuel built his business gradually. He fitted a window here, a door there. He mended carts, he fashioned benches, and he listened to the talk of the times. In the newspapers he read how two of the nation's most famous intellectuals, Ivan Aksakov and Fyodor Dostoyevski, had proclaimed themselves to be Jew haters and accused the Jews of being 'an alien element bent on exploiting the masses and invading all areas of patriotic Russian life'. He learned that the Jews were accused of tainting the purity of the Slav race. To have broad Slavic features and fair hair, the newspaper claimed, was good. To wear Slav national dress, sing Slavic songs and eat Slavic dishes was good. And to be Jewish, surmised Samuel, was bad.

As Samuel made his rounds, he heard that the government was engaged in the movement of thousands of Jews to southern Russia where special towns and factories had been established for them. He also heard tell of a Kovno rabbi by the name of Yitshak Elhanan Spektor[2], who was calling on all Lithuanians to lay aside their religious differences and fight for the liberation of Lithuania from Russia rule.

In 1863 the first anti-Russian riots broke out in Lithuania; and later in Poland. Banned Lithuanian books were smuggled into the country, passed from hand to hand, and read by firesides bounded by bolted doors. People wore the fur-trimmed jackets, embroidered shirts and striped skirts of Lithuanian national dress. And the haunting 'music box' songs of the medieval troubadours rang out through the tavern yards.

And elsewhere, while Lithuania sought to shake herself free of Russia; the upper echelons of Jewish society fought to shed the shroud of discrimination. Affluent and aspiring, they affected to camouflage their faith; and to hide it behind a façade of gracious homes, extensive estates, rich clothing and select intellectual gatherings.

The 14th century Black Madonna in the Chapel of the
Gates of Dawn, which is said to have miraculous powers

THE SOLTZ FAMILY

Everything that happens happens as it should, and if you observe carefully,
you will find this to be so.
–Marcus Aurelius Antoninus Augustus (121-180 BC)

1870 was a black year for Russia. There had been a merciless drought and the crops had failed; the livestock had perished and the peasants had faced starvation. Fire had arrived and, fanned by the hot dry winds of a cruel summer, it had swept through the stubble and flared into orange tongues of flame. Columns of thick black smoke had twisted up into the sky like whirling demons, and sparks had been tossed on the wind to catch alight in the dry thatch of the cottages.

Then the fire had consumed all that lay in its path.

It was an ill wind but it profited Samuel Block. He had spent his time wisely in Vilnius. He had acquired horses, carts and tools; and he had carved a reputation for himself as a man who dealt well with emergencies. When the fires reached the town of Birzai[1], which lay some distance from Vilnius, a message was sent from a wealthy merchant who resided there. His name was Lazarus Soltz[2] and his yard had been ravaged by fire; he needed a man who could repair his outhouses without delay. The message was given to Samuel Block, and he set out immediately with his horse and cart and a team of workers.

Locked between the Rivers Apascia and Agluona, not far from the Latvian border, Birzai was both rural and elegant. It was an area that had once been owned by the Princes of Radzivil, whose moated castles still stood amid its lakes and pastures. It was quiet and green and its rivers ran placidly amid pollarded willows; and those with the money to do so liked to build their country retreats there.

Birzai stood amid fields of pale blue flax, and it was famous for the fineness of its linen. In the interests of preserving the town's picturesque gentility, the threshing of the flax was done in the mills of Siauliai, which was an ugly textile town that was discreetly separated from Birzai by a short stretch of single-gauge railway.

Birzai had a Jewish community, which was separated from the town by the waters of a large lake known as Lake Siruinis. Too extensive to be called a *shtetl*, the community lived in *Birzu Dvaras*, the Birzai Estate. With more wealth and standing than others of their faith, the Birzai Jews had arrived on the Estate in the 13th century at the specific invitation of Prince Christopher Radzivil. In the intervening centuries they had brought considerable affluence to the area, they were gracious and wealthy; and they enjoyed excellent relations with their neighbours.

By far the largest house on the Birzai Estate was that of the Soltz family. It stood a few miles beyond the rest and had originally been owned by a member of the Radzivil family, whose debts had caused him to surrender it to the Soltzs.

Enclosed within high walls of butter-coloured stone, it was a gracious white-painted residence with a steep-sloped pale gray roof. Double rows of green-shuttered windows extended to the right and left of the front door, which stood between twin columns. A flight of shallow stone steps led down to a gravelled carriage-sweep. Behind the house was a flagged courtyard enclosed by outhouses, stables and carriage houses. A lane led to the orchards, which were pink over in cherry time.

Abraham Soltz had made his fortune in flax, and his judicious investment of his profits had allowed him to leave his business affairs in the hands of a manager. This left him at liberty to devote his time to his family and to the local Jewish community. Mr Soltz was a devout man, but he was proud of the fact that it was with Soltz money that the lavish Birzai synagogue had been built. Mr Soltz liked to think of himself as a humble man, but he could not help but be gratified by the fact that his gracious drawing room served as the backdrop for a series of literary and religious soirees that attracted scholars from far beyond the boundaries of Birzai.

When the brilliant young Rabbi Sinson had first begun to attend these gatherings, Mr Soltz had flattered himself into believing that the Rabbi was attracted by the earnestness of the discussions. But then his wife had explained to him that the gifted young Rabbi had found time to look up from his texts and take notice their eldest daughter, Fanny. Mr Soltz had accepted this, and thereafter the Rabbi's visits had became even more frequent.

Since the Rabbi came from a good family with both land and connections, he offered all that a man might desire in a son-in-law, and Mr Soltz promoted the match. But Fanny herself was too gentle and shy to encourage the young man. Instead, she sat with her gleaming black braids wound up and over her brow in traditional Lithuanian fashion, and bent her lovely eyes to her embroidery.

This exasperated Fanny's younger sister, Ettel, beyond all measure. It was well known that the eldest daughter must be married before the younger could look for suitors, and Ettel was approaching twenty years of age. Ettel willed her beautiful sister to look up from her embroidery and smile upon the Rabbi. But for all that she willed it, it took an entire year for the couple to be married and moved to a house of their own. It was only when Fanny was gone that Ettel realized how much she missed her sister; and how fortunate Fanny had been in attracting the one man amongst their father's friends who was below the age of forty.

CHAPTER 6

ETTEL SOLTZ

The great question … which I have not been able to answer, despite my thirty years
of research into the feminine soul, is 'What does a woman want?'
–Sigmund Freud (1856-1939)

ARRIVING ON THE SOLTZ ESTATE, Samuel surveyed the damage done to the yard. It was ringed by blackened fingers of timber, some still sullenly hissing; and it was strewn with all that had been dragged from the outhouses. There were crates of apples, sacks of grain, strings of onions, wheels of cheese and flagons of mead all piled in a heap at its centre. Samuel estimated that the fire had dealt him at least a month of work, maybe more.

In the centre of the yard, surrounded by peasants, stood a young woman. She was traditionally dressed in Lithuanian style in a tight-laced black bodice, a white linen blouse, and a red skirt that fell to just above her ankles. A red shawl was crossed tightly across her bosom and tucked into her embroidered apron. On her feet were wooden clogs.

She looked, Samuel thought, like a farmer's daughter.

When he looked again, he realized his error. While all around her lifted, hauled and stacked, the young woman did nothing but direct. And the hands that pointed to the spilled fruit and the fractured crates had never seen manual work. Samuel stared. The woman had strong features framed by thick, glossy braids. She was striking, she was commanding. Feeling Samuel's eyes on upon her, the woman looked towards him.

Her lip curled, she tossed her braids, and turned and left the yard.

Unmarried at the age of twenty-six, Samuel Block was well aware of his need of a wife. But the matchmakers of Vilnius had found him strangely hard to please. His mother had contrived to have all manner of personable girls pass through her kitchen, but she had not been successful either. The difficulty, or so Samuel believed, lay in the fact that the girls had been sleek, plump, attractive, well bred and domestically faultless, but they had been docile. They had shown no desire to look beyond the walls of their community or to test the boundaries of their faith; and this had bored him. The woman in the courtyard was different.

The next time Samuel saw her, the woman was changed; and any idea of her being a farmer's daughter was rendered ridiculous. The rustic costume had been replaced by a black silk gown; it was severely tailored from throat to lace-edged wrist. The clogs had been replaced by high-heeled, buttoned boots. The peasant-girl braids were gone and her dark hair was drawn severely back into a chignon at the nape of her neck.

Whisking her skirts clear of the dust and debris, the lady swept through the yard. She had been picking flowers and held a basket of blooms in her hand. She passed close enough to Samuel for him to catch a breath of lavender, but she took no notice of him. Samuel asked a kitchen maid who the lady was. The girl laughed and told him the lady was Miss Ettel Soltz, the second-eldest daughter of the house. Samuel could see why the girl had laughed: the lady was clearly far beyond his reach. But this did not deter him.

Miss Soltz's movements were easily charted. Samuel worked all day in the yard, and since this was the centre of all domestic activity he saw everything that went on in the house. Careful observance told him that it was Miss Soltz's morning habit to visit her married sister, who lived a short distance away. Sometimes the married sister paid a return visit bringing her small boy with her.

In the afternoons Miss Soltz was to be found in the drawing room with her mother and those of her younger sisters who were not in the schoolroom. Sometimes the sound of a piano would drift from the house; sometimes the strings of a harp could be heard. Sometimes the staccato commands of a dancing master would issue from behind the polished panes, and occasionally groups of ladies might call for tea. But the routine rarely varied and Samuel was at a loss to know how he might break its tight bonds of propriety.

The winds had died and the orchards lay still when Samuel's opportunity came. He was returning in his cart from Birzai, whence he had gone to buy nails, when he saw a small pony trap halted in the carriage drive. One of its red-painted wheels stood out at an unnatural angle, the pony was free of its shafts, and Miss Ettel Soltz held its reigns. Her sister sat on a tree stump. The small boy walked his white button-boots up and down the hill she had made of her skirts.

Samuel pulled his cart alongside; he doffed his cap and asked if he might be permitted to help. Seeing a handsome young man, neatly attired and with a pleasing politeness of address, the ladies accepted. Samuel stripped off his jacket, rolled up his sleeves and set to work. The damage was minimal and the wheel was soon hefted back in to position, its bolts secured. Samuel wiped his hands carefully on a white handkerchief. Then he handed the ladies back into their little carriage. He smiled at Ettel as he did so.

Ettel liked what she saw. He was a tall man with broad shoulders and sunburned forearms, he was handsome and he clasped her fingers with warm dry hands. He held them too long; and she blushed. A brief conversation was held; Samuel explained the reason for his presence on the estate, and he effected a formal introduction that the ladies could not avoid. As he bade them farewell, Samuel bent his gaze very directly upon Miss Ettel Soltz. There was no mistaking his intention.

Once introduced, Samuel made it his business to encounter Ettel wherever and whenever he could. At first their exchanges were stiffly polite: he would comment on the weather and enquire after her health; her replies would be brief, her eyes downcast. Later they grew familiar enough to exchange words on other topics. They found they shared similar ideas and had read the same books. He made her laugh. She found this unusual and intimate.

One morning instead of the brief touch of Ettel's gloves that he was wont to offer, Samuel raised his eyes to hers and very deliberately bent his handsome head to kiss her fingers. She did not pull them away.

Thereafter, though not a word was said, neither Ettel nor Samuel remained in any doubt as to where events were leading. But time was running out: Samuel's work was coming to an end.

The daughter of a family that prided itself on the cleverness of its men and the beauty of its women, Ettel knew that in her case such pride was misplaced. She was aware that her family had cast her in the role of spinster and that they looked to her to care for Mr and Mrs Soltz in their dotage. But having encountered the bold gaze of Mr Samuel Block Ettel had other ideas.

When Samuel Block asked her to marry him she accepted without demur.

The opposition from the Soltz family was intense, and it took all Ettel's considerable determination to withstand it. She was told that Mr Block was not a gentleman and that she, a lady, had not been brought up to marry a cabinetmaker. Her father said Mr Block did not have sufficient wealth to support her. Her mother said Ettel risked marrying beneath her station in life Only Fanny gave her any encouragement, but Fanny was far too gentle and caught up with her babies and her husband to be of any real support.

So Ettel battled for a husband alone.

Samuel met the opposition with a calm that surprised Ettel. Nor would he be denied his bride. Seeking an interview with Mr Soltz, Samuel presented him with a set of plans for a substantial farmhouse; and he showed him the lease on a goodly expanse of land. He proffered a sound set of accounts; he stated how the house would be built and what crops would be planted. As the year of 1878 drew to a close Mr Soltz realized that his opposition to the marriage was futile: Samuel Block would have his daughter whether her father agreed or not. To the disgust of his wife, Mr Soltz gave his consent. He made only one stipulation: that the farmhouse be built and equipped before the marriage took place.

It took over a year for the farmhouse to be made ready and during this time Ettel amassed a collection of fine linen, silver and china that was utterly unsuited to it. The ceremony was held in traditional style, the entire community was invited and Ettel wore a coronet of rue on her dark hair. As the newlyweds left in a cart piled high with their belongings, Ettel's family waved from the lawn. Her mother was heard to say that Ettel would rue the day.

Old Lithuanian farmhouse

Old Lithuanian cottages

CHAPTER 7

SAMUEL AND ETTEL BLOCK

Who so findeth a wife findeth a good thing.
—Proverbs

THE FARMHOUSE IN WHICH SAMUEL and Ettel Block began their married life lay equidistant between the Soltz Estates and the town of Vilnius. It stood amid rolling farmland and was encircled by thick forest. Just within sight of the tiny *shtetl* of Gilwan[1], it had two floors and was finished with a shingled roof with twin gables. With the intention of pleasing his wife, Samuel had fashioned a fanlight above the front door and pannelled the walls of the small parlour.

But it was still a farmhouse.

Outside the kitchen door was a pond fringed by bulrushes. There was a duck house and a bench from which Samuel fished. To one side of the house was a small paddock for the horses and to the other there were outhouses for the chickens, geese, goats and cows. At the front of the house there was a flagged yard and a cluster of stables. A lane wound away through the apple orchards to join the main road into Vilnius.

Ettel, though well satisfied with her husband, was less so with her new station in life. She was shocked to learn just how much hardship she had been shielded from while living in the affluence of Birzai, and how hard the life of a farmer's wife was.

Determined to keep up appearances Ettel kept the silver polished, the floors waxed and the linen lavender scented. When visitors came she served tea in china cups and affected to spend her days in embroidery. In reality she lived as a drudge and was forced to learn a whole new set of skills in an exceptionally short period of time.

In the dairy, there were cows to be milked, butter to be churned and cheese to be made. In the kitchen garden, there were herbs to be grown and dried from the rafters of the kitchen. There was a smokehouse and a henhouse to be kept, hives to be maintained, honey to be made into mead, and barley into vodka. In summer, there was bottling and pickling to be done; in winter there was meat to be smoked. When the rye was harvested, bread flavoured with onion and caraway seeds had to be made. When the potatoes were lifted, traditional *Cepelinai* dumplings had to be stuffed, and when the cabbages were pulled the leaves had to be rolled and stuffed with meat and baked into packages known as 'little doves'.

It was hard work and it changed Ettel.

Within months of her marriage her silk gowns had been packed away in layers of camphor and lavender; her caps, jewellery and lace too. A year later they were unpacked and, clad in her finery, Ettel travelled with Samuel to Vilnius. In a dingy studio they posed together before a dapper man with a box camera and a flash that went off with a pop and a stench of cordite. Their faces were blank and unfamiliar in the photographic image he supplied. But they framed it and placed it on the mantelpiece.

And with every year that passed, it looked less like them.

In 1879, biting down hard on a knotted sheet tied tight between the bedposts, Ettel gave birth to her first child.

It was not the boy she had hoped for.

They called the child Anna and placed her in a cradle that Samuel had made and painted with garlands of roses. When the family visited Ettel dressed the baby in a gown edged with the lace she no longer wore. And she tried not to think of all the many ways in which the farmhouse fell short of her mother's expectations.

But she was, she reflected, happy.

CHAPTER 8

PERSECUTION

Time is like a river made up of the events which happen, and its current is strong: no sooner does anything appear than it is swept away, and another comes in its place and will be swept away too.

–Marcus Aurelius Antoninus (121-180 BC)

Far beyond the Blocks' farmhouse, the face of Russia was changing. Though emancipated, the people had come to realize that they were no better off as peasants than they had been as serfs. They were bitter and disillusioned, and easily swayed by the emotive speeches of the radicals who called themselves Communists. Revolution was in the air.

In 1881 the Tsar, Alexander II was assassinated and, though it was well known that the Communists were responsible for the deed, the government sought an easier scapegoat: they blamed the Jews. A wave of pogroms immediately broke out and thousands of refugees flooded into Europe. Alarmed, the crowned heads of Europe remonstrated. Surely, they said, the new Tsar, Alexander III, could bring the violence to an end.

All compliance, Alexander called for an investigation into the underlying causes of the pogroms. But when the results were announced, the Jews knew they could expect no mercy from him. The report revealed that the pogroms had been orchestrated by the Jews themselves, and the Tsar's advisors suggested that their only solution lay in the exertion of even tighter control over Jewish movements.

In the wake of the Tsar's announcement, the Patriarch of the Russian Orthodox Church made a speech. He said it was his fervent hope that one third of Russia's Jews would convert, one third would die and one third would flee the country.

The message was clear.

In Birzai, the Soltz, Block and Sinson families gathered to discuss the matter. Conversion, all were agreed, was not an option. In the first place, their faith would not allow it, and in the second it would make no difference: a converted Jew would always be a Jew in Gentile eyes; and hated all the more for his weakness. This left only one option: flight.

Mr Soltz, cocooned for all his life in the relative safety of the Birzai backwater, was violently opposed to this. He said the family risked arriving as destitute refugees in a strange land, and he could not face this prospect. Better, he said, that they should wait, as the Jews had always done, until the storm of hatred had passed over them. Samuel Block and the Rabbi Sinson exchanged glances, and the Rabbi said he would look into the matter of escape.

The results of the Rabbi's enquiries, conducted with his usual thoroughness, were not encouraging. There was only one proven escape route from Lithuania and this was via the steamships that sailed to Britain from the Baltic ports of Libau, Königsberg and Szczecin (Liepaja, Kaliningrad and Stettin) . The journey to the ports, without the correct travel papers, was hazardous and many died on the way. Some were shot by the Russian border guards, who were typically drunk; most were betrayed by the very agents they had paid to help them. And that was not all: those who chose to leave Russia could carry nothing but money with them and, by the time they reached the Baltic ports, most of them had been cheated out of this.

Another decision faced those refugees that reached Western Europe: whether to stay there or to travel on to America or South Africa? For the people of the Kovno region, however, there was only one logical destination: the British textile town of Leeds.

Leeds was linked directly to Libau by the port of Hull, and had a flourishing and long-established Jewish community originating from the Kovno region. It had a booming textile industry, jobs in the mills were easily had, and accommodation could be easily found with the help of the local Jewish community, who, the Rabbi learned, stood at the dockside to welcome every incoming boat. Better than all this, the Rabbi had a number of acquaintances already resident in Leeds.

With four boys rapidly approaching the age of conscription into the Russian army the Rabbi Sinson began to formulate his plans for departure.

CHAPTER 9

A GILWAN EDUCATION

The roots of education are bitter, but the fruit is sweet.
—Aristotle (384-322 BC)

To ETTEL BLOCK, NOW IN her late twenties, the years on the farm had been cruel. Though never beautiful she was now plain; and often rather sour of face. In the wake of her first child, Ettel's waistline had thickened; and she had grown stouter and shorter of temper with every child that followed.

The children had arrived in orderly succession. Annie was born in 1879, Abraham Lazarus in 1883, Lily in 1888 and Freda in 1891. When Freda was placed in the rose-garlanded cradle, Annie was thirteen and approaching womanhood; Abraham was ten and already helping on the farm; and Lily had grown into a determined four-year-old with a puckishly pretty face framed by a cloud of black curls.

Ettel was determined that the children should not grow up as peasants. She insisted that they be properly clothed, fed and educated. But in this, Ettel's determination, which was considerable, failed her. The children were healthy but, because they were raised on a farm, they were forever muddied, torn, and tumbled; and they lacked manners. As for their education, unlike Fanny Sinson's children, who had private tutors, the Block children attended the local Jewish school.

Ettel disapproved of this school wholeheartedly, but there was no alternative to it.

The schoolhouse was small and ramshackle and had been built by the community. The community also provided the schoolmaster's salary, but much of it arrived in kind, and all of it was stored in the schoolroom. This, piled high with sacks of grain, boxes of salted herrings, bags of nails and barrels of butter, grew to resemble a general store. The schoolmaster's wife spent her days bartering goods, spinning flax, and hammering out spinning tops from bits of old tin. So the pupils fought for their education against a backdrop of clanking scales, clinking coins, and determined haggling.

This education, though hard earned, was perplexing. According to the dictates of the state, it was a Russian education: all Lithuanian books were banned, the use of the distinctive Lithuanian Cyrillic script was forbidden, and all references to Lithuanian culture or history were wiped from the text books. Yet at home the exact opposite prevailed. It was a secular education, stripped bare of all Jewish belief, language and tradition. Yet at home all these things were held sacred.

So it was that the Block children grew up fluent in Russian, Yiddish, Hebrew and Lithuanian; but unable to read or write properly in any of these languages. At school they were required to be good Russians; but at home they were expected to be loyal Lithuanians. At school they were encouraged to convert from Judaism to Christianity, while at home they were urged to cling to their Jewish faith. And beyond the narrow confines of the *shtetl* and its chaotic little school it was best not to admit to being Jewish at all.

Ettel Block with Abraham Lazarus and Lily circa 1890, Vilnius

Similar contradictions affected the entire region. Though part of the Russian Empire, the Vilnius region was fiercely Lithuanian; and it refused to sever its age-old ties with Poland. Beyond the sleepy insularity of Gilwan, it was passionately revolutionary. Close to Russia's borders, it seethed with radicals and patriots; and it acted as an illegal entry point for anti-Russian propaganda. In every tavern there were agents peddling escape routes to Europe; and on every street corner there were government agents known as the Secret Police, who waited and watched to catch the revolutionaries red-handed. Anti-Semitism was rife, and anyone caught in anti-Russian behaviour was either shot or sent to Siberia.

Boy soldiers in the armies of the Tsar 1800s

CHAPTER 10

TROUBLE COMES

When sorrows come, they come not single spies, but in battalions.
–*Hamlet*, William Shakespeare (1564-1616)

I T WAS MARCH 1892; THE snow was melting, but the leaves remained stiff and crystal-laced with frost. Night had fallen on the Gilwan farm, and Samuel and Ettel Block had retired early to their bedchamber. The nursery was quiet. Freda was asleep in her rose-garlanded cradle. Lily and Annie lay rolled together in the deep trough of their feather bed, and Abraham lay in the little truckle bed that pulled out from beneath it. He was awake, curled beneath his patchwork quilt, watching the shadow-fingers of the trees as they crept across the ceiling.

The sounds came from far away; and they were as yet indistinct. He heard shouting; and it moved steadily closer. There were galloping horses and urgent men; and they had left the main road and were heading down the lane. They were calling to each other; and they were drawing closer; they would soon be in the yard.

Running to the window, Abraham saw two horses plunge out of the dark tunnel of the lane and into the pale moonlight of the yard. They skittered to a halt, their iron shoes sparking off the flagstones. They were lathered in white and their nostrils flared blood red. Two men, booted and spurred, flung themselves from the horses. One strode to the front door of the farmhouse and hammered on it. The other held the horses' heads; he looked upwards as the lamplight flared in Samuel and Ettel's chamber. 'Someone's coming,' he said.

Samuel Block flung himself down the stairs; he opened the door and raised his lantern. Butter-yellow light pooled around the man standing on the doorstep. His face, red and sweating, was familiar to Samuel. He was a member of the Secret Police.

'There is a Polish insurgent[1] on the run,' said the man.

Samuel said nothing.

'He is heading across your land; towards Gilwan,' said the man, 'we have to head him off! We need fresh horses, these are spent!' The man spoke with lumbering importance and he stank of vodka.

Samuel surveyed the men; they were both drunk; they would ride his horses to their deaths, and perhaps their own; and he would bear the blame.

'Bring the horses, now!' The man belched and swayed back on his heels.

Still Samuel did nothing.

The man's expression changed; it grew clumsily sly.

'Ah ha! That's how it is, is it? The insurgent has already arrived here and you are hiding him!'

Samuel had learned the lessons of the Jewish Quarter of Vilnius well.

'I am sorry, gentlemen,' he said. He lifted his shoulders; he extended his hands; cupped palms up.

'I would gladly give you horses,' he said, 'but they are all rented out for the beet pulling.' He indicated the stables. 'There are no horses in there, but for a mare in foal, and she'll be no good to you.'

He affected to wring his hands and cringe.

The man flicked a glance towards the darkened stables. He swore. He strode to his horse and hauled himself up into the saddle; his companion did likewise. The spokesman wrenched his horse brutally around until he was level with Samuel.

'You are lying, Jew,' he said, 'like all your kind. But I have an insurgent to catch.'

He reigned in his horse, which was now eager to be gone.

'But I shall return, and I will search your barn; and you know what I will find there don't you Jew?'

He let the horse have its head.

'Anti-Russian propaganda,' he shouted back over his shoulder, 'that's what I shall find there, Jew. And it will be Siberia for you.'

The riders careered into the dark lane and were gone.

Samuel lowered the lantern and stood in its shrunken pool of light. He turned into the house, slammed the door and stood with his back against it.

In the narrow hallway, Ettel stood white-faced; her fingers scrabbled at her shawl.

'I must go,' Samuel said.

Ettel stared at him, her face ghoulish in the glare of the lantern.

'Get me a bag with food and water,' Samuel said. He strode to the stairs and swung himself violently around the newel post. He bounded up them. Minutes later he was back, wrestling his arms into the sleeves of his greatcoat.

'Where?' said Ettel.

'As far away as I can get,' Samuel said.

She handed him the knapsack; he shouldered it.

'I'll send for you,' he said.

He pulled a peaked cap low over his eyes and was gone.

CHAPTER 11

SALCININKAI

Nothing has more strength than dire necessity.
–Euripides (480-406 BC)

THE CHILDREN CREPT DOWN THE stairs in the chill of the early morning. They found their mother rocking and hugging herself in the fireside chair. The grate was cold, the range unlit. Ettel's hair was lank and loose; she was still clad in her nightgown and her shawl hung askew from her shoulders.

'Mamma?' said Annie, timorous.

Ettel halted her rocking and stared at them unfocussed. Freda began to wail in Abraham's arms; Lily clung to Annie's hand.

Ettel squared her shoulders. She rose from the chair; she pressed her hands into the small of her back as if it pained her.

'Your father is gone,' she said. 'Get dressed and go to school.'

There was an almost festive air in the absence of the children's father. The rules were suspended, the routines laid aside. But it did not last. When the children realized that Samuel was not coming back, their world grew cold and frightening.

The crops rotted in the furrows, the labourers spat gouts of tobacco on to the flagstones and stumped off up the lane. Ettel sold the contents of the timber store; then she sold the contents of the smoke shed. She sold the hay, the horses, the cows and the goats. She packed the chickens into coops made of bent reeds and sold them too.

When the farm had nothing left to yield, Ettel sold the contents of her chests; she sold the silver; the linen; and the china. Finally she sold the brass-bottomed pans and the samovar. All that was left to her was a rusty black silk dress and a pair of boots so old that they were moulded to the exact shape of her feet.

At school, the other children shrank away from the Blocks; and they whispered about them behind their hands. In the village Ettel's neighbours whisked their skirts away from her, and they did not look her in the eye; she knew that they feared the taint of association with one so clearly fallen from grace. But it did not stop them from haggling down the price of her possessions, or from crowding in to her kitchen to see what else she might be forced to sell.

The family survived on borsht, rye bread and orchard fruit throughout the long pale summer. Sometimes, Abraham pulled a pike from the dark waters of the pond. Its flesh was muddy-grey and tasteless, but they ate it all the same.

When winter came the family piled on clothes, one layer upon another, until it was all they could do to move their arms. Ettel began to burn the timber from the outhouses; and when that was gone she started on the furniture.

She was determined not to ask her family for help; her pride would not allow it.

And in all this time, there had been no word from Samuel.

It was a clear, crisp, blue morning. The ice could be heard cracking on the pond and the rooks cawed in the bare black branches of the trees. Carriage wheels rattled across the iced flagstones of the yard.

Ettel rubbed a hole in the frost ferns of the window. A large black travelling coach stood in the yard. The breath of the horses plumed into the air, the coachman stamped his feet to restore circulation. The carriage door opened and a pair of neat little boots could be seen kicking down the folding steps. A figure descended, wreathed in a thick black cloak, its capacious hood drawn up.

Fanny Sinson, her hands thrust into her white fur muff, made her way gingerly across the ice to the front door.

Banished to the nursery, the children strained to hear what was being said in the parlour below. The hum of female conversation rose and fell; pacing was heard; raised voices. Chairs scraped back, the parlour door opened and Ettel's clogs clattered down the passageway and up the stairs.

When she entered the nursery, Ettel's face was expressionless, but her nose was rose red and pinched.

'Pack everything,' she said, 'we are going to stay with your Aunt Sinson'.

Bundled into the dank old-leather-smelling gloom of the carriage, Ettel, her sister, Fanny, and the children jolted their way through the watery afternoon sunshine and into the smoke-tainted gloom of evening.

As the children slept, Ettel stared out of the window; it was steamed over, but her eyes were glazed and unfocussed. Fanny, normally so timid, had been uncharacteristically firm in their discussion. Ettel had been over ruled; her views discounted. Ettel turned down her mouth and pressed her lips together when she remembered this. But then she consoled herself with the thought that at least she had never had to ask for help from her family. She had never had to beg. They could not say that she had brought it all on herself.

The carriage lurched along the deeply rutted tracks; it crunched on the ice and slithered on the grimy snow. They passed through dim forests where a carpet of pine needles deadened all sound; and where hunting owls hooted to each other and foxes barked. They rattled down narrow lanes, through sleeping villages, and across narrow packhorse bridges.

Slowly the soot-black of night bleached to indigo, the stars went out and the sky grew pink and silvered-grey. From the brow of a mist-wreathed heath, the smudge of a town could be made out in the far distance. Chimneys stood out black and jagged. The coach slowed its pace and turned between a pair of tall gateposts; the wrought iron gates were flung back; the gateman doffed his cap and blew on his fingers.

The Grange, for that was the name of Fanny Sinson's home, was large, square, and reassuring. It stood on the very outskirts of the town of Salcininkai[1], which lay in the east of Lithuania. Rows of long pale windows winked in the misty light and a half-moon of yellow light illuminated the double doors.

As the carriage drew up, the doors were flung open, a wedge of light extended down the steps and across the gravel, and the Rabbi Sinson emerged. He had his fur collar turned up, but his smile could be seen. He ran down the steps and wrenched the carriage door open.

'Thank God you are come,' he said, 'I was about to ride out to look for you.'

It was late in the morning, when the children were pushed down the long length of a corridor. Their mother was behind them delivering small shoves to their backs. Their aunt swept ahead of them, leading the way. It was a corridor such as the Block children had never seen before. It had black-and-white tiles on the floor and pale-blue watered silk panels on the walls. The ceiling was wreathed with dancing nymphs, long white shutters were folded back from the windows, and long white curtains hung from brass poles. Fragile tables with bowed legs stood against the panels and lozenges of crystal hung from the lamp brackets. Ettel reflected sourly that the Rabbi had done well for himself.

In the drawing room, a fire blazed. Above a pink-veined marble mantelpiece a square mirror rose to the ceiling; it was edged in heavy gilt. There were Turkish rugs, leather wing chairs with button backs, a blue velvet chaise longue, and a stuffed squirrel beneath a glass dome.

Gathered into a neat circle, the Sinson children awaited their cousins. The boys, slightly older than Abraham, wore suits with sailor-collars; the girls stood stiff in flounced frocks and frilled pinafores; they had large bows in their hair. Mary Sinson stepped forward to greet Annie. The girls were the same age, but Mary looked much older in her high-necked blouse and long blue skirt.

The cousins eyed each other across a deep divide.

Ettel realized just how far she had drifted from the gracious scene that lay before her. Fanny glanced at her sister's weathered face, reddened hands and rusty black gown and wondered what the Rabbi's intellectual callers would make of her.

The Rabbi Sinson smiled at his wife, embraced his sister-in-law, and pushed the Block children closer to the fire.

Russian travelling carriage c. 1890

The forests of Lithuania in the snow

CHAPTER 12

AT THE GRANGE

Courage is knowing what not to fear.

–Plato (427-327)

THE RABBI WAS A PRUDENT man and he had arranged for a cottage to be made ready for the Block family. In reality, it was more of a summerhouse than a cottage, and it stood amid birch trees on the edge of a small lake. There was a pot-bellied boiler that devoured logs, and heat shimmered in the air immediately around it; but it was bitterly cold elsewhere in the summerhouse so the family spent most of their time at The Grange, where fires blazed in every room. Ettel sat stiffly with her sister in the parlour and jabbed at her embroidery. The children joined their cousins in the schoolroom.

The first day of lessons did not go well. The schoolmaster, Yehuda Lev[1], was very young and very clever. He was a protégé of the Rabbi's and, when he discovered how far the Block children lagged behind their cousins in educational competence, he was shocked. Then he made the discovery that Lily was more than worthy of his intellectual attention, and he relaxed his disapproval.

Six months passed; the chill spring dawned and the pale summer waned; and the two families grew accustomed to each other. The Block children learned manners, the Sinson children learned appreciation, and Lily showed herself to be brighter than them all.

One morning, the Rabbi Sinson strode into the parlour with a bundle of letters in his hand. His eyes were on Ettel and he handed her a letter. It was from Samuel. Ettel ripped it open and began to read. Fanny dropped her embroidery and did not pick it up.

Ettel's face fell into lines of blank amazement.

'He is in South Africa,' she said, 'he joined the Gold Rush but it has come to nothing. He has set up as a cabinetmaker in a place called Johannesburg,' she pursed her lips and frowned.

'And what else, Sister,' said Fanny.

'He says it is a good place. He bids us join him there.'

Ettel was torn between relief and horror. She said nothing for some moments, but clenched the letter in her hand.

'But he does not know our situation,' she said eventually, 'and when he learns that we are far from Gilwan, and that the danger is passed, he will return.'

'Better that he does not, sister,' said Fanny.

'He will return,' said Ettel. 'I will write and tell him to join us here.'

'He does not speak of returning,' said Fanny.

'Then he *must* speak of it,' said Ettel. She glowered at her sister.

'He may have found a better life in Africa,' said Fanny, 'it might be—'

'Africa? What do I know of Africa?' said Ettel.

'But—'

'And what do I *want* to know of Africa?' Ettel said.

She folded the letter away and picked up her embroidery.

'He will return,' she said.

And thereafter she froze into a state of denial that would admit no contradiction.

As the year of 1895 drew to a close, it began to seem as if all the news to arrive at The Grange was unsettling. First came word that the Tsar, Alexander III had died of a chill caught on the battlefields; and that he was to be succeeded by his son, Nicholas II.

Then came the news that Nicholas's coronation had been tainted by disaster. Thousands had been trampled to death as they surged forward to seize the food and ale that had been laid out for them in the vast parade ground known as the Khodynka Field, just outside Moscow. The newspapers spoke of bad omens and a doomed reign.

There was news of unrest, of peasant revolt, of brutal suppression and escalating calls for a final revolution. There was news of violent pogroms. And it was said that the new Tsar applauded them.

In Birzai, the Rabbi's weekly intellectual discussion groups grew gradually more heated as the scholars debated the relative merits of the three new political factions. On the right stood a coalition of capitalists and nobility; they urged for peaceful social reform and the retention of the monarchy. In the centre stood the communists; they called for power to be put into the hands of the peasants. And, on the left, stood the Marxist revolutionaries; they would accept nothing less than total social, economic and political revolution. It was not clear which, if any of these factions, held any goodwill for the Jews.

Shortly after the outbreak of the Sino-Russian War, a letter arrived for the Rabbi. It was written on thick yellow governmental paper, stamped in purple and countersigned in red. It stated that the eldest of the Sinson boys, Eli, had been called up for service in the Russian army; Eli Sinson was just twelve-years-old.

The Rabbi stared at the letter in disbelief. He had hoped that amid the morass of Russian bureaucracy, the confusion of Nicholas's doomed reign, and the rumblings of revolution, the fact that his son had arrived at the age of conscription might have gone unnoticed.

He read the letter again: Eli was to report to the Military Academy in Vilnius within a week; and his failure to do so would attract the harshest of penalties.

White-faced the Rabbi rushed in search of Fanny. Their discussion was short. The Rabbi put his carefully laid plans for flight into action.

'You will come with us,' said Fanny to her sister.

'No,' said Ettel, 'I am waiting for Samuel.'

'And if he does not come?'

'He will come.'

'Then let us at least take the children,' said Fanny.

'No,' said Ettel, 'we will wait for Samuel.'

'Please, Mamma,' said Annie Block.

'Certainly not,' said Ettel.

'Let her go,' said Fanny.

Ettel looked in surprise at her sister.

'Let her go, Ettel. She is seventeen; old enough to decide for herself,' said Fanny. She eyed Ettel steadily.

'Very well,' said Ettel. She glared at Annie, 'forsake us if you must, but your father will be displeased by your desertion,' she said.

'Papa will not come back,' said Annie.

'You are a stupid girl,' said her mother, 'and you know nothing.'

Three days later, amid a flurry of confusion and tears, the Sinson family left for the port of Libau.

In her hand, Ettel held the address of their agent in Salcininkai.

CHAPTER 13

ALONE IN RUSSIA

The die is cast.
–Julius Caesar (100-44 BC)

ALONE IN THE EMPTY ROOMS of The Grange, Lily, Abraham, Freda and Ettel Block struggled to survive. Ettel was now forty-years-old; she looked much older, but her determination remained undiminished. No amount of determination, however, could keep the great house warm. The family retreated into the kitchens, which were cavernous and echoing in the absence of the army of cooks and maids that had once scurried there. A small fire was kept alight below the great black iron range, and its warmth was welcome.

Ettel had pinned her hopes on the return of Samuel. She had written to him and told him to join them at The Grange. But when Samuel's letter arrived it spoke only of his new life; and it urged them to delay no longer in leaving Russia.

'Ah,' said Ettel, 'he has not received my letter.'

The next letter from Samuel destroyed all her pretensions. He made it clear that there was no question of his return to Russia; he offered only instructions as to how she and the children should make their way to Africa.

Faced with a blank refusal, Ettel said nothing, but in her heart she began to resent Samuel.

A letter arrived from Fanny Sinson; it was brief. The family had arrived safely in Leeds, she said, where kindly friends had taken them in. Annie was well and the Rabbi hoped to find work in a textile mill. Fanny made no mention of how their journey had been. She said merely that she would send money when she could.

The empty months rolled by, but the money never came; and Fanny's letters grew shorter and more infrequent until, in the end, they ceased to come at all. Ettel did not pause to ask herself why this might be; but she railed constantly against the cruelty of her sister and her husband.

Ettel did not go to the local village often, but when she did, she came to realize that the villagers were shunning her. She was angry and demanded to know what she had done to deserve such treatment. The answer shocked her.

'We are being made to pay for the sins of your family,' she was told, 'the army has been denied your sons; so it is taking ours.'

A few weeks later a man arrived at The Grange. He stood on the front steps with a piece of government paper in his hand.

'We have received information,' he said, 'that this house serves as a depository for revolutionary literature.'

'What nonsense!' said Ettel. Unlike Samuel, she had not learned humility.

'Stand aside,' said the man, I have orders to search the house.'

Ettel stood aside, but she glared at him.

The search was desultory and yielded nothing. The man was truculent when he returned to find Ettel in the kitchen. Had she been more perceptive, she might have realized that this was not the time to provoke him. But this was not Ettel's way.

'So? You found nothing?' she said triumphantly. She folded her arms across her chest.

The man looked beyond Ettel to where the children huddled by the range.

'And what have we here?' he said.

He strode over to Abraham and yanked his chin up.

'How old are you boy?' He said.

Abraham said nothing.

'Old enough,' said the man. He leered at Ettel, 'this time the army will have its boy, eh?'

'You have no authority,' said Ettel.

The man laughed, 'authority is not hard to find in Nicholas's Russia,' he said.

He crammed his peaked cap on his head and strutted down the steps in his high black boots.

Ettel stood silent.

Freda began to wail.

Abraham looked steadily at his mother.

'I have to go,' he said.

Ettel put her hand to her brow and took a deep breath. She walked into the drawing room and reached into the cavity that lay behind one of the tall shutters. It contained an envelope and a pouch of coins. Ettel flung a shawl over her head, pocketed the envelope and the pouch, and returned to the kitchen.

'Stay here,' she said and followed in the wake of the man.

FLIGHT

There are only two mistakes one can make along the road to truth:
not going all the way, and not starting.

–Buddha

Hurrying to the address Rabbi Sinson had given her, Ettel found the agent. He was operating from an upturned barrel in a dimly lit tavern. Rotund and expansive, he had a face like a blighted potato. He told her the boy must go to the Russian port of Libau; and that his steamship ticket must be bought in advance. Ettel bridled and asked why this should be so.

'My good woman,' said the man, 'don't you know that there are thousands of Jews trying to escape Russia every day. It's a seller's market.'

Ettel paid the high price the agent demanded for the ticket. It was for a passage on the *Hero*, a cargo ship operated by Thomas Wilson and Sons of Hull. It was enclosed in a small red pasteboard folder. She thrust this into her pocket.

The cost of escape did not end there; there was also the cost of smuggling Abraham to the port of Libau. Ettel glanced suspiciously at the agent when he named a price for this.

'You won't find anyone willing to do it for less,' he said blandly. His patience was beginning to wear thin, and he began to turn away. Ettel paid the price.

'Does the boy have a passport?' said the man.

'You know he doesn't,' said Ettel.

'Then he will be refused entry to the port of Hull.'

'I have no more money,' said Ettel.

The agent eyed her. He rasped the stubble on his chin and looked her insolently up and down. She bit her lip. The cost of the passport would leave but a few coins in the pouch.

A woman with a haunted face slipped into the tavern. After a brief consultation, she was directed to the agent's barrel.

'Well?' he said to Ettel. She paid the price.

As night fell, Ettel and Lily waited at the bottom of the carriage drive for the cart to arrive. Abraham was bundled between them wearing as many clothes as possible. Sewn into the lining of his overcoat were the ticket, a small amount of money and the address of the Sinson family in Leeds. In his pocket, tied up in a handkerchief, were a hunk of rye bread, a heel of cheese and an apple.

When the cart arrived, much later than had been agreed, it proved to be a high-sided waggon piled with muddied potatoes. Lifting some sacking to its rear, the carter indicated a dark space where another boy was already huddled. Abraham scrambled in beside him.

Before the sackcloth fell over the face of his mother, Abraham opened his mouth to bid her farewell.

'No talking,' barked the carter, his face in shadow beneath a greasy hat. He climbed back up to his box and flicked his whip. The carthorses stamped their great hooves and snorted. Slowly the cart moved forward.

Standing in the lane, Ettel watched the cart until it disappeared around the corner.

It took two days for the cart to reach Libau. Two other boys were picked up along the way; and a head-scarved woman with a silent swaddled baby clamped to her chest. The cart made few stops, they were given no food, and the refills of the stone water flagon were rare. As night fell on the first evening, the cart swayed to a halt, and splinters of light crept between its rough wooden slats. The sounds of a tavern could be heard: shouts, laughter, and the clink of bridals. They could smell food.

But it was not for them.

The carter fed and watered the horses and headed into the tavern. When he returned, he was muttering drunk. Once the glow of the tavern had been swallowed up by the gloom of the forest, he pulled the horses to a halt. He lurched and swore his way down the length of the cart, hoisted the sacking and raised his lantern. The suddenness of its glare blinded the travellers.

'Give me money or get out,' said the carter.

They gave him money; but he was wilier than they, and he knew that they had held some back. In the middle of the night he demanded more; and they gave it to him. The carter had a nose for money, and he knew when he had taken all that they had. So when he stopped the cart the next time he merely raked them with his eyes and pointed.

From Abraham, he took an overcoat, from the boys a watch, a belt and a jacket. From the woman, the carter took her wedding ring. He pointed to the baby's bonnet. The woman removed it and handed it to him; the baby lay silent and still.

The travellers had no way of marking the passage of time, but eventually the scent of the forest was replaced by the bitter tang of peat and heathland. Then came a burr of gentle village talk, which was replaced by the harsh babble of a town. The cart jolted over railway lines and the carter exchanged insults with other drivers. Gulls shrieked, and blasts of chill, damp, salty air seeped into the frowsy warmth of the space beneath the cart.

They had arrived at Libau.

A milky sun rose over the iron-grey waters of the Baltic as the travellers climbed bone-stiff from the cart. They were met with a sluice of rain that needled their cheeks. Through eyes watering from the harsh glare of daylight, they saw that they were surrounded by gaunt blind-eyed buildings that rose to high rain-slicked roofs. There was a sea wall in the distance where a line of derricks stood hunched and idle. Three fat red funnels rose above them. A tangle of masts and the clink-clink of rigging marked where the herring fleet wallowed on its moorings. A sweep of bay rounded into a headland where a black and white striped lighthouse stood. Netted cargos hung motionless from cranes, cargo-shed doors banged; and far away a whistle blew.

The carter shoved his charges towards a squat brick building. Above the door, a sign read Helmsing and Grim, Agents for Thomas Wilson and Sons of Hull. Inside was a small room with an empty grate and two long benches. On one wall was a railway clock, on the other a glass kiosk. There was no one inside it.

The travellers looked around for the carter; but he had left them without a word.

They huddled together for warmth, but the chill crept up through the soles of their boots; and the long hours passed.

There was a great deal of huffing and blowing when the clerk of the shipping line finally appeared. It took some time for him to peel off the layers of his clothing and put his peaked cap on his head. Then he summoned the travellers to the window of his kiosk one by one. He looked very carefully at their tickets, sometimes shooting a glance upwards at their faces as if he might discern some shred of deceit there. But he found nothing to fault. He waved them back to the bench and mimed sleep.

The light was fading when he returned. He held open the door and shepherded them out of the waiting room. Bent into the biting wind, the travellers followed the clerk. The rain bucketed into their faces as he led them alongside a tangle of railway lines; across a cobbled square set with fat black iron bollards, and down to the dockside. A ship was moored on the docks where earlier no ship had been. It reared above them as high as a garrison; and it groaned on its rusted iron hawsers. A metal walkway snaked from the dockside to the ship. It had once been white but was now streaked orange with rust. It was hinged; and it clanked and contorted in time with the ship. Across it shuffled a long line of overcoats.

The clerk shoved Abraham towards the end of the line. He joined it and followed it across the gangway and on to the companionway of the ship. The crowd carried him forward and deposited him in the prow of the ship. It was a sharp space with high iron walls and it sloshed with water rainbowed by oil. The squatting overcoats shuffled up to admit his small haunches.

The ship stank of oil, coal and cattle; and from far below came bellows. Abraham hugged his knees and wiped the drip off the end of his nose with the sleeve of his jacket.

With a crash of chains and a blast on her siren, the ship left the dock and the dull thrum of engines set up from deep within her belly. She wallowed out into the rolling glass-green waters of the Baltic Sea, shrugged herself free of the bay, and settled herself into a steady roll-pitch-and-yaw. The hull reared up to meet the great green crests of the waves; and it smacked down into the deep grey troughs. Icy water hurled itself over the overcoats; and the bilges swilled and sucked. As darkness fell, the crew threw straw pallets up from a black hole in the deck. Seizing one, Abraham squeezed it between an old woman and a girl with purple-ringed eyes.

And then he endured.

Sometimes he slept; sometimes he stared up at the sky. Sometimes he watched the blank faces around him. Eventually he retreated into a space in his mind. He had furnished it with a small truckle bed and a patchwork quilt.

CHAPTER 15

LANDING IN ENGLAND

A good traveler has no fixed plans, and is not intent on arriving.
–Lao Tzu (Zhou Dynasty 4-5th century BC)

AT FIRST NO MORE THAN a slate smudge above pale green water, Britain emerged from the waves and her coastline grew steadily more distinct. Long bleak beaches fringed by rain-shrouded hills broke free of the monotonous blur of sky and sea. An estuary yawned; it was flanked by sullen brown mud-banks where oily-feathered cormorants held their wings out to dry.

As the *Hero* steamed up the Humber Estuary, her crew dragged the straw pallets, now stained and stinking, from beneath the passengers. They set them alight and hurled them over the side of the ship. The air was filled with the smell of burning straw and Abraham was reminded of the stubble-fires of his childhood.

The crew prodded the passengers to their feet and marshalled them into line.

The morning was the colour of seagulls as the *Hero* manoeuvered herself clumsily into position off the port of Hull. She gave a blast on her sirens and churned backwards and forwards through the scud-flecked water until she drew abreast of her moorings. Hawsers were hurled and secured, her iron ribs clanged like monstrous cymbals against the dockside and, raspingly, she came to rest. The gangplank fell with a crash; it bucked and squealed as it fought for a grip on the cobbles; and the huddle of refugees shuffled across it.

The refugees staggered as they hit dry land, and the horizon seemed still to rise and fall before their eyes. Then they steadied into a slow-moving chain gang of a queue that wound sluggishly between oiled ropes and disgorged into a large shed where white soup-plate lights glared down on them.

Orders were shouted in a language they could not comprehend. They were herded into lines and harried into queues. A stethoscope was poked into Abraham's clothing, and a light was shone into his eyes. He was bundled and pushed until he faced a row of white-clad women. They were ladling soup into enamel bowls.

'Smile lad,' said one of them in Yiddish, 'you're safe now.'

They were the kindest words he had heard in a long time.

'All those for Leeds!' a man bellowed.

Toe to heel, toe to heel, the refugees snaked out of the immigration hall and on to the platform of the Great Northern Railway.

'Leeds, LEEDS, all aboard for Leeds.'

Pressed into the iron cage of the mail-van, Abraham hugged his knees and buried his nose in the musty solace of his trousers. Doors slammed and whistles shrilled as the train pulled out of the station, and the racket and clatter of wheels on tracks began.

In the mail van Abraham's eyes stung with grit and soot.
He closed them.

'LEEDS!'
The train slowed and hushed and shunted to a halt.
'LEEDS!'
The windows banged down and the doors were flung open all the way down the length of the train. Steam billowed, people shouted. Without warning, the wall of the mail van rolled back, light flooded in, and faces beneath shiny black peaked caps peered in. Hands lunged and hauled at the mail-sacks; porters swung themselves up into the van and tossed parcels down to their fellows on the platform below.

Bleary-eyed and rank-mouthed, Abraham edged towards the gap that lay between the mail-van and the platform; it was wide but he jumped it.

Before his feet touched the ground a hand punched out of the air and grabbed him by the collar of his jacket. The same hand dumped him on a metal barrow. He craned back to see who his captor might be. He saw bright blue eyes set in a soot-stained ferret of a face.

'Hello, young fellow,' said the man. He spoke Yiddish, but not as a Jew would speak it.

'I'm Jimmy Gilmour,' he said, 'got people coming for you?'

Abraham fished in his pocket for the folded paper that bore the Sinson's address.

'They'll be outside,' said Jimmy Gilmour. He forced a passage through the sea of backs using the barrow as a battering ram. Legs buckled at the knees, people swore but Jimmy Gilmour kept on pushing his barrow down the platform, through the ticket hall and out on to an apron of dirty cobbles.

'Here we are!' he said, and he tipped Abraham off the barrow and on to the cobbles.

Then he left.

Abraham looked up to find himself surrounded by black buildings as uneven as rotted teeth. A crowd surged forward to examine him then retreated disappointed by what it had found. For the first time since the sacking had fallen across the face of his mother, Abraham prayed. From the tail end of the meteor of the crowd, a slight figure in a long black overcoat broke free. A long white face beneath a large black hat drew close; it smiled.

The Rabbi Sinson had come.

Hurrying along, his hand enveloped in the dry warmth of his uncle's palm, Abraham found it hard to raise his eyes from the slippery quilt of the cobbles. But he was dimly aware that they scurried along past squat black buildings, tall gates, yawning yards and redbrick chimneys spewing smoke. There were rows of houses all alike, black lampposts with arms outstretched, scrubbed doorsteps, soapy gutters and apron-wrapped women. Above them, ribbons of smoke curled up into a leaden sky. At street level pincushions of moss clung to the snouts of dribbling drainpipes. And from within the gaunt-grim buildings, came the stop-start whir of machinery, and the clatter of paddled treadles.

'Nearly there,' said the Rabbi.

He turned left.

'Copenhagen Street!'

A flight of black-railed steps led up from the cobbles to an open door on the floor above. A pair of women lolled there, shawls clutched tight to their chests; they looked down without interest. Beneath the steps a dark passage yawned; Abraham and the Rabbi dived into it like rabbits down a burrow. Their footsteps echoed hollowly along it.

They emerged into a dull redbrick yard where a terrace of grimy houses stood. Opposite them, across the yard, was a row of rough green wooden doors, each with a diamond-shaped hole cut into it. A man emerged from one of these doors; he hitched his braces, buttoned his flies and nodded to the Rabbi.

The Rabbi pulled Abraham to a halt in front of one of the houses. He pushed him gently towards a grimy door set in a small outshot building.

'I've got him,' he called.

The door opened. Beyond it lay a narrow scullery with a stone sink and damp-pustuled walls. It led into a small room with only one window. The grate was empty, the floorboards were bare. A length of string ran down the centre of the room; a yellowed blanket was flung over it.

From one side of the blanket emerged his cousins, from the other his aunt.

The Streets of Leyland in 1890

CHAPTER 16

COPENHAGEN STREET

It's not how much or how little you have that makes you great or small,
but how much or how little you are with what you have.
–Rabbi Samson Raphael Hirsch (1808-1888)

BRAHAM SHARED A MATTRESS WITH his male cousins. It was rolled up in the daytime and served as a bench, which was drawn up to the table at which the family dined. Abraham found nothing strange in his new surroundings. His world had changed so often and so drastically since he had left the Gilwan farmhouse, that he was merely grateful for the fact that Copenhagen Street seemed to offer some constancy. He did, however, find it hard to adjust to the new image of his Aunt Sinson.

Fanny Sinson's silken gowns and lace caps had gone, and she wore a calico pinafore, a shawl, a brown headscarf and wooden clogs. Her piano-playing hands were rubbed red raw from scrubbing other people's sheets, and she was constantly in motion where once she had always been still. But Abraham had no time to dwell on all this because he faced the greater challenge of how to find work on the unforgiving streets of Leyland[1].

Leyland had been flung up in 1840 with the sole purpose of providing shelter for the thousands of textile workers that flooded into Leeds in the wake of the Industrial Revolution. No thought had been given to its planning, and its houses were as small and mean as the Victorian social conscience would allow.

It had never been a model village: and now it was a slum.

It covered an exact square mile of yards, alleys, back-to-back terraces and two-up-two-down houses, which glowered at each other across narrow cobbled streets. Four or five families might share one of these houses. Each had a tin bath hung at the head of the cellar steps; and it was taken down every Friday night and filled with hot water. A clotheshorse draped with damp shirts was set up around it, and every member of the house took it in turns to scrub themselves in the grey water it contained. Across every yard ran a row of 'privies', which as many as fifty people might share. But privacy itself was a thing unknown in Leyland.

In its initial incarnation, Leyland had housed Irish immigrants escaping the potato famine: now it housed Jews escaping the pogroms. But certain adjustments had had to be made to allow for the switch of inhabitants. The churches had become synagogues, the billiard halls had become public baths, and the public houses had become meeting rooms called *steibels*, each of which bore the name of a particular Lithuanian village. There were shops and market stalls, but these had remained unchanged, though they bore Jewish names. Solomon Jacobs kept a herd of cows that he swore gave kosher milk. And on Friday nights, the weaving Irish drunks were replaced by people hurrying to bathe before the lighting of the candles for the Shabbat meal.

With the arrival of the Jews, Leyland's commercial character had changed. It had turned its

The Streets of Leyland in 1890

face against the rowdy crash and clatter of the textile mills, and adopted instead the gentle whir of the garment industry. The tenement blocks of the mill workers had been turned into sweatshops, and here the workers paddled their treadles for twelve hours a day. Then they lay down beneath their machines to sleep the night.

It was a Leyland man, John Barran, who had invented the concept of piecework. And this was the foundation upon which the sweatshops were built. He realized that any worker, no matter how unskilled, could produce one small piece of a greater garment better, cheaper and faster than a lone tailor could produce the whole. But it took a tailor from Kovno to transform Leyland into the 'home of gentlemen's tailoring'.

Mr Moshe Osinsky[2] was gifted; his suits were well cut and affordable, and he couldn't make them fast enough. But he was troubled by the fear that his name might not afford them the cachet he knew they deserved. So Mr Moshe renamed himself Montague Burton, and his clothing chain likewise.

Mr Moshe had never intended it, but this caused a new idiom to enter the English language. As gentlemen the length and breadth of England hurried out to buy one of his superlative suits they were said to have 'gone for a Burton'.

Mr Moshe hated the phrase, but he had to admit that it sold suits.

It was in Mr Montague Burton's factory in Leyland that the fifteen-year-old Abraham Block got his first job.

The Rabbi Sinson had arranged the interview and his Aunt Sinson had ensured that he was clad in one of his cousin's outgrown Knickerbocker suits. He wore a shirt with a celluloid collar that hurt his neck, and on his head was a baker-boy cap.

Abraham and the Rabbi set off early through darkly drizzled streets that rang to the sound of steel toecaps on paving stones. The breath of carthorses billowed out into the air, and regiments of glass milk bottles rattled. The factory, which was known simply as 'Burton's', occupied an entire block and stood behind large black wrought iron gates. Across its towering Gothic frontage was a large sign. It read Montague Burton's Tailoring for Gentlemen wrought in iron letters as tall as a man.

Burton's Front Office stood between the factory and the world. It had a half-glassed door with a brass bell that jangled to announce Abraham and the Rabbi. The Front Office had a green-marbled linoleum floor worn bare in places; and a row of hard-backed chairs with shiny green seats that stood uncompromisingly along one wall. A large round clock ticked above the chairs, and through the thin ceiling came the steady bump and grind of sewing machines. At a small desk, her legs shielded by a modesty panel, sat a lady. As they entered, she was engaged in inserting a sheet of paper into the platen of a heavy gold and black typewriter.

'Good morning,' said the Rabbi, raising his hat. 'We have an appointment with Mr Burton.'
'Indeed?' said the lady.

She looked at her diary.

'Please take a seat,' she said, and indicated the row of chairs.

Abraham sat on the very edge of his chair so that his feet might reach the floor, and he turned his cap around and around in his hands. The Rabbi, his eyes straight ahead, put out one white hand to still this motion.

They were ushered into a large office with frosted glass panels. Abraham saw an expanse of pale green blotting paper enclosed in tooled red Morocco leather. Mr Montague Burton reared from beyond this sheet of green to greet them. He was slight, balding, dapper and bespectacled and he smelled of camphor. He gestured to the two chairs drawn up before his desk.

'So this is the boy,' he said.

He shook the Rabbi's hand and ignored Abraham.

The two men talked and Abraham waited. Eventually both men turned to look at him.

'Yes,' said Mr Burton, 'we will start him as a Burton's Boy for the sum agreed?'

His glasses flashed towards the Rabbi, who nodded.

'Six to six, bring a packed lunch, must be neat, must be nimble, must be on time,' said Mr Burton.

He tapped his blotter with his pencil as he pronounced each condition.

'Yes, Mr Burton. Thank you, Mr Burton,' said the Rabbi.

Mr Burton beamed upon Abraham.

'Report to the factory gates Monday next,' he said 'and be sure to wear a pair of strong strong boots!'

CHAPTER 17

TAILORING FOR GENTLEMEN

When a man tells you that he got rich through hard work, ask him: 'Whose?'
–Don Marquis, American Poet (1878-1937)

WHEN MONDAY MORNING ARRIVED, HIS stomach hollow, a flat cap on his head, and boots a size too large on his feet, Abraham presented himself at the factory gates. He was half-an-hour early and it was not quite light as he stood in the persistent drizzle outside 'Deliveries'. It was a small building, rather like a military guardhouse, and it stood just within the great iron scrolls of the gates. Shafts of yellow light spilled out on to the wet pavement; and voices could be heard from within.

Abraham removed his cap and stepped inside.

'Deliveries' was lined with shelves; they were stacked high with brown-paper parcels, and each parcel was tied with string and hung with a luggage label upon which a number was written. A high counter divided the room. On one side of the counter a line of boys waited. Each had a large leather satchel worn crosswise across his short jacket.

On the other side of the counter stood a clerk in a beige apron, with his sleeves rolled up. As each boy stepped smartly up to the counter, the clerk pulled a parcel down from the shelves and handed it to the boy. He noted its number in his large green ledger, and dismissed the boy with an impatient flick of his fingers.

When Abraham's turn came to step up to the counter, he found he could barely see over it. The clerk, leaning on one elbow, craned down to look at him.

'New boy,' he observed. 'Speak English?'

'Learning,' said Abraham.

'Must learn English,' said the clerk in Yiddish. 'Mr Burton is very hot on the speaking of English. Oh yes, he's very hot indeed.'

The clerk explained the nature of Abraham's task; it was not complicated. He had to deliver the parcels allocated to him, to the destinations written upon them; and then he had to return for more.

'Know Leyland?' said the clerk.

'Yes, sir,' said Abraham, who had spent the previous days pacing it out with his cousins. He had memorized the street names phonetically.

'Hmm,' said the clerk. He was skeptical, but he handed Abraham his first Burton's parcel.

The first week was hard, the second was easier, and thereafter Abraham was confident that he knew the maze of Leyland's dark streets as intimately as he knew its huddles of sweatshops.

Most of the sweatshops were tight-packed with sewing machines, but not all. Some had long wooden benches on which the button-holers worked. Others had vast tables on which the cutters wielded their shears. Some had steaming black ranges where the irons of the pressers were heated.

But all the shops stank of sweat, new-milled fabric, and the thin, honey-gold oil that the workers dripped into their machines. The lighting was poor and the workers hunched crook-backed to their tasks; and they rarely spoke to each other. At first Abraham decided that this was because speech was forbidden; but later he realized that the workers did not have time to speak because they were paid by the piece. He learned from this: he ran at full tilt to complete all his deliveries; and he never loitered on corners to catcall like the other boys. His diligence was rewarded: the clerk pronounced him to be the 'Best of Burton's Boys'; and promoted him to Priority Parcels. This, a portal to another realm, concerned the delivery of the finished Burton's suits to the Burton's Emporiums.

It was in one of these establishments that Abraham got his first glimpse of the mythical 'gentlemen' for whom Leyland slaved. Peeping around a door, where he should not have been peeping, he saw a stiff, stout man being eased into a white-chalked jacket; it sprouted tufts of white thread and was missing one sleeve. The gentlemen stood before a large oval mirror. His chest was thrust out and he was being patted and smoothed by a purse-lipped young man with brilliantly crimped hair.

An unusually observant boy, Abraham decided that a gentleman was the thing to be; but he guessed that to be one required money.

From that day, Abraham ensured that for every Burton delivery he made on his outward journeys, he picked up a private commission for his return. He had to run faster, and he had to be circumspect lest his duplicity be discovered, but within weeks he had doubled his wages.

And he had reached the limits of his capacity.

Abraham collected the staves of the broken crates that lay around outside the factory, the yards and the sweatshops. He nailed them together to make a cart, and his Aunt Sinson acquired the chassis of an old perambulator for him.

Abraham Block was in business.

CHAPTER 18

ANNIE BLOCK

Marriage is an adventure, like going to war.
–Gilbert K. Chesterton (1874-1936)

I T HAD NOT TAKEN LONG for Rabbi Sinson's scholarly brilliance to be recognized, and he now officiated at a number of synagogues. He gave evening classes in the Talmud, and he chaired a number of theological discussion groups, to which all manner of earnest intellectuals were drawn. All these things fulfilled the Rabbi's desire to serve his fellow man, but they also made it possible for him to move his family into a house of their own: it stood in Trafalgar Street.

It was in Trafalgar Street that life for the family began to improve. Fanny Sinson ceased taking in washing and began teaching at the local school. She acquired a treadle sewing machine, she took in piecework, and she did fine embroidery work for one of Leyland's fashion houses.

Eli Sinson worked on the printing presses of the *Leeds Herald*, Lev Sinson worked at the Tetley Brewery, and the younger Sinson children worked their evenings as sweepers on the factory floors. Mary Sinson was fortunate; she worked as a pattern-cutter on the production line of the famous nine-gored skirt, which every lady desired. And Annie Block worked as a packer in the local *matzo* biscuit factory.

The Rakusen[1] biscuit factory was almost aggressively modern. At one end of its expanse of bright lights, sacks of flour were delivered. And at the other end of its white tiled corridors cartons of biscuits emerged. And these were loaded on to horse-drawn vans in navy blue and gold livery. Meanwhile, the Rakusen ovens scrawled furls of black smoke over Leyland's skies and the Rakusen vats filled its streets with the rank reek of sour dough.

Mr Rakusen had been a watchmaker before he fled the pogroms of Minsk. And, when he first arrived in Leyland, he continued in this trade. But then Mr Rakusen made a discovery, which was that Leyland folk had no interest in charting the passage of time; for the simple reason that they had so little of it to expend as they wished. So he decided to take a leap of faith on one of his hobbies.

Mr Rakusen liked to bake, and his brittle-thin, crispy-white *matzo* biscuits were especially popular for the feast of Passover. At first Mr Rakusen had been flattered by the success of his biscuits, and he had been happy to give them away to his family and friends. But then total strangers arrived on his doorstep and proffered money for the biscuits; and this made him think.

Mr Rakusen gave up watchmaking and invested his savings in the installation of an automated production line. His faith was justified and, virtually over night, the Rakusen *matzo* became the biscuit of choice of British Jewry. As Mr Rakusen's time shrank, he realized that he needed a manager and, since he had no sons, he advertised for a young 'lieutenant': Nathan Harris got the job.

Sharp of elbow in his Burton's suit, Nathan Harris was a man made for success, or so thought Annie Block[2], who observed his rise to fame from her position on a stool on the production line. She determined to marry him and escape the chaos of the Sinson household and the lowliness of her stool.

Like her mother, Ettel, Annie was no beauty. But she was shapely and dark and people liked to call her striking. She had inherited her mother's determination, and she had no doubt in her ability to get what she wanted. She also believed in Ettel's tales regarding the ills of marrying beneath oneself; and Annie was determined not to do likewise.

The conquest of Mr Harris was swiftly executed.

Mary Sinson was persuaded to bring home a pattern for the famous nine-gore skirt and Fanny Sinson was prevailed upon to make it. Annie sewed rows of pin-tucks into the fashionable bodice of the so-called 'pigeon pouter' shirt, and she clinched her waist into a broad black belt so as to create the illusion of an hourglass figure. She trimmed a hat, and set off on a bright Saturday morning to encounter Mr Harris: by chance.

Nathan Harris liked to think of himself as ruthless, but he was no match for Annie Block; and he had proposed marriage before he had realized he desired it. It was then that Annie told him that she wanted to get married immediately; that she could not wait. Annie lowered her lashes as she said this; and Mr Harris sweated in his tight celluloid collar and studs.

Within a matter of weeks they were married and had moved to a small house in Broad Street.

CHAPTER 19

ROSIE DANIELS

All paid jobs absorb and degrade the mind.

–Aristotle, Greek philosopher (384-322 BC)

Rosie Daniels[1] was Mr Rakusen's secretary. She was also his wife's younger sister, and she shared their marital home. This was not an arrangement that suited Mrs Rakusen, who knew her sister to be beautiful and her husband to be susceptible. So when she learned that 'young Mr Harris' had married and moved into a house much larger than he, in her opinion, had any right to, Mrs Rakusen skewered her hat to her head and set off to the biscuit factory.

'Well, Mr Harris,' she said, 'I hear you are married.'

'Indeed, Mrs Rakusen,' said Mr Harris.

'And moved into a new house in Broad Street?' said Mrs Rakusen, an eyebrow raised.

'Indeed,' said Mr Harris.

'So much expense in getting married and setting up home,' said Mrs Rakusen.

'Oh, not—'

'Oh yes,' said Mrs Rakusen, 'in fact Mr Rakusen and I are very concerned that you should not over reach yourself, Mr Harris,' said Mrs Rakusen

'Over reach myself…?'

'Financially,' said Mrs Rakusen, sharply.

'Ah…' said Mr Harris.

'We have decided that you must take a lodger,' said Mrs Rakusen, all gentleness again.

Mr Harris said nothing.

'My sister, Rosie,' said Mrs Rakusen.

'Ah…' said Mr Harris.

'Dear Rosie has been looking for lodgings for some time,' confided Mrs Rakusen, 'but nothing has proved quite suitable. Not for a girl of her background, you understand.'

'Oh, err, quite…' said Mr Harris.

'But of course with you and Annie,' Mrs Rakusen smiled, 'whom we like to think of as family,' she smiled again, 'it would be quite a different proposition.'

'I—'

'And Mr Rakusen is quite delighted by the idea,' said Mrs Rakusen.

Mr Harris wavered, but not for long.

'You are very kind to think of us, Mrs Rakusen,' he said, 'Annie will be delighted.'

Annie was not delighted. Rosie was not the kind of girl that any woman would want to find at her breakfast table, newly married or not. But she could not deny the favour that Rosie's presence would bestow upon them.

When Abraham next visited his sister, he did not stay long. He had received a letter from Ettel that he wished to share with Annie and, when this had been done, he made his farewells and stepped out on to the wet pavement.

And there he found Rosie with her hand raised to insert her key in the lock of the front door.

At the age of eighteen Abraham Block had seen many girls and quite a number of them had noted his good looks and smiled upon him. But he had never seen the like of Rosie Daniels.

Sublimely curved, tiny of waist and full of chest Rosie had the sort of figure, face and hair that every woman of the late Victorian age prayed for; and she knew it.

With the faintest of smiles, Rosie slipped past Abraham and into the house. Before she closed the door, she raised one hand to remove the sailor hat set so casually askew on her tight blonde curls. It was a gesture that she knew displayed her figure to its very best advantage.

As the door closed, Abraham stood in the street and stared at its blank panels.

Rosie Daniels had hit him hard.

Abraham became an avid family visitor; and was always to be found in the narrow little house in Broad Street. And, when he wasn't sitting in the front parlour looking at Rosie Daniels, he was out on the streets looking for a better job. Rosie, he reasoned, could not be expected to look at a barrow boy.

Jobs were not easily found in Leyland and those that paid the kind of sums that Abraham had in mind were as needles in haystacks. He persevered, but he grew impatient. Then his thoughts lighted upon Mr Nathan Harris and his position of privilege at the Rakusen biscuit factory.

The job that Nathan Harris secured for Abraham was at the hot end of the production line. His task was to feed the greased trays of pallid paper-thin biscuits into the maw of the vast wood-fired oven.

And he hated it.

He hated the blast of raw heat that rushed from the oven, and he hated the doleful clang of its closing door. He hated the glare from the stark-white walls, and he hated the torture of having to stand in one place all day long; until his feet in their white gumboots went numb.

But more than anything else he loathed the dank-sour stink of the dough, which slunk into every crevice of his being. Soon, just to look at the clammy squares as they sweated in the heat made Abraham's gorge rise.

But he endured because he had purpose: Rosie Daniels.

CHAPTER 20

LILY BLOCK

You will never do anything in this world without courage.
It is the greatest quality of the mind next to honor.
–Aristotle, Greek philosopher (384-322 BC)

IT DID NOT TAKE THE Lithuanian Secret Police long to discover that yet another bird had flown the despised Sinson nest; and they determined to make life as hard as they could for Ettel Block. There were numerous ways in which they might do this. They could stop her and search her in the village. They could read or withhold her mail, and they could threaten to search the house for anti-Russian propaganda.

They did all of these things, but Ettel Block remained impervious.

Then Lily Block delivered herself into their hands.

It was Lily's custom to meet with her former schoolmaster, Yehuda Lev, in the empty gatehouse that stood by the gates to The Grange. It was cold there, but they managed to discuss politics, ethics, philosophy and the coming revolution, all of which interested them both greatly.

It had not been long after the departure of the Sinson family that Lily and Yehuda had met once again in the village. He, keen to retain his brightest pupil, had offered to continue with Lily's literary education. And she, hungry for knowledge, had accepted.

In Yehuda, Lily believed she had found her intellectual soul mate. He, like her, was a believer in the Haskalah Movement, which was devoted towards furthering Jewish enlightenment. He was well read, he was a gifted teacher, he was inspired; and he was inspiring.

In Lily, Yehuda believed he had found the ideal disciple. She was intelligent, she learned quickly and she challenged him. He wished that this were all that he saw in Lily, but it was not. Though just fifteen, Lily looked much older than her years. She was tall and strongly built; her figure was good, and she retained her cloud of dark curls, and Yehuda Lev was attracted to her.

But he was not the only one.

It was when she was returning from one of her meetings with Yehuda that Lily found herself confronted by a government agent. He was a sweaty fellow with a pockmarked face and brown teeth; and he had accosted her before.

On that occasion the agent had claimed the right to search her, and he had run his fat hands all over her body searching, he said, for revolutionary literature. On this occasion, Lily could not afford him any such right. Because in her pocket she carried a letter from the Rabbi Sinson; and it laid out in detail how the family might escape Russia.

Lily forced a smile and greeted the agent politely, but it made no difference. His patting and squeezing began. Within minutes the letter had been found. It was in Yiddish and he could not fully comprehend its meaning; but he could guess.

'Corresponding with enemies of the state,' the man said, 'now here's a pretty tale.'

'Just my uncle,' said Lily.

'Your uncle is a Jewish plotter,' said the agent, 'and this letter will put you all in jail.'

'Please, I've done you no harm,' said Lily.

'Oh, please is it now?' The agent mimicked her; he licked his lips and stared at the rise and fall of her breasts beneath the simple white blouse.

'Well if you've done me no harm, little girl,' he said, 'do me some good.' His hands clutched at her.

Lily slapped them away and ran.

'Little bitch,' the man called after her.

'Little Jewish bitch, you are going to regret that!'

The next day, Lily followed the instructions contained in the Rabbi's letter. They outlined how the family should go secretly to the town of Lida, where they would be met by his friends, who would arrange their onward journey.

But Lily planned only for her own escape.

And she did not tell Ettel, because she knew that Ettel would not let her go.

Within a week the Rabbi's friends had sent Lily a ticket for the Great Northern Line's steamship the *Kew Bridge*. They directed her to take the train to Lida where they said she would be met.

It was winter and the station lay a four-hour walk away, and the area was thick with government agents. Lily told Yehuda what she planned and asked him to accompany her.

On the appointed day, dressed in as many clothes as possible, Lily crept from The Grange and met Yehuda at the gatehouse. The sky was heavy with snow and, as they set off, it began to fall in flakes as large and soft as cherry blossom.

As their boots crunched through the frozen puddles, and the snowflakes melted on their cheeks, Lily said little; but she thought deeply.

What would her mother do without her?

Would the Secret Police punish her mother and her little sister, Freda?

Had she put them in danger?

It was dark when Lily and Yehuda reached the station and the platform was already lined with people, and piled with crates, bales of linen and sacks of mail.

'We don't have long,' said Yehuda, 'the train is coming.'

Lily reached a decision.

'Please return to my mother,' she said, 'and tell her that I have gone.'

'Is that wise?' said Yehuda.

'No,' said Lily, 'but I don't want her to worry. But, please, I beg of you, do not tell her where I have gone.'

Yehuda nodded.

'You will write to me?' he said.

'Of course.'

'I will miss you, I've—'

'It's here!' said Lily staring at the great black disc of the engine as it pulled into the station amid clouds of smoke and steam.

'Help me up!' she said. She struggled to reach the door, which towered high above her. He cupped his hands and she used them as a step. Then she was gone from him and seated inside the carriage.

The train did not wait.

As the doors slammed and the windows banged up and down, the guard's flag descended, his whistle blew, and the huge pistons that drove the iron wheels began to turn. Yehuda ran alongside the train as it gathered speed, he pressed his hand to Lily's soot-covered window.

She saw his mouth moving, but she could not make out the words.

As the train outpaced him, Yehuda stood panting on the platform.

He waved until it disappeared around a bend in the tracks.

He did not suppose it would have made any difference had she understood what he had been trying to tell her.

Union Castle liners in dock 1900

CHAPTER 21

EARNING A LIVING

Gravitation is not responsible for people falling in love.
–Albert Einstein, German physicist (1879-1955)

V ISITING HIS SISTER AS OFTEN as he did in the year of 1898, it was inevitable that Abraham and Rosie should fall in love. They came from starkly different backgrounds, and they were attracted by the sheer extremes of their oppositeness. He was so dark, she was so fair; he was so Lithuanian; she was so northern British. He had known harshness; she had been cherished. But these things apart, they shared the characteristics of astuteness, ambition, a raw awareness and an unshakeable conviction that better times lay ahead. They also shared the same disdain for the values that Annie and Nathan held so dear.

And Abraham made Rosie laugh.

Rosie loved to laugh. She laughed at Abraham's guttural English, and how his clothes smelt of *matzo* dough; she laughed at his tales of his homeland, and she laughed at his dreams for the future. She laughed at his obvious devotion to her, and she laughed at his frequent despair over it. But Abraham didn't care. When Rosie laughed he was happy, and if it was at his expense so be it.

Abraham never laughed at Rosie. He knew that she was easily hurt and slow to forgive and he had no wish to shake her faith in herself, which he knew was largely based on her looks. Nor did he flatter her and tell her how pretty she was: because every other factory lad in Leyland did that. And she expected it.

But they made an attractive pair. Sometimes, when they walked out together, hard-faced women would halt their doorstep conversations and smile as the couple passed. Though whether they smiled at the remembrance of their own love, or the foolishness of love in general was not clear.

Sometimes Abraham and Rosie walked the banks of the canal, where blinkered horses trudged the towpaths and hauled their painted barges behind them. Sometimes they paused at the locks and they watched as the massive gates opened, and the broth-brown water emptied into the sud-flecked basin below.

But wherever they walked, they talked of the future.

Rosie's future held a hat shop and a large house on the outskirts of Leeds. It had curved glass in its huge front windows, a porcelain bell push, a porticoed porch and a tall monkey-puzzle tree in the front garden.

Abraham's future held his father, South Africa and the making of his fortune. He was not clear how this would become reality, but he painted a graphic picture of a large house not entirely dissimilar to the one on the outskirts of Leeds.

It was only a brief leap between their future apart and their future together. And when that leap was made Abraham realized that his time in Leyland was over. Life in the biscuit factory was taking him nowhere. It would never make him wealthy and it would never allow him to marry Rosie. And he hated it still.

As he approached his seventeenth birthday, Abraham wrote to his father.

It was not until the September of 1900 that Abraham received his reply; and its contents surprised him. His father wrote that he had joined the British Army and was fighting the Boers of the Transvaal and Orange Free State. He spoke of a battle won, and how the towns of Johannesburg and Pretoria were now in British hands. He said he thought it would not be long before the war was over, and he said that he looked forward greatly to Abraham's arrival. But he also said that he could not guarantee when he would be back at his home on the outskirts of Johannesburg. It was not an overly encouraging letter, or a completely discouraging one, but it was all that Abraham needed.

As Christmas approached, he worked all the hours he could in the Rakusen biscuit factory. And as he fed the pallid biscuits into the roaring oven he planned his departure; and he realized that the stench of the dough no longer sickened him. As the time for his departure grew close, Abraham tried to make Rosie promise that she would wait for him to return and marry her. But Rosie only laughed.

'You'd best make your fortune first, Abraham Block,' she said, 'and then we'll talk of marriage.'

On New Year's Day, 1901, Abraham took the train from Leeds to Hull. He retraced the journey he had made three years earlier, and he found his way easily to the shipping office of the Union Line. He asked the cost of a passage to Cape Town.

The answer stunned him.

It was far higher than he had been led to believe and much more than he had.

'It's the New Year,' said the clerk, 'everyone's off to make a new life, the price goes up.'

The clerk was used to seeing desperate young men with their hopes dashed, but there was something about Abraham's despair that touched him.

'Are you willing to work the passage?' he said.

'Yes,' said Abraham, 'but I'm not a sailor.'

'No need to be,' said the clerk, 'they want deck hands, but these days they can get them for next to nothing. You won't be paid, but you'll get there all the same.'

It was a long shot, but Abraham had come to believe in long shots. He followed the clerk's directions and walked from ship to ship asking, in his eager, open-faced way, if there was any possibility of work. It took him two days before he struck lucky. It was a passenger ship heading to Cape Town and the sailors said the engine room needed grease monkeys.

Abraham had no idea what a grease monkey was, but since he had neither a passport nor his seaman's papers, he deemed himself fortunate to become one. He heaved his kitbag on to his shoulder and followed the sailors up the gangplank and on to the ship.

And far away on a Baltic shore, his sister Lily did likewise.

CHAPTER 22

LILY BETRAYED

It's good to trust others but not to do so is much better.
—Benito Mussolini, Italian politician (1883-1945)

WHEN YEHUDA TOLD ETTEL THAT her daughter had left on a train, a wave of fury broke over him such as he had never experienced before. And when he refused to tell Ettel exactly where Lily had gone, she grabbed him by the shoulders and shook him until he bit straight through his tongue. His mouth flooded with blood.

'She's gone to Lida,' he said. He spat and looked in some disbelief at the blood on the back of his hand.

'Lida? Why Lida?' said Ettel.

But this Yehuda could not tell her, because the prudent Lily had kept these details to herself. Ettel fumed and glowered: then it came to her: the Rabbi Sinsen had a scholarly colleague in Lida: Eli Mieikus.

The next morning, armed with a tightly furled umbrella and a small valise, Ettel trudged to the station and boarded a train to Lida. She arrived at the town's famous Talmudic School and demanded the address of Eli Mieikus[1].

When she arrived there, she found her daughter Lily.

Lily listened to her mother's tirade in silence. And when it was finished she made no attempt to defend her actions.

Ettel drew on her gloves and picked up her valise.

'Come,' she said, 'let us end this madness and return to the station.'

Lily stood up and faced her mother.

'All my life, Mamma,' she said, 'you have told me of how privileged you were to have grown up in Birzai, and to have had a fine education.'

'And what of it?' said Ettel, impatient.

'I had no such privileges and my only chance of finding them lie in Britain,' said Lily.

'That's not the—'

'And all my life, Mamma,' continued Lily, 'you have told me of how you married beneath yourself.'

'That is so, but—'

'And you have warned me not to make the same mistake,' said Lily.

'Yes, I have but—'

'But for all that, Mamma, you won't allow me to better myself, you deny me any chance of a good marriage, and you wish to force me into becoming as bitter as you are,' said Lily.

For several minutes, Ettel said nothing.

She tapped the ferule of her umbrella on the floor.

Then she took some money from her bag and handed it to Lily.

'Very well,' she said, 'go to England like your sister Annie and your brother Abraham. And leave me here like your father has done. But when you have bettered yourself, remember this: it was only my sacrifice that made it possible.'

When the agent arrived to collect Lily, he seemed credible enough. His price was high but this was, he said, because he guaranteed success. He told Lily that they would travel by cart to a place close to the Prussian border, where he would help her to cross. He said she would be met on the other side and taken to the port. He explained that they must travel as man and wife, and he handed her a peasant shawl to cover her dark hair.

The cart journey was long and slow. But Lily, hunched into her coat, with her scarf pulled low over her brow to hide her face, saw little of it. They were challenged by uniformed soldiers, but on every occasion the carter would pull Lily roughly into his arms and he would wink at the guards and tell them how they were newly married.

'Can't wait to get her home,' he would say with a leer. And he would slip his hands inside her coat and squeeze her breasts.

It was a good act and it served them well.

They reached a pair of high green gates beyond which lay a winding drive. A sign over the gates read Dr Stretzl's Vapour Baths. At the end of the drive was a large building, it was tiled in green and had white marble columns; and it looked, Lily thought, like a Greek temple. The agent pushed her through a door into a green tiled chamber that stank of sweat and eucalyptus. It was full of people huddled on to the green marble benches that lined the walls.

'Wait here for your medical examination,' the agent said, 'and then we will proceed'.

In the far corner of the chamber was a dirty white hospital screen. It stood on rusty wheels and shoes could be seen shuffling beyond them. One by one, the people were called behind this screen. There would be a brief murmur of conversation and then a voice would call out, 'passed,' or, 'unfit to travel'.

Those who waited remained silent as the people emerged from behind the screen with their fate decided. Some of these people sobbed, others pleaded, some fumbled with money or jewellery, but it made no difference. Many left grey-faced.

When her time came to go behind the screen, Lily passed the examination with ease, but she found it hard to meet the gaze of those who waited.

The light was fading as the agent returned. He drove a covered cart and there was another woman already seated within it. Looking at her, Lily found it hard to believe that she had passed the medical. She was in late middle age, stooped and her breathing was laboured and rattled in her scrawny chest. The woman threw Lily a hard, assessing glance and dismissed her.

They travelled in silence.

It was a miserable journey and took them across wild heathland pitted with bogs. More than once the agent called for them to climb down from the cart and push. Their feet sank ankle-deep in the black peat; it clutched and sucked at them as the agent urged the horse forward. As the light dwindled, the heath was replaced by thick forest; and all sound was muffled but for the clink of the bridle and the rasp of the woman's breathing.

The cart drew to a halt and the agent helped them down. Behind them lay the forest; ahead lay a wide stretch of cleared land; and tree-stumps poked through the snow. In the distance was a bank of earth.

'That is the border,' whispered the agent.

He tethered the horse, indicated silence, and beckoned them to follow him as he picked his way through the stumps and the snow. At a certain point, he motioned them to the ground. They lay flat with their faces in the snow.

'There are guards all around,' the agent whispered, 'wait here, keep completely still and when you hear a low whistle from me run.'

They stared at him in terror.

'Don't stop, don't look back,' he said, 'when you get there, climb up the bank and drop down into the trench. Climb the other side and run to the forest. It is not far, and someone will be waiting for you.'

He did not wish them luck.

His boots crunched away through the snow; and silence fell.

The women waited, tensed for the sound of the whistle, or for the cold click of a rifle.

But there was nothing.

And still nothing.

The cold crept through their clothing and deep into the marrow of their bones, numbing their faces and deadening their feet. Slowly, Lily came to realize that if she did not run soon, she would never run again. With dull resignation she realized that the agent had left them; and that his signal would never come.

She forced her head around in the snow and looked at the woman. From within the dark huddle of clothing that lay as still as death, a pair of deep-set black eyes stared back at her.

The woman knew.

They had been betrayed.

CHAPTER 23

SOUTH AFRICA

Youth is easily deceived because it is quick to hope.
–Aristotle, Greek philosopher (384-322 BC)

ABRAHAM DID NOT KNOW WHAT a grease monkey was when he boarded the freighter bound for Cape Town, but he soon found out.

He worked in the engine room, and it was a searing hot hell with narrow ladders up and down which men swung like monkeys. The domain of a foul-tempered Irishman whose filthy cap proclaimed him to be the Chief Engineer, the engine room lay at the very heart of the ship. It never slept and it never saw daylight. It was a place of perpetual clanking, hissing and spewing; a realm of barely contained chaos where crises came and went amid a flurry of spanners and oaths; where pistons pumped and half-clad men with smut-smeared faces cajoled the cussed beast of an engine down the edge of Europe, down the west coast of Africa, and around the Cape of Good Hope into Cape Town.

Somewhere between Morocco and the Bight of Benin, Abraham turned eighteen, and somewhere before that he learned to strip down to his breeches, coat himself in thick brown grease, eat when he could, sleep when he might, and to slide down ladders without touching the rungs. He also discovered a world where it made no difference whether a man was Lascar or Jamaican; Chinaman or Jew; the rules were the same.

And this was novel.

The engine room bred its own camaraderie. It was of a kind that Abraham had never known before; and he was immediately admitted into its embrace. The men of the engine room were an elite; they were muscled like prizefighters and they bent pipes with their bare hands. They hefted sledgehammers and they shovelled tons of coal into the roaring maw of the engine until they were as strong as oxen. Oiled and naked they had black skull-and-cross-bones faces with white eye-sockets and grinning teeth; and the rest of the crew feared them.

When the freighter pulled into the great sweep of Table Mountain Bay, the youth that had left Leyland was gone and a sturdy fellow with a rough tongue and a ready swing of a calloused fist had taken his place. As he looked over the glinting waters of Cape Town, where seal snouts bobbed, and the African sun shone down from a serene blue sky, Abraham Block swore that he would never again spend his days under the drizzled grey skies of Northern Europe.

The men of the engine room had a creed: they looked after their own; and an insult to one was an insult to all. For them Cape Town was just another layover in an endless reel of ports, but Abraham was their brother and they undertook to find him work on the dockside. They smuggled him ashore and they passed him into the hands of one of their own; they did their duty by him. Then they tipped their blackened nails to their greasy quiffs and swaggered back to their world.

The job to which his comrades had committed him was that of a humper; and it suited Abraham well. Cape Town was a meat depot and the transit point from which all carcasses left Africa. The dockside was lined with stinking warehouses where countless carcasses swung on greasy hooks. And an army of men humped them from hook to chain, chain to ship.

It was tough work but Abraham's muscles were now trained to it. He was blood-smeared and rancid but he didn't care because he was guaranteed a hammock, three meals a day and a wage that would allow him to continue his port hopping until he got to Johannesburg. His next stop was the naval depot of Simonstown, which lay just up the coast.

Simonstown was linked to Cape Town by a busy little single-gauge railway. It hugged the spectacular coastline and rattled through bay after blue bay. They were all beautiful; and they were all enfolded by the hills and vineyards of the Cape; and eventually they opened into the bay of Simonstown.

It was a Navy town, it was square and ordered, roped and flagged; its brass was polished and it knew precisely what could be done and what could not. It took Abraham less than a day to pick up his next job; and it returned him to the comforting hell of the engine room.

It was a troopship bound for Durban, the nearest port to Johannesburg, and it carried a wry and raucous company of British Fusiliers. They cursed, gambled and smoked their way up the coast of Africa to feature in the next act of a war they barely understood. From them, Abraham learned that his father had been only half right in his predictions about the end of the Boer War: the First Boer War had ended, but the Second Boer War had begun almost immediately afterwards. And the Second Boer War, he learned, was radically different from the First; it was hand-to-hand, hot and dusty, and it was played out in the blazing bush of the African veld, where the Boers had the upper hand. Unused to this, the British had elected to play dirty. Under the command of General Kitchener they had been ordered to 'sweep the veld clean and starve the enemy into submission'. And they had done so. Thousands of Boers had been herded into concentration camps where they were dying amid shameful squalor and disease. It was a cruel, mean, ill-fated war, and nobody was proud of it. But it was still going on.

When the troopship docked in Durban, the khaki-clad soldiers disembarked with their knapsacks on their backs, their billycans clanking and their half-smoked cigarettes in their top pockets; and they shuffled into a close line on the dockside. At a given command they moved off. Freed from the engine room with his pay in his pocket, Abraham hefted his kitbag and followed them. He slipped in to place at the back of the line and tramped forward like they did with the peculiarly shuffling gait of an army on the move with no idea of its direction.

In the drill yard the soldiers bumped to a halt. A sergeant with a clipboard in his hand bellowed orders. Lines formed, boots scuffed, men elbowed, jostled, spat, swore and waited for their names to be called. Then they marched smartly forward to receive their orders.

When Abraham's turn came, there was no one behind him and he faced the sergeant alone across the courtyard. The man looked up from his list.

'Well, lad?' he said. 'Why aren't you in uniform?'

It was almost too easy. Thanking God for the superb simplicity of this intervention, Abraham asked if he might sign up for the British Army[1]. The British Army was desperate for men and accepted him. It uniformed him, equipped him, armed him and sent him to the railway station. No tickets were required on the troop train, and when the British Army arrived in Johannesburg

The operation tent, field hospital, Boer War

Faces from the Boer War

it marched itself briskly into the barracks.

Locally engaged, untrained and, as far as the Army could see, unskilled, Abraham was assigned to the duties of a hospital orderly. The barracks had a field hospital; it was hurled together from rope and canvas; it was brutish, barely clean and barely human. Abraham's role was simple: he cleaned. On certain days he pounded calico sheets in stone sinks, on others he boiled bloodied bandages. On some days he stirred vats of boiling shirts, and on others he scrubbed potatoes.

And in six-months he rarely left the barracks.

In January 1902 Cecil Rhodes, the man who had set the Boer War in motion, died at the young age of forty-eight. His death was totally unexpected; thousands of mourners, black and white, filed past his coffin; and thousands more lined the railway line. Encased in his heavy lead coffin, Rhodes was carried high up in to the Matopo Hills where he was buried deep within their huge rocky outcrops. Shortly afterwards the Boers surrendered to the British.

Now the British Army no longer had any use for Abraham Block. He surrendered his uniform, collected his pay and walked out of the barracks. And, since the British Army no longer cared where or how he travelled, he walked into Johannesburg.

Abraham trudged along the road. To either side of him the dust whipped itself into whirling devils that danced off into the dry bush. He had no idea where he was going, but he surmised that if the British Army was done with him, it would be done with his father too; so he might have some hope of finding him.

He thought about Rosie; he had written to her, but had received no reply. This did not particularly surprise him since neither she nor the British Army cared particularly for letters.

CHAPTER 24

PRUSSIA

All the world is full of suffering. It is also full of overcoming.
–Helen Keller (1880-1968)

L ILY BLOCK LAY WITH HER face down in the snow. She knew that if she did not move she would die where she lay. Still on her stomach, she used her arms to propel herself forward across the brittle mantle of snow. Her eyes were fixed on the brown mound of the border trench ahead. Behind her, she heard the harsh rasping of breath. The woman was following her.

It was a long, hard, ungainly squirm and scrabble across the deceitful snow, which collapsed beneath her like the rind on a half-set cheese. She could hear her own panting and the scuffing of her boots. Then she realized that she could not hear the rattle and rasp of the woman. Lily halted and looked back. The woman was still. She lay spread-eagled amid the severed tree stumps face down in the snow. Lily pivoted on her stomach and made her way back. She grabbed the headscarf and yanked the woman's face up. The eyes were dull, the thin mouth was clamped.

'Leave me alone,' said the woman.

It was the first time Lily had heard her speak, she had the gruff, cracked voice of a peasant.

'I want to die here in peace,' said the woman. She looked away. 'Not in agony when the bullets come,' she said. And she returned her face to its death mask in the snow.

Something in the pathos of this miserable defeat made Lily angry; and it gave her strength. She stood up, straddled the woman, grabbed the sodden collar of her coat and hauled her to her feet. The woman swayed in her short, ugly black boots. Lily punched her in the small of the back and forced her forward, then she put her arm about the broad waist, and they lurched forward together.

They were upright; they were clearly visible, and the tree stumps had ceased. Now only white snow lay between them and the bank of earth that marked the border. They stumbled forward exposed and vulnerable. Lily expected the shouts to begin, the shots to come, the black figures to run towards them across the white.

But they did not.

Wrenching the woman along with her, Lily wondered how her life could have tunnelled to the point where all that mattered was the placing of one foot in front of the other in a world of glaring white. And then the white ended and the brown bank of earth rose in front of her.

For a moment Lily stared stupidly at it.

Shots rang out.

Lily pushed the woman up the bank of frozen earth until she was balanced like a square black parcel on its rim. Then she pushed the woman over the edge so that she rolled down into the trench. Lily followed. The trench was deep and filled with water. A thin skein of ice lay on top of it, but this gave way and the icy water closed around their ankles like manacles. They cowered, waiting for the faces to appear above the sparkling white ridge; for the black barrels to be slithered into position, pointing down at them.

But they did not.

More shots rang out. There was shouting. There was screaming. All in an instant, Lily realized that another group of refugees was trying to cross the border nearby. But they had been caught, and the guards were killing them. Lily forced the woman up on to the edge of the trench and scrabbled up beside her. They crouched there. A dark line of firs lay beyond a wide expanse of pure white.

'Run,' said Lily.

And she set off across the snow.

She did not stop and she did not look back. And it was a wedge of time that she would remember for the rest of her life. She bounded across the snow, her heart pounding and her long legs pumping. Shots rang out all around.

Even when she had reached the tree line, Lily kept running. She leapt and crashed through the undergrowth; it tore at her clothing and scratched her face. When she could go no further, she collapsed in a tumble of brushwood. She could hear the woman blundering in her wake. It was dark now. It was silent. Lily listened for the sound of pursuit for as long as she could. But in the end she slept.

'Get up!' The voice spoke Yiddish.

'Get up, girl, GET UP!' Someone was shaking her.

Opening her eyes, Lily saw an old man. He was bundled into a thick coat, which was held together with farming twine. On his head was a fur hat, the earflaps stuck out at odd angles. He was smiling and showing empty gums.

'Come,' he said. He held out his hand to help her up. 'I will take you to safety but we must go now. Hurry!'

Hoisted to her feet, Lily looked around for the woman.

She was gone.

Clutched by fear, Lily reached for the purse, which had been strapped around her waist. It contained all her money.

It was gone.

Lily scrabbled through her pockets for the boat ticket.

It was gone.

The woman had taken everything.

Lily crammed her fist into her mouth to stop herself from whimpering.

Then she remembered: she had sewn the ticket into the lining of her coat.

And it was still there.

The old man had watched this small, bitter drama with knowing pity. But now he beckoned urgently. She followed him through the trees. The forest came to a sudden end. They had walked through a dark world of pine needles, bare trunks and shafts of eerie light that glancing down from above, but suddenly there was pale winter sky, a bank of frozen bracken, and a cart track. Beyond the track was a rough line of bushes, and beyond this were rolling fields of snowy furrows. Lone trees stood out as if sketched in charcoal against the heavy white sky.

The old man set off down the track. Every now and then he threw a glance over his shoulder to see that Lily was following. He moved with a swift but lolloping gait and his breath clouded the air.

The town emerged from the shoulder of frozen furrows spire first; the spire was followed by a scrawl of buildings; they were dark and indistinct, but extensive. The old man picked up his pace.

The light was fading as they arrived on the fringes of the town, but the houses still straggled thinly; and habitation had only just begun. A tight huddle of buildings stood slightly apart from the rest. The roof of the central building was bowed and a thin scribble of smoke seeped from a hole cut in its sagging thatch. A square sign hung outside, but it was mantled in snow and could not be made out. There was a hitching rail bare of horses. A glimmer of light leaked from small windows draped in sacks, and the thatch straggled low over them. In the centre of the building was a door: rough nailed planks with a black latch. The old man put his shoulder against the door and shoved it open. He stood back and waved Lily inside. He smiled through cracked lips.

It was murky inside. The roof was low and the floor no more than hard-packed earth. It was smoky; and a poor fire smouldered in the hearth. The place smelt of old tobacco and stale ale. From one of the low, smoke-blackened beams hung a single lantern. In the corner, hunched over a three-legged table, sat two men.

They stared at Lily.

Lily turned to the old man for reassurance. But he was gone. Backing against the wall with her eyes locked on the two men, Lily felt her way along it until she reached a door. She scrabbled for the latch, lifted it and backed through the door. She found herself in a small yard.

The yard was enclosed by low buildings; there was a trough and a pump, some straw and a pile of manure. Across the flagstones was a green door with a hole cut into it to admit the light. Lily ran to the door and slammed it behind her. There was a bolt on the inside and she worked it across into the hasp with clumsy fingers. She slid down the door until she sat with her back to it, her arms around her knees. There was a filth-caked hole in the floor and it stank, but Lily forced herself to breath in the stench. She put her head on her knees and stilled her breathing. The light from the small square hole in the door darkened into indigo and was steadily punched through with a pinprick of stars.

Lily awoke to the sound of knocking. The square hole was filled with blue. Someone was rattling the door and shouting for it to be opened.

A girl stood on the step, her shawl clasped tight around her. When she saw Lily she took a step backwards and then turned and ran across the yard into the tavern.

Numb and uncaring, Lily stood where she was. She scraped the bubbled paint off the door of the privy with her nail.

When the girl returned, she pulled Lily out into the yard.

'You looked like a ghost,' she said.

She proffered a white enamel mug with a blue rim; steam rose from it.

'It's coffee, drink it,' the girl said.

Thick, sweet, gritty and strong, the coffee jolted Lily back into urgency. She questioned the girl; and she found that her luck had changed. The tavern stood on the outskirts of Konigsberg and it was but an hour's walk to the docks.

The old man had served her well.

The clerk of the shipping office did not like refugees. Their hunching and desperation disturbed him; he avoided looking into their empty eyes. But he had never seen a refugee quite like Lily Block before. She was wafer thin and black clad. She was smeared in earth and she stank, but she stood before him with a halo of black curls framing her white face. The light was behind her and the curls glowed with violet, pink and blue lights. Beneath a pair of black winging brows, dark eyes surveyed him with some impatience.

The girl thrust a ticket at him. She took a step backwards as he inspected it, as if preparing to run. He could feel her eyes upon him as he checked the ticket. She was feral and hungry for his pronouncement on her destiny.

'I don't know where you've come from my girl,' he said, 'and I don't want to. But your ship is due in today.'

The girl took a gulp of air and her thin shoulders dropped. She had been holding herself as taut as a catapult ready to let fly. 'Thank you,' she said.

'You need to rest,' said the clerk. He surprised himself; he was not characteristically kind. He waved her to a bench in the waiting room. He got down on his knees and lit the fire, blowing on it until it caught light.

'I'll call you when the time comes,' he said.

He smiled at her.

When he returned, the clerk found Lily asleep and it hurt him to wake her. But she sprang to her feet; she was strong; and she was ready. He led her down to the dockside. A ship had docked and people flocked around it. The clerk hustled Lily through the crowd and on to the decks of the ship. He had some small authority and he used it. He put her into a cabin, although she had not paid for such.

There was only one small porthole and the cabin was dark. It took seconds for Lily's vision to adjust to the gloom: she realized the cabin was tight packed with people.

'Move up,' shouted the clerk, 'come on, move up and let her sit down.'

A space was made for Lily on the wooden benches.

'Good luck,' said the clerk and turned to go, 'keep your wits about you,' he said, turning to look at her for the last time.

Lily smiled at him. It transformed her and he was amply repaid.

'Oh I will,' she said, 'there is nothing that can stop me now.'

It was a grim journey. The seas were high and the old freighter seemed to take every wave head on. A bucket of water was passed around the cabin and the refugees dipped their cold hands into it and lapped like dogs; then they lurched and vomited in sync with the roll of the ship.

A lantern swung from the roof but on the first night it went out without warning. In the musty darkness, not daring to sleep, Lily felt hands probing her pockets. She scratched at them with her nails and they pulled away. As the cabin door opened, she saw the bulky sea coat and the peaked cap of a sailor silhouetted in the light.

The following night she heard the door opening again.

'Wake up, wake up!' she shouted, 'we are being robbed.'

The sailor swore. He had to fight his way back to the door. The hands grasped at him in the dark from all sides; they rasped and clutched like the claws of blind ravens. When he had slammed the cabin door behind him, he realized that gobbets of spit were slithering down his face and that they trailed all over his coat.

In the morning, the passengers took it in turns to peep out of the porthole and when Lily's turn came she saw the long dull brown bulk of land. The roll and yaw of the ship steadied. They had arrived in calmer water.

As the pogroms of Eastern Europe had worsened, so the tide of refugees had risen. Now it threatened to engulf the British ports. In Hull the Jewish community had rallied to help its own. They had formed into work groups, and they waited on the dockside to greet every incoming refugee ship. They wore armbands marked with the Star of David and they carried out their duties gladly. Many had been refugees themselves. Some guided the arrivals through the immigration lines; some provided them with kosher food. Some comforted the fearful and some led the shuffling lines away from the docks and on to the platform of the Paradise Street Station, which was not far away.

One of these work groups was composed of women; they were wealthy women and they had a special task; they met and cared for all the single young women who arrived on the dockside. This was so that they could not be preyed upon by the ruthless and sold into prostitution, as had happened in the past. It was one of these women whose sharp eyes picked out Lily. She thrust her way through the crowds towards the thin back figure using her umbrella.

Swept into the perfumed arms of a plump lady in a fur-trimmed costume, Lily was startled. And she was even more startled when she was bundled into the back of a long dark car. Lily had never travelled in a car before; she had rarely even seen one. But she took little notice of the journey. She was drained. It was enough that the woman spoke kindly to her. That she gave her water and biscuits; and that she stroked her hair and crooned to her in Yiddish.

The car drew into the drive of a great dark house and the lady led Lily up a wide staircase to a room hung with velvet curtains and beribboned pictures. There was a maid in a lace apron and she put Lily in a tin bath and scrubbed her. She dried her, and dressed her in a white lace nightgown; she brushed out her hair, and she put her between the starched sheets of a huge bed that looked like a sleigh.

And Lily slept.

In the morning the maid came again. She dressed Lily in a stiff dress with a large sash that tied at the back; she forced her feet into stockings and polished black boots. She led her down the broad staircase to the entrance hall below.

A familiar voice drifted out of a room that opened off it.

The Rabbi Sinson had come.

CHAPTER 25

JOHANNESBURG

A consistent soul believes in destiny, a capricious one in chance.
–Benjamin Disraeli, Statesman (1804-1881)

THE YEAR WAS 1902 AND Johannesburg was the heartbeat of the South African Gold Rush. It was a night-grown mushroom of a town; and more buildings sprang up out of its mire daily. Its streets were jammed with jostling carts and horse-drawn trams. The buildings seemed to have been thrown together and many were not finished; most were made out of corrugated iron and sacking. The ramshackle spew of construction drifted in all directions without form or purpose. It was unplanned and unsavoury and, as Abraham walked through the streets, doors were flung open and pails of grey water were hurled out into the dust.

It was a sharp, jagged, rusty town only recently emerged from war. The snouts of battered field guns could be seen poking from rings of wagons still chained together and packed with sandbags. Dogs barked behind rusting reels of barbed wire that were strung between high wooden watchtowers. There seemed to be no plan to the buildings, no blocks, no squares, no signs. And all the people that scurried and hurried in the streets had no time to stop, no inclination to issue directions, no interest in yet another newcomer to town.

In the centre of the town stood the offices of The Victoria Gold Mining Company. They were grandiose and fronted by a long covered verandah. In its shade lounged a crowd of men; they were chewing tobacco and spitting into the street. The men wore tattered khaki shirts, leather waistcoats and slouch hats; some had bandoliers strung around them; some had goatskin water bottles lashed across their chests. They seemed to be waiting for something; they were wary and poised for flight. Most seemed to carry their worldly goods strapped to their backs, shovels and all. In the shade of a wall, a line of Chinese waited impassive and blank-eyed.

Abraham caught the glance of a man still clad in his khaki uniform; he had his British Army sun helmet pushed back on his brow. Abraham asked the soldier where he might find food and he pointed to a corrugated iron shack. On its rusting walls were daubed the words, The Silver Grill, in white paint.

The Silver Grill's menu was brief: bully beef and rice. It was served on an enamel plate with a bent spoon and an enamel mug of water. Abraham was hungry and he did not look up from his plate until he had finished his beef and rice. He felt better, and he looked around

The shack was dim and it buzzed with blue-black flies. There was a long table at its centre with benches set to either side. Seated at intervals along the benches was a disparate selection of men. There were neat clerks in dark suits, tight collars and stringy ties; there were rough men in torn shirts and drooping braces; there were tough men in slouch hats and leather waistcoats. One man sat with his saddle on the bench beside him. Another kept his pickaxe across his knees as he shovelled food into his mouth on the blade of his hunting knife.

Across the table from where Abraham sat was a pair of men who stood out from the rest. They seemed to be gentlemen. They wore shooting jackets with leather edged cuffs; and their trousers were tucked into buckled leather gaiters.

Abraham bent his ear to catch their conversation. They spoke of farming, of crops and land, acreage and labour. When a natural break came in their conversation, Abraham leant deferentially across the table and he asked if they knew where any farming work might be had.

One of the men flicked a glance at Abraham. He had yellow eyes like those of a cat.

'You might try Jeppe's African Farms,' he said. He spoke with the clipped, slightly superior correctness of a British gentleman.

'Jeppe's African Farms?' repeated Abraham.

'Yes, they've just bought up more than a million acres of prime Transvaal farmland,' said the man, 'so I think we can deduce that they need all the labour they can get.'

Abraham was about to ask where Jeppe's African Farms might be found, but the yellow eyes had turned away from him and he knew himself to have been dismissed.

The man was speaking to his companion, 'all the labour they can get and divine intervention to rid them of the plague of puff adders I hear they've inherited,' he said.

His companion gave a bark of derision.

'There's not much you don't know is there, Grogan[1]?' he said.

The offices of Jeppe's African Farms were rough; they leaned slightly backwards and they were fashioned from the preferred combination of corrugated iron and sackcloth. Along the front of the building ran a rickety verandah. It had a tin roof, which emitted sudden loud cracks as it expanded in the heat. There was a rail and a number of horses were hitched to it. They twitched their tails. One stamped its back foot periodically.

The door to Jeppe's African Farms stood open.

It was gloomy inside, and narrow shafts of light fell from the meagre windows on to the tamped earth floor. At the far end of the shed stood two large oil cans. Planks had been laid across them and behind this makeshift desk sat a man on a high stool. His shirtsleeves were rolled up, his waistcoat was unbuttoned and his collar was missing. He had a pair of round glasses pushed up on his forehead. A line of men snaked back from his desk. They were roughly clothed and held their hats in their hands.

The hiring was brisk.

The queue shuffled forward and the man at its head stepped up to the desk. He was handed a piece of paper, but he did not read it. He either signed his name or ground his thumb-print on to the paper; then he turned and left. When Abraham's turn came, he read the paper; it was a contract for a week's work and the sum offered was good. He signed it.

'Where do I go?' he said.

The clerk looked up sharply and dropped his glasses down on to his nose. He peered at Abraham suspiciously. 'You've signed for Good Hope Chicken Farm,' he said, 'there's a waggon outside. Get on it.'

As Abraham was walking away, the man spoke again.

'I've just had another by the same name as you,' he said, 'he was asking for carpentry work. Any relation?'

Abraham strode to the door. He blinked in the sudden glare and surveyed the faces of the men who stood outside. A cart was pulling away. It was loaded with planks and driven by a man with a black hat pulled low. He had broad shoulders and there was something familiar about the way he hunched over the reigns. A small golden dog ran behind the cart.

'Anymore for Good Hope?' shouted a voice.

By the hitching rail a large wagon waited. It was full of men, some standing, some lounging against its high sides. A man ran across to it; he grasped the hand of one of those already aboard and hauled himself up. The driver stood by the tailgate.

'Anymore? Anymore for Good Hope Farm?' he shouted.

Abraham raised his hand and moved towards the wagon. As he did so he cast a glance down the road. The cart was disappearing around the corner and the golden dog had to run to keep up with it. For a split second its tail seemed to form a question mark.

Abraham swerved around the labour wagon and out into the street. He ran as fast as he could in the wake of the cart. When he was in earshot of the driver he began to shout.

'Father? Father!' The dog turned and barked at him.

'Father! Wait! Stop!'

The cart slowed to a halt. The dog ran around his ankles yapping and making small feints as if to bite him.

Samuel Block threw the reigns on to the broad back of his horse. He jumped down from his seat and strode back to where the sturdy young man stood in the middle of the road. The golden dog was making rings around him.

Samuel's face split into a smile; he strode forward.

'Welcome, my son,' he said, and threw his arms around Abraham[2].

Samuel's carpentry yard lay in East London, a half-day's journey from the town of Johannesburg, and he and Abraham travelled there together, seated on the narrow bench of the cart. At first Abraham was awkward in his father's presence and Samuel struggled to draw replies from him. But the strangeness passed, and the years fell away. Abraham glanced frequently at his father as they talked, as if to check that his presence was real. And when their eyes met, they smiled conspiratorially at each other.

At fifty-one, Samuel was burned by the sun. A delicate fan of white lines radiated from the corners of his eyes; his hair had greyed at the temples but he was still a handsome man. And the hands that held the reigns, though brown-spotted by the sun, were those that Abraham remembered from his boyhood on the Gilwan farm.

Samuel's yard was a simple enclosure pallisaded by rough offcuts of timber. There was an iron hut at its centre and there were piles of timber lying beneath sheets of canvas around its perimeter. The hut contained a bed, a table and two chairs, and served as a workshop. It took many hours of conversation for Samuel and Abraham to span the years of their separation; and the golden dog curled up on the floor beneath the table, its sharp nose tucked into its extravagantly feathered tail, and went to sleep. They spoke of many things; the dark days in the wake of Samuel's departure, Abraham's journey to Britain, and Samuel's war. They spoke of Ettel, her stubbornness, and her refusal to leave Russia.

'She and Freda have to get out,' said Samuel, 'there is nothing left for them there. But Ettel will not listen to me.' He stared down at his clasped hands. 'There may come a time when she cannot get out,' he said, 'there is revolution coming.'

'The British speak of closing their doors against any more refugees,' said Abraham.

Samuel shook his head and remained silent for a while.

'I have had a letter from your sister, Lily,' he said eventually, 'she arrived in Leyland just weeks after you had left. She is brave and stubborn like her mother. She refuses to remain in Leyland and insists that she will come here. I cannot stop her coming, but it is no life for a girl.'

Abraham frowned.

'It can be made to be so,' he said, 'it must be made to be so.'

'You'll marry this girl, Rosie?' said Samuel.

'Yes. But I need money,' said Abraham.

'Best turn your hand to schmussing then,' said Samuel.

East London lay at the centre of the South African wool industry. It was a rough place full of men with crooks and dogs and rushing bolting herds of sheep. Around its perimeter stood rows of long shearing sheds and beyond these lay many acres of pens where the herds waited until they could be funnelled through the shearing sheds.

'You go to the pens and you pick the wool off the fences,' said Samuel, 'when you have a sack full of wool you sell it to the spinners. They call it schmussing.'

'And that makes money?' said Abraham, skeptical.

'Try it for yourself,' said Samuel.

He was correct; a living could be made from schmussing but Abraham was not the only one trying to do so. There were a number of sharp-faced men hanging around the pens and they did not welcome competition. There were fights, the work was hard, and the income was meagre and slow in coming.

'Why don't you try shearing, mate?' said one of the sharp-faced men. He had come up against Abraham's fists on several occasions and they had taken an odd kind of liking to each other.

'You have to be as strong as an ox,' he said. He grinned at Abraham, 'but I can vouch for you in that regard, and the money's good. I'll introduce you; you can pay me a commission.'

It took Abraham time to learn how to seize a sheep, clamp it between his knees and slide a sharp knife beneath its thick oily fleece without cutting its soft pink flesh. And it took even longer for him to learn how to remove the fleece in one lanolin sodden sleight of hand. But once he had mastered the art he was paid well for his skill.

But not enough.

Abraham considered how he might supplement his income. He thought about how he might carry the fleeces from the sheds to the spinners; and from the spinners to the port. But this required a cart.

One day, one of the sheep drovers asked Abraham if he knew of anyone who might like to buy a pair of Basutos.

'What are Basutos?' said Abraham

'Ponies,' said the drover, 'they're bred in the Transvaal and they're so tough that they were used to drag the guns through the war. Plucky little beasts, can't work 'em too hard.'

'I'll have them,' said Abraham.

The ponies were white, short of leg and exceptionally broad of back. They were well trained and immensely strong, and Abraham was well pleased with his bargain. He built a cart and put them into harness and within months he had more work than he could handle.

And his savings grew.

It was January 1903, and Abraham had saved sufficient money to buy a plot of land. He drove the ponies into Johannesburg and hitched them to the rail outside Jeppe's African Farms. They had no land to sell, but they directed him to Bentley Brothers who were selling plots in the southern Cape.

'Abraham Block?'

Abraham turned to see who was calling him. It was Eli Levy[3]. He had worked alongside Abraham in the British Army Barracks. Abraham was pleased to see him and they exchanged news, but he was short of time.

'I must leave you, Eli,' he said, 'I've come here to buy land and I must leave before nightfall.'

'You don't want to buy land here,' said Eli.

'Why not?' said Abraham.

'Haven't you heard? There's a new Jewish homeland. It's here, in Africa. They call it the New Zion and there's land for free for those willing to settle there.'

Abraham gazed steadily at Eli.

'Where,' he said.

'North of here,' said Eli, 'in a British Colony. There's a meeting being held in Cape Town about it next week. The British Colonial Secretary, Joseph Chamberlain[4], is to speak. People are flocking there. If you're going I will come with you.'

The Rt. Hon. Joseph Chamberlain (1836-1914)

THE NEW ZION

We believe that salvation is to be found in wholesome work in a beloved land.
Work will provide our people with the bread of tomorrow, and moreover,
with the honor of the tomorrow, the freedom of the tomorrow.
–Theodor Benyamin Ze'ev Herzl, The Father of Zionism (1860-1904)

IT WAS HOT IN THE marquee that had been erected in the gardens of the Mount Pleasant Hotel, which was one of the finest in Cape Town. The air was rank with the smell of trampled grass, cigars and sweat. Rows of canvas chairs had been set up inside the marquee: and a rough stage stood at its farthest end. The chairs immediately below the stage were filled with tailored backs and they rippled as their owners leant to speak to each other. The chairs behind them were filled with untailored backs and their owners sat more still and stolid in their seats.

Abraham and Eli pushed through the crowds that jostled the central aisle and secured seats as close to the stage as they could. There was a buzz of conversation, people called out to each other, and it grew steadily hotter. Men began to fan themselves with their hats; the rows of seats filled and soon there was standing room only at the back.

It was stiflingly hot.

At a given signal, the white canvas flaps at the rear of the marquee were rolled down. There was a rustle of expectancy, the front rows craned to the left. The crowd fell silent.

A tall, elderly man strode on to the stage.

The front rows clapped and a wave of applause rippled back through the marquee.

Joseph Chamberlain, The British Colonial Secretary, needed no introduction; his face was a regular fixture on the front pages of South Africa's newspapers. He was elegantly attired in a dark grey frock coat. In his buttonhole was a red rose, across his dove-grey waistcoat was looped a gold watch; and into his right eye was screwed a monocle. He was sixty-seven years old, but he had the elasticity of step of a much younger man.

Mr Chamberlain raised his hand to acknowledge his applause and to indicate that it might end. He grasped the lectern with both hands and looked out over the crowd. As he began to speak, the audience relaxed, aware that they were in the hands of an orator. He spoke to them of the war, his sorrow at the losses sustained by both sides, his delight that South Africa had joined the British Empire.

'It is a great Empire,' he said, 'and it is my belief that it will grow to be a historic federation of Anglo-Saxon nations whose power will extend all over the globe.'

Mr Chamberlain paused to mop his brow.

'I have an all-abiding faith in the power of imperialism,' he said and his monocle flashed around the marquee. 'I am proud to be British, and I believe that the British race is the greatest of the governing races that the world has ever seen.'

He leant back from the lectern; and then forward again, as if to share a confidence.

'But it is not enough,' he said, 'to occupy the great spaces of the world's surface unless you can make the best of them; and it is the duty of a landlord to develop his estate.'

A whisper of unease ran through his listeners. Did the great man regard South Africa as his estate?

Joseph Chamberlain knew his audience well. He smiled out over it; he was indulgent to it. 'And that estate is Kenya, in the British Protectorate of East Africa,' he said.

Mr Chamberlain explained that he had visited Kenya and had developed a great love for the country. He described it as an extraordinarily diverse land, where the scenery ranged from the shores of the Indian Ocean to the alpine peaks of Mount Kenya. He spoke of its beauty, its superb climate and its fertile soil.

'I have it on reliable authority,' he said, 'that there is a climate of perpetual summer in Kenya. That the cabbages are as big as bicycle wheels! And that they turn the scales, gentlemen, at thirty pounds!' He brought his fist down on the lectern.

'And I am also told that ostriches can be had for the trouble of catching them!' he said. There was laughter; members of the audience turned to look at each other and raise eyebrows. But Mr Chamberlain swept on. The British, he said, had built a glorious railway in Kenya. The Uganda Railway ran from the port of Mombasa, through Kenya, to the shores of Lake Victoria in Uganda; and it would link the heart of Africa to the rest of the world. The volume of trade expected from the railway was unheard of in the annals of British Imperial history. Fortunes were waiting to be made.

'A hardy band of dedicated men and women have already gone to Kenya to claim their land,' Chamberlain said, 'and their fortunes are already being made! Their dynasties are already being founded! Their lives are already being changed!'

The crowd stirred.

'And what is needed to succeed in this land, you ask?' said Chamberlain.

The audience craned.

'Courage and determination!' declared Chamberlain, 'that is all!'

The crowd was his.

'So now let me tell you of the suggestion I have made to Mr Theodor Herzl, the founder of the Zionist Movement, to whom I was introduced by my friend, Mr Nathan Rothschild,' he said. 'I have suggested to Mr Herzl that an area of five thousand square miles of this beautiful land called Kenya can be given to the Jewish people!'

The audience roared.

'To serve as an ante chamber to the Holy Land, a place of apprenticeship, a place where the Jewish people can prepare to enter into their rightful inheritance like the followers of Moses, who spent forty years in preparation to settle in the land of Canaan!'

All around Abraham and Eli, people leapt to their feet and cheered.

On the stage, Chamberlain opened his arms wide and benevolent.

'Go there! And build a new Zion!' he said.

People leapt from their seats and began to battle their way to the rear of the tent. Abraham turned to Eli, whose face was shining.

'We have work to do, Eli,' was all he said.

Once decided upon his course of action, Abraham Block was hungry to proceed. His enquiries told him that each new settler in the land of Kenya was required to clear and plant his own land; though nobody, it seemed, knew which crops would grow best in Kenya. The British Government suggested coffee, cocoa or indigo rubber, but others said that peas and potatoes did better. Abraham bought a bag of Early Rose potato seeds, and a bag each of linseed, bean and pea seeds.

He decided to take the Basuto ponies with him.

Having bought his ticket and paid for the shipment of the ponies, Abraham was left with the sum of twenty pounds from his savings.

It would have to be enough.

Into his kit bag he put his one set of clothes and his few personal possessions.

Samuel handed Abraham a small leather pouch. In it was the gold watch that his own father, Lazarus Block, had given to him when he left for Vilnius.

'Sell it if you have to,' Samuel said, 'or return it to me when I come to join you.'

CHAPTER 27

ABOARD THE *FELDMARSCHALL*

The 'Rund-um-Afrika' (round Africa) route was operated by the Deutsche Ost-Afrika-Linie
(DOAL). For this the "Kronprinz" (1900/5,645 gt) and consorts were introduced,
steamers with a grey hull, white superstructure and a buff funnel,
topped with an arrangement of black/white/red rings, pointing the national colours.

ABRAHAM'S PASSAGE TO KENYA WAS booked on the Deutsch-Ost-Africa-Linie. It was a German line, known as the DOAL and its tramp steamer, the *Feldmarschall*, was one of the few ships to sail between Europe and East Africa. It stopped at eleven ports between Trieste and Mombasa, but it made only one call in South Africa, and this was to the port of Delagoa Bay[1], which was linked to the town of Pretoria by a small railway.

It took three days for Abraham to walk his ponies to Pretoria and when he arrived he loaded them into the goods van of the Delagoa Bay Railway. The ponies remained with their heads in their nosebags for the entire journey and, when the train arrived at its destination, they walked placidly to the quayside.

Delagoa Bay docks were unlike any docks Abraham had ever encountered. They stood against a backdrop of waving coconut palms and they looked out over the blue waters of the Indian Ocean. There were not many buildings, and those that existed were squat and engulfed in creeping torrents of fuchsia and orange blossom. There was an apron of rough white coral stone, fiercely hot in the glare of the sun, a pair of wooden hoists and a lone derrick. The dockside itself was little more than a high sea wall built from giant sugar-white cubes of coral.

A ship was moored to it.

On the dockside, teams of sweating stevedores scurried back and forth. Some were engaged in loading cargo into nets; others dragged trolleys piled high with crates. Teams of boys wheeled barrows of teetering luggage.

A group of passengers appeared to have disembarked from the ship to take the air. The ladies wore white and held parasols. The gentlemen fanned themselves with their sun helmets. There were a number of officials clad in the white and gold uniform of the DOAL; they stood on a raised platform in the blazing sun and tried to direct the chaotic operations; but these seemed to proceed at their own pace regardless.

Around the rusted grey hull of the *Feldmarschall*, flocked a small flotilla of dugouts and lighters.

Abraham stood in the shade until the time came for his ponies to be loaded. They were strapped into large canvas slings and hoisted high above the dockside and down into the hold of the ship. They pawed the air as they swung over Abraham's head, but seemed otherwise undisturbed by the experience, and he hurried down into the hold to make sure they were secured. It was much against his better judgment, but he had become fond of them.

The hold was murky. It clanked and echoed and stank of cargos past. It took time for Abraham's eyes to adjust to the gloom, but when this was done he saw that his ponies were not the only creatures to be sailing with the *Feldmarschall*. There was pile of crated chickens, there were two sturdy brown dogs in a wooden crate, and there were four metal cages of cats. The cats mewled piteously. Abraham settled his ponies with hay and water. As he walked past the cats their almond eyes peeped out of the gloom at him and their small pink mouths cranked opened into snarls. He gave them some water and the remains of the food that he carried in his pocket.

When Abraham found his Third Class cabin, he discovered it to be already full. There were six narrow wooden bunks. On the bottom one sat Eli Levy; and above and around him lounged a selection of fresh-faced young men. Eli introduced them as Messrs Sulsky, Medicks, Hotz, London and Moskow[2].

'They're bound for the New Zion,' Eli said, 'like us.'

It took three weeks for the *Feldmarschall* to wallow her way up the coast of East Africa stopping at every port on the way. The cabin was cramped, so the young men spent most of their time on deck and it was here, in the mornings, that the German beer drinkers foregathered.

There were about forty of them, all male, and they made up at least half of the passenger manifest. They were boisterous and, according to the traditions of the DOAL, they spent their days in beer drinking competitions.

The rules were simple; the competitors were required to drink a glass of beer every two minutes until only one man was left standing. The record was set at sixty glasses of beer, but most of the *Feldmarschall*'s competitors could drink no more than thirty glasses. The reigning champions of the voyage were a pair of Bavarian farmers, who took it in turns to win the prize, which was a glass of beer. Then they spent the next two hours vomiting cheerfully over the side. It was an ugly pastime and greatly disapproved of by the British passengers. They spent their time organizing relay races up and down the deck, or playing deck quoits in neatly starched flannel shorts.

Since neither the British nor the Germans offered to include Abraham and his fellows in their pursuits, the young men spent their time discussing their future; and they disembarked in every port to gather news.

It was in Dar es Salaam that Maurice London learned of The Kishinev Pogrom, and he brought the news, white-faced, to the cabin.

'There has been a pogrom far worse than any other,' he said, 'seven hundred Jewish homes razed, fifty Jews dead, hundreds injured.'

His friends stared at him.

'What happened?' said Abraham.

'A Christian boy named Mikhail Rybachenko was found with his throat cut in the Ukrainian town of Dubossary. Later a Christian girl was found there too: she had been poisoned. The anti-Jewish newspaper, *Bessarabetz*, claimed that they had both been murdered by the Jews, who had used their blood to make *matzos* for Passover.'

'And then?' said Sulsky.

'Then the Orthodox Bishop of Kishinev called on his congregation to take revenge,' said Maurice, 'and there were three days of rioting. The man who told me this story said the people ran through the streets screaming "Death to the Jews" and "Crusade Against the Hate Race". It was on Easter Sunday that most of the killing was done.'

'And what was the truth of the matter?' said Abraham.

'The boy was murdered by his uncle, the girl had committed suicide when her father assaulted her,' said Maurice.

Abraham said nothing.

He thought of Ettel and Freda left behind in Russia.

They would have to be brought out.

Once Dar es Salaam, the capital of Tanganyika, with its grand white Germanic buildings and its neat and ordered docks, had been left behind, the coastline grew steadily more desolate. There were long sweeps of silver-white beaches backed by swaying palms; but they seemed devoid of life. A line of white breakers developed; it lay perhaps half a mile off shore and beyond it lay aquamarine lagoons where fishermen with harpoons and nets waded.

In the wake of the *Feldmarschall*, sharp black fins scythed through the waters; the sharks were unable to breach the reef and trailed the ship in the hope of food.

As dawn broke on the final day of the voyage, squat grey trees with trunks as wide as houses and branches that stretched up into the sky like plump women's arms, began to replace the coconut palms. Some were hung with tufts of white; others were showered with large pink flowers. A string of coral islands rose abruptly out of the water, they were white and sculpted into fanciful shapes, and tiny figures waved from their narrow beaches. There were craggy grey cliffs on the mainland; and they were dotted with small white buildings with palm roofs. The ship rounded a headland and swung into the wide mouth of a creek. On one side stood a large fortress. It was rusty-pink, blind-eyed and menacing.

'Fort Jesus,' said Eli, 'I heard the British passengers talking about it. It was built by the Portuguese in the 17th century; it's a prison now.'

The fort had crenellated battlements, and at each corner was a domed lookout tower set with archery slits. Its massive bulbous walls were streaked with black. On the shoreline, black cannons were trained out to sea, and a green-slimed slipway led to an archway now tumbled into the waves. Beyond the Fort was a haphazard mosaic of buildings; most were whitewashed and had rusty-red iron roofs. A stone harbour could be made out, its dockside lined with high-sided seagoing dhows.

The water in the creek was calm and clear but it was too shallow to admit the *Feldmarschall*. With a rolling out of chains, she dropped anchor; and from the harbour a flotilla of small boats took to the glittering water and skimmed out across it to meet her. The passengers leaned over the side of the ship to watch them come.

There were rowing boats, canoes and dugouts, and they clustered around the waterline of the

Fort Jesus, Mombasa

ship like ants on a carcass. On one side the luggage was roped and swung down to the lighters, on the other a flurry of rowing boats sculled back and forth. Most were simple crafts with a single man at the oars, but some were broad bellied and fitted with scarlet cushions and fringed canopies; these were manned by oarsmen in white uniforms with red cummerbunds.

Abraham swung with ease down the ship's rusted ladder and hailed the most unassuming craft he could see. He sat in its prow as the oarsman pulled towards the shore. And, as the little fleet drew nearer to the beach, all the oarsmen began to sing. It was a strange, lilting chant and it gave the scene something of the air of a Venetian carnival. There was gold and blue, scarlet and white and the headland was laced with iridescent green fronds. The breeze was warm and carried a light, sweet, floral scent. And the sun glinted off the clear water.

Abraham smiled.

From the beach a group of native men waded out. As each rowing boat grounded, they stepped forward to lift the passengers up and out of the boats. Then they waded through the shallows and deposited their burdens on the sand. When Abraham's turn came, a gleaming brown fellow with teeth as white as his tattered shorts arrived alongside the boat. He grinned broadly and then turned around. He motioned for Abraham to climb aboard his back. So Abraham Block arrived in Kenya clinging like a monkey to the back of a black giant, and both of them were laughing.

Abraham took up position outside the customs shed, a creaking lean-to at the end of the causeway. And there he remained as the ship slowly disgorged her passengers, her cargo and her crew. The ponies were to be taken off the ship by a wooden crane, which stood on a headland a little further down the bay.

It was late afternoon when a large wooden crate came in to view. It was being hauled by a team of chanting men, who rolled it to a halt by the customs shed. Inside were the ponies in their habitual state of calm. They whickered at Abraham. By now the customs shed was empty so Abraham shouldered his kit bag, lashed the sacks of seeds to the backs of the ponies, and set off up the ramp into town.

Immediately beyond the docks lay a dusty square. There was a customs house, a fish market and a few rows of merchants' houses. All manner of people passed through the square, but none stopped to look at Abraham and his ponies. There were Arabs in flowing white robes and golden slippers, there were groups of ladies veiled in black with only their eyes showing, and there were packs of ragged children trailed by packs of skeletal dogs. There were scurrying Indian traders and busy clerks, and plump women in brightly coloured wraps with turbans on their heads. And there where white men in white suits with sun helmets on the their heads. But nobody paid Abraham any attention. Perplexed, he stood in the square with his ponies and scratched his head. Night was not far off and he knew that it would fall suddenly.

A man dressed in a khaki tunic and white trousers walked past. He glanced at the ponies appreciatively.

'Lovely little beasts,' he said, 'you'll be needing stabling for them?'

'Yes,' said Abraham.

'Better follow me,' said the man. He stuck out a hand. 'McJohn[3],' he said.

The man led them through a maze of narrow streets where the houses stood close and tall; they afforded fleeting glimpses into high-ceilinged rooms where families squatted in pools of lamplight. There was laughter, and the scent of spices, rice and meat drifted from within.

The ponies' hooves clattered on the cobbles.

'Where are you from?' said the man.

'Lithuania,' said Abraham.

The man smiled.

'You'd not think so from my name,' he said, 'but I am an Armenian Jew. I run a trading post for a European trading company called Smith McKenzie. They couldn't pronounce my real name, so they called me McJohn.' He glanced at Abraham, 'you'll need a bed for the night I presume?'

Abraham nodded.

'I run a small bar in the evenings, and let out a couple of rooms,' said McJohn, 'they aren't much but they'll do you for a few nights.

It was late by the time Abraham had settled the ponies into the stables of the Cecil Hotel, which stood next to Mr McJohn's bar. He had not lied; the room was not much. It held nothing but a narrow bed and a hurricane lantern. The walls were thin and the hubbub from the bar went on until late at night. But it did not prevent Abraham from sleeping.

The next morning, the bar was closed, McJohn was gone, and a bucket of cold water stood outside his room.

The Cecil Hotel, Mombasa, c.1900

CHAPTER 28

IN MOMBASA

The sea at Mombasa is as blue as a cornflower and, outside the inlet to the harbour,
the long breakers of the Indian Ocean draw a thin crooked white line,
and give out a low thunder even in the calmest weather.
–Karen Blixen, *Out of Africa*

MOMBASA STOOD ON AN ISLAND, though this was not immediately apparent. It was separated from the mainland by a series of creeks so narrow that the men of the town were in the habit of swimming across them in lieu of their morning ablutions.

The town was a tight-seamed patchwork of new and old. On the waterfront, the ancient Fort Jesus glowered out to sea; and immediately next to it stood a startlingly new courthouse. The dhow harbour was said to date back to the time of King Solomon; but it shared a wall with a bright new mosque with a gleaming emerald green dome and aqua blue walls. The fish market was dank and rotting and patrolled by hundreds of wall-eyed tomcats; but behind it stood a bright red post office with a flag that could be hoisted to announce the incoming mail ship. There were shiny new warehouses, and there were dusty-dark emporiums; and these were sunk below the level of the street and were the domain of betel-chewing traders who squatted behind sacks of lentils, bags of rice, towers of soap, and neat piles of cloves, chilli and turmeric.

There was a jumble of ancient Swahili houses with overhanging balconies encased in wooden fretwork; and they leaned so close that the people could chat with their neighbours. Below the old Fort stood The New Mombasa Club, a gathering place for British gentlemen. It had white walls, a grass-green corrugated iron roof, and a view out to sea. Next to it crouched the old Seamen's Mission with a rusted anchor outside its door.

In the centre of the island stood the railway station. It was neatly painted in brown and cream and ringed by a white picket fence. It might have been transported straight from Britain, but for the fact that all around it was hot and humid; and the sun beat down on white buildings shaded by palm, mango and tamarind trees.

The narrow streets were thronged with people, dogs and donkey carts; and the Europeans rode about in small hooded trolleys known as *gharries*. They ran on narrow gauge railway lines, which had once been intended to form the Central African Railway but this had never been extended beyond the Treasury, the British Residency and the Mombasa Sports Club. The *gharries* were painted in bright colours and carried four passengers: two in front and two behind. They were propelled by Africans, clad in white shorts and blue sailor blouses, who started them with a violent shove and then jumped aboard behind and clung on.

The *gharrie* boys called to each other as they worked. They gave their clients names and would exchange gossip as to where 'elephant belly' was going, what 'tomato head' had said, and whether or not 'hyena breath' was in a bad mood. They spoke in vernacular Swahili, and their clients affected not to understand a word they said: but since the British Foreign Office required its people to be fluent in Swahili, this may not have been the case.

Because Mombasa stood on a hill, the *gharries* were prone to hurtling down the inclines at great speed, and screeching to a halt to avoid dogs, goats and people. And because they ran on single tracks, a strict order of precedence had to be observed. When meeting an oncoming *gharrie*, for example, a junior member of the Administration was required to defer to his seniors by leaping of his *gharrie* and dragging it off the rails. It was an odd system, Abraham thought, and it served its purpose, but he had no wish to ride on it.

Abraham found his companions at The Grand Hotel[1]. It was imposing on the outside but less so within. It was run by a Mr Anderson, his Belgian wife Maia, and their close friend Rudolf Mayer. It was a relationship that prompted much speculation. People also wondered why the trio had elected to run a hotel at all, since none of them seemed to know anything about the business. Most of the rooms had neither windows nor doors, and the reservation system was so untrustworthy that guests were regularly forced to sleep beneath the billiard table.

Abraham found Eli, London, Hotz, Medicks, Sulsky and Moskow on the terrace. They were seated around a pockmarked metal table beneath the palms. Hundreds of black-and-white Indian house crows cawed from above.

'Be thankful you did not stay here last night,' said Sulsky, 'we were all five of us crammed into a single room, there were no windows, there was no door, no lamp and we were eaten alive by the mosquitoes.'

'And Moskow woke up to find rats climbing over him,' said Hotz

'I complained,' said Moskow, 'but they said they lived in the water tank.'

'As if that explained it,' said Medicks.

'We can't stand another night of it,' said Eli, 'so we've decided to take the train to Nairobi this morning.'

'And what will you do when you get there?' said Abraham.

'We picked up some information last night in the bar,' said London, 'and we're going straight to the Land Commission to claim our land.'

'Come with us,' said Eli.

'I will come,' said Abraham, but I want to take a look around Mombasa first.'

He did not tell them that he had barely the money for the rail ticket. The crating of the ponies off the ship had been costlier than expected.

McJohn had suggested that Abraham commence his search for work at the offices of the DOAL.

'Can't miss 'em,' he had said, 'they're so new the paint's still wet. They are the first and only prefabricated building ever to have been imported into East Africa. They're on the harbour front and they have the words The East African Trading Company written along the tin roof in letters as high as a man.'

McJohn was correct. The newness of the offices set them utterly apart from the rest. But they did not smell of paint; they smelt of incense. The double doors stood open and in the reception area Abraham found a small Indian clerk seated behind a large desk. A cone of incense burned in a brass dish in front of him.

'Deters mosquitoes,' he said. He waved Abraham to a row of chairs. 'You'll be wanting to meet the partners I expect?' he said. And, without waiting for a reply, he set off down a corridor. When he returned, the little clerk was accompanied by a man so tiny and delicate that the clerk himself appeared huge. And Abraham, who was not much more than five feet tall, felt clumsy.

'Mr Loy[2],' said the clerk, and returned to his desk.

Mr Loy was dressed from head to toe in white. He wore a white tropical suit, a white waistcoat, a white shirt, a white tie and a pair of white leather shoes with white laces. He had very dark hair lavishly oiled, parted and plastered to his brow. And he wore a dark moustache that drooped over his rosebud mouth.

'Rudolf Loy,' he said and clicked his heels together in the Austrian manner, 'how can I be of service?'

Abraham began to speak in his, still heavily accented, English.

Mr Loy smiled and dropped into Yiddish.

'You have found friends,' he said, 'and you are most welcome. My partner and I were also forced to leave Europe, but I suspect that our journey was somewhat easier than yours, will you share your story?'

As he spoke, another man entered the room. He was at least twice the size of Mr Loy both in breadth and height. He was dressed entirely in white and possessed of the most impressive set of whiskers Abraham had ever seen. The two men stood side by side. They presented a ludicrous image. But Abraham did not smile.

'May I present my partner, Mr Otto Markus,' said Mr Loy.

The introductions were made and Abraham told his story. He tried to be concise but he was interrupted constantly by his listeners, who took it in turns to ask questions. When their curiosity had been satisfied, Abraham asked Mr Markus and Mr Loy how they had come to be in Mombasa.

'We met at the Vienna Export Akademi,' said Mr Loy

'Europe's first and premier business school,' said Mr Markus.

'We knew immediately that we were destined for partnership,' said Mr Loy.

'And for Africa,' said Mr Markus

'You find us only just arrived in Mombasa,' said Mr Loy.

'Being just returned from a two year walk to the Congo,' said Mr Markus.

'And back,' said Mr Loy.

'We took one hundred porters and brought them all back laden with ivory,' said Mr Markus

'Not a single man died on the way,' said Mr Loy.

'We have invested our profits wisely,' said Mr Markus.

'Very wisely,' said Mr Loy, 'we have set up the East African Trading Company.'

'Dealing in coffee curing and the export of hides and skins,' said Mr Markus.

'My partner is also the acting consul for the Austrian Government and the agent for a number of shipping lines,' said Mr Loy.

The railway coming into Mombasa circa 1900 (Binks)

Leaving Mombasa on the Uganda Railway

Mombasa main street with gharrie tracks and Africa Hotel (Kenya National Archives)

Mr Markus said nothing, but beamed.

'Markus and Loy at your service,' said both men.

They bowed.

Mesmerized by the exchange, Abraham said nothing.

'And what are your plans, Mr Block,' said Mr Markus.

'I want to claim a plot of land and farm it,' said Abraham, recovering himself.

'Excellent plan,' said Mr Loy.

'Excellent,' said Mr Markus, 'and we know just the man to assist you.'

'Mr John Ainsworth,' said Mr Loy.

'The sub-district Commissioner of Nairobi,' said Mr Markus.

'Land Allocation Office,' said Mr Loy.

'We will write a letter of introduction,' said Mr Markus.

Abraham had not intended to leave Mombasa so soon, but the possession of a letter of introduction to one of the most important men in the colony was no small thing. He decided to take the train on the following day. It was only when he had made his farewells to Messrs Markus and Loy that he realized they had made no mention of the New Zion.

And neither had he.

He supposed it was of no consequence.

Rudolf Loy and Otto Markus outside their office in Mombasa circa 1906

CHAPTER 29

RIDING THE LUNATIC LINE

What it will cost no words can express;
What is its object no brain can suppose;
Where it will start from no one can guess;
Where it is going to nobody knows;
What is the use of it none can conjecture;
What it will carry there's none can define;
And in spite of George Curzon's superior lecture,
It clearly is naught but a lunatic line.

–Henry Labouchere[1], *The Truth*

ACCORDING TO McJOHN, WHO WAS a mine of information on all topics, the Nairobi train left from Mombasa Station twice a week at eleven o'clock prompt. As to when it would arrive in Nairobi, some 327 miles up the track, this was not so certain.

'Depends,' said McJohn.

'On what?'

'Floods, fires, bent tracks, faulty engines, buffalos, elephants.'

'So?'

'Best say twenty-four hours. Could be thirty-six,' said McJohn.

Begun in 1898 and completed as far as Lake Victoria in 1901, the Uganda Railway[2] was one of the greatest feats of Victorian engineering. It climbed from sea level at Mombasa through deserts, plains, mountains and forest to cross the equator at 6, 300 feet above sea level. Over six hundred miles long, it had 43 stations, 35 viaducts and 1, 280 bridges. Its engines, each of which weighed 600 tons, had been shipped from England in pieces and reassembled in Mombasa. It had cost five million pounds and the lives of 2, 500 Indian workers. But it was a white elephant of mammoth proportions.

'It's known as the Lunatic Express,' said McJohn.

'Why?' said Abraham.

'Because nobody knows why it was built, not even the British Government.'

McJohn was an authority on the train.

'The trick is,' he said 'to get to the station at around six o'clock so as to be sure of getting a seat at the front.'

'I don't need a seat at the front,' said Abraham.

'You do,' said McJohn, 'the farther back you travel, the dustier you get. If you're not at the front you'll arrive looking like a Red Indian. Most people wear goggles. Some travel in rags and throw them out of the window as the train pulls into Nairobi. Travel at the front and don't wear false teeth.'

'Why?' said Abraham.

'Rattles so much they fall out.'

Once launched, there was no stopping McJohn. The carriages were so rough they were known as 'loose boxes', they leaked, there was no bedding, and the train was regularly halted by rhinoceros, he recounted.

'One punctured the boiler only last week,' he said.

'What happened?' said Abraham.

'Train was three days late. Watch out for the sparks.'

'Why?'

'Fly in through the windows, set fire to everything,' said McJohn, 'and don't forget to carry a bottle of whisky.'

'I don't drink it.'

'No. But Tom O'Reilly does and he's the driver. Prone to stopping and refusing to continue unless he's given whisky. Everyone carries it,' said McJohn, 'and keep an eye open for lion cubs.'

'On the train?'

'British upper classes like to carry them: pet monkeys, gazelles, lion cubs. Scares the Goan ticket collectors half out of their wits,' said McJohn.

Abraham took McJohn's tales lightly but he arrived at the station early. He wanted to secure a place for his ponies in the goods wagon and McJohn had warned that it filled up quickly.

'Lion cubs and such,' he had said.

Long and low, Mombasa Railway Station was an impressive building approached by a broad gravel sweep that ended in a rough yard. This was already full of horses and carts when Abraham arrived in it. He hitched the ponies to a rail and went into the ticket hall where people already jostled at the glass ticket window.

'Go First Class,' had said McJohn, 'anything else is unbearable.'

Abraham bought a Second Class ticket. He did not have enough money for First Class and he would not have spent it even if he had. He pushed his way through the crowd to the platform, which was shaded by a corrugated iron roof.

The train was already in the station. It was painted in brown and cream and each of the carriages bore a large metal number slotted into a holder on its side. A First Class carriage stood immediately next to Abraham, so he opened the door and peered inside. It was built in the Indian style with no corridor and just four bare bunks, and it was already occupied. There was a pile of blankets, several red velvet cushions, a large picnic basket, a number of jerry cans of water, a primus stove and a bull terrier.

The terrier growled at Abraham and he retreated hurriedly.

As he closed the door he found a short man glowering at him. He had very pale blue eyes, long red hair and a large white sun helmet.

'Wrong carriage,' Abraham said.

'Humph,' said the man.

Returning to his ponies, Abraham walked them down the platform to the goods van. It was already full. There was a heifer tethered to one wall and a stuffed elephant foot and two tusks lashed to the other. In the corner was a pile of cages. They were full of cats: and they were the same cats that had travelled with the *Feldmarschall* from Delagoa Bay.

They were sodden and stained; and they mewled.

The platform seethed. There were passengers of all types, porters, baggage carts, piles of trunks and mountains of canvas sacks. There were baskets of mangoes, bunches of green bananas, sacks of coconuts and rolled lion skins. Towards the end of the platform stood a grand piano swathed in calico.

At a quarter to eleven, the engine started to belch steam. Railway men ran up and down the train fetching great blows to its wheels with sledgehammers. Porters hurled sacks into the goods van. Passengers hung out of the windows. Women walked up and down its length with baskets of bananas on their heads.

Locating his carriage, Abraham found it to be occupied by a group of Indian traders. They were sitting cross-legged on their bunks and playing cards. They did not look up as he joined them.

At eleven o'clock, wreathed in steam, the train pulled out of the station. People ran alongside it until it outpaced them, and ragged children dived for coins thrown from the windows. The train wound its way through warehouses and shantytowns; it hurried across the Salisbury Bridge, which linked Mombasa Island to the mainland, and to either side of the track lay midnight blue water and half rotted mangrove swamps.

As the train pulled up through the Rabai Hills, the temperature in the carriage rose; and Abraham's shirt and the robes of his fellow travellers were plastered to their bodies. He stuck his nose out of the window. The air was almost too hot to breathe. As the train barrelled into the burning wastes of the Taru Desert, it passed through waves of grey-green bush that rolled away into the far distance and shimmered in the heat. The soil was iron-red and the acacia trees were sprinkled with white blossom. Hornbills swooped between them. A line of boulders revealed themselves to be elephants coated with thick red dust. Then they melted away into the bush as if they had never been. Atop a huge rock a lion stretched.

Towards the end of the day, as the heat waned, more wildlife emerged. There were antelopes, gazelles and pairs of tiny dik-diks. They gazed big-eyed at the passing train and then bounded away into the undergrowth.

As darkness fell, the train pulled into a station. A long brown sign read, Voi. With much shunting and blowing the train ground to a halt. Doors banged, people jumped down on to the track. There was no platform. Abraham turned to his companions.

'What happens here?' he said.

'It's the *dak* bungalow of Mr Nazareth,' they told him, 'here we eat,' and they swung themselves down from the carriage.

The dak bungalow was not much more than a hut. Inside it was gloomy and tightly packed with tables and benches. Hurricane lanterns hung from the rafters flaring the iron-sheeted ceiling with soot. Towers of moths fluttered around them.

There were stewards clad in white uniforms with silver buttons weaving their way through the tables. Abraham sat down on a bench. Immediately a white-gloved hand served him with a glass of warm beer and an enamel bowl of soup; and this was followed by a plate bearing tinned salmon and meatballs. It was a strange combination, but he ate it. Above him the moths danced around the flames, singed and slithered down the oily glass on to the table. A good number landed in the food. The white-gloved hand reappeared, this time with a bowl of tinned fruit

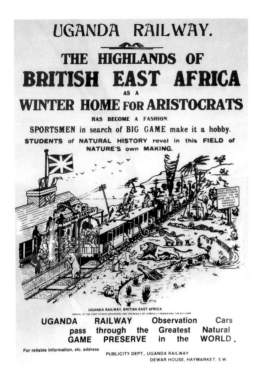

Riding a gharrie

Florence Preston lays the last sleeper on the railway on the shores of Lake Victoria

and hot custard. All around him people complained bitterly about the food. Many left their plates untouched.

Abraham slipped meatballs and tinned salmon into his handkerchief.

Outside in the dark-blue light people were sitting on the embankment. Outside First Class they were drinking whisky. Back in his own carriage, Abraham found the Indians stretching out on their bunks, rolling their jackets under the heads and hawking on to the floor.

'Do we not travel on?' he said.

'The train doesn't travel at night,' they said, 'there are bends in the track'.

From down the track came shouts of laughter from the whisky drinkers. And the ping, ping of bullets hitting tin cans. Later the sounds faded, doors slammed and those who had windows pulled them up.

With a long wail of its whistle, the train fell silent.

Outside hyenas whooped. Inside it was swelteringly hot, the Indians snored and the mosquitoes whined; and from far away came the cough of a lion.

Abraham awoke to the sound of doors slamming. Dawn was breaking and by its watery light he could see figures jumping down on to the track; they headed to the dak bungalow where there were earth closets and buckets of cold water. As he passed the First Class carriages, Abraham noticed that the gentlemen were shaving using steaming bowls of water from the engine. One of them was the man in the large white sun helmet into whose carriage he had blundered. Now the man had the bull terrier wedged under one arm and was addressed by the others as 'D'. They seemed to defer to him.

Hoisting himself up on to the goods wagon and rolling back the heavy wooden door, Abraham found his ponies in their habitual state of calm. In the corner the cats lay in a tangle of soiled fur. He gave them the meatballs and the tinned salmon. They mewed.

Breakfast was a simple affair: boiled eggs, tea and a banana. The bill, when it came, was pitifully small, but all around him the passengers continued to complain. Mr Nazareth, a small rounded Indian gentleman, received all the complaints with a smile and a polite 'thank you'.

On the tracks, the engine built up steam, the whistle blew, the doors slammed and the train ground into motion.

As the train laboured across the bush, sparks from its engine blew back down the carriages and in through the windows, where the passengers stamped them out. It ground through the volcanoes of Tsavo, and enormous baobab trees began to dot the landscape; their fat grey branches decked in pink flowers. Now the air cooled and freshened, and the hills could be seen to be crowned with tufts of pine trees. Now, men swung themselves along the outside of the carriages to chat with friends elsewhere; they wore goggles and they laughed.

The great white mound of Mount Kilimanjaro passed by, its snows tinged rose pink and dripping down its sides like cream on a pudding. Below it columns of dust as a high as a house danced across the plains. Now the train strained and heaved to achieve its final gradient, but it triumphed and the whistle shrilled.

All around the carriages huge green plains opened up and a carnival of animals bounded and lolloped alongside the train. Perhaps they raced it, perhaps they drew speed from its motion, but there were great herds of them: eland, antelope, gazelle and giraffe. Beyond the plunging hooves and bucking heads, placid rhinos grazed, ostriches careered, and warthogs charged with their tails erect.

As the train hurtled across the Athi Plains, Abraham's fellow passengers began to pack up their belongings, wind their turbans, and swill the remains of their water around their mouths and on to the floor. Sticking his head out of the window, Abraham saw the glint of corrugated iron, and shacks began to line the track.

People walked alongside it.

Railway sidings appeared, goods sheds and a platform.

They had arrived in Nairobi.

Abraham looked down at himself; he was covered in thick red dust.

Train leaving Nairobi Railway Station circa 1900

CHAPTER 30

ARRIVING IN NAIROBI

Nairobi is the result of some momentary mental aberration.
–Lord Hindlip, *British East Africa Past, Present and Future*

As Abraham jumped down from the train he was hit by the cool clarity of the highland air. He looked around. The station was little more than a large iron hut. There was an old clock strung up over the door, and a mass of people surged down the rough platform. Several men had climbed on to crates to get a better view of the arrivals. It seemed that the coming of the train was an event of great interest to the people of Nairobi.

Some of the people who greeted the train had come to collect goods; some had come to meet friends. Some had come out of simple curiosity to see what the train might have brought. A number came specifically to see if it had brought any women. With one woman to every fifty men, wives were hard to come by, and fresh females were best appropriated quickly.

Abraham pushed his way to the goods van. The doors were already rolled back and he hoisted himself up. The ponies were safe. The tusks and the elephant's foot were gone, the heifer as well. In the corner stood a thickset man with ripples of wiry brown hair. He was untying the cages of cats from the wall. They were snarling at him, but when they saw Abraham they fell silent, and their small pink noses twitched.

'Are they yours?' said Abraham.

'Aye,' said the man, straightening up. He eyed Abraham belligerently.

'And what's it to you?'

Something in his accent reminded Abraham of Leeds.

'Nothing,' he said, 'but for the fact that I've travelled from Delagoa Bay with them; and I have cared for them along the way, which is just as well, because nobody else did.'

The man's expression lightened, and he held out his hand.

'Tommy Wood[1],' he said, 'originally from Sheffield, latterly from South Africa. I'm grateful for your care of the animals. I paid for their food and keep in advance. I should have known better eh?'

Abraham shrugged. 'What are you going to do with them?' he said.

'Breed 'em and sell 'em as mousers,' said Tommy Wood. He glanced curiously at Abraham, 'you must be new to town? Or you'd know them to be a valuable commodity.'

'Yes, I am' said Abraham. He held out his hand. 'Abraham Block, originally from Lithuania, latterly from Leeds and South Africa.'

'Welcome to Nairobi, Mr Block,' said Tommy Wood, 'do you have somewhere to stay?'

'Not yet,' said Abraham.

'Stay with me then,' said Tommy Wood, 'I have what passes for a hotel, and the first night's on me. We'll call it a thank you for taking care of my cats. Four Rupees[2] a night thereafter, and

Nairobi in the early 1900s

that includes three meals a day. You won't get better. Should be able to fix up stabling for your ponies too. Basutos aren't they? You'll get a good price for them.'

'Maybe, but I've no mind to sell them,' said Abraham, 'and as to your offer, I'm much obliged.'

The ponies picked their way carefully down the plank from the carriage and they followed Abraham down the platform with no more than a cursory glance to either side. Tommy Wood led the way with the cages of cats in his arms.

'We'll nip down the side here,' he said and headed around a corner to emerge at the front of the station.

Abraham looked around. Beyond the few horses and carts that were hitched to a rail, there was nothing to be seen. A swamp stretched away into the distance and a few shacks dotted the landscape; it was flat, bare, grey and dolorous.

'How far to the town?' he said.

'This is the town,' replied Tommy Wood. He grinned, 'Come on. I'll show you the sights.'

Tommy gestured towards the huddle of station buildings.

'That's known as Railwayville,' he said, 'though I can't think why: the whole town is the bastard child of the railway and without it there would be no Nairobi at all.'

'And why is the railway here?'

'Heaven only knows, nobody else does. I mean, I ask you? Who, in their right mind, would have chosen to build a town in a Godforsaken place like this?'

Abraham looked around. A swamp lay ahead of them. Around its perimeter stood a jumble of tattered army tents.

'That's Tentfontein,' said Tommy, 'where the South Africans camp until they can find something better.' He waved to a shantytown in the distance. 'That's the Indian Bazaar,' he said. 'Filthy place. We burned it down last year: bubonic plague. But they've built it up again. Painted it purple and yellow. Can't imagine why. Not complaining though, I sell 'em the paint.'

He squinted into the distance at the Bazaar.

'But I'll tell you what?' he said, 'you can buy anything there. Hippo teeth, guns, anything the settler might desire.'

'Are there many settlers?' said Abraham.

'Oh, about a hundred and thirty, I should say: in Nairobi at least. Excluding the Asians,' said Tommy, 'upcountry maybe another thirty. So counting the ones on the coast? Say five hundred at most?'

'And what about in the New Zion?' said Abraham.

'The what?'

'The Jewish homeland?'

'Oh, no! You've not fallen for that cock and bull story, have you?' said Tommy Wood.

'Is it not true?'

'There's been talk. Joseph Chamberlain's all for it. But I wouldn't hold your breath,' said Tommy Wood, 'it's still only talk. And we colonials are good at that.'

They passed through a small cemetery. Abraham noticed that on a number of the rough wooden crosses the words 'killed by lions' had been scratched.

'Are there many lions?' he said.

'Hundreds,' said Tommy Wood, 'but only at night. So best not to walk around then.'

They had traversed the swamp now, and reached a rough highway. It was strung with tents, iron shacks and makeshift workshops; some rough taverns and boarding houses had appeared. A ditch ran along its centre and people emptied buckets in to it.

'This is Victoria Street,' said Tommy, 'hypothetically'.

The ponies picked their way delicately through the mud.

'And here we are at The Victoria Hotel, better known as Tommy Wood's', said Mr Wood.

It was a simple building made out of galvanized iron sheeting and sacking. It had two floors and an outside staircase. In front of it, sitting on sardine crates, were a number of men; they were talking and drinking beer.

'Leave the ponies here,' said Tommy; he indicating a rail. He left the cat crates in the shade of the building and led Abraham through the crowd. When they reached the outside staircase, he waved Abraham up it.

'Shop's below, hotel upstairs, butchery out the back yard,' he said, 'and my safe is the only bank in town.'

At the top of the stairs was a dark room containing a battered table and twelve rickety dining chairs of assorted design. There was a simple bar hung with paraffin lanterns and beyond it lay four small rooms divided by calico and wood partitions. Pushing open the rough wooden door to one of these rooms, Tommy indicated a narrow bed, a stool and a ewer of water standing in a round enamel basin.

'Not much, as I said, but—'

'It's more than I am used to, said Abraham, I'm grateful Mr Wood.'

'Call me Tommy, my friend,' said Tommy Wood.

He glanced at the watch strung across his waistcoat, 'I'd best be getting on,' he said, 'follow me.'

He strode to the staircase and dived headlong down it. At the foot of the steps he swung around a post, he bent his head and he unlocked a door.

Inside the room he turned to Abraham and flung his arms open wide.

'My emporium,' he said.

It was a long low-ceilinged room lit by just one paraffin lamp. There were no windows. In one corner were farming implements. There were hoes, seeds, cans of oil, balls of string, coils of wire and milk churns. In another corner stood piles of Lifebuoy soap, canned sardines, bully beef, Epsom's Liver Salts and condensed milk. In the centre of the floor stood a collection of sacks. They were rolled down to reveal their contents. There were nails, grain and beans. By the door, hung a selection of ladies' straw hats.

'I used to have a lady milliner working here,' said Tommy Wood, 'Mayence Bent[3] her name was. She was damned good at her trade; I'll give her that, but saucy with it. We fell out. She's built a hotel down the street. So I've had to take to tailoring myself,' he indicated some bales of suiting material, 'damned good business it is too,' he said. 'But then the truth is that it's all good business. You can't go wrong.'

'Hmm,' said Abraham Block.

'We'd best get those ponies of yours along to Old Jeevanjee,' Tommy Wood said.

CHAPTER 31

OLD JEEVANJEE

A.M. Jeevanjee was liked and respected by the Administration and for many years he represented
Asian interests to the British, both as a private individual and
as the first Asian member of the Kenya Legislative Council.
He was also the sole Asian member of the Nairobi Club, which he had built…

–Cynthia Salvadori, *Through Open Doors*

ABRAHAM AND TOMMY WOOD LEFT the ponies by a bridge over the Nairobi River and walked on until they arrived in an area of savannah grassland. There were several roughly scaffolded structures and a number of newly built houses.

'The Land Office call this area Parklands,' said Tommy Wood, 'but they've not the sense they were born with. And that's Old Jeevanjee's,' he indicated a large pink building.

Like the area, Old Jeevanjee's house was very newly arrived. Fronted by fluted pillars, it rose to two storeys and had many windows. It stood back from the road, which was a mired track, and had four tall stone gateposts; each topped by a black and white carriage lamp. Two were labelled IN and two were labelled OUT.

A broad sweep of gravel drive connected the gates to the house. And a shallow flight of steps led up from it to a pair of thickly varnished double doors. At the foot of these steps sat two stone lions. They were painted rose pink, like the house. At the top of them stood a gentleman.

'Old Jeevanjee,' said Tommy Wood.

Small, round and burnished, Mr Jeevanjee[1] was impeccably presented in white robes embroidered at neck and hem. On his small, plump feet were scarlet slippers, which turned up at the toes. On his head was a golden turban pinned with a brooch and an egret feather. His beard was oiled, scented and forked at the end. He did not look anything like what 'Old Jeevanjee' might have been expected to look like.

'Welcome to my home,' said Mr Jeevanjee and descended to meet them.

'Mr Jeevanjee is a builder,' said Tommy, 'he has built most of Nairobi and he is shortly to present us with our first municipal gardens and a covered market.'

Abraham shook Mr Jeevanjee's hand.

'And his mansion is undoubtedly the finest in Nairobi,' said Tommy.

'Oh no,' said Mr Jeevanjee, and he giggled, 'no, no. Not at all.'

He shepherded them up the steps and paused at the top to cast a look over his estate.
He smiled.

'My neighbour, Mr Alibhai Sharif, is trying to top me, you know?' he said. 'He has built a house that has six more columns than mine! And a roof terrace with a garden swing!' Mr Jeevanjee's voice rose at the end of each statement. Then he sighed. 'And he has painted it lavender,' he said.

He led them through the double doors into a lavish hall.

'But I don't know if he has topped me,' he said, and waved his arms around.

The reception room was grand. The floor was polished parquet; and it was strewn with costly rugs. The swagged curtains were in pink velvet and edged with tiny golden tassels. A staircase with carved balustrades curved upwards to a gallery. At the foot of the staircase stood two identical peacocks. They were fashioned in blue and green enamel and each held a lantern in its beak.

'He can't have rivaled this,' said Tommy Wood, 'it's a palace by anybody's reckoning.'

'Mmm,' said Mr Jeevanjee, 'and lavender is so … obvious.'

'Indeed it is,' said Tommy.

There was a brief pause in the conversation.

'We have called,' said Tommy, indicating Abraham, 'to see if you might be able to help us with a little problem.'

'Delighted,' said Mr Jeevanjee steepling his plump fingers and bowing.

'Mr Abraham Block here is newly arrived in Nairobi,' Mr Jeevanjee bowed in Abraham's direction, 'and he needs somewhere to stable his Basuto ponies. I told him that, as the creator of Nairobi's first racecourse and the owner of its finest racehorses, you might be able to assist him. I understand that the bluebloods like to mix with the commoners from time to time?'

Mr Jeevanjee giggled. 'Oh yes. My racehorses are fond of donkeys, even zebras, but Basuto ponies will do quite as well. Let's go have a look-see shall we?'

Mr Jeevanjee led them around to the rear of the pink house, and through its infant pink gardens to a walled courtyard. At its centre stood a massive fig tree, hung with creepers and buttressed by great grey roots. Around the courtyard stood lines of stables. The heads of some twenty gleaming racehorses nodded from them.

'My pride and joy,' said Mr Jeevanjee steepling his fingers to his mouth and emitting another tiny giggle. He led them along the lines of heads. He pointed to a chestnut horse, its mane plaited with golden ribbons, 'Star of the East,' he said, 'winner of the first race ever to be run at the new Nairobi Racecourse.'

At the end of the line was a shed containing a pair of mules and a donkey, 'will this suit?' said Mr Jeevanjee.

'Topping,' said Tommy.

A modest fee was agreed and Abraham left to fetch his ponies. Later, as they walked back to the hotel, Abraham asked Tommy Wood what he knew of Mr Jeevanjee.

'Came from Karachi around 1890,' he said, 'traded in Australia for a while. Got a contract with the Imperial British East Africa Company to supply Indian coolies on the railway. Owns ships. Rich man. Getting richer.'

'A good man to know then?' said Abraham.

'The best,' said Tommy, 'apart from me and "D".'

'Who is "D"?' said Abraham. The image of the small red-haired man with the large white sun helmet came into his mind.

'Hugh Cholmondeley, Third Baron Delamere[2],' said Tommy, 'you're bound to come across him. He's known as the "Rhodes of Kenya".'

'Small man? Red hair? Large hat?' said Abraham.

'That's him,' said Tommy, 'Inherited enormous wealth. Arrived here in 1897 after a two-thousand-mile camel ride from Somalia, fell in love with the place. Came back for good in 1901. Wild card; terrible temper, awful charm. He's the colonial king pin, unofficial leader; explorer, hunter, settler, farmer. You name it, Delamere's done it.'

'Mmm,' said Abraham.

CHAPTER 32

THE COLONIALS

I choose my friends for their good looks, my acquaintances for their good characters,
and my enemies for their good intellects.

–Oscar Wilde (1854-1900)

BACK AT THE VICTORIA HOTEL, the bar was full and the conversation was loud. Abraham went to his room, but he could hear every word that was said through its thin calico walls, so he decided that it was better to join the conversation than eavesdrop on it.

In the yellow light of the lanterns there was every type of man. There were colonial administrators, speculators, hunters, traders and farmers. There were soldiers, missionaries and railway men. And all of them, Abraham noted, carried a gun.

'In one evening in my bar,' had said Tommy Wood, 'you'll meet everyone who matters.'

It seemed he was correct.

The first person Abraham met was Ali Khan[1]. He wore leather breeches and gaiters, his long black hair was plaited, and his nose was hooked to meet his chin. He wore a pair of black goggles and he carried a bullwhip. A Pathan horse-dealer, Ali ran the town's only taxi service. It was a mule cart driven at breakneck speed. In daylight hours he ferried goods and people; and at night he carried drunks.

'I know where everyone's bed is in this town,' he said, 'not that they're always in 'em.'

He did not know of any work to be had.

The second person Abraham met was an Australian called Tom Deacon[2], who had just acquired a plot of land.

'I got it in payment for a gaming debt,' he said, 'I've tried pigs, but they got swine fever. I planted wheat, but the elephants trampled it. I'm clearing for coffee now. It's a hard land and I've just about had enough.'

'That's what they all say,' said a man in a linen suit, 'but is enough ever enough?'

He was playing Patience alone. As he looked up he revealed an empty socket where once his right eye had been.

'You'd know all about that wouldn't you Williams?' said a square-built fellow in a khaki hunters suit. He had a South African accent and on his head was a hat fashioned from a whole leopard pelt. The tail hung down his back and the snarling face, fangs out, topped his own.

'I guess I would, Mr Bowker,' said the man addressed as Williams.

Later, Abraham asked Tommy what he knew of Williams. He had come to learn that Tommy liked to air his knowledge.

'Greswold Williams[3]?' said Tommy, 'English. Reckons he's upper class. Says he lost his eye in a duel. Likes to cut a romantic figure. But there's nowt romantic to my way of thinking about selling morphine and cocaine to all the young fools that come out here with more money than sense'.

'Have you many of those?'

'Aye. And more arriving by the day,' said Tommy, 'but Williams is not a man of the ilk you'd want to know.' He looked down the bar.

'Unlike young Herbert Binks[4] here,' he said, 'now he's fresh from Yorkshire where all the right 'uns come from.'

Herbert Binks was a slight young man with round glasses. They caught the light as he turned towards Abraham, making him look fleetingly blind.

'Binksie came out here when his ladylove turned him down. Ain't that right lad?' said Tommy.

'Aye. She didn't reckon I'd amount to much,' said Binks, 'smart lass. But I'll do right enough for this place,' he said.

'And what will you do in this place?' said Abraham.

'Whatever seems the most likely', said Binks. He tossed back his whisky and indicated to Tommy that he'd take another.

'I'm a chemist by profession, but I've been a farmer, a miner, a hunter, a photographer and an astronomer too, and one of 'em's bound to suit,' he said.

It was impossible to oversleep at Wood's Hotel. With the dawn came the sound of hawking and spitting, the clank of tin cups on enamel basins. And the grunts of men forcing themselves into tropical garb. According to local lore, the rays of the sun destroyed the spine. It rotted the liver and sent men insane. So they wore red flannel spine pads sewn into their jackets from neck to hips. Their hats were lined with scarlet flannel, and they wore them one on top of the other as a Double Terai.

Abraham had no time for such things, it seemed to him that men rotted their livers and went insane without any help from the sun.

CHAPTER 33

ABRAHAM BLOCK MAKES A DEAL

Buy land. They ain't making any more of the stuff.

–Will Rogers, American cowboy and vaudeville performer (1879-1935)

BREAKFAST WAS SERVED IN THE bar where at least half the complement of men from the night before seemed still to be in residence. Tea was dispensed from an oversized enamel teapot, bread was hot from the baker's, and the butter was scooped out of a metal tin stamped 'Bombay' and referred to as axle grease. Bright yellow, it had acquired the greasy clarity of tallow by being constantly melted and solidified in the heat of Mombasa docks.

'You'll get used to it,' said Tommy Wood, and he rolled a boiled egg down the bar to Abraham.

It was whilst he was peeling the egg, that Abraham became aware of a conversation. It was not quite within his earshot, but since eavesdropping was a way of life at Wood's Hotel, he leaned closer.

'It's a prime piece of land,' said a man, 'best I've seen. Even old Reggie Wright[1] down at the Lands Commission roused himself from his habitual gloom to comment on it. I showed it to him on the map.'

'Where is it?' said a second man.

'Parklands: that new residential area. You know, where Jeevanjee's building?'

'Well he certainly knows what he's doing. How much?'

'I don't know, but I'd pay a hundred pounds and think I'd done very well.'

They were young men and looked like every other settler Abraham had ever met. They were in their shirtsleeves, and their faces were burnished; one wore braces and an open-necked shirt. The other wore a collar but it had curled up like bacon in the heat.

'So buy it?' said the second man.

'I'd like to,' said the first, 'but I've got to report to the new DC at Kiambu this morning and it's a long walk.'

'I suppose it might still be there when you get back?' The tone was doubtful.

'If it is, I'll buy it!'

The conversation ended and the young men left.

Abraham considered. Then he walked to Parklands and called on Mr Jeevanjee.

'Do you know who owns the plot next to you, Mr Jeevanjee?' he said.

'Well I do, Mr Block,' said Mr Jevanjee as if this were obvious.

'I'd like to buy it,' said Abraham.

'Hmm,' said Mr Jeevanjee.

'I'd like to give you a twenty pound deposit now.'

'Hmm?'

'And I guarantee to bring you another fifty pounds by the end of the day. You have my ponies as surety,' said Abraham.

'Hmm.'

Mr Jeevanjee looked Abraham up and down. He steepled his fingers to his small brown rosebud of a mouth and he smiled.

'There's something about you, Mr Block,' he said, 'I don't often see it. But I know it when I do. You attract money. I'll sell you the land for seventy five pounds, no more, no less.'

'Done,' said Abraham, and gave him twenty pounds. It was all the money he had in the world. 'How do I get to Kiambu?' he said.

Abraham caught up with the two men from Wood's bar an hour later. They were walking fast. But he walked faster.

He drew alongside them, smiled and tipped his hat.

'I heard you talking in Tommy Wood's bar,' he said, 'about the land you wanted to buy in Parklands.'

The men stopped. They pushed their sun helmets back on their heads so they could see him.

'And?' said one of them. His tone was slightly insolent.

'And I bought it,' said Abraham, 'and I want to sell it: to you: for one hundred pounds.'

'Well I'll be damned,' said the prospective buyer, 'fast mover aren't you?'

'I am,' said Abraham.

The man threw back his head and laughed. He looked to his friend.

'What do you think Ronnie?'

'Bloke's right. You said you wanted it. He's got it for you. Price you said you'd pay. Can't say fairer.'

'I don't believe you can,' said his friend. He turned to Abraham and held out his hand.

'Done', he said.

They arranged to meet later in Wood's to finalize the deal. And when this was done Abraham Block had more than doubled the money that he had arrived in Nairobi with.

It was later that same day that Abraham found Tommy; he was nailing a notice to the wall of the bar. There was to be a land sale in Nairobi in two day's time.

'Will you buy land?' said Abraham to Tommy.

'No. I'm just the auctioneer.'

'Why not?'

'Why won't I buy land in this place? Because it's a mosquito-ridden swamp. And I believe they will site the Administrative Headquarters of the Protectorate elsewhere,' he said.

On the day of the sale, there was standing room only in Wood's bar. And Abraham found his friends, Eli, Sulsky, London and Moskow there.

'Where have you been?' he said.

'Camped outside the Lands Office,' said Eli.

'Along with a hundred others,' said Sulsky.

'Some of them have been there for months,' said Moskow, 'with not even a sniff at a map of the land available.'

'Why?' said Abraham.

'The word is that the Land Commissioners are overwhelmed,' said Eli, 'though they don't seem to be so. Most of them seem to spend their time catching butterflies along the river.'

'I've a letter of introduction to Mr John Ainsworth, the Sub-District Commissioner for Nairobi?' said Abraham, 'I'm told he is the man to see.' His friends looked at him curiously.

'How did you get *that*?' said London.

From his position behind the bar, Tommy Wood shouted for the sale of land to begin. He shuffled a pile of deeds before him. Instead of a gavel he used a roofing hammer. An hour later, despite a lot of shouting, he had sold nothing: not a single plot of land.

'Told you so,' said Tommy to Abraham, 'nobody wants to risk building in a swamp in the middle of nowhere.'

He turned back to the room.

'So? You lot won't buy land?' he said, 'that's fair enough. But which one of you Scrooges would like to buy a nice pussy? He smiled. 'And don't try and tell me you don't need one,' he said.

CHAPTER 34

THE LAND COMMISSIONERS

The day of small nations has long passed away. The day of Empires has come.
–Joseph Chamberlain 1836-1914

JOHN AINSWORTH, THE SUB-DISTRICT COMMISSIONER for Nairobi, had built his own office. It was a grey tin shack by the slow brown waters of the Nairobi River, and he had also built the bridge across the river. This replaced the stepping-stones that the Kikuyu people had put there; and their village stood close by. Ainsworth's Bridge was grey stone, and it had been washed away three times, but Mr Ainsworth insisted on replacing it every time this happened. Its maintenance had become something of an obsession with him. It was, he felt, the only thing in Nairobi over which he had any real control.

Mr Ainsworth's office, and his living quarters which lay behind them, were surrounded by gardens filled with exotic shrubs. Most of these he had brought with him from his last posting, which had been in Australia. Mr Ainsworth lavished great care on his gardens, and they repaid him twentyfold by attracting clouds of butterflies. There were blue pansy butterflies, green skippers, whites, emperor swallowtails and tawny-red painted ladies. Leading to Ainsworth's Bridge was an avenue of spindly eucalyptus trees, the seedlings for which Mr Ainsworth had also brought from Australia.

Mr Ainsworth disapproved strongly of Nairobi. Or to be more precise, he disapproved of where it stood, which he liked to refer to as 'blighted plain'. But Mr Ainsworth was a realist and he doubted that the town would ever be relocated, so he devoted himself to making the place look, as he put it, 'less damned ghastly' by planting avenues of gum trees all over town. It was because of this that the men of Tommy Wood's bar had dubbed him 'Johnny Gum Tree'. And to their delight the name had stuck.

There was a circle of stones around Mr Ainsworth's shack and these were repainted every week in white paint. By the door, which was a sheet of corrugated iron, there was a flagpole from which flew the Union Jack. It was lowered every evening at six by a gardener clad in long socks, white lace-up shoes, white shorts, a safari jacket and a sun helmet. As the flag came down, the strains of *The Last Post* floated from the fluted trumpet of a wind-up phonograph, which was operated by Mr Ainsworth's cook.

'Johnny Gum Tree', said Wood's bar, was a stickler for form.

Abraham pushed open the door to Mr Ainsworth's office and led the small Jewish deputation inside. Like most of Nairobi's buildings it was hot and gloomy and had creaking corrugated iron walls. A small Indian clerk sat at a desk. He looked enquiringly at them, pen poised. Abraham, pushed forward by his fellows, presented the letter of introduction from Mr Markus. He asked if they might have an audience with the Sub-District Commissioner. The clerk took the letter and waved them towards the usual collection of mismatched dining chairs.

A few minutes later, a short man barrelled in to the room. He wore a safari suit with trousers that stopped several inches short of his highly polished shoes; his trouser creases were knife-edge sharp and starch-shiny.

'John Ainsworth, Sub-District Commissioner for Nairobi' he said. He waved Mr Markus's letter at them. 'I have a high regard for Messrs Markus and Loy,' he said, 'they are exactly the stock of men required to build the Empire. So any request emanating from them finds favour with me. How may I be of assistance?' He jutted his head forward and moved it to left and right like a tortoise. It was evident that Mr Ainsworth's time was short.

'We heard Mr Chamberlain speak in Cape Town,' began Abraham.

Mr Ainsworth drew a deep breath and narrowed his eyes.

'We were impressed by what we heard of the British Protectorate of Kenya and we have come to petition for land,' he said, 'we'd like to settle here. And farm.'

Abraham had decided that the mention of the New Zion would not help them.

'Ah ha,' said Mr Ainsworth, 'then you must go to the Lands Commission.'

He looked down at the letter in his hand.

'The thing is, though,' he said, 'and I wouldn't say this to everyone. The thing is that those fellows in the Lands Commission can be a bit tricky. Seem almost to want to prevent people from getting land.' He mused on this for a second or two then reached a decision.

'So,' he said, 'I'm going to send you straight to the British Commissioner, Sir Charles Eliot. Now he is a man who is very keen on attracting young fellows like you to the Colony. And,' he wagged an admonitory finger, 'he won't allow those land chappies to lead you up the garden path.' Mr Ainsworth strode over to the clerk's desk and dashed off a note. He handed it to Abraham. 'Speaking of which,' he said, 'when you get settled you'll need eucalyptus seedlings. Come to me. I've got more than I know what to do with.'

The Office of the Commissioner stood on The Hill. This was a hump of land that rose abruptly to the east of the swamp and seemed to have acquired an air of official importance that was entirely unwarranted. The office itself was no more prepossessing than that of Mr Ainsworth, but it was slightly larger.

Sir Charles Eliot[1] did not have the appearance of an empire builder: he looked more like an Oxford don. He was softly spoken and he favoured a thick moustache, which he trimmed in a straight line across his thin red lips; he had dark hair severely parted down the centre of his head and plastered to either side of it. Sir Charles was a scholar of some note; he spoke fourteen languages fluently, he gave readings of Mandarin verse nightly, and he was a world authority on sea slugs. Wood's bar had, therefore, christened him 'The Great Sea Slug'.

Sir Charles' office was lined with books. In its centre was a large tank. It was veiled in translucent green slime and Sir Charles was peering into it as Abraham and his flock entered.

'Nudibranchiates.' said Sir Charles. He looked up and directed them to the seats lined up before his ornate desk. 'Utterly fascinating once you get to know them; but I don't suppose you will.' He sat down on the other side of his desk. 'Great shame: they more than reward investigation. But there we are. Now, tell me why you are here?'

When he learned that the young men wished to settle in the Protectorate, Sir Charles's waxy face glowed, and he rubbed his dry white hands together.

'Excellent,' he said, 'and you wish to invest?'

Ainsworth's Bridge, Nairobi, 1906

'Yes,' said Eli, 'but we understand that a sum of three hundred pounds will be sufficient?'

'Have you joy of adventure and an appetite for risk?' said Sir Charles as if reciting from a hymnbook.

'In plenty,' said Eli, and the others nodded vigorously.

'Then that is more than enough,' declared Sir Charles.

He squared his shoulders in preparation for the delivery of a portion of one of his favourite speeches. 'Because if a man comes here with three thousand pounds and expects a safe return on his money,' he said, 'then that is a dangerous man to this colony! But if a man comes here with three hundred pounds and the determination that nothing on God's green earth is going to drive him out of Kenya, then that is the man we want!' [2]

There was silence.

Abraham stood up and proffered the scrawled note.

'Mr Ainsworth hoped you might refer us to the Land Commission,' he said, though it seemed a poor response to the rousing nature of the speech. Moscow helped him out.

'We have been camped outside there for some time,' he said, 'but they tell us they are—'

'Swamped?' said Sir Charles.

'Busy,' said Eli diplomatically.

'Utter nonsense!' said Sir Charles, 'Slackers to a man, no idea of the importance of their work. If only more true settlers came here, rather than all these shooters, we could really build this country.' He placed the knuckles of both hands on his desk and leaned forward. He beamed at them.

'As it happens, however, you have timed your arrival perfectly, gentlemen, because we have just issued some new grants of land. These are divided into three classes.' He held up a pale white finger. 'Firstly, there are farms of 5,000 acres, which are available at a penny per acre per annum. Secondly,' he held up another finger, 'there are 99-year leased farms, which are available at a half penny per acre annually and, thirdly,' he leant towards them, 'there are the 640-acre plots, which make ideal farms for first-timers and are available on exceptionally reasonable terms. These will suit you gentlemen admirably, I think?'

'Indeed,' said Eli.

'Exemplary!' said Sir Charles, 'then I shall instruct my chaps in the Land Commission to show you the maps this very day.' He swept a space clear on his desk, dashed off a note and handed it to them.

As the group filed out of his office Sir Charles shook each of them by the hand; and as the door closed behind them they heard his voice from within; it echoed. 'Exactly what we need my beloveds, he said, '*exactly* my dears.'

When Mr Reginald Wright of the Lands Commission read Sir Charles' note he uttered a snort of exasperation and flung it on his desk.

'It's all very well for him,' he said, closing his eyes briefly, 'he has no idea what we're up against.' He glared at them. 'Show you maps he says! There are no maps. There are sketches. But there are NO maps!' He pulled down one of the many rolled papers that were stacked on the shelves behind him and spread it out before them on the desk. 'See?' he said truculently. The young men, who had no idea what they were looking at, looked puzzled and downcast.

Mr Wright sighed. 'Oh, very well!' he said, 'make rough copies and go and look at the plots with your own eyes. It won't be easy: a chap called Harries[3] had to walk 400 miles before he decided on a plot in Thika, and another chap, Hoey I think his name was, covered a thousand miles before choosing one on the Loita plains. But better that, gentlemen, than to buy sight unseen and then complain.' The unspoken words 'to me' hung in the air.

The group nodded their comprehension.

'When you have found your land,' continued Mr Wright, 'come back to me and I will try to get it surveyed.' He removed his glasses and rubbed his eyes. 'It may take time because I have a severe shortage of surveyors. One of my best men, Cyrill Ortlipp[4], was drowned last week while crossing the Morendat River. And all his papers were swallowed by a python.' Mr Wright wiped his round gold spectacles on his handkerchief. 'It was a tragedy,' he said, 'the loss of those papers has set us back months.'

The great strength of Wood's Hotel lay in the depth of its information pool.

Tommy Wood had an assistant; his name was Mr King, and his tentacles were far reaching. If something needed doing Mr King would get it done. If something had to be acquired Mr King would acquire it. And if something needed to be said Mr King would say it. But he had no use for circumlocution. So when Hotz, London, Moscow, Sulsky and Eli went to him with a complicated list of requirements for their land expedition he held up a hand.

'Condense it,' he said.

Several hours later, they were equipped with horses, guides, camping equipment and supplies.

'Start at dawn,' said Mr King.

Hours later, after carefully cataloguing his equipment, Hotz passed Mr King in the corridor.

'You stink,' said Mr King.

CHAPTER 35

RAISING CAPITAL

The ground squelches under the feet like the crust over a morass and one treads
with care around great piles of garbage and open gutters.
Here, they say, one can cut one's finger and it will fester within an hour.
–Nairobi in 1902 as described by a missionary from the Sagala Mission

NAIROBI WAS GROWING, BUT IT was still little more than a collection of tin huts on a doleful plain. But sitting on the step at the back of Tommy Wood's butchery, Abraham could see for miles. Thirty to be precise, to a great hunch of a mountain called Ol Donyo Sabuk, the Mountain of the Buffalo.

In the space that lay between this mountain and the tin tidemark of Nairobi, lay a broad swathe of savanna plain. And across it moved great cloud shadows of game. In the dry season the plains were tawny gold, in the rains they were a jade green, and in the evenings they turned from soft lilac to bruised plum as the great ball of the sun sank behind them.

Abraham spent many hours looking out over these plains; he liked to trace the stampedes of wildebeest and the steady buffalo trains. He had tamed some gazelles, which had broken free of the herds and ventured closer to the town. They would not take food from his hand, but they would edge close enough to regard him with their large black eyes, and to stamp their small hooves impatiently in the dust. Abraham liked to watch them; and he liked to use the back step of the butchery as a place in which to think.

Now, with his friends departed upcountry to choose their land, his thoughts turned to how he might make sufficient money to do likewise. Later, as Wood's bar filled, he left the step and set to work information gathering. The settler community was set in its ways. It was not considered good form to ask directly about such things as work or money because settlers disliked negatives. It was better, therefore, to sew the seeds of enquiry and wait for them to sprout.

Abraham was good at this.

It took time for his probing to show any return, but eventually Wood's bar delivered. There was a new man in town, they said. His name was Eric Erskine; he had come from India, he was believed to be wealthy, and he had bought thousands of acres of land in the Rift Valley. So, reasoned Wood's bar, he must be in need of a good man: a man such as Abraham Block.

This information was good in parts, except for the fact that Mr Erskine had all the men he needed. But something in Abraham's demeanor, when he approached him, must have pleased Mr Erskine because he said, 'I can't give you work. But I can give you free lodgings. I have a large house on The Hill. It's only half-built but it's habitable and I could do with the company. It would reduce your overheads at least?' he said.

'I appreciate it,' said Abraham, 'and I will repay you with interest.'

Abraham moved his belongings and his ponies to Mr Erskine's plot, which was large and had already received the attentions of Johnny Gum Tree. As was his habit, Abraham paced it out, and viewed the plots on either side. One was rambling and uncleared, and bore a sign proclaiming it to be the property of the railway. The other, which was cleared and planted with Kikuyu grass, had a large tin hut at its centre, and a sign, which read 'The Nairobi Club'.

Abraham was a curious man. He strolled over to the shack and pushed open the door. There was a rough bar with a locked cabinet containing an array of bottles. There was a gilt mirror lacking silver. There were a number of stuffed animal heads hanging at drunken angles on rusty nails. By the door was an elephant's foot fashioned into an umbrella stand, and three sagging sofas, which were pulled up around a stone fireplace, its grandeur at odds with its surroundings. As Abraham left, closing the door behind him, he noticed a neatly painted sign. It read, 'For Officers and Gentlemen Only'.

Abraham smiled; he was beginning to understand the British.

On his return to Mr Erskine's half-built house, Abraham noticed a number of half-built outhouses; and he filed their existence away in his mind. Some weeks later a South African by the name of Kreiger[1] made an announcement to Wood's bar in general. He had two sows for sale. Both, he said, were about to litter and he had nowhere to keep them.

'First man to give me five pounds can have 'em,' he said.

'Lend me five pounds?' said Abraham to Tommy Wood, 'You'll be repaid with interest.'

'First you shift out of my hotel, then you touch me for money,' said Tommy, but he pulled some crumpled notes out of his pocket. Abraham walked across to the owner of the pigs and placed the money on the table in front of him.

'I'll take them,' he said.

When the pigs were installed in the outhouses on Mr Erskine's plot, Abraham went to Tommy.

'Let me have all the swill from the kitchens,' he said, 'you'll be repaid with interest.'

'Aye,' said Tommy Wood, 'that I will.'

By the end of the first month, Abraham had two litters of piglets. By the end of the third month, he had sold them and repaid Tommy Wood with interest.

'You want to watch yourself Abraham Lazarus Block,' Tommy said, 'you're so sharp you'll cut yourself.'

'We could do the same thing with some turkeys,' said Abraham.

'Aye we could, ALB' said Tommy Wood, 'so you'll be wanting the money back again I take it?'

'ALB?'

'Suits you,' said Tommy, 'short and sharp.'

It did suit Abraham Lazarus Block. And it stuck.

Nicknames were popular in the colony. The white men gave them to each other, and the Africans gave them to the white men. The white men did this out of a sense of camaraderie; the Africans did it in the interests of precision. To them, all white men looked much the same and their names were equally indecipherable; so the African made up new names for them. They were typically apt, sometimes cruel, and once bestowed they could not be withdrawn. The Administration drew up a list; on one side was written the name of the white man and on the other was written the name the Africans had given him. When this list was published, it caused great upset. It revealed that Sir Northrup McMillan[2], a wealthy American with a 54-inch waist, was known as 'The Tummy'. He hated this. But nothing he could do or say could change it. Commander Niverson, a blustering red-faced Wood's bar regular, was called 'Bano'. He was proud and pompous and had insisted that the Africans call him *Bwana*. But he couldn't pronounce the word, so he paid the price. A raw Assistant District Commissioner, just arrived from England with his wife and nursemaid, was known as 'The Man with Two Wives', which caused him acute embarrassment. And another gangling new recruit went by the name of 'Squeaky Legs' on account of his new leather gaiters.

Abraham Block was known initially as 'The Midget' because he was short. But in later years, in a monumental departure from tradition, the Africans renamed him: he became known as 'The Prophet' in recognition of his uncanny ability to make money.

'What's your African nickname?' said Abraham to Tommy Wood.

'Don't you know?' said Tommy.

'Why should I?'

'Because I yell it from morning 'til night,' said Tommy. 'They call me *Wataka Nini*, it means "What do you want?"'

'Why?' said Abraham.

'Why? Simple. They're always wandering into my shop: picking things up and putting them down; and laughing and chattering and wasting my time, in the way they do. And eventually I can't stand it. So I shout.'

His glance fell on the two remaining cats.

'It could be worse, I suppose,' he said.

Fred Tate outside the Stanley Hotel

CHAPTER 36

ABRAHAM BLOCK PROVIDES

Business is never so healthy as when,
like a chicken, it must do a certain amount of scratching around for what it gets.
–Henry Ford, American industrialist (1873-1974)

IT TOOK TIME FOR ALB to carve a role for himself out of the unyielding grit of the settler community. But eventually he succeeded; and then it seemed as if he had always been part of it. He was well liked. He had an easy smile and an unassuming manner. He was always willing to proffer his help, but he didn't look for reward. He offered an array of skills, all of which were useful to the infant colony. He was a competent carpenter and could make or mend most things. He was an able farmer, and his time in engine rooms had given him a basic engineering competency.

Abraham Block was also good company. He was both a listener and a raconteur and there was something about his wry wit, his thick Russian accent, and his laconic delivery, which made people laugh. And in the harsh settler world, laughter was the only antidote to setbacks. And these occurred constantly.

ALB also made it his business to know everyone; and he made no distinction in his knowing. He knew the settlers, he knew the Indians and he knew the Africans, and this gave him a vital advantage, because they did not always know each other. Abraham, like the Africans, knew the value of everything. He wasted nothing: he watched and waited and he picked up what the white men threw away. And, like the Indians, he knew that only hard work would deliver wealth, and that only thrift would preserve it. Unlike some of the other settlers, however, Abraham Block had no sense of entitlement and no belief in the luck that they seemed to place so much faith in.

For all these reasons, though he rarely drank more than a tumbler of whisky, Abraham was invited everywhere; and when Mayence Bent declared the Grand Opening of her new hotel, the Stanley, he was one of the first to be invited to the event.

Mayence Bent claimed to be the wife of Mr W. S. Bent[1], a railway engineer who had worked on the building of the Nigerian Railway. He was middle-aged, dry and bookish and he had a love of crosswords and the construction of political essays. Rumour had it that Mayence Bent was not actually married to him. She was in her early thirties, sharply attractive, flirtatious and ambitious. She was also a talented seamstress, though where she had learned her skills was unknown.

When Mayence had first arrived in Nairobi, there had been few women with any use for the tailored costumes or frivolous hats in which she excelled. Most wore the clothes they had arrived in, and patched them as they wore out; and the remainder wore the standard safari costume as prescribed by the safari outfitters of London. This consisted of a pair of gabardine breeches worn beneath an ankle-length skirt with a side split, a manly shirt, high-laced boots and a flannel-lined sun helmet.

Everything changed when Mr Jeevanjee opened his racecourse. Suddenly, Nairobi had a social event of note. Now all the women who had endured the solitary roughness of up-country life had an excuse to come to town; and they needed to dress for it.

Mayence Bent was made.

She set up as a modiste in a small room at the back of Tommy Wood's emporium; and she did well. But then she noticed that whenever one of 'her ladies' was in a state of undress, Tommy Wood would find some excuse to present himself. It was always to discuss a matter of extreme triviality; and they fell out over it.

Mayence decided to build her own shop; but then she thought again. Her time at Tommy Wood's had taught her that Nairobi lacked a hotel suitable for ladies. Of all the boarding houses, Wood's was easily the best, but it presented a number of problems for lady guests, and they were all of a delicate nature. The earth closets could only be reached by walking across the yard, and this was in full view of the bar. The water pump was in the middle of the yard, and the rooms had calico walls. The latter presented by far the most serious problem because, as the ladies dressed, or undressed, in the light of their lanterns, their silhouettes were cast in titillating detail on to the wall of the bar. The effect was that of a *son et lumière* show, which Tommy Wood called 'getting an eyeful' and was known to enjoy.

Mayence Bent decided to build a hotel for gentlefolk; she called it The Stanley.

The Stanley rose swiftly above the squalor of Victoria Street. It was a two-storey structure built from galvanized iron sheeting and wood; and it stood midway between Tommy Wood's hotel and the station. It had a red-painted tin roof, white-painted corrugated-iron walls and a timber veranda, which encircled the first floor. On the ground floor there was a dining room, a bar and a lounge.

In essence, The Stanley was no better than Wood's, but the genius of Mayence lay in her ability to make it appear so. The furniture, though made by local Indian carpenters, echoed the latest designs from the London furnishers, Waring and Gillow. There were oil lamps rather than paraffin lanterns, and there were curtains at the windows, some of which had glass in them. In the lounge there was an upright piano, which had hinged brass candleholders and a tasseled stool that went up and down on a wooden screw. In each bedroom was a carved dressing table on which stood a china ewer and basin; and screens were provided behind which the ladies might change. In the entrance hall there was a palm in a chamber pot and a chintz-covered sofa with claw feet; and its walls boasted two gilt-framed mirrors, a pendulum clock in a wooden case, and an array of animal heads, which had been contributed by the town's latest arrival, a German taxidermist called Hock.

The Stanley also boasted the services of a Goan chef, who had been enticed away from the railway. Known only as Pinto he had an immense black iron range beneath which red-hot fires roared, and a cool room lined with charcoal down which water dripped. His menu was limited; it featured tinned salmon and bully beef; and tinned peaches and tapioca pudding. Custard came with everything; and on Sundays there was goat stew. All this was luxury indeed, and Nairobi was duly captivated.

Mayence Bent had triumphed; but she had a problem; and it lay in the bedrooms. She had stitched the bed linen by hand, stuffed the pillows with ostrich feathers, and had the local blacksmith produce iron bedsteads complete with bed knobs. But she could not obtain any mattresses, and this riled her. The problem lay in the lack of suitable stuffing; neither horsehair nor hay was available in sufficient quantities, and the only solution lay in the use of a rough webbing made out of strips of zebra skin tacked to a wooden frame.

'Of course our Mayence reckons zebra skin is not good enough for her fancy new hotel,' said Tommy Wood as he and Abraham walked to the Grand Opening. 'Mind, she always did have ideas above her station' he continued, 'proper mattresses! I ask you?'

Tommy eyed Abraham and his eyes narrowed.

'Now then, though,' he said slowly, 'you're a canny fellow, Block. Fix up anything you can. What about giving the lady a bit of what she wants? She'd be very grateful I shouldn't wonder.' He grinned.

Abraham made no reply.

The Stanley was already crowded when Tommy and Abraham arrived. People were drinking, smoking and tinkling on the piano. The entire contents of Wood's had migrated there for the evening, though most swore they would never return. Abraham pushed his way through the crowd until he stood before Mayence Bent. He squared his broad shoulders, smoothed his dark hair back from his brow, and smiled. It was no hardship: Mayence was a comely woman. She also had something of Rosie about her. She had an hourglass figure, high piled hair, and she liked to stand with her hands on her tiny waist and her bust thrust out. It was a stance both sensual and challenging.

'Mrs Bent,' said Abraham, 'I'm told you are in want of something in your bedrooms that I might be able to provide.'

'Indeed Mr Block,' said Mayence, her eyebrows raised, 'and what might that be?'

'Mattresses,' said Abraham.

Mrs Bent's rather protuberant pale blue eyes fastened themselves on his.

'Really?' she said. She took Abraham by the arm, pressing her soft full bust into him as she did so, and led him through the crowd and into an alcove.

'Tell me more,' she said.

'I think I can give you what you want,' said Abraham.

Mayence arched one finely pencilled eyebrow.

'I'll bring you a sample mattress within a week,' he said, 'if it pleases you, I will make more. No down payment required. Cash on delivery'.

'I've heard you're quite the man for delivering,' said Mayence. She held her head on one side. Her pearl earring quivered.

'I'm a man of my word,' said Abraham.

'We'll see about that,' said Mayence, 'but I think we have a deal.'

She smiled upon him.

Abraham had only the sketchiest notion of how he would deliver that which he had promised so glibly. His idea hinged on something that he had seen while he was walking alongside the railway.

The following morning Abraham presented himself at the railway station. He asked if he might see the Superintendent, a Scot by the name of McEwan.

'The grass is very tall along your sidings,' he began, when he had been shown into Mr McEwan's small, bare office.

The Stanley Hotel 1902

Abraham Block c. 1910

Fred Tate c. 1930

Mayence Bent c. 1905

The 3rd Lord Delamere

Tommy Wood

'Aye,' said McEwan, 'and what's it to you?'

'I'd like to cut it and cart it away. I have a use for it.'

'Aye,' said McEwan 'and what might that be?'

Abraham had learned that the settler community valued honesty, though it did not always employ it. So he told Mr McEwan about the mattresses for the Stanley Hotel.

'You're a canny fellow, Mr Block,' said the Superintendent, 'you should have been born Scottish. But Jewish is close enough, I dare say. Away with you and cut the grass. But if your plan works I'll be expecting a wee something in return.'

He tapped his rosy red nose.

'I always repay with interest, Mr McEwan,' said ALB and tapped his own.

Abraham's next call was to Mr Marcus[2], a Rumanian Jew who prided himself on the fact that his shop stocked everything a farmer could possibly require. Abraham had sent a number of clients his way and the two men had become pleasantly acquainted.

Mr Marcus was hunched over his accounts, his desk wedged between plough boards, hoes and mattocks; he greeted Abraham with pleasure.

'I need a number of machetes,' Abraham said, and he outlined his plan for the construction of Mayence Bent's mattresses. 'I cannot afford to buy them,' he explained, 'but I will pay you with interest when the job is done.'

'Of course you will,' said Mr Marcus, 'and they're better out in the fields than gathering dust on my shelves. And what about the covering for these mattresses? Do you have a plan for those?'

'I had thought to have them made in the Indian Bazaar,' said Abraham.

'Mr da Souza,' said Mr Marcus, 'he has a stall by the Kikuyu tanning yard. Can't miss it. Smells. Tell him I sent you.'

The stalls of the Indian Bazaar were painted in canary yellow and violet; they were tightly jumbled and anchored in mud. They sold everything from elephant tusks to bolts of silk; and from bags of nails to elephant guns. The Bazaar dealt a blow to the senses that took a while to absorb; it was noisy and rancorous. Merchants yelled, beggars rang their bells, people quarreled, and at every corner a bare-breasted African girl lolled. There were large cans filled with *pombe*, a brew distilled from sugar cane, and men dipped their cups into these cans in return for a few coins; then they drank until they dropped and they slept where they fell.

Mr R. A. da Souza was a squat Goan with an egg-round pate and a large black treadle sewing machine. When Abraham found him, he was engaged in sewing nosebags. Abraham presented him with a detailed drawing of the mattress he had in mind.

'It can be done,' pronounced Mr da Souza after some consideration, 'but you must do the stuffing.'

Abraham recruited a team of African boys from those who habitually hung around outside Wood's. He collected his ponies, he borrowed Tommy Wood's cart, and he loaded the boys and the machetes into it. The weather had been exceptionally hot and the grass on the sidings was dry and easily cut. Back in Wood's yard Abraham had the boys lay it out in sheaves.

The next day Abraham collected the mattress cover from Mr da Souza and set about the task of stuffing it with the sheaves of grass. It wasn't easy and his hands and arms were scratched and bloodied by the time he had stuffed it to his satisfaction.

The mattress looked good; but there was a problem: none of the needles in Wood's shop was long enough to allow him to sew up the hole through which the grass had been pushed.

Abraham sat back on his haunches and contemplated the gaping mattress.

A man wove his way from the bar to the earth closets. On his return, he stopped and surveyed the problem with the concentrated intensity of the very drunk.

'Wharr you want,' he said, 'ish a bicycle spoke.'

Abraham burst into Tommy Wood's shop, demanded a spoke, sharpened one end, punctured the other, and threaded it with baling twine.

Mayence Bent was engaged in emptying her chamber pots over the edge of the first floor balcony when Abraham drew his cart up outside the Stanley Hotel. She paused in her task.

'Your mattress, Mrs Bent,' said Abraham.

'So I see, Mr Block,' said she.

Seconds later, Mayence appeared on the front steps of her hotel. She descended to the cart and poked the mattress in several places. Then she climbed into the cart and bounced up and down on it. 'I'll take it;' she said, 'and thirteen more like it. How fast? And how much?'

'Two weeks, ten Rupees each,' said Abraham.

'Done,' said Mayence Bent.

'If you'll take my advice, Mrs Bent,' said Abraham, 'you'll cover the mattresses with a thick blanket when you finally make up the beds,' he indicated his bleeding arms and hands, 'or you'll have some sorely pricked customers in your bedrooms.'

'Oh I've plenty of those already, Mr Block,' said Mrs Bent.

And she whisked back up the steps.

CHAPTER 37

THE FIRST FARM

Success is not final, failure is not fatal: it is the courage to continue that counts.
—Winston Churchill, Statesman (1874-1965)

ABRAHAM'S BUSINESS VENTURES HAD EARNED him money. And, as was his way, he had repaid all those who had helped him. Now he had money to invest, but the question was: in what?

One evening he fell into conversation with an assured young man with thickly brilliantined hair. He introduced himself as Lieutenant Richard Meinertzhagen[1], of the 3rd King's African Rifles.

'Do you know the Indian Bazaar?' said the Lieutenant.

'I do,' said Abraham.

'Did you know that you can get a Somali girl there for five Rupees, a Seychellois for four, a Masai for three, and a half-caste for one?' Meinertzhagen said.

'I did not,' said Abraham.

'Of course most fellows don't bother paying for it,' said Meinertzhagen, blowing cigar smoke out of the side of his mouth, 'they all keep a native woman, mostly Maasai.'

'Oh.'

'You should get one yourself,' Meinertzhagen said. His manner was condescending but not unfriendly.

'I've no time for that,' said Abraham, 'I have to double my money so I can marry a girl in Britain. If you were in my position what would you do with the sum of fifty pounds?'

'Buy land,' said Meinertzhagen.

'Where?' said Abraham.

'Anywhere,' said Meinertzhagen.

'What kind of land?'

'Farming land,' said Meinertzhagen. He pulled on his cigar, 'and the sooner the better.'

Abraham said nothing.

'The majority of settlers are all scallywags, you see,' said Meinertzhagen, 'they do nothing but grumble if they're not given what they ask for by the Administration. They want the easy way out.' He eyed Abraham. 'You, on the other hand,' he said, 'are enthusiastic, full of ideas, Jewish and you'll do well'.

He offered Abraham a cigar.

'Good luck to you,' he said.

Abraham accepted both.

Wood's hotel served both as Nairobi's unofficial land agency and its auction house. And, since he spent a lot of time there, Abraham was well acquainted with land prices. So when he fell into conversation with a pair of German farmers with land for sale, he knew that the deal they offered was good.

Dr Ufferman and Mr Lauterbach[2] had a farm to sell. It was called Njuna and it was in the Kiambu district, north of Nairobi.

'It's a 640-acre plot, already cleared of bush,' said Mr Lauterbach.

'It belongs to our neighbour, Mr Corren,' said Dr Ufferman, 'it broke him. He has left for England. He will not return. He has put it into our hands for a quick sale.'

'But we have several buyers interested,' said Mr Lauterbach hastily.

'And what price did you have in mind?' said Abraham.

'One-hundred-and-fifty pounds,' said Mr Lauterbach.

Abraham nodded, his eyes on the far horizon.

'It was a fair price. It was a good price.'

'Mmm,' he said. And he waited.

'One-hundred-and-forty-five,' said Dr Ufferman.

Abraham considered. He did not have one-hundred-and-forty-five pounds but it was a good price and a good deal; he knew that. It was also seventeen miles to Kiambu where the farm lay and it would take time to view it. He might lose the deal in the process. He deliberated, but instinct triumphed over caution.

'I'll take it, sight unseen, with a deposit of fifty pounds,' said Abraham.

'Done. Full payment within five years,' said Mr Lauterbach.

The road to Kiambu was rough and the ponies struggled with its mud and ruts. The new cart was heavily laden with tools and supplies, and the road lay largely up hill.

Abraham found that he was glad to put Nairobi behind him; and he was surprised to discover that beyond its dull and dismal plains the hills rose glossy-green, the soil was rich and red, and the land was scored by deep ravines through which rivers tumbled. There were meadows and they reminded him of England; there was heath land, and it reminded him of Lithuania. There were numerous farming plots; and most had already been marked out with small posts and green twine. There were simple farmhouses on some of them; and they were round, mud-built and topped with a conical thatch. A rough gate marked the entrance to plot twenty-seven and a sign read 'Njuna Farm'. There was a mud hut with a conical roof; and chickens scratched in the dust at its base. The door, four planks of wood nailed together, was held to with string.

Abraham pushed it open.

It was dark inside the hut, but Abraham flung open the rough wooden shutters and light flooded in. There was a wooden bed set on an earth floor; there were a few oilcans, two logs with a plank balanced on top of them, and a ring of stones with the remains of a fire in their centre. Above them a blackened hole opened in the roof.

It was more than Abraham had expected.

From outside the hut came the sound of whining. A golden dog with a curled tail and a face like a jackal stood there. It was very thin.

'Poor fellow,' said Abraham, 'did Farmer Corren leave you to fend for yourself?'

He reached into his pocket for a hunk of bread. The dog crept forward on its belly and seized it. 'Good dog, Corren,' he said, 'we shall do well together.'

Corren was faithful. Wherever Abraham went, he went. Whatever Abraham threw him he ate. And he slept outside the door at night.

Over the next few weeks, Abraham reviewed his purchase. The land had been cleared but it had not been ploughed and this needed to be done before he could plant. The Germans had spoken of 'plentiful native labour', but Abraham could see none in evidence. He was walking his land when he saw a group of women digging a plot on the horizon. When he reached it, the women dropped their tools and ran away. Abraham could see a cluster of pointed thatched roofs nearby.

The next day, with Corren at his heels, Abraham walked to the village. It had only six or seven mud huts; and chickens and naked babies scrabbled in the dust. When Abraham arrived all the women in the village ran to hide in their huts; they laughed behind their hands. They were clad in short leather aprons and beads. Out of the central hut strode a tall man clad in a monkey-skin cloak. Abraham had picked up a few words in Kikuyu and he used them. He mimed the action of tilling and showed the man a few coins.

'Tomorrow?' he said, 'you send men?'

Smiling the man nodded, and held out his hand for the coins.

When the man arrived several days later, he had a group of women in his wake. They were clad, as before, in short leather skirts and beads, and they laughed at him behind their hands. Abraham indicated his tools, paced out a patch of land, and mimed the action of breaking the soil. Still laughing the women took up the tools and began to work. The man held out his hand for money. The women were good workers, but they made little impression on the land. Despite two week's of their concentrated efforts, Abraham had less than an acre ready for seed.

The rains were coming: he needed a plough.

Abraham thought back to the South African 'Rudsek' plough that Mr Marcus had shown him. He decided that it would not fit on his cart.

The next day he selected four women from his team and, with much giggling, they climbed into the cart. Two hours later, Abraham arrived at Mr Marcus's shop. But there he met with disappointment. Although Mr Marcus offered his very best price and excellent terms, Abraham still could not afford the 'Rudsek' plough.

'Why don't you sell those Basuto ponies', said Mr Marcus.

'No,' said Abraham shaking his head decisively

'You'll get an excellent price for them.'

'No, really, I can't.'

'Bano Niverson[3] is in the market for a pair of horses and a cart.'

'No, Mr Marcus, I cannot sell them.'

'I'll broker the deal. Leave the ponies and the cart with me, and you can take the plough with you. How's that for a deal. Done?'

Abraham was struck by a great sadness. The ponies had been the most faithful creatures he had ever known and he was much attached to them.

'Your harem can carry the plough,' said Mr Marcus, sensing his advantage.

'Will Mr Niverson look after them properly?' said Abraham. He was wavering and he was miserable.

'Bano? Sure. He's proud but he's not stupid.'

Abraham led the ponies into Mr Marcus's yard, he petted them and they whickered.

It hurt him to leave them behind.

The way back to Njuna Farm lay past Wood's Hotel. Abraham walked in the lead and behind him trailed the four scantily clad ladies. Each was bent double and had a section of plough on her back. As they passed the drinkers sitting outside the bar, a cheer went up.

'One not enough for you, ALB?' someone said.

'They'll be good for nothing when you get them back to Kiambu, you know,' said another.

Leaning down from the first floor Tommy Wood grinned.

'Take no notice lad,' he said, 'you'll make more money than this lot put together, and in half the time I shouldn't wonder.'

Abraham forced a smile on to his face.

'But the one on the left is a right little cracker,' said Tommy, 'I'd let the others carry her load if I were you.'

The first year of farming was hard for everyone, and most of the crops that were planted by Abraham's neighbours failed. He learned that only maize, millet, wheat, barley, lentils and fenugreek had withstood the unusually harsh conditions of the colony. He had been lucky: he had planted an acre with his South African seeds and they had done well. But they only supplied him with enough food to live on. He devoted himself to ploughing the land, but it was a heartbreaking business. He had acquired a pair of oxen, but it took time to train them to the halter, and when he had finally done so one died of a bite from a tsetse fly and the other one bolted. Abraham trained a second team; then he taught some village boys how to guide them down the furrow, but the boys ran away. Finally, when the land had been ploughed, Abraham learned that it must lie fallow for six months; and that then it would have to be ploughed all over again.

It was a lonely and dispiriting existence. Of his neighbours, few ever visited and Abraham was left with nothing to do but collect odd nails and straighten them for future use, and whittle bits of wood into spoons. He had written many times to Rosie and he had supplied her with the address of Wood's hotel, but he had received no reply.

He lived on potatoes and beans; and he began to wonder if he had made a serious mistake in coming to Kenya.

CHAPTER 38

THE JEWISH PROBLEM

'I feel very strongly that it is vital for us to constantly keep in mind the fact that
the Jewish problem is but a phase of the world problem.'
–Louis Finkelstein, American Talmudic scholar (1895-1991)

WHILE ABRAHAM STRUGGLED TO TAME his farm, Nairobi struggled with the Jewish Problem. It was not the same Jewish Problem that had plagued the Tsars, and it was not new to Nairobi, but it was vexing nonetheless.

The settlers were well aware of the fact that Joseph Chamberlain had offered five thousand square miles of Kenyan land to the Zionist Association, and they knew that he intended it as a Jewish homeland. But they did not believe that the offer would ever be accepted. When they learned that a deputation was to arrive in Kenya to review the land, they realized their mistake. There was talk of a Jewish invasion, protest meetings were held, and the local news writers grew ever more anti-Semitic in their columns.

Then came the news that Chamberlain was talking of settling twenty thousand Jews in Kenya. And a week later this number rose to a million. Now the settlers became outraged. The Colonialists Association was formed, and its meetings were held in Tommy Wood's bar. Tempers ran high, and people took sides.

On the surface of things, Joseph Chamberlain's plan was sound. He had genuine compassion for the plight of the thousands of Jews fleeing the pogroms of Eastern Europe, and he was committed to giving them a homeland. But he was also aware that the Jews were flooding the British labour market and causing a rise in anti-Semitic feeling there. He wanted to make the British investment in the Uganda Railway pay; but there was only one way he could do this, and that was by encouraging mass settlement in Kenya. Chamberlain did his best; he made extensive speaking tours and he lauded Kenya's virtues to whoever would listen, but still the settlers did not arrive in the numbers he required. So, when the opportunity arose to deposit twenty thousand industrious Jews in the colony, overnight and at little cost, Chamberlain seized it.

But he had reckoned without the settlers.

In the settlers' view, if Chamberlain was to give away five thousand acres of prime agricultural land, to the Jews or to anyone else, then he might just as well give it to them. They believed they deserved it; and they launched their anti-Semitic campaign solely in the interests of getting it.

Tommy Wood agreed to act as chairman for the Anti-Zionist Immigration Committee, which met in his bar[1]. The settlers arrived in droves and clamoured to have their say. The Reverend 'Pa' Bennett said that, in his Christian opinion, the Jews were, 'a people who were alien in their habits, thoughts and actions.' Mr McClellan Wilson, Abraham's neighbour, said that, in his opinion, the Jews 'rendered themselves obnoxious to the people of every country they went to, and would be a hindrance rather than a help to British East Africa.'

Tommy Wood took the floor.

'It is the duty of this gathering,' he said, 'to bring forward every objection to these undesirables being landed in our midst. The British taxpayers want people to settle here who will give a return on the money they have invested in the railway. But how can they expect this if the government locates possibly the lowest class of white men there is in the very heart of the country?'

There were shouts of assent.

'I call on every settler to contribute to an action fund to fight the invasion,' said Tommy.

Lieutenant Richard Meinertzhagen got up.

'This whole scheme is just asking for trouble,' he said in his lazy drawl, 'the Jews' home is in Palestine. They are not good mixers and never have been. They have their own religion, customs and habits and will constitute a most indigestible element in East Africa if they come in any numbers.'

A few days later, Lord Delamere cabled *The Times* in London. The cable was long and reportedly cost him twenty pounds. He spoke of how feeling in the colony ran high against Jewish settlement and he accused the British Government of swamping the bright future of Kenya. While waiting for a response to the cable, Delamere had a series of pamphlets printed. They were widely circulated and described the Zionists as 'parasites not agriculturalists, who would immediately form a poor white class'. In *The African Standard*, Sir Charles Eliot referred to the Zionists as 'a body of alien Israelites.'

None of this was good, but Abraham had heard worse.

He walked into Nairobi for supplies and saw a sign over Tommy Wood's bar. It read 'East Africa may be Jewed but you will not be if you deal with T.A. Wood's Nairobi Stores.'

He was disappointed, but he was not surprised.

When the Zionist deputation returned from their journey to survey the land in question, it was learned that their trip had been plagued by trouble. Their luggage had been lost, their oxen had disappeared, their Masai guides had gone missing; and they had been attacked by Nandi tribesmen. Wood's bar found all of this highly amusing, but when the Congress of Zionists in Basle declared Kenya to be 'a swamp', they found it slightly less so. The Zionists, they learned, had rejected the land on the basis that it was 'pastoral rather than agricultural, and that it had insufficient raw materials to support the settlement of twenty thousand Jews.'

Fleetingly, Tommy Wood wondered whether Abraham had read any of Delamere's pamphlets or heard any of the invective that had been leveled against the Zionists. He told himself that this was most unlikely since Abraham had been away on his farm.

Tommy was wrong; considerable damage had been done to Jewish-Christian relations in general. And Abraham Block, in particular, was thinking of leaving Kenya forever.

CHAPTER 39

LORD DELAMERE MAKES A DIFFERENCE

*Treat a man as he appears to be, and you make him worse. But treat a man as if he were
what he potentially could be, and you make him what he should be.*
–Johann Wolfgang von Goethe, German dramatist (1749-1832)

ABRAHAM'S FIRST YEAR ON THE farm had been hard; but in his second he had more success.

He had planted oats and potatoes, both of which had grown well and earned him a handsome profit. One morning a man called Mr W. J. King[1] rode up to Njuna Farm and asked for samples of Abraham's Early Rose potatoes.

'I want to try selling them in South Africa,' said Mr King, 'they're crying out for potatoes there.'

A few months later Mr King returned triumphant.

'Kenyan spuds are selling for two pounds a ton in the Transvaal,' he said, 'plant more!'

Everyone planted potatoes, but when they arrived in Cape Town they were found to be blackened and sprouting.

'The idiots shipped them next to the boiler room,' said Mr King.

The price of potatoes collapsed and Abraham was forced to let all his crops rot in the ground. Abraham's peas grew well. He picked them and walked seventeen miles into Nairobi to sell them; but nobody wanted to buy. It was the same with his carrots and his lettuce; and his chickens were taken by a mongoose. Alone but for Corren, Abraham lived on sweet potatoes and bananas, and he began to consider making plans to leave Kenya.

Then came the news that decided him.

It was a beautiful morning. The sky was blue, the acacia was in blossom, and the trees were wreathed in garlands of tiny yellow puffballs. Clouds of butterflies danced above the puddles in the track that led to the farm. A man rode up it on horseback. He stopped and handed a letter over the gate to Abraham.

'It's been lying at Wood's for three weeks,' he said, 'but Tommy went to England to collect a wife and he's only just got back. He asked me to deliver it to you.'

Abraham looked at the letter. It was from Rosie[2].

And it was short.

Rosie said that she had received a proposal of marriage from a cousin of Mr Rakusen. She did not love the man, but he seemed likely to inherit the business. Things had not gone well for her whilst Abraham had been away. She had lost her job and she had been forced to return to live with her sister, which was intolerable.

As he reached the end of the letter, Abraham realized that Rosie was to marry someone else. He dragged the door of his hut shut and bound it with string. He whistled for Corren and he set off for Nairobi. He had had enough. He would call on Mr Marcus and ask him how much he would give him for all his farm equipment. Then he would advertise the land for sale at Tommy Wood's.

Mr Marcus's shop was, as usual, crammed with every conceivable kind of agricultural equipment, and Mr Marcus himself was squeezed behind his desk. In front of him, seated on a high stool, with his feet not quite touching the floor, was Lord Delamere. He had taken his sun helmet off and his red curls reached his shoulders. He was wearing a fraying grey cardigan and his breeches were worn so bare that his combinations showed through the holes.

'You're welcome, Abraham,' said Mr Marcus, and he turned to Lord Delamere.

'May I intro—', he began.

'No need,' said Delamere, 'I have heard tell of Mr Block.' He turned to Abraham, 'Call me 'D',' he said, 'everyone else does.'

He looked more closely at Abraham. 'But all is not well with you, young man,' he said, 'I can see it in your face. What is wrong? Tell us.'

For once in his life, Abraham poured out his troubles. He told Lord Delamere and Mr Marcus of his struggle with the farm, his failure to sell his crops, and his loss of the only girl he had ever loved.

'I have had enough,' he said, 'I have decided to return to South Africa.'

'Nonsense,' said Delamere, 'I won't hear of it. You are exactly the kind of chap we need here.'

Abraham glanced at him. It was not what he had expected to hear, but it made no difference. 'My mind is made up,' he said.

'It is not,' said Delamere, 'but mine is. Now, tell me exactly what you need in order to turn yourself around; and I will see what can be done.'

Abraham remained silent; he looked from Mr Marcus to Lord Delamere.

'Come on man, let's have it, I don't have all day!' said Lord Delamere.

Abraham squared his shoulders; he had nothing to lose.

'I need a double farrow plough and at least two more oxen to pull it. I need the materials to build a house, and I need to sink a well,' he said, 'My Lord.'

''D', I've told you,' said Delamere irritable as ever.

He turned to Mr Marcus, 'you'll oblige me by giving our friend 100 Rupees every month,' he said, 'start now and debit my account. Charge the plough to me,' he said.

'I—' began Abraham.

'And give me pen and paper if you will,' said Lord Delamere.

He scrawled a note.

'I am sending this to my farm manager at Njoro,' he said to Abraham, 'I have asked him to send twelve of my best oxen and a couple of good dairy cows to Limuru Station. Can you collect them from there on Friday?'

Abraham blinked.

'Mmm. We'll assume that you can then, shall we?' said Delamere and he grinned at Abraham. It rendered him devilishly amusing; he looked like a naughty schoolboy, or perhaps an evil goblin.

'Thank you, Sir,' said Abraham, 'I will repay you with interest.'

'You'll be the first one who ever has,' said Delamere.

The oxen arrived as Lord Delamere had promised and with them came two dairy cows. Using

Lord Delamere at the Nairobi Races

his new plough, Abraham ploughed his land and planted peas, oats, beans and potatoes. They did well.

A careful man, Abraham turned his old hut into a cow byre, and he built a new house in the traditional manner. It had a kitchen, a parlour, an office and two bedrooms. He drove his oxcart into town to buy blankets, pots and pans. From Mayence Bent he commissioned a pair of curtains.

'Nothing fancy, Mrs Bent', he said, 'just something to keep out the light of the moon.'

'The light of the moon has its uses, Mr Block,' said Mayence. 'Shall I introduce you to some ladies?'

'I can't afford a wife yet, Mrs Bent,' said Abraham.

'You'd best work harder then, Mr Block,' said Mayence, 'because it's my belief you've need of one.' As she ran up the steps to the Stanley Hotel, she threw a smile over her shoulder.

By the end of 1904, Abraham's circumstances had improved considerably. His crops were doing well and his home was comfortable. He had trained some local lads to run his farm, and he had taken paying work on a neighbouring farm. It took him an hour to walk there; so he left Njuna Farm at dawn and returned at nightfall.

It was a hard life, but after three years, Abraham had earned enough money to repay Lord Delamere with interest, and to pay off what he owed on Njuna Farm.

'I knew you'd make a go of it, Block,' said Delamere.

'Thanks to you,' said Abraham.

'Rot,' said Delamere, 'now come and look at these Maasai cattle I've bought.'

CHAPTER 40

NAIROBI GROWS UP

Baa, baa, black sheep,
Have you any wool?
Yes, sir, yes, sir,
Three bags full;
One for the master,
And one for the dame,
And one for the little boy
Who lives down the lane.

–English nursery rhyme

B Y 1904 NAIROBI WAS NO longer the scruffy by-blow of the railway; it was a burgeoning town with a character and purpose entirely its own. The tented encampments had gone, the swamp had been drained, and the appearance of a lion was an event worthy of mention. The streets were lit with paraffin lanterns on poles, a night soil cart toured, and a rudimentary drainage system had been installed.

The Indian Bazaar had burned down for the fifth time in its history and it had been replaced by a stone structure, which had been presented to the town by Mr Jeevanjee. At first the traders refused to use the new market. Then they dug up its lead drainage pipes, flooded its alleys, and stole all its flagstones; and thereafter it flourished.

Mr Jeevanjee had also presented Nairobi with the Jubilee Gardens, which were liberally planted with scented neem trees and pink hibiscus, and laid with velvet green lawns. They featured a life-sized statue of Queen Victoria beneath which was a brass plaque stating that it had been unveiled by His Royal Highness the Duke of Connaught[1].

Securing the services of the Duke to officiate at the opening of his gardens had taxed Mr Jeevanjee's ingenuity since the Duke and his party had been merely passing through Nairobi on their way to join a game-shooting safari. But Mr Jeevanjee had taken up patient station outside their rooms at the Norfolk Hotel and had remained there, beaming and confident, until the Duke capitulated.

The opening ceremony was an event of some note. The gardens were hung with bunting, tea and cucumber sandwiches were served, a brass band played, and a Maasai warrior had to be hastily draped in a tablecloth lest his nakedness shock the Duke's daughter, the Princess Patricia.

Around the perimeter of the Jubilee Gardens, Mr Jevanjee had erected the Jubilee Buildings; it was a collection of commercial premises, which were raised above street level and shaded by verandas. They sheltered a collection of Indian *dukas*[2], which were dim and dark and piled floor to ceiling with bales of assorted stock. Each had a small stool set in its doorway, and its owner sat there typically picking his teeth or chewing betel; and hurling scarlet spital out in to the street.

Government Road, Nairobi in 1912

There were butcheries hung with yellow-fat-veined carcasses, which were sliced on demand. There were hawkers of roasted maize cobs, cardamom tea, caged chickens and rat traps. There were Indian tailors, taxidermists, gunsmiths and safari outfitters.

In the centre of town, close to the Stanley Hotel, there was a clock tower around which the professions clustered. There were accountants, lawyers and medical men, but the most colourful of them all was Dr Ribeiro[3]. He wore a black Stetson hat and rode a tame zebra, which stood outside his premises awaiting emergencies. Dr Ribeiro, a Goan, wore blue glasses, profound whiskers, a black frock coat and a black and white striped waistcoat. He was plump and he had to struggle to mount the zebra, and this caused the silver buttons to pop off his waistcoat, and the street urchins collected them and sold them back to him.

Close to Dr Ribeiro's dispensary were the premises of Messrs Gailey and Roberts[4], a pair of railway engineers who had elected to remain in the colony and act as surveyors and land agents. Beyond Gailey and Roberts was the photographic emporium of Mr Binks, who also sold tin windmills and was known to be building an aeroplane out of canvas and wood.

Ali Khan, the Pathan horse dealer, still did a brisk trade in ferrying people around the town on his mule cart, but several new forms of transportation had arrived to join him. The first was the *gharrie*, a two man horse-drawn carriage with a large black leather hood, which creaked and cracked and could be folded back on demand. The second was the rickshaw, which was sometimes fitted with a gaudy parasol and always drawn by a man clad in a white safari jacket, shorts and a sun helmet. The third was a bicycle, which was unloaded from the train and carried down the platform on a porter's head having been shipped from England by a man named MacDonald[5].

Mr MacDonald was the first man to plant tea in Kenya, so he enjoyed something of a reputation as an innovator; and he and his bicycle were closely observed. At first he could only ride it up and down Victoria Street, because all the other streets were too rutted. Then he employed two boys; one to push and the other to pull him through the ruts. This was successful, so Mr MacDonald employed a team of boys to push and pull him through the ravines that lay between Nairobi and his upcountry farm. When the rains arrived the ravines flooded, so Mr MacDonald dismantled his bicycle and swam backwards and forwards across the floods with its various parts strapped to his back. When all were assembled on the far side, he remounted and continued his journey, drying his clothes in the wind as he went.

Nairobi was impressed by Mr MacDonald's bicycle and several more machines were ordered. In Wood's bar, ever the barometer of Nairobi's passions, bicycling tales became all the rage. The most popular concerned Randall Swift and his partner Ernest Rutherfoord[6], who had established Kenya's first sisal plantation, which lay forty-seven miles out of Nairobi. The gentlemen purchased a bicycle but since there were two of them they were forced to invent an ingenious relay system for its use. Rutherfoord would rise at dawn and walk until he was overtaken by Swift on the bicycle. Swift would relinquish the bicycle to Rutherfoord, who would ride it for ten miles before leaving it by the wayside for Swift, and so they would continue until they reached Nairobi.

This tale delighted Wood's bar; and then they learned that Rutherfoord's African nickname was 'the one who remains young' because he maintained his startling physique by striding the margins of the sisal plantation with three bags full of maize; one on his back and one under each arm. It was irresistible: Rutherfoord became known as Baa Baa.

CHAPTER 41

THE NORFOLK HOTEL

The key is to keep company only with people who uplift you, whose presence calls forth your best.
–Epictetus, Greek philosopher (55-135 BC)

O N Christmas Day, 1904, The Norfolk Hotel opened in Nairobi and instantly all other hotels were flung into the shade. It was built on one of Lord Delamere's old hunting sites, close to the river, and was but a short walk from Ainsworth's Bridge.

'All other Nairobi hotels are doss houses where rooms can be rented by the hour,' said Mr R. Aylmer Winearls, who financed its building. 'This hotel is what we like to call a Fashionable Rendezvous of the Highlands.'

'Oh for heaven's sakes,' said Tommy Wood, 'have you seen the advertisement the bloody man has put in the paper?'

'No,' said Abraham.

'Listen to this,' said Tommy and he read aloud, '"The hotel has good stabling, carriages and *gharries* to meet every train, hot and cold baths, a billiard room, and a French chef late of the Waldorf Astoria Hotel, New York."'

'Mmm,' said Abraham.

'French chef my foot,' said Tommy

But for all his scoffing, even Tommy Wood was impressed by the new hotel.

It was white-painted with black Tudor crossbeams and it was encircled by a white picket fence. It had a turret, a red tiled roof, and a broad verandah, and it was set in extensive gardens. It offered thirty-four bedrooms, a number of bathrooms, two cottages for married couples, a dining room to seat one hundred guests, and electric light throughout.

'Excellent stabling too,' said Major Charles Ringer[1], racehorse owner and co-owner of the new hotel, 'main reason we built the place. Only yesterday a lion mauled one of my horses out at the farm, and you just can't be having that sort of thing can you?'

Portly and with only a few strands of ginger hair to comb across his brown-freckled scalp, Major Ringer was almost a caricature of a colonial. He wore a sharply starched safari suit with the breeches tucked into the top of his high-laced boots. He wore a large white sun helmet, sometimes with the strap beneath his chin, and he liked to carry a riding crop. He had, as he liked to recount, spent his soldiering years on the West African coast.

'Bloody place,' he would say, 'atrocities left right and centre. My finest hour was being in at the kill of the fall of Benin City. Got my juju there.'

'Juju?' said Tommy Wood licking his lips.

'Ivory fetish, carved in the shape of a head, took it from one the most feared witch doctors in Benin,' said Major Ringer, 'it has a huge amount of power, brings me luck, named my farm out on Ol Donyo Sabuk after it'.

'Well it's certainly brought you luck with the horses,' said Tommy.

This was true, Major Ringer's racing stables were superb, and his mare 'The Skate', imported from Australia, was one of the finest the colony had ever seen.

It was his love of the races that had prompted the Major to suggest to his wealthy partner, 'Pop' Winearls, that Nairobi required a first class hotel.

'Need to raise the tone of the place,' he had said.

And in this the gentlemen had certainly succeeded.

The opening ceremony of the Norfolk was magnificent. The eucalyptus trees around the hotel were draped in red-white-and-blue bunting, a brass band marched up and down in front of the white picket fence, cocktails and caviar were served on the terrace, and a tame lion cub on a silver chain was walked up and down by a waiter.

Standing on a podium, in a dress suit several sizes too small for him, Major Ringer made an impressive speech. It went well until his attention was caught by his gun bearer, who had pushed his way through the crowd and was waving the major's elephant gun in his face. The Major, irritated, bent to hear what the man had to say; he stared angrily at him for a few seconds, grabbed the gun and strode off.

'Damned elephant in the stables,' he was heard to say.

When he returned, the Major informed the crowd that he had shot the elephant and planned to have its foot made into an umbrella stand.

Some called Major Ringer a snob because he courted the company of the affluent. He made much of his acquaintance with his neighbour, William Northrup McMillan, an American millionaire who had made a fortune out of Rumanian oilfields and Malayan rubber. Northrup had arrived in Kenya via a camel trek down the Nile and, finding it to his liking, he had built a faithful replica of an English mansion at the base of Ol Donyo Sabuk Mountain.

'Of course he's called the place Juja,' said Major Ringer.

'Go on,' said Tommy, 'tell us why?'

'Juju is the big fetish and Juja is the small fetish,' said the Major.

'Got it the wrong way round hasn't he?' said Tommy, 'I hear he is so fat he has had to have the sides removed from all his motorcars just so that he can get into them, and that he's just taken delivery of a custom-built Buick with detachable doors.'

'Ah, American cars! Wonderful,' said the Major, 'but then you see McMillan needs them – so many American guests, all staying at the Norfolk of course.'

'Of course,' said Tommy Wood.

But Tommy lost business to the Major. Over the years all the great names of hunting began their safaris from the Norfolk Hotel. It hosted Frederick Selous, Sir Frederick Jackson, 'Karamoja' Bell, Major Hugh Chauncy Stigand, Captain Jim Sutherland, Paul Rainy, Phil Percival, and Denys Finch-Hatton; and it also hosted their clients, such as Theodore Roosevelt and his son Kermit, Winston Churchill and a glittering selection of counts, barons and European princes.

The Norfolk could always be relied upon to supply gossip. There was the tale of the colonial administrator and his pet leopard, 'Starpit'[2]. It was young and playful and particularly fond of ripping up cushions, and he spent much of his time smacking its nose and drawling, 'Oh for goodness sake, stop it!'

There was the fact that the bar attracted so many noblemen that it became known as The House of Lords. There were the scandalous liaisons that were reported to have taken place on the billiard table, and there was the fact that the French chef, Louis Le Blanc, became so incensed by one of his Somali underlings that he chased him around and around the kitchen with a deboning knife and finally speared his cheek to a chopping block.

Finally, there was the much-loved tale of the elderly widow of an administrator in the Indian Civil Service who arrived to stay at the Norfolk on a night when it hosted a particularly riotous gathering of young men. Major Ringer, fearful for her safety, had her bedroom door nailed shut with six-inch nails.

CHAPTER 42

SAMUEL AND LILY ARRIVE

Happiness depends upon ourselves.
–Aristotle, Greek philosopher (384-322 BC)

ABRAHAM WAS DRIVING HIS OXCART past the Norfolk Hotel on his way back to Njuna Farm when he was hailed from the terrace.

'Letter for you ALB,' said Major Ringer, 'South African postmark.'

Abraham called a boy to hold the heads of his oxen. Beyond the bright daylight of the terrace, the reception room was gloomy. It had thick velvet curtains and contained two button-back wing chairs and a writing desk. There was a long polished counter with a round brass button bell-push at its centre; and behind the counter stood a tall Somali in a long white gown buttoned high to the neck. His face was impassive and he wore a red fez. He was engaged in posting letters into the row of pigeonholes that ran behind the counter.

'You have a letter for me?' said Abraham.

The Somali surveyed him without any change of expression. He walked majestically to a tray of letters. His long fingers rifled through them, extracted one, and handed it to Abraham.

The postmark on the letter showed it to have been posted four weeks ago in Johannesburg. Abraham ripped it open and read it where he stood. Then he sat down suddenly in one of the wing chairs.

The Somali raised one elegant eyebrow.

The letter was from Samuel and it was typically brief. Lily had left Leeds, he said, and travelled to South Africa to join him. She had read Abraham's letters describing life in Kenya and had persuaded Samuel to accompany her there. They would be arriving in Mombasa in three week's time. Abraham glanced again at the postmark. His father and his sister would be arriving in Mombasa on the steamer, The *Carisbrook Castle*, in one week's time.

Abraham took the train to Mombasa. The descent was markedly faster than the ascent had been, and the train fairly rattled across the Athi Plains before plunging down through the baobab trees, the perfumed acacia and the red-hot wastes of the Taru Desert. It stopped only briefly in Voi, where Mr Nazareth's menu remained unchanged, and it thundered on down through the palm trees to the coast. There, the midnight blue creeks opened up on either side of the Salisbury Bridge, and the train puffed its way importantly across it. As it slowed into the station, laughing children held up wedges of pineapple, paper-screws of cashew nuts and green coconuts with their tops cut off.

Abraham found Mombasa to be utterly unchanged. The streets were as tight and dark, as muddled and jumbled as ever; and the black-veiled women flitted along them with their dark eyes darting. The traders hunched and spat, the cats prowled, the dogs fought, and the call of the muezzin battled with the cawing of the black-and-white crows. In the dhow harbour, washing fluttered from the decks of the dhows, and boys leapt with splayed legs and held noses into the oily black water below. Down on the dockside, the white buildings shimmered like mirages in the glare, and the blue-green creeks glittered beneath the brooding gaze of Fort Jesus.

The *Carisbrook Castle* was expected to dock later that day.

When the ship arrived, Abraham watched as the flotilla of boats paddled out to meet it. He saw the tiny figures clambering down its sides and dropping into the little white boats; and he saw the tall black figures as they strode out to meet them in the shallows. It did not surprise Abraham that his father elected to wade ashore, but he smiled at the sight of his sister, Lily, in the arms of a tall African, her white petticoats fluttering over his great forearms, and her boots dangling just inches above the waves. She was tall, regal of features and her black hair stood out around her head in a riot of ringlets; she was a woman and not the schoolgirl that Abraham had left behind in Russia.

When Lily saw her brother, she demanded to be set down immediately, though she and her porter had not yet reached the beach. Her skirts billowed briefly before being dragged down by the weight of the water. She strode towards Abraham, the waves frothing around her boots. She held out her strong hands and smiled.

'My beloved brother,' she said, 'I have come to take care of you.'

The train's return to Nairobi was hot and slow, and it allowed many hours for Abraham, Samuel and Lily to discuss all that had taken place during their various times of separation. The conversation turned to Ettel and Freda, who still remained in Russia; and Lily was well informed.

'The pogroms continue,' she said, 'but every wave is worse than the last. Even within Russia they are condemned by such respected figures as Tolstoy and Maxim Gorkey; and outside Russia they have been censured by Theodore Roosevelt, the President of the United States; and he has pressured the Tsar for reform.'

'But it does no good,' said Samuel

'No, the Tsar does not listen,' said Lily, 'but his power is waning. He suffered a resounding defeat in the Russo-Japanese War. He has lost face in Europe and he has lost face with the Russian people.'

'Which encourages the government to fan the flames of the pogroms,' said Samuel, 'last month it was Odessa, this month it is Kiev, next month it could be Salcininkai, where Ettel and Freda are.'

'And the revolution draws closer,' said Lily.

'Does our mother not realize the danger she is in?' said Abraham.

'She does, but she fears change,' said Lily, 'she lives in the past, she sits stiff-backed in her old black silk dress, and she talks of the wealth and connections of her family.

'They are no good to her now,' said Samuel, 'she lives on the money I send her, and it is not much.'

'And our sister, Freda, how is she?' said Abraham

'Sixteen, clever, but dominated by our mother,' said Lily

Samuel sighed. 'The time has come,' he said, 'for us to force Ettel and Freda to leave Russia.' He looked at Abraham, 'and that, my son, is why Lily and I have come to Kenya,' he said.

'What has Kenya to do with it?' said Abraham.

'I know my wife,' said Samuel, 'she is stubborn and she is proud, but once she realizes that

The train arrives at Nairobi Railway Station 1916

Nairobi Railway Station 1911

her family has gathered together without her she will come. I have arranged for an agent to escort them to Danzig.'

'And then?'

'Then your sister, Annie, and the Rabbi Sinson will meet them in Hull.'

'They will go to Leeds?' said Abraham. He could not envisage his mother in Leyland.

'Briefly; then they will travel on to Mombasa,'

Abraham gazed out of the window of the train at the hornbills swooping through the shimmering red heat. It seemed that his world, insular for so long, was to become peopled once again by his family. 'Then we have much to do,' he said.

Abraham told Lily and Samuel about Njuna Farm, the land, the livestock, the empty house and the new life that lay ahead of them. And as he spoke he reached a decision.

'I am going to leave the farm in your hands,' he said.

Samuel looked up at him in surprise.

'I am going to begin cattle trading,' said Abraham, 'I have received word that a large consignment of cattle has been confiscated from the Nandi tribesmen. It is their punishment for having attempted to rebel against the British. The cattle are to be sold by auction in the north of Kenya. And those that take the trouble to go there will make money.'

By the time the train had reached Nairobi, the Block Family had laid their plans.

The time of Abraham's solitude was past, and with it the time of his toil upon the land.

Abraham Block had made up his mind to make some money.

CHAPTER 43

CATTLE TRADING

Whatever you can do or dream, begin it.
–Johann Wolfgang von Goethe, German dramatist, (1749-1832)

EVERYTHING CHANGED WHEN LILY AND Samuel arrived at Njuna Farm. Lily threw down her bags and began looking through cupboards and writing lists immediately. 'There is much to be done before Mother and Freda arrive,' she said, 'I need pans, dairy equipment, bedding…'

She opened the door of the range, 'and this won't draw,' she said. She pulled a calico apron out of her valise.

'And get that dog out of my kitchen,' she said.

Abraham whistled Corren to his heels and went to join his father.

Samuel was equally thorough; he examined the oxen, he kicked the cartwheels, he ran his finger along the blades of the plough, and he squinted at the Kikuyu maidens; they were pulling cabbages clad in their habitual garb of short leather aprons and strings of beads.

'Rain expected?' said Samuel.

'Next month,' said Abraham.

'Better get on,' said Samuel, and he strode off in the direction of the barns.

'When's that cattle sale?' he called over his shoulder.

Abraham did not bother to reply.

He was released from the toils of Njuna Farm.

Abraham's horse was squat, piebald, laden with saddlebags, and Corren ran at its heels. The cattle sale was to be held in the lands of the Maasai, and these lay a day's ride to the north. As they drew closer a tower of dust could be seen rising above the bush.

It was a harsh landscape backed by purple-shadowed hills and it was flecked with stunted acacia laden with great brown bulbous seed casings. The wind whistled through them and they wailed like souls lost in limbo. There was no clearly defined road across the plains, but there were hundreds of thin tracks; and they met and parted, split and merged like so many giant braids. As the dust cloud drew closer, so a dull lowing could be heard, and Abraham was joined in his journey by striding groups of Maasai. They walked swiftly and easily, springing off their heels; and they carried ropes around their shoulders. Swathed in scarlet cloaks, they had short staffs and knives thrust into their leather belts. Some had large holes in their earlobes; others wore long swinging earrings. All were strung around with coloured beads. The younger ones favoured intricate hairstyles; they were plaited and wound around their heads, stuck with feathers and daubed in red river mud. The older men, stooped and spare, had skull-like faces, toothless mouths and close shaven scalps.

Groups of maidens followed the men; their red, yellow and blue capes fluttering in the breeze. The gaze of all was locked on the dust cloud. And the smell of the cattle coiled towards them and drew them forward.

When he arrived in the dust bowl where the cattle sale was to be held Abraham was overwhelmed. The air was thick with khaki dust, the flies swarmed and the cattle blundered and cavorted – a sea of russet, white, grey, brown and black hides. They came in all sizes. Some had fluted velvet dewlaps; some had tall humps, some had wide horns. Each one was subtly different and the gaze of the Maasai devoured them all.

There was little conversation.

Sensing the adoration of their audience the steers kicked their heels and whisked their tails. A few settlers stood around regarding the herds. Abraham did not know any of them.

'When does the sale begin?' he said.

'When the Maasai say it will begin,' said a wizened fellow chewing on a stick.

'And how is the bidding done?' he asked.

'Depends on the Maasai,' he was told and the ranks of the settlers closed against him.

It was not going to be easy.

A large white sun helmet appeared on a short figure surrounded by tall red-cloaked warriors. Delamere was clad in his usual battered cardigan, drooping breeches and high-laced boots. He held a flywhisk made from the tail of a cow in one hand, and he whirled it around his head. In his other hand he held a long stick, and he used it to point at those cows that interested him. His warriors surveyed his choices gravely and either shook their heads or nodded. Sometimes they would walk over to a particular cow, bend close to it and loop an arm around its neck; and the communication might span minutes. When judgment was pronounced it was final and Delamere never argued. The chosen cattle were directed into the care of his warriors, the others were shooed on their way.

Abraham hitched the piebald horse to an acacia bush and forced his way through the snorting, bucking skittering cattle until he drew close to Delamere and his phalanx of warriors. He waited to be noticed. Sensing a presence, Delamere spun around.

'Block,' he said, 'always in the right place at the right time ain't you?'

'Maybe,' said Abraham, 'but I have no chance against these men. Cow flesh is a religion to them, I see.'

Delamere grinned.

'You're a canny fellow Block,' he said, 'you see more than other men. When it comes to judging cattle, the Maasai have almost divine powers. They believe all cows to be theirs by right and they love them like children. Are you buying?'

'I came to buy and I have money. I had hoped to be a cattle trader, but—'

'And so you shall be,' said Delamere, 'but only if these fellows will it.'

He spoke to his warriors. They surveyed Abraham. They whispered in Delamere's ear.

'You have the luck of the devil, Block,' said Delamere, 'give them your money and you'll get a bargain like no other. Don't watch, don't argue, don't interfere. And when it is finished give them the payment they ask of you.

Maasai cattle herder

Abraham handed over all the money he had carried with him. Delamere gave it to the warriors.

'Now go,' he said, 'I will call you when the trading is done.'

Abraham sat in the shade with Corren and his piebald horse. Much later he noticed Delamere looking his way and patting the top of his head. It seemed he was beckoning to him.

'You've done well,' said Delamere when Abraham reached him. He indicated a herd of multicoloured cows. They waited patiently in the care of the Maasai.

'They have chosen well for you. But I'm afraid you may find the price high,' he said.

Abraham waited.

'They've a fancy for your gold watch[1],' said Delamere.

It was Samuel's watch, the one that he had been given by his own father, Lazarus.

Abraham unhooked it from his waistcoat and held it out to the half-circle of red-cloaked men. Silently, one stepped forward and took the watch. Holding it to his ear, he smiled broadly.

'Excellent bargain,' said 'D', 'the value of their patronage is beyond price.'

'Thank you,' said Abraham, 'so is the value of yours.'

Abraham tripled his capital in weeks. Taken under the wing of Delamere, whose love of cattle equalled that of the Maasai, he could not fail. He was alerted in advance to every sale, and guided in his purchases by Delamere's men. And Delamere himself treated him with easy and open-handed kindness. Abraham counted himself fortunate indeed.

He grew to love driving the docile trains of swaying cattle back to the farm. He knew instinctively which cow was the natural leader and should wear the brass bell around its neck. He had learned from the masters and he knew what to look for in a cow.

But he also knew the value of diversification.

'We need to get in to the butchery business,' he said to Samuel.

'And hides,' said Samuel.

When he was next in Nairobi, Abraham visited Tommy Wood.

'I'd like to buy your butchery,' he said.

'How did you know I wanted to sell?' said Tommy

'It was time,' replied Abraham.

The Victoria Butchery was Abraham's first Nairobi business and it did well. But once having set it up he distanced himself from it. He put Lily in charge of the books and Samuel in charge of the stock. Then, whenever he found himself in Nairobi, Abraham visited his shop. He always arrived unannounced.

Arriving outside, he would survey the shop, hands clasped behind his back. He would walk around it. Inside he would tap and poke at things, pick them up, put them down. If there were customers he would smile and raise his hat. Sometimes he would sit on the stool by the door and watch. He did not ask questions. He didn't need to. He knew instinctively if anything was wrong.

Abraham's next business venture concerned his purchase of a share in a pig farm in the Ngong Hills. The farm belonged to a missionary by the name of Mr Kreiger.

'How did you know that I wanted to sell a share in the business?' said Mr Kreiger.

'I assumed you had more important work to do,' said Abraham.

Mr Kreiger laughed, 'I do indeed,' he said, 'and by the way, Max Nightingale's looking for investment in his turkey farm. It's just down the road, why not take a walk over there?'

'Thank you, Mr Kreiger,' said Abraham, 'I will indeed.'

The New Stanley Hotel

CHAPTER 44

BUYING AND SELLING

Try not to become a man of success, but rather try to become a man of value.

–Albert Einstein, physicist (1879-1955)

IT WAS, PERHAPS, AN ODD alliance but Mayence Bent and Abraham Block had become friends. And they remained so.

With the death of Mr Bent, Mayence had married again. Fred Tate[1] was young, handsome and ambitious. He was wily too, and he knew how to handle Mayence. Fred persuaded her to renovate the Stanley, to expand the menu, to soften the furnishings and to invest in a billiard table. He also dissuaded her from regarding the Norfolk Hotel as a rival. The Stanley, Fred said, had its own niche.

Fred's instincts were sound. The titles, the wealth and the would-be glamorous headed to the Norfolk. The rakish, the raffish and the harder of head chose the Stanley. It became the haunt of the railway men, the farmers, the hunters and the military men. The Norfolk forged a reputation for wild parties and exotic behavior. The Stanley established itself as a place where business could be done.

Then Tommy Wood's hotel, the Victoria, burned down. And, since Tommy swore he would not rebuild it, his entire clientele took up residence in the Stanley's long bar. Abraham went with them. He felt uncomfortable at the Norfolk; its grandeur did not suit him. And there was something in Major Ringer's attitude towards him that he did not quite like.

When Abraham was next in Nairobi, he called at the Stanley for lunch. It was Friday and goat stew was on the menu.

'Still not married, Mr Block?' said Mayence, who couldn't bear the waste of a good man.

'Not yet, Mrs Tate,' said Abraham, 'I still can't afford it.'

'That's not what I hear,' said Mayence, 'you're quite the catch now. Money, land, farmhouse, livestock; and with friends in high places,' she said: she like the rest of the settler community found the friendship of Block and Delamere fascinating.

'The love of cows, Mrs Tate,' said Abraham, 'can bring men together.'

'Cows!' said Mayence, 'they're all anyone talks about these days, I'm sick to the back teeth of them. That lot over there,' she jutted her chin at a smoke-wreathed group, 'are off to Uganda to buy cows. What's wrong with the ones we've got here? That's what I'd like to know?'

Abraham looked towards the group she indicated. He recognized some faces from Wood's bar. There was a giant of a man called Ben Garland[2], known to his friends as 'Fatty', and his thin partner, Fred Raper, who was a saddler. The rest of the men, in slouch hats and khaki shirts, he did not know.

Abraham shook hands with Garland and nodded to Raper.

'We're talking about Ugandan cattle, ALB' said Garland, 'according to these gents they knock

The New Stanley under construction in 1913

the spots off the ones we've got here.'

'Is that so,' said Abraham, nodding to the group.

"D"s been sniffing around them. Maasai love 'em, and they can be had cheaply I'm told' said Garland.

'Just got to go up there and get them,' said Raper, bobbing behind Garland.

Abraham sipped his whisky and said nothing. He knew that the settler community loved nothing better than the idea that something could be had for nothing; but he did not subscribe to it.

'Three hundred of the little darlings going begging,' said Garland.

'There for the taking,' said Raper.

Fatty Garland eyed Abraham. 'God works in mysterious ways, Block,' he said at length.

'He does?' said Abraham.

'Yes,' said Garland, waving his cigar, 'here's us ready and willing to buy these cattle, but without the time and inclination to fetch 'em and there's you—'

'At a loose end?' Raper had a face like a terrier.

'I am never at a loose end,' said Abraham to Raper. He turned to Garland, 'but I am always open to suggestions,' he said.

It took time, but a deal was hammered out.

Garland and Raper would finance the purchase of two hundred prime Ankole cattle. They would cover the cost of Abraham's travel to Uganda and his return to the market town of Nakuru in Kenya. In Nakuru, Abraham would sell the cattle and the profits would be split three ways. Abraham liked the deal. There was only one problem: he had received word from Samuel that Ettel and Freda were due to arrive in Mombasa in three month's time.

'How long will it take?' he said.

'Three months I reckon,' said Garland, 'the Nakuru cattle sale is the week before Christmas, so you've got to be back by then.'

Abraham considered. Lily and Samuel could meet Ettel and Freda in Mombasa, and he had waited nearly ten years to see them; so a few more weeks would not make any difference.

'I'll do it,' said Abraham.

Abraham took the train to Kisumu. He had not travelled much in Kenya and he was impressed by what he saw. North of Nairobi the earth was rent by the gigantic gash of The Great Rift Valley. On one side rose the smoky blue hills of the Mau Escarpment, on the other the humps of the Aberdare Range. In the cleft of the Rift sparkled a chain of lakes, some fringed with thousands of pink flamingos. Beyond the lakes the land rose to verdant plains that were dotted with flat-topped acacia, then it plunged into deep valleys before broiling over miles and miles of acacia bush. In western Kenya, the land rolled down in gracious folds to the town of Kisumu and there it embraced the sparkling waters of Lake Victoria, one of the largest inland lakes in the world.

Abraham crossed the lake on one of the fat-bellied tramp steamers that plied the shores between Kenya and Uganda. Landing in Uganda, he was surprised to find himself in an utterly different world. It was hot and humid, low-lying, sultry and gloriously green. Thousands of islands floated in the sparkling blue waters of the lake and its shores were edged by low hills thickly embroidered with banana trees. They grew so densely that their long vivid green leaves formed a kind of tropical forest, a lush jungle broken only by the small round villages of the Buganda people.

The humidity in Port Bell was vicious. Within minutes of stepping off the rusty decks of the steamer, where a soft breeze had cooled the passengers, Abraham was drenched in perspiration. Dumping his bags beneath a banana tree, he settled down to wait.

Fatty Garland had told him that a man would meet him and lead him to the cattle sale.

But it was not a man who arrived: it was a woman.

She wore a long purple dress with peaked puffed sleeves and a broad yellow sash with golden fringes. The sash was tied around her waist and fell to her bare ankles, which were clasped by heavy hinged bangles. On the woman's head was a large turban tied in yellow, violet and mauve damask; and in her ears swung long golden earrings. Abraham supposed her to be somewhere in middle age. She was startlingly handsome; and at her back stood two young men leaning on their spears.

The woman fell to her knees in front of Abraham and offered him a note. Shocked by this display of obeisance, Abraham bent to help her rise. He put a hand under her elbow. The two young men stepped forward spears horizontal. Abraham took the note and read it. Garland's agent had malaria. He could not come.

'The Lady Abambara³, a princess of the Nkole tribe, will take you to the cattle sale,' read the note, 'without her introduction, you will not be permitted to buy, since all the cattle are the property of the king. In return for her help you will give her a cow'.

The cost of a cow had not been part of the original deal, but Abraham had no choice in the matter. He nodded to the woman and indicated that she should lead the way. She rose gracefully to her feet, motioned imperiously for her warriors to fall in behind her, and set off into the green vaults of the bananas.

The road wound as sinuous as a snake and its aspect never varied. To either side the banana trees were so dense that they presented a wall of almost unbroken iridescent green that arched and rustled, whispered and sighed. Some of the trees thrust forth pointed buds. Voluptuous and claret-red, they glistened and wept syrupy tears at the end of craning stalks. Many of the trees were laden down with huge bunches of tiny green bananas. Pairs of small green birds with yellow heads and red eyes swung upside down in these and whistled. They looked like miniature parrots.

From time to time as the land rose, the trees would part to reveal the sparkle of the lake and its drifting shoals of islands. If there were people amid the trees, or on the shores, they did not reveal themselves, and the lady never spoke and never paused in her steady gait.

Abraham concentrated on hefting his bags, mopping his brow, and preparing himself for what lay ahead.

It was a revelation.

Abraham thought he had seen cattle of every shape, size and hue in Kenya. But he had seen nothing. The glory of the Ankole transcended them all. Though in size and colour, they were similar to the Zebu cattle of the Maasai, the Ankole bore enormous horns. Their span was immense and they were so heavy that the cows walked with heads lowered. The horns, more like tusks, swayed gracefully from side to side. Sometimes it seemed as if their weight were too great for the animals to bear.

For a moment, Abraham doubted his ability to judge. The creatures were magnificent, and he was awed. Then his Maasai learning came to his aid: the Ankole might be awesome but they were still cows. The selection took long hours. The haggling was intense. But a bargain was a bargain in any language and ALB knew how to drive one.

Then came the task of driving the herd back through the banana groves to the shores of the lake at Port Bell.

When they reached the dockside, Abraham turned to the lady and invited her to select one of the cows. It did not surprise him that she selected easily the most regal of the bulls.

She slipped a woven halter around its lavishly dewlapped neck, dipped in curtsy to Abraham, waved her warriors behind her, and set off into the banana trees.

They closed behind her as if she had never been.

Ankole cow

CHAPTER 45

BRINGING HOME THE HERD

There is a time for everything and a season for every activity under heaven.

–Ecclesiastes 3:1

I T HAD ALL SEEMED TOO simple.

Abraham stood on the rocky headland that stretched out into Lake Victoria just beyond the town of Kisumu. To his left a raft of cormorants dried their oily wings in the sun, to his right two hundred Ankole cattle grazed placidly on the thin grass that grew just beyond the reed beds. In the shallow waters of the lake, two ebony-black young men stretched a net between them and began to wade into the water.

Shouldering his panniers, Abraham came to a decision.

'Can you herd cows?' he said.

The youths stared at him, their dark, handsome faces blank. Reaching into his pocket, Abraham showed them some coins. Then he pointed to the cows and mimicked walking with his fingers. The faces remained blank. Opening his arms wide, Abraham made as if to sweep the herd of cows before him. Obediently, the herd moved forward.

This was all that was required.

Smitten by the beauty of the alien cows, the young men discarded their nets, cut themselves flexible sticks, and moved into position at the rear of the herd. Abraham noted that they had the easy grace of lifelong herders.

He surveyed the herd. He was looking for its natural leader. From its centre walked a white cow. The colour of rain clouds with the sun shining through them, her pumice-grey dewlap fell to her knees like a fall of the finest lace. She walked up to Abraham and nudged him. Then she turned and walked away, her rump swaying regally from side to side. In her wake the other cows fell in to order, each according to a hierarchy that only they understood.

As the days progressed, the colours of the herd shifted and wove themselves into intricate patterns. They seemed vague but they were magically precise. If a cow wandered from its position, the pattern changed, and so the boys knew that a member of the herd had strayed.

Driving the cows was not difficult; the problem lay in finding ample water for them. Abraham took to walking ahead and scanning the landscape for rivers or ponds. When he found a suitable spot he would prepare for their arrival. Then a fire would be lit and the boys would create a rough *boma* of brushwood. Herded inside its thorny walls, the cattle would settle for the night and Abraham and the boys would take it in turns to watch over them.

It occurred to Abraham that it would be all too easy for the boys to steal some of the cattle whilst he slept. Then he realized that the herd would only move as one.

It took forty weary days for Abraham, his herd, and his boys to walk down through the red-dusty heat of the Tugen Hills, alongside the sparkling lakes of the Rift, and through the green pastures that swept down to the shores of Lake Nakuru.

As the lake came into view, its fringes laced with the coral pink of thousands of flamingoes, Abraham realized he had lost all track of time. He wondered if the cattle sale had already taken place. Then, shrugging, he shouldered his stick, hung his elbows across the ends of it and continued walking.

Nakuru was little more than an upcountry trading post with a railway halt. It was a farmer's town, set in its ways. And it was unprepared for the arrival of two hundred Ankole cattle, wreathed in dust, and with a gentle momentum that threatened to sweep them through the town without halt. People ran to see them, stopped in their tracks and stared. Children whooped, old men pointed their sticks. Impervious to it all, the cavalcade of cattle swung serenely onwards until they reached the lake, and then they drank.

Abraham left the herd and walked back to town. He enquired when the cattle sale would take place. His timing had been good, it was to be held in two days time and buyers were already gathering.

News of the arrival of the Ankole herd spread fast. All manner of sharp-eyed buyers arrived on the shores of the lake. They circled the cattle like hyena, sniffing, poking, eyeing. Then they began to bark their offers.

'I shall sell on the day prescribed and not before,' said Abraham. But the more he refused the traders' offers, the more the value of the cattle rose.

On the day of the sale, the Ankole swayed into the market square in the wake of the white cow. She halted at Abraham's command.

A hush fell.

The buyers pushed forward and grasped the rails around the auction ring.

The white cow surveyed the crowds serenely and whisked her tail.

The first Ankole was led forward to face the buyers.

'What am I bid?' said the auctioneer.

And all hell broke loose.

Abraham could not watch. He retired to the Nakuru Hotel[1] and sat on the veranda where he drank cup after cup of hot, sweet tea. As evening fell the buyers began to arrive on the veranda. Drinks were ordered. Great plumes of dust marked the passage of their purchases out of town.

Garland and Raper arrived. They were smiling broadly.

'Block! You are a magician,' Garland said, 'do you have any idea how much money we've made out of this little venture?'

'No,' said Abraham, 'but I'd like my share of it. I need to get back to Nairobi. My mother arrives in less than week.'

'From Mombasa?' said Garland.

'From Lithuania.'

'Where's that?'

'You wouldn't want to know.'

'Better get cracking then, old chap,' said Garland and they sat down to apportion the profits of the sale. When it was all over, Abraham bade Garland and Raper farewell.

'Oh, there's just one more thing,' said Garland.

'Big thing,' said Raper.

'There's a "thank you" waiting for you in the back yard. Your herders chose it for you.'

'Knew what they were doing,' said Raper

Shouldering his bags, Abraham walked through the hotel and out into the yard. There was a long hitching rail. Tethered to it was the white cow.

Abraham was ready to start walking at dawn the next day, but the boys still waited by the white cow; he had paid them off handsomely but they seemed loath to leave him.

'You belong on the lake,' he told them, 'we all have our place in this world, and that is yours.' He wondered, as he said this, where his own place in the world might be. And whether it would always be in this land of endless sky. Then he clicked the white cow forward, placed his stick across his shoulders, hung his elbows over either end, and set off in her wake.

CHAPTER 46

CHRISTMAS WITH THE DELAMERES

No act of kindness, no matter how small, is ever wasted.

–Aesop, *The Lion and the Mouse*, Greek slave and fable author (620-560 BC)

ABRAHAM HAD BEEN ON THE road for so long that it seemed as though he had always been there. Every day was the same. Every night he would light a small fire, cook whatever food he had foraged along the way, roll himself in his red blanket and sleep. Now that they were alone, the white cow stood over him like a silver wraith in the moonlight.

One morning Abraham awoke to find a small boy looking at him. Shrugging off his blanket, he stood up. The boy ran off. Abraham stamped out the remains of the fire and cleaned his teeth with an aromatic twig. The boy returned. He thrust a folded note in Abraham's direction. Opening it, Abraham saw that it bore the Delamere crest.

'My boy tells me you are camping on our land,' said the note. 'Since it is Christmas Eve, it would give us great pleasure if you would join our group for the festivities. The boy will guide you to us.'

The note was signed Florence Delamere.

'Thank your mistress,' said Abraham to the boy, 'but tell her that I have been twelve weeks on the road and I am too rough and dirty to join her party.'

And too Jewish, he thought to himself.

He was touched nonetheless. Lady Delamere had no idea who the white man camped on her land might be and her generosity of spirit was admirable.

He called the white cow and they set off down the track.

They had not travelled far when there was a creak of wheels and the jingle of a bridle. Around a bend in the track came a small yellow and black buggy. It was drawn by a mule, and in it sat a lady. She was dressed in a simple white shirt and a flared khaki skirt. She wore a large white sun helmet tied with a gauze scarf. The lady drew up alongside Abraham and the white cow, and she smiled. She had white teeth and dimples.

'I'm not used to being refused,' she said, 'and all my other guests are dirty and rough, so you'll fit in well,' she extended a gloved hand, 'Florence Delamere,' she said.

'Abraham Block, my lady,' said Abraham and bowed in the Lithuanian manner.

'I don't believe it!' said Lady Delamere, 'Mr Block! Do you know you are one of the few men in this country that my husband actually likes? He will be so pleased to see you… and so absolutely furious if I don't make you come,' she motioned to the mule.

'Just take his head and turn him around would you?' she said.

Abraham did as he was bid.

'But I'm—' he began.

'Now do jump up here beside me, Mr Block' said Lady Delamere, 'and throw your bags in the back. I expect that quite *beautiful* cow will follow behind us.'

Once again, Abraham did as he was bid.

He was not sure what he had expected of the Delamere Ranch but he could never have imagined its extreme simplicity. It was certainly no mansion and little more than a collection of huts built in the traditional manner from mud and sticks. These were topped with untidy grass thatch, and rough windows had been punched through their wattle walls and draped with gunnysacks.

Lady Delamere jumped down from the buggy and tossed the reigns to the boy who ran forward. She gestured to Abraham to follow her into the largest of the huts.

In the centre of the room, which rose to a pointed ceiling, stood an elegant dining table draped in a green chenille cloth. Eight lyre-backed dining chairs stood at drunken angles on the uneven earth floor. A chandelier was lashed to one of the beams that spanned the room. On a polished mahogany sideboard, crystal decanters stood. Propped against the mud walls were gilt-framed oil paintings. A silver punch bowl had been filled with earth and planted with candles. Hurricane lanterns were nailed to the walls. There were packing crates everywhere, some unpacked, some still bound and labelled. In one corner stood an enormous four-poster bed with red damask curtains and a plume of feathers atop its canopy. In front of the huge grey stone fireplace, a bull terrier chewed a box. On its lid the words Fortnum and Mason could still be made out.

'Do sit down, Mr Block,' said Lady Delamere, 'I'll go and find 'D'.' She swept out of the room pausing only to remove the box from the dog.

'Tsk,' she said, and tapped it on the nose.

Abraham sat on a dining chair and turned his dusty hat around in his hands. He felt like a small boy.

'I've put your bags in the blue room,' said Lady Delamere when she returned, 'it's not blue and it's not a room, but there we are. Dinner *may* be at eight. The turkey is exceptionally large and the oven is an oilcan set on coals.' She smiled gently upon Abraham.

The bull terrier sniffed his boots.

There was a commotion outside the hut, the hessian sacking was thrust aside and a small figure barrelled into the room.

'Block! Block, my dear fellow!' said Lord Delamere, 'you do turn up in the most unexpected places.'

He was clad in his usual torn grey cardigan and had a red Maasai blanket slung over one shoulder. His greasy red curls flowed free.

'And just in time!' he continued.

He clapped Abraham on the shoulder and hustled him through another hessian curtain into the room beyond.

'Only two minutes to go!' he said.

It was a large room piled high with tea chests, gun cases and metal trunks with 'Delamere' stencilled on them. Against the walls leant a selection of paintings, mirrors and cricket bats. In the centre of the room, flanked by four wing chairs, stood a green chaise longue. Beside it on an upturned china chamber pot, was a wind-up phonograph with a large, fluted brass trumpet.

Lake Elmenteita and the crater known as Lord Delamere's Nose

'Sit down, sit down,' said 'D', 'they'll all be here in a minute. Then we can get started!' He knelt by the side of the phonograph and lifted the needle on to the thick black disc that lay there.

Dazed, Abraham sat down on a packing case.

Lady Delamere entered the room, her arm around the waist of a willowy young lady who was introduced to Abraham as 'dear Daisy'. The ladies were followed by a group of young men, seemingly just returned from riding. There was also an elderly lady with a lorgnette, and a pair of cigar-smoking gentlemen in shooting jackets.

And a group of Maasai warriors.

Lady Delamere stood by the fireplace, one white hand resting lightly upon it. The guests seated themselves where they might, and the Maasai took up position in a half circle to the rear of the phonograph.

'Ready?' shouted 'D'.

'Absolutely darling,' said his wife.

Squatting on all fours, 'D' wound the handle on the side of the phonograph. There was a scratching sound and then a rising wail. Then came the strains of the popular vaudeville song *All Aboard for Margate*.

The warriors swayed, the young men careered, the elderly aunt kept time with her lorgnette.

'May I?' said 'D' to Dear Daisy. Then he jigged up and down the room with one arm around Dear Daisy and the other in the air.

'Splendid ain't it?' he cried to Abraham.

'I cannot think of anything better,' said Abraham, and he meant it.

The evening spent with the Delameres was one of the best that Abraham had ever known. The turkey, hand-reared by Lady 'D', made a feast in itself. The table was decked with branches of green acacia; and the conversation was led by 'D' and rolled from politics to cattle poultices. Bottles of claret were wrenched from straw-packed cases and Abraham drank more than he had ever drunk before.

He found himself telling the story of his flight from Lithuania and the pogroms that had prompted it. Tears shone in Lady Delamere's eyes in the candlelight.

'The evil that is done in the name of religion,' she said. She patting Abraham's hand, 'but you're safe now and Kenya is your home. Surely here in Africa all religious differences can be forgotten.'

'Not a chance, my dear,' said 'D', 'now let's hear all about those Ankole cattle, Block, I've waited quite long enough.'

CHAPTER 47

THE ARRIVAL OF THE MATRIARCH

Conscience is a mother-in-law whose visit never ends.
–H. L. Mencken, American editor (1880-1956)

A<small>S ABRAHAM DROVE THE WHITE</small> cow up the narrow track to Njuna Farm, Corren ran to meet him.

'Still banished?' said Abraham and bent to pat him.

He wondered if his mother had arrived.

The last time he had seen Ettel Block, Abraham had been a small boy cowering in the back of a cart. Now he was a man. At that time, his mother had seemed invincible. He wondered if she would seem so now.

As he opened the door into the kitchen a wave of Yiddish washed out to meet him. The faces turned to the door and the Yiddish halted. His mother sat at the head of the kitchen table.

Now nearly sixty, Ettel Block seemed smaller than he had remembered her to be. She was, he thought, diminished. Her iron-grey hair was scraped back from a lined face. Her body had thickened into bulky squareness. Her dress was as alien to settler life as the lace cap skewered to her head.

'Abraham, my son,' she said. She did not get up. She looked him up and down, 'you are too thin,' she said, 'you must eat.'

The years rolled back.

The tale of Ettel's departure from Lithuania was many hours in the telling and she would not be hurried. She had been outraged by the demands of the agent, horrified by the conditions on the ship, disgusted by the squalor of Leyland, and sick 'unto death' on the long sea passage.

Freda, her face unnaturally pale after the long years in the Baltic cold, said little. She looked from speaker to speaker seemingly overwhelmed.

Samuel sat silent. It had been sixteen years since he had bade farewell to his wife. The years in between had been kind to him, but not to her. Ettel, wax-skinned, squat and glowering looked more like his mother than his wife; and they were both keenly aware of this.

'I have purchased land in your absence, Brother,' Lily said.

'And I have cleared it ready to sell, my son,' said Samuel.

'I've seen another plot I want to buy, said Lily, 'near to Simon Haller's Farm'.

There was something about the way she said 'Simon Haller[1]', and Ettel pounced on it.

'And who might he be?' she demanded.

'He's from the Ukraine, Mamma,' said Lily.

'He fled like I did to avoid the draft,' said Abraham, 'port-crawled the meat ships from Durban to Mombasa. The last I heard, he was working with John Rifkin[2]. They make tin baths and water-tanks,' he turned to Lily.

Aunt Lily's wedding 1913

'So he has a farm in Kiambu now?' he said.

'Growing potatoes, beans and oats,' said Lily. 'I thought I might do likewise.'

'And you my son?' said Ettel sweeping all this aside, 'do you intend to continue cattle rustling with your jailbird friends?'

'I—'

'Or are you going to find a nice Jewish girl and settle down?'

'I—'

'Because it's time I had grandchildren,' said Ettel, her hand lifted at every threatened interruption.

'It's hardly cattle rustling, Mamma,' said Abraham, 'and my friends are not jailbirds'.

'Hmm,' said Ettel.

Abraham's decision to leave Njuna Farm in the hands of Lily and Samuel had proven to be a good one. Lily had turned the empty rooms into a home. The kitchen range blazed, pots hung from a rack on the ceiling, and washing blew on the line. Samuel had made furniture; there was a dining room with a dresser; a parlour with a rocking chair and a chintz-covered sofa.

Down the once echoing passages, doors opened on to bedrooms furnished with iron beds. At the end of the corridor was a room containing a cast iron bath. There was a circular smoke house, a preserving room, a dairy and a herb garden. Lily had planted it with rue, rosemary, tarragon and chamomile.

'It's a proper Lithuanian farmhouse, eh Mamma?' said Lily.

'This,' said Ettel heavily, 'is nothing like a Lithuanian farmhouse, and it is not at all what I am used to.'

She sniffed.

Samuel sighed.

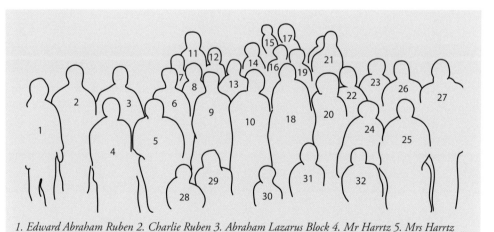

1. Edward Abraham Ruben 2. Charlie Ruben 3. Abraham Lazarus Block 4. Mr Harrtz 5. Mrs Harrtz
6. Mrs Medicks 7. Helen Ruben (Biemer) 8. Mr Medicks 9. Freda Block Kirkel 10. Lily Block Haller
11. Mrs M. Biemer 12. Dora Katzler (Biemer) 13. Shimon Branitzky 14. Philip Rifkin 15. Sophie Somen
(Biemer) 16. Revi's child 17. Mr G. Biemer 18. Simon Haller (Eddie and Charlie Ruben's uncle)
19. Reverend (name unknown) 20. Becky Rifkin Levitan 21. Unknown 22. Mrs Langman
23. Mr Langman 24. Mrs Block 25. Mrs Rifkin 26. Sam Block 27. John Rifkin 28. Charles Medicks
29. Langman's daughter 30. Sophie Rifkin 31. Langman's daughter 32. Alec Medicks.

CHAPTER 48

OF BIRDS AND BEASTS

It is discouraging how many people are shocked by honesty and how few by deceit.
–Noel Coward, playwright (1899-1973)

AT THE CONCLUSION OF THEIR Ankole cattle venture, Abraham and Fatty Garland had remained in partnership. They made an odd couple. Garland was over six-feet tall and built, as he himself put it, 'like a brick shit house'; and Abraham was a dapper five-feet-six inches tall with the growing air of the dandy about him. But for all this, their partnership was sound. They had worked hard to establish a reputation for supplying the best steers at the best price, but in order to maintain it they had to look increasingly far afield for their herds. They had even considered travelling to Ethiopia to buy cattle.

Garland and Block were not the only ones herding cattle up and down the country: everyone was doing it. And, as more and more cattle traversed the land, they began to spread disease from one area to another. In the north of Kenya there was an outbreak of pleuro-pneumonia, which decimated several herds, and this resulted in the southerly movement of all cattle being stopped. Then came a wave of East Coast Fever, which was equally deadly. The colonial government moved swiftly to contain the spread of these diseases. All the infected areas were declared 'dirty' while all the uninfected areas were declared 'clean': and movement of cattle between the two was banned. This hampered Garland and Block whose success lay in the speed with which they were able to put their herds up for auction in the Nakuru market place.

As the next Nakuru sale approached, Fatty made a proposal.

'Why don't we just nip across a corner of the dirty land above Nakuru?' he said. 'Then we'll get our steers up for auction before anyone else. We'll make a killing.'

'That would mean breaking the law,' said Abraham.

'They've only just announced it,' said Garland, 'ink's hardly dry, probably not even legal. Besides; nobody will know.'

Abraham doubted this, and it came as no surprise to him when they were caught. They were cutting across of a corner of dirty land when a man appeared.

'See your quarantine papers?' he said.

'Back at the farm,' said Fatty.

'And I'm the Queen of Sheba,' said the man, 'you'll come with me, gentlemen, if you please.'

As they emerged from a week in Naivasha jail, Abraham turned to Fatty.

'Don't tell my mother,' he said.

'What's it worth?' said Fatty.

The following year, Fatty Garland came up with another idea.

'Ostriches[1],' he said. 'Everyone's doing them. Can't go wrong.'

'Who's everyone?' said Abraham.

'Everyone,' said Fatty, 'those South African brothers, Clifford and Harold Hill, have made a fortune selling feathers for ladies' fancy hats. F.O.B Wilson, Phil Percival and Archie Lambert are doing it down at Ulu. Leslie Tarlton's doing it, 'D' Delamere's doing. In fact 'D' reckons he can herd around a hundred cocks at a time without injury'.

'Why *would* he be injured?' said Abraham suspiciously.

'Ah well,' said Fatty, 'they can fetch you a cruel blow with those feet, ostriches can. Nasty claws you know. Horny. Chap was disemboweled only last week. There's a fellow up at Naivasha who has a cock bird that has a reputation for rushing up to folk, knocking them down, and standing guard over them.'

'Then what happens?'

'They die. People put bets on how many people this bird can kill in a week.'

'Is there money to be made?'

'Well, I lost my bet.'

'In ostriches.'

'Plenty', said Fatty, 'you can pick up chicks for nothing in the bush. You just go out there and grab 'em. Easy money.'

'No such thing,' said Abraham, 'and anyway, what do we do with the chicks when we've caught them?'

'Cage them, feed them, put a sock over their heads and clip their feathers.'

'And the birds allow you to do all this?'

'Up until the age of three they do.'

'And then?'

'Then you employ boys with long metal sticks to do the clipping. Simple really,' said Fatty.

Abraham was skeptical but he felt that the time had come to cease trading in cattle. Boys were hired and sent into the bush with nets. Ostrich chicks were captured, cages were built, green leaves were chopped and fed through the bars. But as the birds grew to adulthood they became ever harder to control. They launched attacks on their keepers and when they were put in the auction ring at Nakuru some rushed at the barbed wire fences and decapitated themselves and others leapt clean over them and ran away. Then it was discovered that the boys were stealing the ostrich feathers.

'Pull 'em out and stick them under their coats,' said Fatty.

'What do they do with them?' said Abraham.

'Sell 'em to the Nandi warriors as headdresses', said Garland as if this were obvious. Shortly afterwards the wearing of ostrich feathers fell from favour in Edwardian Britain.

'What's next?' said Fatty.

'What makes you think I know?'

'Not called The Prophet for nothing are you?'

'Safaris,' said Abraham.

'To get into the safari business we need to get chummy with Newland and Tarlton[2],' said Fatty, 'they're the best safari outfitters in Kenya. Got any chums there, ALB?'

'As a matter of fact I have,' said Abraham, 'David Tulipman[3] a young Jewish friend of mine, is their accountant and Billy Judd[4] takes out some of their safaris.'

'Who's Billy Judd?'

'Met him in the Boer War; he hunts for Northrup McMillan. A few months ago McMillan invited a group of British lords to stay at his mansion at Ol Donyo Sabuk. Billy took them out and they collected so many trophies that Billy's tip allowed him to buy half a plot of land in Kabete.'

'Who bought the other half?'

'I did, we're growing experimental barley.'

'You know, Block,' said Fatty, 'your ingenuity never fails to amaze me. Is there anything you won't try?'

'Not if there's a profit to be made,' said Block.

CHAPTER 49

IN THE SAFARI BUSINESS

One secret of success in life is for a man to be ready for his opportunity when it comes.
–Benjamin Disraeli, Statesman (1804-1881)

LIKE EVERY OTHER SETTLER, ABRAHAM Block knew that the profits to be made in the safari business were immense. Game shooting was fashionable; Kenya was the place to shoot; and everyone wanted to be seen to be going on safari there. First came men like Theodore Roosevelt and Winston Churchill; then came the crowned heads of Europe and the aristocracy; and Hollywood brought up the rear. In one month alone, the Norfolk hosted several earls, numerous lords, two Indian princes and so many European counts and barons that they ceased to deserve a mention; and the relative merits of hunters such as Denys Finch Hatton[1] and Bror von Blixen were argued from Europe to America and back again.

All safaris departed from outside the Norfolk Hotel, which described itself as 'The True Home of the Big Game Shooter'; and the sight of a safari 'going out' caused people to line the streets for hours in advance of its departure. Soon the Norfolk had earned the reputation of being the only place to stay when going on safari. Major Ringer was delighted, as were Newland and Tarlton, a pair of hunters from Australia, who ran the most prestigious safari outfitters in the world.

Newland and Tarlton had offices in London, Paris and New York; they ran a desk in the foyer of the Norfolk Hotel, and they ran their empire from an office in Station Road; and it was to the latter office that Abraham went to visit his friend, David Tulipman.

David's office was so small that the door hit his desk whenever it opened to admit a visitor, but this did not concern him because he lived in a world of ledgers, files, bills of sale and chits stuffed on spikes. He was young, but he was respected because safari business was big business. A typical Newland and Tarlton safari might leave the Norfolk with a stream of men and goods over a mile long. It might remain in the bush for three months, and its guests would expect eight-course suppers nightly. The cost of such safaris was considerable and it required a small army of men to make them possible.

'One fellow had a grand piano hauled through the bush,' said David Tulipman to Abraham Block.

'Why?' said Abraham.

'So he could play in the moonlight,' said David, 'and another insisted on having the vegetables boiled in champagne. Said he didn't trust the water.'

'Who supplies your safaris?' said Abraham.

'That depends,' said David, 'usually it all happens at such short notice that we take what we can, from whoever we can, cost no object.'

'Mmm…' said Abraham, 'how do I become a supplier?'

'Best way is to get close to one of the hunters, they rule the roost around here,' said David.

'Which hunter takes out the most safaris?'

'Denys Finch Hatton,' said David, 'he's got it all; looks and charm for the ladies. Gifted tracker, crack shot too.'

'Where do I find him?'

'You won't. He spends most of his time in the bush. The only way would be to catch him when he's putting a safari together.' David consulted a chart on the wall. 'He'll be doing that next month.'

'Where?'

'He puts up at the Norfolk until the safari pulls out. He usually hires storage there too,' said David.

The following month Abraham walked to the Norfolk. Major Ringer was, as usual, taking his coffee on the terrace.

'I've a message from Billy Judd for Mr Finch Hatton,' Abraham said.

'Room 19, across the courtyard,' said Major Ringer without looking up from his newspaper.

Abraham stood outside Room 19; there was music playing inside. He knocked.

'Come,' said a voice.

It was a small room and it was full of boxes. Denys Finch Hatton was long and thin with a baldhead and a sharply aquiline nose; he was folded into a chair too low for him. Around the walls, he had rigged up a system of strings, to which were clipped bunches of paper, lists and maps. He looked up as Abraham entered. His eyes were a rich hazel-brown. They stood out against his tanned skin.

'And?' he said.

'Billy Judd suggested I call on you,' said Abraham. 'He and I are farming partners, he said you had a safari going out soon.'

'And what if I have?'

'I'd like to equip it,' said Abraham.

'And you are?' said Finch Hatton.

'Abraham Block.'

'Block. I've heard that name. Friend of 'D's aren't you?'

'Yes.'

'So why should I engage you?'

'I'll get everything you need cheaper, better and faster than anyone else.'

'And what proof do I have of that, Mr Block?'

'You don't. But I'll work for you for nothing on your next safari. If you like my work, you'll pay me. If you don't, you won't.'

'Bit of a risk for you isn't it?' said Finch Hatton.

'No,' said Abraham.

Then he waited.

Denys Finch Hatton surveyed him. He smiled, 'Oh sit down man,' he said, 'move those papers, pass me that list. I like your style.'

Denys Finch Hatton gave Abraham a lecture.

'I insist upon a smoothly run safari,' he said, 'so that I can relax and enjoy myself. A safari can be a misery if the organization is slapdash; and I don't tolerate that. A safari is like being marooned in the desert: stores are everything.' He had tapped the list on the desk. 'And the secret of stores,' he said, 'is to know the life of a tin of sardines.'

Abraham narrowed his eyes, but said nothing.

'Law of averages,' said Finch Hatton, 'a pound of tea will last one man a fortnight, while a tin of marmalade will last that same man a week.'

Abraham nodded.

'All tents must be eight-feet high; every hunter requires thirty porters, and each porter will carry a sixty pound load. There will be forty porters to every client. A second set of ratios applies to such things as cooks, gun bearers, pack animals, chop-boxes, medicine chests, folding baths, mosquito nets, salt and ammunition'.

'Salt?'

'For preserving the animal skins,' said Finch Hatton, 'shoot do you?'

'As well as any farmer,'

'Good. Any other skills?'

'Gun smith, carpenter, upholsterer, butcher, saddler, horse dealer, grease monkey, sheep shearer; I can turn my hand to most things. I speak Russian, Lithuanian, Yiddish, German and English.'

'Excellent. I'm beginning to be glad you turned up, Mr Block,' said Finch Hatton, 'but right now I need you to find me a clown. We'll call it a test of your skills.'

'A clown?'

'Every safari has a jester, a man to keep the porters smiling at the end of a long day's march. He runs up and down the lines, pulls faces, tells lewd jokes, mimics his employers, the porters love it,' said Finch Hatton, 'can't run a safari without one, but I've got a safari going out soon, and I still have not found my clown.'

'I will find one', said Abraham.

Several hours later, when Abraham emerged from the Norfolk Hotel, he was smiling.

'All sunny in the world of Block?' said Major Ringer.

'Yes,' said Abraham.

It took Abraham a few hours to track down Mr King, but when he had done so he came straight to the point. 'I need a clown for the porters on a Finch Hatton safari,' he said.

'When?'

'Now.'

'Kikuyu or Akamba?'

'The best.'

'I only deal in the best, Mr Block. Room 19 is it?'

'Yes.'

Abraham returned to the office of David Tulipman.

'I need you to tell me the price that Finch Hatton paid for everything on his last safari,' he said, 'and who his suppliers were. We will work with Billy Judd and we will split the profits three-ways.'

'Done,' said David Tulipmann.

Abraham rode out to see Billy Judd. He laid his plans before him.

'We can also kit out your safaris, Billy' he said, 'and you can bring us more work from all the other hunters that you know; your recommendation is worth a lot. All profits will be shared.' Billy Judd grinned.

'Cornering the safari market are we now Block?' he said.

'Safari supplies,' said Abraham, 'there's a difference.'

Abraham called on Denys Finch Hatton again.

'Clown acceptable?' he said.

'More than.'

'Here's the list of everything else that I believe will be required,' said Abraham, 'you will want to check it.'

'I will indeed.'

Denys Finch Hatton approved the list and Abraham marshalled his contacts. Markus and Loy sent goods up by train from Mombasa; Tommy Wood and Mr Marcus supplied the hardware; Mayence Tate supplied the fine linens; Mr da Souza made the uniforms; Fred Raper supplied the leather goods and the boots for the porters; Fatty Garland supplied the pack animals; Mr Nazareth supplied the Goan chefs; Mr Jeevanjee supplied tinned goods and storage, and Mr King supplied what nobody else could. The safari pickles, jams and other preserves came from Lily and Ettel.

'Keep it in the family,' said Lily.

'Family? What family? I will make them,' said Ettel, '*you* are not capable.'

On the appointed day, the crowds gathered outside the Norfolk Hotel. It was draped in red, white and blue bunting. The railway band sat on campstools along the white picket fence; and the bandleader adjusted his music stand and buttoned his white gloves. Along the terrace the guests gathered, the ladies carrying parasols and wearing large hats; champagne cocktails were served. Beneath the eucalyptus trees stood mountains of boxes, crates and baskets.

Out in the hot sun, the safari slowly shuffled itself into shape. At its head was a long line of porters clad in navy blue jerseys, each carrying a pair of new boots around his neck, a length of rope to secure his load, and his daily rations. Behind the porters came the gun-bearers, cooks, stewards, and syces. Behind them came the pack animals, and to the front and the rear were bands of *askaris* armed with muskets. Finally came the horses for the clients and the carts that carried their personal baggage.

Of the clients themselves, and of Denys Finch Hatton, there was no sign.

At a given signal, the porters stepped forward to receive their loads and hoisted them on to their heads. The clown, clad in monkey skins with a pair of cow horns strapped to his head, danced up and down the line. The cooks shouldered their pots, the gun bearers hoisted the gun cases on to their heads. The bandleader raised his baton and looked towards the door of the hotel. Out on to the terrace stepped Major Ringer. The crowds cheered; and Major Ringer shepherded the clients into view. There were four gentlemen in safari suits and two ladies.

The band began to play.

Finally, Denys Finch Hatton stepped out on to the terrace. He was laughing; and the ladies moved closer to him. Abraham Block stood at the foot of the steps.

'Ready, Block?' said Denys Finch Hatton.

'Ready, Sir,' said Abraham.

Denys turned to the ladies. 'Shall we?' he said.

Behind his back, he gave Block a thumbs up.

At the front of the line, a boy beat a roll on a goatskin drum and marched off in the direction of Ainsworth's Bridge. Behind him, the safari fell in to line. The band played *Jerusalem*, the crowd cheered and waved, children ran alongside the moving ranks, and donkeys brayed. As the last packhorse swayed off into the dust cloud, Denys Finch Hatton made his way in a leisurely manner down the steps; he handed the ladies into their small buggy, and he indicated to the gentlemen that they might mount. Finch Hatton swung himself up into the saddle, he waved to the terrace, and he set off. There was now no sign of the safari: just a large cloud of dust.

Word had it in the long bar of the Stanley that it had stretched for at least half a mile.

CHAPTER 50

MARRIAGE PLANS

Many go fishing without knowing it is fish they are after.
–Henry David Thoreau (1817-1862)

OVER THE NEXT THREE YEARS, Abraham Block and his partners, David Tulipman and Billy Judd equipped numerous safaris. It was hard work. But it paid very well. And they became so successful that they were forced to turn contracts away.

By the end of 1913 Abraham had come to realize that he was a relatively wealthy man. But he did not feel like one, because going without had become something of a religion with him.

'What are you *doing* man?' said Finch Hatton as Abraham picked up a bent nail and put it in his pocket.

'Might come in useful,' Abraham said, 'save a bit of money.'

'Good Lord, man,' said Finch Hatton, 'there's more to life than money! You can't take it with you when you go, you know.'

'If I can't take it with me,' said Abraham, 'I'm not going.'

'Well I am,' said David Tulipman, when Abraham recounted the conversation.

'Where to?' said Abraham.

'Back to Palestine.'

'Why?' said Abraham.

'To visit my family,' said David, 'you should come. I have two beautiful sisters. And you can afford a wife now.'

He proffered a photograph of two dark, serious eyed girls.

'You could become my brother-in-law,' he said, 'then we could really make some money.'

'There's more to life than money,' said Abraham.

'Such as?' said David.

'I don't know,' said Abraham.

Abraham had continued to expand his farming interests, which were managed by Lily and Samuel. They had bought and sold a number of farms. And some they had put under the management of the Boer trekkers, who were newly arrived from South Africa. The Boers were thrifty and diligent and the Block's profits soared.

Lily diversified into planting tea and coffee. She had made it her business to learn everything she could about farming and she was an authority on experimental crops. At first, when Simon Haller began to call, Lily assumed he came to mine her considerable reserves of agricultural knowledge.

Ettel snorted. 'You may think like a man,' she said, 'but you don't look like one.'

'He is interested in my seed trials,' said Lily.

'He is interested in your child bearing ability,' said Ettel.

'We are on the committee for the building of Nairobi's first synagogue,' said Lily, we have things to discuss, Mamma.'

'I may be old, but I know what the look in his eye means', said Ettel, avoiding Samuel's gaze. 'Best translate it into marriage before *you* realize what it leads to.'

Ettel was right.

At the end of 1912, Simon Haller proposed and was accepted.

'There is only one problem,' he said.

'What is that?' said Lily.

'I have already asked my brother in the Ukraine to send his young sons to help me on the farm,' said Simon.

'And this is a problem?' said Lily.

'Eddie, Archie, Charlie and David Ruben[1] arrive on the day before the wedding,' said Simon.

'So selfish,' said Ettel, when she heard. 'You might at least let me get my grandchild before you start mothering other people's children. And *Ukrainians* at that!'

It was after the wedding ceremony that Ettel finally released a piece of news she had been saving. The wedding cavalcade left the District Commissioner's office, where all ceremonies took place, and wound its crocodile of buggies, rickshaws, bicycles and mules, to the Stanley Hotel, where Mayence Tate had laid out a feast. Ettel sat at the head of the table, as was her habit, and grimaced over the tinned peaches.

'So cheap, we would never have had tinned peaches in Lithuania,' she said to Abraham, who sat next to her.

Abraham said nothing.

'Talking of weddings, I heard from your sister, Annie, the other day,' said Ettel, casually.

'Mmm,' said Abraham.

'Yes. She said that the young woman you had wished to marry has still not found a man.'

'What?' said Abraham.

'How fortunate you did not marry her, my son,' said Ettel, 'she obviously has faults.'

Abraham held up a hand.

Ettel put her spoon down and stared at him.

'Is my Rosie not married, then?' Abraham said.

'Your Rosie?' said his mother.

'What did Annie say, Mother?' said Abraham, 'Tell me!'

Something in Abraham's tone reminded Ettel of Samuel.

'According to your sister, the young woman's engagement was broken off,' she said. She sniffed and resumed her tinned peaches.

'Why?' said Abraham.

'How would I know that, my son?' said Ettel airily, 'you would have to ask her that yourself.'

'I will,' said Abraham.

The next day Abraham announced that he was leaving for Europe immediately.

The Synagogue Building Committee and Mr Gain at the laying of the foundation stone, 1912.

Front row: David Goldberg, Robertson, Mark Solomon (slightly behind), H. Fein (with hat), Sammy Jacobs, W.A.Gain, Simon Medicks.
Back row: H.J.Wolffe, Philip Raphael, Linton (slightly to the fore), B. Levinson, David Tulipman, Michael Haartz, John Rifkin.

'What can you mean, my son?' said his mother. 'What will you do in Europe? Don't you know they're talking of war there?'

'I have something that must be done,' said Abraham.

Ettel brought the flat of her hand down on the kitchen table.

'How can you think of leaving now?' she said, 'I've only just arrived!'

'I'm going to ask Rosie Daniels to marry me,' said Abraham.

'How wonderful,' said Freda, 'it might be my turn next.'

CHAPTER 51

A MAN ON A MISSION

Blessed are the hearts that can bend; they shall never be broken.
–Albert Camus, Philosopher 1913-1960

Leeds seemed unchanged. The bricks were perhaps a little blacker, the chimneys a little sootier, the doorsteps scrubbed a little whiter. Arriving at the Sinson's home, Abraham found them to have prospered. His Aunt Sinson looked half the age of her sister, Ettel.

'Your uncle has done so well,' said Fanny. 'He has established reading rooms, schools, baths, soup kitchens for our people all over Leeds. Everyone loves him. He's so respected. Learned men come from all over just to talk to him. And he never turns anyone away. Such a good man I married,' she said.

'Speaking of that, Aunt Sinson,' said Abraham, 'I have come with a purpose. I have heard that Rosie Daniels is not married, yet she herself told me that she had married a cousin of Mr Rakusen.'

'Wally Rakusen died in the flu epidemic,' said his aunt.

'I see,' said Abraham, 'then I will ask her to marry me.'

'You may be too late,' said his aunt.

'Why?'

'I hear she has just become engaged to Solomon Peers, the dentist.'

'Where can I find her?' said Abraham.

'Wally left her some money, she bought a hat shop,' said Fanny Sinson, 'it's on Crimea Street, next to the public baths.'

Abraham wondered if Rosie had changed; and whether she would find him changed. He was nervous as he approached Crimea Street. He could feel the sweat trickling down the inside of his shirt; it was cold on his hot skin. He thought of the sweat patches that would soon stain his suit; and he held out his arms for ventilation.

Looking out of her shop window, Rosie saw Abraham Block; he seemed to be flying down the street towards her.

'Abraham Block!' she said, and she stepped out into the street to halt his progress.

'I never thought to see you again!' she said. She placed her hands on her waist and let out a great shout of laughter. The years rolled back, Rosie was as lovely as ever.

'You look just the same, Rosie,' said Abraham, stupidly.

'Can't say the same for you,' said Rosie, 'quite the swell you look. Done well for yourself have you?'

'I—'

'I can see that you have! Come in!' said Rosie.

Abraham followed her into the shop.

'On my life! I can't believe it,' said Rosie, 'Abraham Block, back from darkest Africa. Now. Tell me all about it!'

Rosie fired questions at him; and she hugged herself with glee over his replies.

'Elephants? Really? And lions and tigers?'

No tigers Rosie, now what I wanted to say was—'

'You! Owning four farms! Imagine!'

'Rosie—'

'Growing tea, well I never did!'

'Rosie! There's something I want to say…'

Rosie halted. Abraham seized the moment.

'Will you marry me Rosie?' he said. He had forgotten to kneel.

Rosie looked at him.

The world stilled.

They stared into each other's eyes.

Then Rosie gave her head a little shake.

'Oh Abraham,' she said, 'for so many years it was all that I dreamed of. But that's all over now. I'm well set up here. My own place, and doing well, though I say so myself.'

She smiled and gestured around the shop.

'But I love you, Rosie,' Abraham said. He leaned forward on his chair and tried to take her hands, but she would not let him.

'Oh Abraham,' she said, 'I can't leave all this and go to Africa. What would I do there? I don't belong there. And besides, I'm to marry Sol Peers, the dentist. We'll do well together.' She gave him a falsely cheery smile, 'I'm sorry, Abraham,' she said.

Abraham did not know what to say.

Rosie placed her hands decisively on her knees. 'Plenty more fish in the sea though' she said, 'well set up fellow like you; you'll have the girls throwing themselves at you, you see if you don't.'

Abraham sat back on his chair; it was not how he had thought it would be. He could read her face and he knew that she wanted the awkward conversation to end; she wanted him to go. It was a clumsy goodbye. They searched for words; they shook hands. Then they laughed at the ridiculousness of the gesture; and for a second the years rolled back; but nothing had changed.

Or rather, everything had.

As he walked off down the street, Abraham sensed Rosie's eyes on his back; and the world seemed leached of colour; the greyness of Leyland washed around him; and he determined to put it behind him forever.

He had a new life to lead and he was suddenly eager to begin it.

For the next two months, Abraham Block drifted through Europe; and he spent money. It was an odd feeling. In Paris, he bought suits, in Rome he bought cigars, in Budapest, he steamed down the river. In Romania, he went around castles with a guidebook in his hand, and in Constantinople he watched the Dervishes whirl.

But eventually he decided that what he really wanted was to go home.

Abraham was standing on the dockside in Constantinople; his ship was in and he was waiting to go aboard.

'Abraham?'

David Tulipman[1] stood before him.

It took time for them to marvel over the startling improbability of this meeting, but when it was done David asked Abraham why he was in Europe, and Abraham found it a relief to tell him.

'Well it's obvious what you have to do next,' said David.

'Is it?'

'Yes. You must come with me to Palestine and meet my sisters. They are the ideal cure for a broken heart,' said David clapping him on the back

'Do you know, David?' said Abraham slowly, as the realization dawned on him, 'I'm not sure I *have* a broken heart.'

'Even better! Come and give your whole heart to one of my sisters.'

Abraham hesitated.

Then he made his decision.

'I will, David,' he said, and he smiled. 'Yes! I will!'

CHAPTER 52

RISHON LE ZION

Who forces time is pushed back by time; who yields to time finds time on his side.
—The Talmud

A

S THEY PACED THE DECKS of the tramp steamer, where the travellers hunched on the rusty white benches and braced against the November cold, David told Abraham about his family.

'My father, Alexander Tulipman[1], grew up in Odessa,' he said. 'He was a farmer growing oilseed. He had a small press and made a reasonable living producing kosher cooking oil. In 1890, as the pogroms swept through Russia, he and my mother decided it was time to leave. But unlike their neighbours, all of whom were heading to America, they went to Palestine. They lived in one room in Jaffa, but it was a struggle to survive and my father despaired. He was a religious man, a Talmudic scholar, so he prayed for guidance and the very next day a friend mentioned that the Baron Rothschild had set up the first Jewish colony. It was called Rishon Le Zion, meaning 'The First To Zion'. My father took this as a sign. He had no money, so he walked to Rishon, it took him four days but when he arrived he was given a job working in the vineyards of the Carmel Winery. And has been there ever since.'

'A remarkable story,' said Abraham.

'Rishon is a remarkable place,' said David, 'it was founded by just seventeen families, all fleeing the pogroms of the Ukraine. They're religion is strong, and even today they speak only Hebrew; and when they discovered that my father was a Talmudic scholar they gave him a small house next to the Great Synagogue. He and my mother live there still.'

Rishon Le Zion stood high on a hill looking out over miles of vineyards and Abraham found it startlingly intense and bright. The buildings were domed and sharply white against the deep blue of the sky. The vines were vividly green against the gnarled grey of their roots. The soil was chalk-white against the strips of grass that divided the vines, and the vines marched across the land in straight rows. At the end of each row was a rose bush. Some were red, some pink, and some golden yellow. The people working the vines were hunched beneath broad brimmed hats. They pruned and snipped, wound and trained the soft green tendrils around their trellises. Above the vines, crumbling white cliffs rose in crags and into them were carved ancient caves, their mouths blocked with iron gates. It was a scene both ancient and timeless.

Mr Tulipman's house was small and square and white painted and it hugged the walls of the Great Synagogue, which stood in the central square of Rishon Le Zion. Over the years, he had extended it to accommodate his family with a series of small white cube-like rooms, which looked like children's building bricks. He had also built a small white reading room with a flat roof and here he taught rows of boys, who sat cross-legged on the floor, their small black slates balanced on their knees.

David Tulipman's parents had not expected his visit. His mother cried, his father beamed, David was hugged, Abraham was pressed to sit first in one chair, and then another. Mrs Tulipman brought out slices of fruit, dishes of salted nuts, slabs of dates, honey cakes, jugs of milk, flagons of grape juice. There was talk of family and business; talk of Kenya; and talk of the war brewing in Europe. It continued for many hours.

'Where are my sisters?' said David eventually.

'Rachel will be here soon,' said Mrs Tulipman, 'Sarah will come later.'

Mrs Tulipman glanced at Abraham.

'My girls have had a very sheltered upbringing, Mr Block,' she said, 'they are not used to the society of young men, other than that of their brother.'

'I have sisters of my own, Mrs Tulipman,' said Abraham, 'and my mother is as careful of them as I am sure you are of your girls.'

'Ah,' said Mrs Tulipman, 'tell us more about your family.'

'My eldest sister is married and lives in England, my sister Lily is newly married and lives in Kenya; and my youngest sister, Freda, is unmarried and lives with my mother and father in Nairobi. My mother is newly arrived from Russia; and my father is taking care of my farms,' he said.

'Farms?' said Mrs Tulipman.

'Yes,' said Abraham; and he spoke of the tea and the coffee, the livestock and the butchery.

'So you own all these farms, Mr Block?' said Mrs Tulipman.

'Yes.'

'And you own other farms, which you rent out. And you own cattle herds?' said Mrs Tulipman.

'And he is the largest supplier to the safari trade,' said David.

'Our son is fortunate in having such a wealthy friend,' said Mrs Tulipman; she glanced expressively at her husband.

'Oh I—'

'Abraham has just toured Europe,' said David, seeking to deflect his mother, 'in the past three months he has seen all the sights. Have you not Abraham?'

'Yes indeed, I—'

'And what brought you to Europe, Mr Block,' said Mrs Tulipman unwilling to relinquish her train of thought.

Abraham glanced at David, who shrugged and waved him on in encouragement.

'I had intentions of marriage, Mrs Tulipman,' said Abraham.

'Indeed?' said Mrs Tulipman.

'But my proposal was turned down.'

'I'm sorry to hear that, Mr Block,' said Mrs Tulipman.

The door opened and a girl entered. Rachel Tulipman was very small, almost doll-like. She wore a red-spotted headscarf and her bell of black skirts dropped to her white-stockinged ankles. Her black hair streamed to her waist; and she wore red shoes.

'My dearest sister!' said David, 'Meet my friend, Mr Abraham Block, from Kenya.'

Rachel Tulipman raised her dark eyes gravely to Abraham's face.

'I have heard much about you, Mr Block,' she said, 'my brother has written and told us all about your work together in the safari business.'

Abraham nodded and smiled. He could think of nothing to say.

The light, shafting down from the high, square window illuminated the down on Rachel's cheeks, so that her face seemed surrounded by light. She turned to her brother and she smiled with the trusting grace of a child; she ran to embrace him.

Abraham Block was lost.

Later, lying on his bed with his hands clasped behind his head, in the room he shared with David, Abraham stared at the ceiling.

'So what did you think of my sister?' said David, 'I adore her.'

'So do I', said Abraham.

David turned on his elbow and looked across at Abraham. He smiled and raised his eyebrows.

'What did I tell you?' he said.

Workers in the Mt Carmel vinyards of Richon in 1910

CHAPTER 53

A SECOND PROPOSAL IS MADE

It is a truth universally acknowledged, that a single man in possession of a good fortune,
must be in want of a wife.
–Jane Austen, English novelist (1775-1817)

IT WAS DAWN IN RISHON and the owls still called amid the olive trees. A gossamer scarf of mist hung across the vineyards. Cut off from the land below, the town seemed to float disembodied.

Abraham walked across the empty square and followed the chalky track that led from the town to the vineyards. He walked up and down the rows of vines, and as he did so, he questioned himself.

How could he be so fickle?

How could he be so desperate to marry Rosie and now be equally desperate to marry Rachel?

Had he forgotten Rosie so soon?

He kicked the white stones and they bounced along the track in front of him.

Then the truth came to him: the old Rosie, 'his Rosie' was gone; and the new Rosie was grown-up. And somewhere in her growing up she had left him far behind. And she was going to marry someone else.

The vineyard workers arrived and they began to bend to the vines.

Abraham made up his mind.

He would ask Mr Tulipman for his daughter's hand in marriage.

Mr Tulipman was delighted when he heard what Abraham had to say.

'Abraham, my dear fellow,' he said, 'I have only just met you, and yet nothing could give me more happiness! But...' His face clouded slightly. He clapped Abraham on the back and led him to a chair.

'But?' said Abraham.

'But I have another daughter.'

Abraham said nothing.

'And she must be married before our little Rachel can be married. You know how it is? The younger cannot wed until the elder is wed. It has always been this way.'

'I see,' said Abraham, cast down.

'But why the long face, my boy?' said Mr Tulipman, 'my second-born daughter, Sarah, is as lovely as my third-born, Rachel. You must marry Sarah! Ach! Wait till I tell Bathsheva!'

'But Mr Tulipman,' said Abraham, 'I have not met your daughter Sarah.'

'You have not?'

'No, I have not.'

'But then come! Meet her! What could be more simple?' said Mr Tulipman, 'I will call my wife. Bathsheva!'

It was a small house and Mrs Tulipman arrived so tumultuously that she must have been outside the door.

'Bathsheva!' said Mr Tulipman, 'you will never believe it but Mr Block wishes to marry our daughter, Sarah!'

'But Mr Block has not met our daughter, Sarah,' said Mrs Tulipman, who had a much keener grip on the situation than her husband.

'What matter my dear? I had not met you when our marriage was arranged.'

Mrs Tulipman looked from her husband to Abraham; and she perceived the situation.

'Abraham, my son!' said Mr Tulipman, now rapturous. 'What joy! Let us sit down together and talk of the wedding. Ach, Bathsheva, can you believe the goodness of our God in sending us such happiness?'

Mrs Tulipman could not.

Abraham struggled against the tide of Tulipman. But there came a point when he realized he could not win.

He tried to make them understand that because he had not seen their daughter, Sarah, he did not know if he wished to marry her or not. But this made things worse.

'But then see her!' shouted Mr Tulipman, triumphant.

And Abraham knew himself to be vanquished. If he saw the girl and refused to marry her, it would seem as though he had found her repulsive. This would insult her, insult the family and hurt his friend, David. His only hope lay in the thought that Sarah Tulipman might refuse him. She, after all, had not met him either.

It was a vain hope.

Later that day Abraham was summoned to the parlour. Mrs Tulipman was seated on the sofa, David Tulipman stood behind her. On the olivewood dresser, stood several bottles of Baron Rothschild's best wine, there were bowls of olives, fresh-baked bread and a large sugar-dusted cake on a silver stand; celebration was expected.

A chair had been placed in the centre of the room.

'Sit down my boy,' said Mr Tulipman; and he waved Abraham towards it.

'Now, my dear,' he said to his wife, 'where is our daughter?'

Sarah Tulipman was nothing like her sister. Where Rachel's face had been heart shaped, Sarah's was square. Where Rachel's hair had been straight, Sarah's lay in waves. Where Rachel's expression had been gently trusting, Sarah's was stricken.

White and pinched of face she sat next to her mother on the sofa. The phrase, 'like a lamb to the slaughter' came into Abraham's mind.

Silence fell in the room.

Sarah clasped her hands together and crossed her ankles. She took a deep breath. Then, gathering her courage, she looked up at Abraham; and she managed a small tight smile.

His heart went out to her.

'Miss Tulipman, he said, 'your father has suggested…' He faltered.

'Go on, my boy,' said Mr Tulipman.

'Your father has suggested that I might have the honour of requesting your hand in marriage,' Abraham said; he had rushed the sentence and Sarah's eyes were huge upon him.

She said nothing.

David patted Sarah on the shoulder; Mrs Tulipman nudged her.

'Sarah, my beloved child? What is your answer to David's dear friend, Mr Block?' she said.

Once again Sarah summoned a smile.

'I shall be honoured to accept, Mr Block,' she said.

And there it was.

Done.

Mr Tulipman rushed for the wine, Mrs Tulipman tugged a lace handkerchief from her pocket; she wept and blew her nose. David strode over to Abraham and embraced him.

Across the room, Sarah rose, smoothed her skirts and moved stiffly towards Abraham. They stood opposite each other, her black boots almost touching the rounded toecaps of his boots, still dusted with chalk from his wrestle with his conscience. Abraham leant forward and planted a kiss on her cold cheek. She smelt of almonds.

The war in Europe seemed imminent, so Mr Tulipman declared that the wedding must take place within as short a space of time as possible.

'The Imperial Navy of the Kaiser is ready to leave Kiel,' he said, 'soon every steamship in Europe will be confined to port. We must obtain your tickets immediately.'

There was only one ship sailing to Mombasa and it was German. To Abraham's surprise, Mr Tulipman announced that he would accompany the couple as far as Jaffa.

'I want to see you on your way,' he said.

In the weeks that followed the Tulipmans struggled to put together a trousseau for Sarah, and the entire town of Rishon was invited to the wedding, which was to take place in the Great Synagogue.

The 26th of July dawned bright and clear; there was no escape.

As the timeless rituals of a Jewish wedding were enacted, Abraham played his part mechanically. Sarah's face remained set, calm and white throughout. She wore an ivory silk gown sewn with seed pearls. Her hair was covered in a lace veil and she wore a circlet of orange blossoms.

She was not tiny and pretty and sparkling like her sister. She was not blonde, shapely and laughing like Rosie. But Sarah's square-jawed face, with its high-planed cheekbones and its strong black brows, was poised. She radiated calm and determination. Frightened she might be, but Sarah Block was not about to let anyone know it. And Abraham was proud of her.

It was late when the family withdrew from Mr Tulipman's reading room, which had been made into a honeymoon chamber. Sarah sat on the edge of the bed with her back straight and her hands clasped in her lap. She wore a stiffly starched white nightgown that descended to her small white ankles. Her black hair tumbled around her shoulders.

Abraham took off his jacket and slipped his braces down. From the corner of his eye he saw Sarah tense. She bit her lip and raised her chin. Abraham felt profoundly sorry for her.

'Sarah, my dear,' he said, 'it's been a long day and you are exhausted. It is time you slept.'

He crossed over to the bed and sat down beside her. She gave him the first genuine smile he had ever had from her.

'Why don't you slip under the covers?' he said. He held them invitingly back for her.

'Rest!' he said and he lay down beside her on top of the covers, fully dressed.

'Go to sleep, little Mrs Block,' he said, 'it will all seem so much better in the morning.'

And so it did.

In the flurry of departure, as her father checked and re-checked their steamer tickets and her mother tried not to cry, Sarah saw that her new husband had decided to protect her. When voices were raised, he silenced them. When things were lost, he found them. And whenever he caught her eye, he smiled at her. When the time came for her to say goodbye to her mother and her sisters, she found Abraham's arm encircling her waist. On the dockside, as their fellow passengers jostled to climb the gangplank, Abraham blocked them and smilingly ushered her aboard.

When their cabins were allocated, they found that Mr Tulipman's adjoined theirs. They could hear him gargling and saying his prayers as they prepared for bed.

'It will be hard to say goodbye to my father in Jaffa,' said Sarah carefully, 'but I look forward to the time when we can be alone together.'

Abraham glanced at her.

'Don't you, Abraham?' said Sarah, and she gave him a small, contained smile.

'I do, my love,' he said. 'Very much indeed.'

When they docked in Mombasa on the 4th of August, Sarah was pregnant, though she did not know it.

And the First World War had been declared.

The Great Synagogue in Richon where Abraham and Sarah were married.

The Wedding of Abraham Block and Sarah Tulipman 26th July 1914.

On the front on the steps, the bride's sisters. Next to the bride, her mother Batsheva. To the left behind the groom, the bride's father. Behind the couple, with beard, the bride's grandfather Alexander Dockelman. Behind the bride, her elder sister Rivka. Old lady with the scarf, the bride's grandmother Itta Dockelman.

CHAPTER 54

ARRIVING IN BRITISH EAST AFRICA

The sudden disappointment of a hope leaves a scar which the ultimate fulfillment
of that hope never entirely removes.
–Thomas Hardy, novelist (1840-1928)

In Abraham's absence, Ettel, Samuel and Freda had moved in to a house in the Parklands district of Nairobi. The move had been planned before Abraham left for Europe. It had been Mr Jeevanjee who had suggested the house. He had built it.

'You can have it for a very reasonable rent, Mr Block, he had said, 'I wish to have you as my neighbour. We shall socialize, I will build a tennis court.'

The house stood not far from Ainsworth's Bridge on Crooked Lane. This was an exceptionally rough track and it swerved sharply halfway along its length to avoid one of the last remaining portions of Nairobi's swamp. This was little more than a pond, but it served as a watering hole for cattle, and people did their laundry there.

'Most unsavoury,' said Ettel.

'Useful,' said Samuel. Freda said nothing; she was relieved to have left the farm, every aspect of which she had hated.

Sarah and Abraham drew up outside the house in a pony and trap piled high with their luggage. Sarah stared at the house in disbelief. It was low and square and built from roughly-dressed stone. It had a corrugated iron roof pierced by a single redbrick chimney. The windows were fitted with warped wooden shutters; on the ledges was a collection of old tin cans planted with seedlings.

At the front of the house was an expanse of red earth where chickens scratched. There was a rough kennel with a rusty chain and a small white dog on the end of it. To one side of the house was a circle of round mud huts, smoke snaking from the holes in their conical roofs. Beside the front door was a ledge on which stood a row of dented milk churns. On the front step sat a fat African cook in a long dirty white robe. He was shelling peas.

Abraham jumped down from the trap. The cook looked up; he ran back into the house and could be heard shouting. Samuel Block appeared in the doorway. Behind him came Ettel in her rusty black silk gown. Samuel strode across the yard and clasped his son in an embrace. He smiled at Sarah over Abraham's shoulder.

Ettel glowered.

'Two weeks we have waited,' she said, 'no news, no telegram. What way is this for a son to treat his mother?' Her small black eyes raked Sarah who stood white-faced in the dusty yard.

'And *this* is the bride you have brought us?' said Ettel. Her tone was incredulous.

Samuel stepped forward and embraced Sarah.

'You have brought home a beauty, my son,' he said, 'is that not so, Wife?' He looked towards

Ettel. She stepped forward, her arms clamped firmly to her sides. Sarah moved to meet her and planted a small kiss on her cheek. Ettel smelt of camphor, and she emanated disapproval.

'You will call me Mother,' she said.

Sarah thought of the warmth of her own mother and pressed her lips together.

'Thank you, Mother,' she said.

Ettel turned and swept into the house. Samuel passed the back of his hand across his brow and exchanged a glance with Abraham.

Inside it was bleak. There was a scrubbed table surrounded by hoop-backed chairs, a dark and dirty fireplace with no fire laid, and a series of cupboards with wire-mesh doors. Padlocks hung from all of them. A large set of keys clanked at Ettel's waist.

The room was chill and it smelt of paraffin. Beyond it, a long stone-flagged passageway stretched away in to the gloom. Its walls were roughly limed and they had bubbled into blisters. All the doors in the passage were closed.

From the shadows, a slight young woman stepped forward.

'Sarah,' said Samuel, 'this is Freda, your new sister-in-law.' He gave Freda a small push in Sarah's direction. Freda embraced Sarah stiffly. Then she pulled away and rushed to embrace her brother.

Sarah was shown into a whitewashed room. It was empty but for an iron bedstead, a washstand, and an alcove fitted with a rail. Sarah sat on the edge of the bed and clasped her hands. Her mother had told her that Abraham Block was a great landowner, a man of wealth. If that was so, why had he brought her to this dismal house?

And why was she expected to share it with these cold-eyed in-laws?

She waited until the servants had deposited her trunks. She screwed her eyes tight; she could feel hot tears coming. Rubbing her nose with the back of her hand, she forced them back.

She could hear the voices of the Blocks echoing down the corridor, the occasional exclamation from Freda, a deep shout of laughter from Samuel. Pressing a hand to her forehead Sarah forced herself to think. She would write to her father and beg that he come and collect her. She would explain that Abraham had deceived them. She would leave this horrible place.

Sarah returned to the parlour and gave a small tight smile to her new family. She sat in silence as the ebb and flow of family conversation washed around her. Then, Samuel said something that caused her eyes to fly to his face.

'You were lucky to get here at all,' he said, 'Germany has declared war on France. So there will be no more ships in or out of Mombasa.'

'Our ship was full of German troops,' said Abraham, 'they seemed to think that war in East Africa was imminent. Will we be involved do you think?'

'Sir Edward Grey, the British Foreign Secretary has said that he will do everything in his power to avoid Britain's becoming involved in this imperialist squabble,' Samuel said, 'and the Tsar has agreed. It will blow over.'

The next morning, when Sarah entered the parlour, having delayed her arrival there for as long as she could, she found the Block family silent. Ettel was twisting her handkerchief; Samuel was staring out of the window. And Freda was crying. As his eyes fell on Sarah, Abraham's expression softened. He sighed and held out a hand towards her.

'I'm sorry, Sarah,' he said, 'Britain has declared war on Germany.'

The fact that an Austrian Archduke had been assassinated in the Balkans had not caused much of a stir in Nairobi. Indeed when the news that Europe was at war reached them, the members of Kenya's government were busily engaged in discussing whether or not there should be a closed season for duck shooting on Lake Naivasha. Nor was the news that British East Africa and German East Africa were now at war taken seriously.

'War?' said Tommy Wood, 'there won't be a war. Not in Africa at least.'

'It'll all be over by Christmas,' said Delamere.

The Governor of Kenya, Sir Henry Conway Belfield, agreed with him.

'Neither I, nor the British East African Protectorate have any interest in the war,' he said.

Governor Heinrich Schnee of German East Africa responded immediately.

'No action will be taken,' he said.

The two governors had met many times and they knew that neither of them had any troops to speak of.

'We shall remain neutral in accordance with the Congo Act of 1885,' said Sir Henry, 'it states very clearly that the colonies of warring nations should remain neutral in the event of a European war.'

'Gentlemen's agreement?' said Governor Schnee.

'Oh, absolutely,' said Sir Henry, 'but in the interests of being prepared I shall call for volunteers to protect the colony.'

Sir Henry's call was met with an immediate and overwhelming response; action and adventure was exactly the kind of thing the settler community relished. First to sign up for the protection of Kenya were the Boers.

Fourteen years earlier they had fought against the British, but now they were anxious to fight for them. The Boers had gathered for an agricultural meeting in the town of Eldoret when the news of Sir Henry's call for defenders of the realm reached them. With one accord they rushed out of the town hall, leapt on to their waiting mules and rode through the night to the railway station at Londiani. Thirty-six hours later they had arrived in Nairobi, dirty, unshaven and without money or weapons.

'Where's the fight?' they said.

They were not alone.

There was an immediate outbreak of patriotic fever.

CHAPTER 55

IN CROOKED LANE

Men are by nature merely indifferent to one another; but women are by nature enemies.
–Arthur Schopenhauer, German philosopher (1788-1860)

TWO DAYS AFTER HER ARRIVAL in Kenya, and a little over a month since she had first laid eyes on her husband, Sarah Block learned that Abraham had volunteered to defend the British Colony of Kenya.

'Why should you volunteer to fight their war?' she said, 'you're not even British?'

'It is my duty,' he said, 'I have no choice.'

'You'll go away! You'll leave me? Here? With them?' she said. She drew her dark brows together in disbelief.

'I will come back as soon as I can,' said Abraham, 'and find us a new home. I can see you are not happy here, but what choice do I have? I can't leave you alone in a new house, can I?'

She gazed at him.

'Can I, Sarah?' he said more softly.

Desolate, she shook her head.

The next morning Abraham mounted his pony. It was strung around with water bottles, blankets, and ammunition. He bent to kiss her goodbye.

When he had gone, Sarah remained standing in the middle of the road.

Watching from his workshop, Samuel waited until she turned back to the house, and then he walked to meet her.

'He'll be back soon enough,' he said, 'it'll be over before it's started. Everyone says so.'

She gave him a tight smile.

'Meanwhile,' said Samuel, 'I have something to show you.'

In one of the outhouses was a pony and a small trap with a black leather hood.

'It's for you,' said Samuel, 'I made it. I thought we could take a drive around Nairobi. Would that please you?'

Sarah's dark world brightened.

They left the grey house behind. On either side of the rust-red track stretched an avenue of jacaranda trees, their lilac blossoms arching over it. The sky was blue, the air clear. Outside Mr Ainsworth's hut, the Union Jack fluttered, and along the banks of the river clouds of butterflies swirled in columns of blue and yellow.

Beyond the bridge, shaded by eucalyptus trees, stood the Norfolk Hotel. And beyond the Norfolk stood the town. It seemed very large to Sarah. And very dirty and alien too. In a dusty shop in Government Road, she purchased a bolt of material. When she arrived back at the house she rolled it out on the kitchen table and began to cut it into curtain lengths.

'Your husband will not approve,' said Ettel, 'you don't need curtains.'

Abraham and Sarah Block in 1914

'I do need curtains,' said Sarah, 'I shall make them myself. And the money was a gift from my mother.'

The following day Sarah purchased some embroidery threads.

'More expenditure?' said Ettel.

'Only a small amount,' said Sarah with a sweet smile, 'to make some pretty things.'

'And where are the pretty things from your trousseau?' said Ettel, 'is your new family not to be allowed to enjoy them?'

'Abraham has said we will be moving into a new house soon,' said Sarah, 'I thought it was better to leave them packed.'

Ettel raised her brows.

'And what need do we have of a new house?' she said.

'I think Sarah means that she and Abraham need a new house,' said Freda.

Ettel's brows rose still further.

Sarah made no reply. She had learned that Samuel was her only friend, that Freda was jealous of his affection, and that Ettel would find fault wherever she could.

The next day she cooked a meal for the family in the traditional style of Rishon Le Zion.

'Too rich,' said Ettel. But she ate it.

Sarah made preserves.

'Mmm,' said Ettel grimacing. She pushed a pickled cucumber to the side of her plate.

'Freda! Bring me my recipe book,' she said.

Finally Sarah presented Ettel and Freda with some gifts she had stitched for them; there was a needle case for Freda and a spectacle case for Ettel.

'You would be better employed gardening than wasting time with such fripperies,' said Ettel.

3rd King's African Rifles on parade in Nairobi

Leaving Nairobi for the Taveta front (by kind permission Brian Stutchbury)

CHAPTER 56

THE ICE-CREAM WAR

There was never a good war or a bad peace
–Benjamin Franklin (1706-1790)

THE VOLUNTEER ENLISTMENT OFFICE[1] WAS not yet open. It stood on The Hill and hundreds of settlers were gathered outside it. Some of them were mounted on mules, others on polo ponies. Some of them had donkeys; others were on foot. Several came on bicycles; others on motorcycles. Some carried massive double-barrelled elephant guns; others had rifles. Most wore slouch hats or sun helmets; one man wore a flat cap. Some had their breeches tucked into puttees; and some wore gaiters. Most favoured a many-pocketed shooting jacket. But when one man cut the sleeves off his jacket, everyone else did likewise. Some strung bandoliers around their jackets; others wore a red scarf tied at its neck. Into every belt was thrust a selection of hunting knives. Footwear ranged from brogues to tennis shoes.

'More like a fancy dress party than a war,' said Tommy Wood.

When the Enlistment Office opened, the settlers gathered around their natural leaders, and a string of small regiments sprang up. There was Bowker's Horse, Arnoldi's Scouts, Ross's Scouts and Wessel's Scouts. The Boers declared themselves to be The Plateau South Africans.

Abraham was swept into the ranks of Bowker's Horse[2]. It was led by the towering figure of Russell Bowker. On his head he wore a snarling leopard's head and its tail hung down his back.

Berkeley Cole, Delamere's brother-in-law, arrived in command of eight hundred Somalis on mules. Cole wore a felt hat with a large ostrich feather drooping across one eye.

'Go on. Don't tell me! Berkeley's Beaus?' shouted Tommy Wood.

'Cole's Mounted Scouts,' said Cole coldly; he tossed his red Maasai cloak across his shoulder.

Delamere had no time for such posturing. He simply gathered together his Maasai warriors, loaded a mule and set off to scout the border.

'Never know when the square heads might come over it,' he said.

'They're calling it The Ice-Cream War3,' said Billy Judd.

'Why?' said Abraham.

'Have to be over soon, or we'll all melt in the sun.'

At the Norfolk Hotel Abraham found Major Ringer on the verandah. He was armed with a rifle and was standing guard over a small huddle of people.

'Prisoners of War,' he said importantly.

'Oh for goodness sake,' said Tommy Wood, 'that's poor old Dr Konrad Schauer and his wife you've got there. They wouldn't harm a fly. And what's poor old Rudolf Mayer done? He's only the Editor of *The East African Standard*?'

'He has a printing press, he is German, and he may print maps,' said Major Ringer.

'And who's that other fellow?' Said Tommy.

Leaving Nairobi for the Taveta front (by kind permission Brian Stutchbury)

'Turkish Ali,' said the Major.

'But he signed up with us for Bowker's Horse,' said Tommy Wood.

'That was before we knew that Turkey was on the other side,' said the Major.

'What will you do with them?' said Abraham.

'Intern them as Enemies of the Empire,' said Major Ringer.

'Where?'

'Detention barracks behind the Nairobi Club', said the Major. He glared at Abraham.

'Your pals Markus and Loy are being put in there too,' he said.

Abraham changed the subject before the Major could decide that he too was an Enemy of the Empire.

'Do you know where we go now, Major?' he said.

'Racecourse,' said Major Ringer.

'Why?'

'New training ground for the East African Mounted Rifles,' said the Major.

'Who are they?' said Abraham.

'You are,' said the Major, 'the Governor has decided to merge all the battalions into one. Create a crack fighting force. We'll show those square heads.'

Arriving at the racecourse, Abraham found the crack fighting force milling about aimlessly. In the jockey's weighing room, odd items of uniform were being handed out; they seemed principally to be red flannel spine pads, khaki shorts and white sun helmets. On the track, tea was being brewed. Rumour was rife.

'So who, exactly, are we fighting?' said Tommy Wood.

'The forces of German East Africa led by General Paul von Lettow Vorbeck[4],' said Billy Judd.

'And what's he got?'

'Two hundred and sixty German soldiers, 2,472 African troops, forty rifles and seventy machine guns.'

'And what have we got?' said Abraham.

'Seven hundred local troops, three hundred Kings African Rifles, and us,' said Billy Judd

'Have we any weapons?'

'Whatever we can cobble together ourselves, two Maxim guns bolted on to a Model T Ford, and two Hotchkiss guns that haven't been fired since 1891, and they jammed then,' said Billy.

'So we're fairly evenly matched then?' Said Abraham.

'Difficult to say, but we're expecting reinforcements from India. And the German East Africans have got an air force,' said Billy.

'An air force?'

'Well only if you believe all the sightings of bright lights moving around in the Northern Frontier District,' said Billy.

'Are they not to be believed?'

'Well, Berkeley Cole sent a brigade of his Mounted Scouts out to the border yesterday, to prevent the German planes from landing.'

'What happened?'

'It was a forty mile journey and their mules refused to gallop. Devil of a job getting them to do so at the best of times.'

Captain Denys Finch Hatton (right) and Captain Appleby (by kind permission of Brian Stutchbury and Sue Deverall)

'About the air force?'

'Turned out the bright lights in the north were Venus.'

The next day, a trooper was arrested for firing his rifle in the night.

'Said he was firing at the plane that was firing at him,' said Billy, 'turned out it wasn't a plane but a crested crane. They've already made up a rhyme about it.'

'A rhyme?' said Abraham.

'Yes, it's quite good actually. It goes like this:

I thought I saw an aeroplane

Upon the Athi plain:

I looked again and saw it was

A Kavirondo crane.'

Royal Navy Air Service Caudron G3 taking off on the Taveta front

Loading the mules on the train (by kind permission Sue Deverall)

CHAPTER 57

IN THE EAST AFRICAN MOUNTED RIFLES

Military intelligence is a contradiction in terms.
–Groucho Marx, (1890-1977)

THE EAST AFRICAN MOUNTED RIFLES were camped at the racecourse where they were being trained by a group of officers from the King's African Rifles. The more aristocratic members of the EAMR moved into the Norfolk Hotel, where parties were held nightly.

'Heard the latest?' said Denys Finch Hatton, 'Troopers Ridley and Thomson were found missing from their posts last night. Their commanding officer asked where they were, and somebody said, "they're at a party at Government House but H.E.'s promised to send them home early in his car".

The EAMR were not the only troops to be camped at the racecourse. There was also the East African Transport Corps, which was largely ox-carts; the East African Regiment, which was a settler's infantry unit; the East African Medical Corps, which was an odd collection of doctors and nurses; the East African Pioneer Corps, which was all African; the East African Motor Transport Corps, which was made up of settlers, most of whom had to be taught to drive; and the Carrier Corps, made up of three thousand African porters.

There was also The East African Lancers, which was commanded by an ex-lancer who insisted on his men carrying lances, but since no such things existed they had to be made out of bamboo poles with red and white pennants attached.

After three weeks, the troops were told that their training was complete.

'Your training is finished,' said the commanding officer, 'but do not leave with the impression that you are trained. You are not.'

'We're having a passing out parade,' said Billy Judd, 'outside the Norfolk Hotel. The Governor's going to address us.'

Abraham and Billy Judd arrived outside the Norfolk Hotel with the rest of their platoon and lined up alongside the white picket fence. They were mounted and carried water, ammunition and food.

'I've been cheated,' said the man next to Abraham, 'I bought this mule from a Syrian outside the Indian Bazaar.'

'Uh huh,' said Abraham.

'He said it was broken in,' said the man, 'and it seemed fine at first, trotted nice as you like. But then it seemed to go stark raving mad.'

Abraham surveyed the beast. It seemed docile enough.

'Oh, I know what you're thinking,' said the man, 'its as quiet as a mouse now, but the minute it sees the red and white handkerchiefs those idiot lancers have stuck on their poles it bucks like a bronco. It's had me off twice already.'

At the end of the parade, the Governor, Sir Henry Belfield, took the salute. He was clad in a Norfolk shooting jacket, a pair of cycling breeches and a large white sun helmet; and he had a monocle screwed into his left eye. As he dismissed the troops somebody shouted, 'Three cheers for the Governor!'

The crowd roared.

The lancers raised their lances, and the mules bolted.

The troops reassembled at Nairobi Railway Station.

'Do we know where we're going?' said Abraham

'German border at Kajiado,' said one of his fellow troopers, a rather laconic fellow by the name of Bob Hawke who had a cigarette perpetually stuck in the corner of his mouth.

'Rumour has it we'll have conquered German East Africa by next week,' said Ridley Scott; another member of Abraham's platoon, 'What a lark!'

When the troops descended from the train at Kajiado they found the place to be little more than a collection of railway houses. Parched bush stretched in all directions.

Abraham led his pony down the platform. It was thronged with mules, oxen and men and the latter seemed to be in jovial mood. As they jostled their way off the platform, Bob Hawkes slipped his arms into the straps of his accordion and played the opening bars of the anthem of the American Civil War, *When we were marching through Georgia*.

Obligingly the troops broke into their newly composed song.

'Hurray! Hurray! We're off to G.E.A.

Hurray! Hurray! The square heads we will slay.

Ands so we sing this happy song

Upon this happy day

As we go marching to Tabora.'

The happy days were short lived. The bush was thick and the men had to hack their way through it. The thorns tore at their hands and feet and the wounds festered. Tsetse flies stung all day, mosquitoes whined all night. There was not enough water. The men began to go down with malaria, yellow fever and black water fever. Then dysentery set in. There were no medical supplies and no stretcher-bearers.

The army had departed in haste and without proper supplies, so it lived off what it could carry or shoot. But shooting became impossible in the dense bush. Within a week the army was marching on a bowl of biltong soup a day.

As the troops crossed the border into German East Africa, the pack animals began to die of starvation, thirst and fever. The mules dropped one by one, and the vultures descended to strip their flesh; soon the army's progress was marked by a trail of rotting carcasses.

The men slept beneath the stars using their saddles as pillows, but many awoke to find that the saddles had been dragged from beneath their heads by hyenas. Lions stalked the army. At night their yellow eyes could be seen gleaming in the bush, but nobody dared to fire on them for fear of alerting the German troops. So they threw stones at them instead.

After a few weeks, word came that Bowker's Horse was to return to the railhead.

'Why?' asked Abraham.

'Seems the Germans have attacked the town of Kisumu, and there are no troops stationed

Abraham Block (far right with mule) and fellow members of the East African Mounted Rifles

up there on our side of Lake Victoria, so they're sending us,' said Ridley Scott. He relit a cigarette butt.

Bowker's Horse fought its way back down the line of dead mules and bloated oxen carcasses. But now there were dead men lying alongside them. At first the men of Bowker's Horse tried to bury the corpses, but there were so many of them that in the end they were forced to leave them where they lay, being consumed by ants.

Slumped on his pony in the punishing heat, Abraham saw a dead face he recognized. It was that of Lionel, the eighteen-year-old son of Leslie Tarleton, the safari outfitter. One of the foot soldiers stooped over the corpse. When he stood up, he had Lionel's hunting knife, his water bottle and a strip of dried meat in his hands.

The trooper glanced up at Abraham.

'My need is greater than his,' he said, 'and where he's gone he won't care.'

Abraham shrugged and rode on.

The acacia bush was wreathed in delicate white blossom, and its sweet scent laced the stink of decay. Bowker's Horse arrived at the railhead exhausted and sick to its stomach. The men were silent on the train. War, Abraham reflected, was a lark no longer.

When the train reached Kisumu, the troops were loaded directly on to a small steamer; it had once belonged to the Uganda Railway and had run a shuttle service between the Kenyan and Ugandan sides of the lake. The steamer had the name *Winifred* on its hull, and a rusted gun lashed to its deck. Standing in its prow with his pony, Abraham surveyed the lake. Nothing could have appeared more peaceful. The sky was a deep, cloudless blue. The lake sparkled, the hippos wallowed in the shallows, and a skein of sacred ibis flew shrieking overhead.

When the *Winifred* reached the Ugandan shore she found it silent, thick with banana plantations, lush and green. A small gunboat pulled almost lazily out of the reeds and headed towards them.

It was a German gunboat.

'Man the Hotchkiss!' came the cry.

Men rushed to swing the rusted gun around to face the gunboat.

'Fire!'

'It's jammed, sir,' said a lad little out of his teens.

With a sense of unreality, Abraham realized that the German gunboat was firing on them. He ducked below the sides of the steamer and pulled the mule's head down with him.

Bullets whined overhead.

A mule brayed.

'Turn her around!' came the command.

Amid a hail of bullets, the *Winifred* wallowed her way around in a clumsy circle and steamed back in the direction she had come. Gingerly, Abraham raised his head and looked back.

The men on the deck of the German gunboat were cheering.

At dawn the following day, Bowker's Horse was ordered back on to the *Winifred*. But this time she was accompanied by the *Kavirondo*, a larger steamer with two guns bolted to her decks.

'Now we'll get the bastards,' said someone.

On the Ugandan shore, the reed beds lay silent; and the lake flies swarmed in black columns. On the deck of the *Winifred* the troops waited as a landing party was sent ashore in a rowing boat. When they returned, they reported that the Germans had evacuated overnight.

Bowker's Horse cheered.

'First battle won against the Germans!' said Ridley Scott.

'I don't think we're fighting the Germans,' said Abraham.

'Well who the hell are we fighting then?

'The African bush,' said Abraham.

Berkeley Cole in the uniform of the Somali Scounts (by kind permission of Brian Stutchbury and Sue Deverall)

Images from the Ice-Cream War (by kind permission of Brian Stutchbury and Sue Deverall)

CHAPTER 58

THE BATTLE FOR THE BUNDU

War does not determine who is right - only who is left.
–Bertrand Russell, British philosopher (1874-1936)

Bowker's Horse returned to Kajiado and limped its way back along the grim line of corpses to rejoin the army. They found it depleted, emaciated and wild eyed. The men had been assailed by sunstroke, gangrene and dysentery; they had been charged by rhinos, bitten by snakes, and stung by scorpions. They had been attacked by rampaging packs of baboons whose yellow teeth and sharp nails could tear a man's stomach open. Shiny-black rivers of soldier ants had marched through the encampments devouring everything that lay in their path. One man had wakened to find his body a writhing mass of ants. He had screamed and his comrades had doused him in petrol. 'Got a light, boy?' had said the platoon wag with the gallows humour that only war can breed.

The border with German East Africa was a hellish place; and Abraham believed that every day there would be his last. He was dry-mouthed and covered in suppurating sores; he was caked in dust and, as his blisters festered, and the cut on his arm began to smell of corruption, he found that he didn't really care whether he lived or died.

Abraham was one of the last men in his platoon to remain mounted; everyone else's mounts had died; and the jokers had renamed the platoon Bowker's Foot. Abraham used the ration of paraffin intended to fuel his lantern to rub down his pony at night.

'Why are you doing that, Block?' asked Bob Hawkes.

'Stop it being bitten by tsetse,' Abraham replied.

'But you can't see your hand in front of your face when night falls,' said Bob.

'I can see you're on foot,' said Abraham.

As the heat rose and the supplies of water dwindled, the working life of a mule shrank to just six weeks. And when they became so thin that they could no longer carry a load, the mules were shot and their carcasses were dragged out of camp; but before they could be burned, most were butchered for their meat. As the pack animals died, their role was taken over by the African soldiers of the Carrier Corps. They worked under appalling conditions; they were resourceful and uncomplaining, and they died in thousands.

'Poor blighters are at the beck and call of everyone,' said Tommy Wood, 'and they achieve the well nigh impossible all the time.'

'And it's not even their war,' said Bob Hawkes.

For many months the EAMR pursued the German *Schuztruppe* in and out of the bush, and back and forth across the border. It was a bitter game of cat and mouse, and both sides fought in a vacuum without any idea of what was happening outside their small arena of war.

In 1915 the long-awaited British reinforcements arrived from India and the bush was flooded

On the Taveta Front (by kind permission Brian Stutchbury)

with Rajput, Punjabi and Baluchi warriors in turbans and pantaloons.

'They're about as much use as a polar bear in the Sahara,' said Tommy Wood, 'they don't speak the lingo, they don't understand the territory, and they have no idea what to do with a charging rhino.'

'And you do?' said Bob Hawke.

In May 1915 a message came down the line from the railhead.

'For you, Block,' said Abraham's commanding officer.

It was from Samuel.

'Sarah about to give birth,' was all that it said.

Abraham stared at the words for a long time. Then he saddled up his pony and rode up to the field headquarters.

'My wife is about to give birth,' he said to the colonel, 'I didn't even know she was pregnant. May I have compassionate leave?'

'Luckily for you, Block' said the colonel, 'I've got more bloody Indians than I know what to do with. Go before I change my mind.'

Abraham rode for three days and nights through a landscape strewn with carcasses, burning pyres, shell cases, and burial parties.

When he strode into the house in Parklands. Ettel was in the kitchen.

'You could have—' she began.

'Where is she?' Abraham said, and he pushed his mother out of the way.

'I was about to tell you, my son, had you not pushed me aside,' said Ettel. She folded her arms and assumed a stubborn expression; and then she saw the look on his face.

'Your wife is with Lily at the farm,' she said.

'Why?' said Abraham.

'She said she needed someone to tell her what to do,' said Ettel, 'what nonsense! Every woman should know what to do. I did.'

Russel Bowker and his troops

233

Denys Finch Hatton interrogating a mutineer from the Somali Scouts (by kind permission of Brian Stutchbury and Sue Deverall)

CHAPTER 59

THE FIRST OF A DYNASTY

Listen to the cry of a woman in labour at the hour of giving birth - look at the dying man's struggle at his last extremity, and then tell me whether something that begins and ends thus could be intended for enjoyment.

–Soren Kierkegaard, Danish philosopher (1813-1855)

IT WAS LATE IN THE evening when Abraham arrived at the Limuru farm. The lamps had been lit and pools of light spilled out into the yard. In the kitchen, large black pans rattled on the range, and towels hung from the drying rack hoisted above it. Only Elijah, the cook, was in the room.

'*Bwana*[1]!' he said, 'God is great!' Only two of his teeth remained and spittle spumed down his chin as he spoke.

'Where is the *memsahib*?' said Abraham.

Elijah pointed down the corridor, 'First born coming,' he said, 'coming now.'

An iron bedstead stood in the centre of the room; and Sarah lay propped on a mountain of pillows. A grey-haired lady knitted in the corner.

'Abraham!' said Lily, 'Thank God!'

Abraham embraced his sister and strode over to his wife. Sarah was drenched in sweat, her hair matted around her face.

'We waited for you,' she said and clung to his hand.

It was not an easy birth. For an entire day the house rang with Sarah's screams. Elijah keened in the kitchen, boiling water, and rocking Lily's newborn son, Arthur. In the yard Corren howled. In the paddock the horses laid back their ears and flared their nostrils.

Abraham and Lily held Sarah as the pain wrenched her. She jabbered in terror. She begged them to stop its terrible roiling, ripping horror; but they could not. Granny Shelton[2], the midwife, had a watch pinned to her apron; she timed the contractions and she signaled the onslaught of the next one with a terse nod. With every one, Sarah grew weaker.

'Send for Dr Burkitt[3],' said Granny Shelton eventually.

Abraham ran from the room, when he returned he said, 'Simon has gone on the Harley Davidson.'

'How long will it be before the doctor arrives?' said Lily.

'The roads are bad. An hour? Maybe two?' said Abraham.

Sarah reared up between them. She arched her back and screamed.

'She can't stand much more of this!' said Abraham.

'Yes she can,' said Lily 'she's stronger than you think.' She mopped Sarah's brow and crooned over her. 'There's nothing little Mrs Sarah Block can't take, is there my love?' she said.

It was dawn when Dr Roland Burkitt arrived. He was clad in a Jaeger dressing gown, carpet slippers and a red scarf. He had received the call at five in the morning; and this was the time at which he conducted his bible studies.

'Cold water!' he yelled, 'Now!'

'Kill or Cure Burkitt' was famous for his belief in the power of cold water, which he used to cure anything from malaria to miscarriage.

'Out of the way woman!' he said, elbowing Granny Shelton aside, 'and get those sheets off your wife,' he said to Abraham, 'Now! Spray her with cold water, man. Go on! Do it!'

An hour later, streaked red and white like a raspberry plucked from a bowl of cream, Rita Block was torn from her mother and thrust into the arms of Granny Shelton.

In the silence that followed the birth, Sarah lay in a stupor. Lily and Abraham lay slumped in their chairs staring at the ceiling; and Dr Burkitt sat in his nightshirt with a towel around his shoulders. Granny Shelton fanned herself with her knitting.

'That's my last birth,' she said, 'I'm too old.'

Rita Rachel Block was swaddled in a towel, and she lay in a drawer that Lily had wrenched from the dresser.

Abraham remained with his wife and daughter for a period of six weeks but at its end, he rode into Nairobi, and when he returned his face was grim.

'I asked for a discharge,' he said, 'but they're sending me back to the battle front.'

'Where?' said Lily.

'Dar es Salaam,' he said.

'Is that bad?'

'It's not good,' said Abraham, but we'll put a brave face on it for Sarah's sake.'

An hour later he was gone.

Sarah stood in the yard and watched as Abraham and his pony disappeared down the lane. Lily stood next to her; she had baby Arthur on one arm, and baby Rita on the other.

Simon Haller had been called up for military service the week before.

'I'm not going back to my mother-in-law and the Nairobi house,' said Sarah.

'No,' said Lily, 'I'm pregnant again, and we have four farms to run between us.'

CHAPTER 60

CLOSE UNTO DEATH

War is not an adventure. It is a disease. It is like typhus.
–Antoine de Saint-Exupery, French novelist, (1900-1944)

THE TRAIN WAS FULL OF troops.

'What's the latest?' asked Abraham of those who shared his carriage.

'Same as always,' said one, 'cat and mouse. Huns pop up. We charge after them. They disappear; those in charge call it "tip and run". The only winner is the bloody bundu. But that South African, Jan Smuts, has taken over from the Indians. Sent 'em packing.'

'Not a bad thing by all accounts,' said Abraham.

'Don't know about that,' said the trooper, chewing on his cigarette, 'better the bloody coolies in the line of fire than us, don't you think?'

'I'm not sure who "us" is anymore,' said Abraham.

'South Africans, Rhodesians, Belgians, Brits, Africans, you name it: they're all running around in the bush.'

Another trooper joined the discussion.

'Yup, there's two thousand of us by all accounts,' he said, 'but at least we've got that slippery bastard, von Lettow, hemmed in on all sides.'

'We've been saying that for the last two years,' said Abraham.

'We've got him this time, though,' said the trooper, 'the port of Dar es Salaam is blockaded. He hasn't had supplies for months. Can't go on much longer.'

'Trouble is, the bastard makes his own supplies,' said the first trooper, 'makes gunpowder, makes bandages out of rice. Makes quinine out of tree bark; they call it von Lettow's schnapps.'

'Rumour has it he's only got one car left' said the other man, 'and it's held together with string.'

'Won't stop him,' said Abraham, 'nothing will.'

He was right. The so-called 'Forgotten War' raged for another two years as von Lettow fought a series of heroic if crazed rearguard actions. He was supported by a few German officers, his ferociously loyal African troops, and ten guns salvaged from the sunken battleship *SMS Konigsberg*, each of which took 400 porters to haul it through the bush.

By 1917 von Lettow had been forced to retreat into Portuguese East Africa, and from there he was harried into Northern Rhodesia. Just as he was planning to blow up the gold mines, von Lettow received news that Germany had surrendered. It came several days late, but with typical cool von Lettow donned what remained of his uniform and had his staff push his car to the British post at Abercorn. After four years of combat the war had cost the allies nine hundred and seventy six officers, 17,650 men, 44,572 African porters, 60,000 horses and mules, and 120,000 oxen.

It had also nearly cost Abraham Block his life.

The troops hung over the side of the ship as it entered the bay off Dar es Salaam, in Tanganyika. The waters were riddled with wrecks, which reared out of the waves snapping like rusted sharks. Abraham peered through a porthole as the blur of blue, silver and gold sharpened into a coastline.

Dar es Salaam, the former German stronghold, had been reduced to rubble by the bombardment of the British Navy. The shell of the Governor's palace stood on the headland, its flagpole sticking up like a splintered match. Below it wallowed the hulk of a scuttled German freighter, the waves crashing over its decks and blowing spumes of foam up through its funnel.

The troop ship dropped anchor in the bay and swung on her chains as a flotilla of launches cast off from the remains of the docks. Abraham clambered down the oily nets that hung from its sides and hung there until a small launch appeared beneath him.

The dockside of Dar es Salaam lay in ruins. Rickshaws darted in all directions. Mule carts tangled with donkeys, and the air was thick with the smell of oil, rotten fish and decayed fruit. With his uniform now plastered to his back, Abraham shouldered his kit bag and walked up the beach.

An officer with a clipboard held up a hand to stop him.

'Papers?' he said, and Abraham handed them to him.

'Mgorogoro,' said the officer, 'Train. Straight ahead.'

The station had been shelled, but somehow it had managed to retain something of the air of a Bavarian chalet. It had a long platform with a glass roof, large segments of which had been blown away. An assortment of troops shuffled along the platform; there were Boers, Indians, Belgians and British.

'Where are we going?' Abraham asked one of them.

'Headquarters of General Van Deteren at Mgorogoro,' he was told.

'How long will it take?'

'Who bloody knows mate?'

Abraham hurled his kitbag into the luggage rack of the soot-grimed railway carriage. He slumped down on the hard wooden bench. The humidity was high and he was dripping in sweat. Unaccountably, he began to shiver, and his teeth chattered.

'You alright mate?' asked one of the troopers.

Abraham nodded.

'You look bloody ghastly.'

Abraham huddled into a corner and tried to sleep.

His head ached and he felt nauseous.

Night had fallen when Abraham awoke, and the train was still moving. Peering through the bars at the window, he could see rows of coconut palms, their trunks thick and grey like a forest of elephant legs. From time to time a large white plantation house would flash out of the gloom. As the gradient of the track increased so the labour of the train intensified until it was puffing and panting along at a snail's pace. It toiled through countless small stations but it rarely stopped other than to take on water from vast canvas pipes, which hung like elephant trunks across the

Red Cross hospital ship in Dar es Salaam harbour

lines. As it did so, billows of steam blew back down its length, and into the carriages. Abraham wondered if it was the steam that was causing the faces of his fellow troopers to swing in and out of focus. He slumped forward.

'Watch out, mate!'

'He's going!'

'Catch him!'

'Oh my Gawd! That's all I need down my uniform.'

The train was stationary and empty. Abraham could see a platform with people hurrying along it. Doors banged. He was lying on the floor, but he could not move. Along the corridor came the patter of bare feet. Two porters struggled to introduce a long stretcher into the confined space of the carriage. As they lifted him on to it, Abraham tried to speak, but they seemed not to hear him.

The next time Abraham awoke he was enveloped in white. There were white ceilings, white walls and white-clad people. A white enamel lampshade hung high above his head and its light hurt his eyes. White rails stood at the foot of his bed. Shoes squeaked on linoleum and the air was laced with the smell of disinfectant.

A face appeared above him. It was black and it smiled. For a second or two, it blotted out the light, and the pain receded. Then the face moved and the pain returned.

For how long he hung in the white limbo of Dodoma Military Hospital, Abraham did not know. He swallowed alternate doses of quinine and Epsom salts, and at the end of it all he found that his malaria had turned into black water fever.

'You're lucky,' said the doctor, some weeks later, 'black water fever is nearly always fatal.'

Abraham regarded him through half-closed eyes. The brightness was unbearable and his eyeballs swam in tears.

'What happens to me now?' he said.

'Train to Dar. Ship to Mombasa,' said the doctor, 'your war is over.'

'Thank God,' said Abraham.

'Still think there is one?' said the doctor.

He turned to his orderly, 'stretcher to the train for this one, quick as you like,' he said.

The train rattled its way down the track to Dar es Salaam, but all that Abraham saw of the journey was the roof of the carriage. He was lashed to a stretcher and swaddled in a sheet. Sometimes an orderly would pass by and force a tin mug between his lips. Abraham grew to dread this because his cracked lips bled. His tongue was swollen and stuck like a slug to the roof of his mouth.

In Dar es Salaam, the train shunted back and forth, spewed steam, whistled and drew to a halt. Abraham's stretcher was carried to the dockside and deposited beneath a palm-thatched awning. His feet were bare and a brown manila tag had been tied to his toe. The flies swarmed around his filthy sheets; he allowed them to feast on the skin that flaked off his face.

The sun inched its way slowly below the fronds of palm thatch.

Without warning Abraham's stretcher was hoisted into the air. His body slithered down its length and crumpled at its foot. The orderlies staggered up the gangplank of a ship. One held his feet, the other his head. The stretcher was chained to the rails on the deck of a ship; and Abraham heard the orderlies laughing as they padded away.

He watched as the sky turned from blue to indigo; and the ship cast off.

From below came a stench so thick that it seemed to cling and coat everything it touched. As the ship rolled with the pitch of the waves, a chorus of groans rose from the hold.

Later, Abraham learned that the troops were jammed so tightly in its fetid darkness that all those who didn't have dysentery when they set sail from Dar es Salaam had got it by the time they arrived in Mombasa.

It came as no surprise to him to learn that he had it too.

CHAPTER 61

A SICKLY CHILD

Intelligent people know of what they speak; fools speak of what they know.
–Minchas Shabbos Pirkei Avos, *Ethics of the Fathers 3:18*

WHEN ABRAHAM LEFT THE KIAMBU farm to return to the war, Rita screamed. And thereafter, day in day out, she screamed, until her small red face was dominated by the square black hole of her mouth. Nothing that Sarah or Lily could do would stop her. Only Elijah could silence her by walking her up and down the kitchen, and singing to her.

Then one day Rita stopped screaming and fell silent.

And that was much worse.

Sarah sent for Dr Burkitt, but by the time he arrived Rita had turned yellow and her small fists lay clenched on her blanket.

'Mmm,' he said, 'my guess is she's got jaundice, is she feeding properly?'

'No,' said Sarah, 'I can hardly get her to take any milk at all.'

'I'm no paediatrician', said Dr Burkitt, frowning, 'but I know you need to get this child to Dr Cook as fast as you can.'

'Where will I find him?' said Sarah.

'Kampala,' said Dr Burkitt.

Sarah stared at him, 'Kampala, Uganda?' she said.

'Yes, my dear, I'm afraid so,' said Dr Burkitt. 'Pack a bag, take a friend, go on the train to Kisumu, take the steamer across the lake and a rickshaw from Entebbe in to Kampala. I'll cable Dr Cook today and tell him to expect you.

'But—'

'But don't waste time, my dear. You don't have it.'

Lily found Sarah sitting at the kitchen table with her head in her hands. Sarah recounted the conversation.

'Dr Burkitt said I had to take a friend,' she said, bleakly, 'but I don't have one.'

'Don't be ridiculous,' said Lily, 'you will travel there with Eddie Ruben[1].'

'Eddie Ruben?' said Sarah, 'Simon's nephew? But he's only seventeen and he doesn't speak English.'

'Yes he does. He's been here three years. And if he managed to get here from the Ukraine, he can get you and Rita to Kampala.'

Eddie, Archie, Charlie and David Ruben had arrived in Kenya the week before their uncle, Simon Haller, had married Lily Block. Since they were all below the age of twelve, Lily had brought them up. But she had not complained; they were tough, rosy-cheeked Ukrainian farm boys, perpetually hungry, perpetually scrape-kneed and perpetually cheerful.

Eddie Ruben in the Ukraine

In August 1914, though technically too young to enlist, Eddie had signed up to join the East African Mounted Rifles. Some weeks later, when training had already begun, his commanding officer pulled up short in front of him.

'How old are you lad?' he said.

Still not fluent in English, Eddie remained silent.

'Not old enough to fight,' said the officer.

The boy's face fell.

'Never mind,' continued the officer, 'I've got just the job for you.'

So it was that Eddie Ruben became a prison warder at the POW internment camp in the stables of The Nairobi Club.

During his time in Nairobi, Eddie Ruben had taken up lodgings with Michael Harrtz[2], who was also from the Ukraine. Michael had arrived in Nairobi in 1901 and had taken up residence in a tent in the backyard of Mr Markus's hardware store. From there he had offered his services as a tinsmith and, in a town largely built from tin, he had done well. He had acquired business premises and had rented a ramshackle house overlooking the racecourse. One day, while pacing its echoing corridors Michael Harrtz came to a decision. The following morning he went to Nairobi's central post office and sent a cable to his hometown in the Ukraine.

'Have need of wife,' it said, 'young, healthy and able to cook.'

He thought it stated the facts clearly enough.

When she arrived, Gertrude was all of these things. But where her bridegroom was small and slight, with hunched shoulders and spindly legs, Gertrude was hefty of bosom and had arms like hams. Where Michael was pale and drawn, Gertrude was rounded and rosy, and where he was shy and retiring, she had a laugh like a donkey and a voice that boomed like a bittern.

They fell instantly in love.

The Harrtz household was shambolic. Shortly after Eddie had taken up lodgings there, so had his three younger brothers, and they had strewn the house with schoolbooks, satchels, cricket bats and muddy boots. Michael Harrtz reveled in the chaos and thought himself a lucky man.

Sarah arrived outside the Harrtz household to collect Eddie Ruben. Rita lay limp and yellow in her arms; Sarah had a small valise in one hand and a straw boater pinned to her dark hair.

There was no one in sight.

Gertie's broad Slavic face rose from the onion beds of her front garden.

'Oh my dear,' she said, 'there you are! I'll make tea. Eddie's shift will be over in an hour and then he'll be home.' She ushered Sarah into the house and swept aside balls of knitting wool and seed packets from the sofa.

'Sit down, my dear,' she said, 'and tell me all about it.'

Eddie Ruben, Sarah and Gertie went to Nairobi Railway Station together. The train to Kampala was to travel through the night, so they arrived there in the evening. As the steam began to billow back down the train, Gertie helped Sarah aboard. Eddie was already in the carriage strapping the luggage into the overhead racks.

'You'll be back in no time,' said Gertie, 'Eddie will take care of you.'

As the train pulled out of the station, Eddie took the baby from Sarah; he settled it competently in the crook of his arm, and he seemed much more proficient with babies than she was. Handsome, open faced, broad shouldered and utterly guileless, Eddie reminded her of her brother, David Tulipman.

'Now Mrs Block,' said Eddie, 'you leave everything to me. I may be only seventeen but now that my prisoners of war have been shipped to India, I'm off to join the Royal North Lancashire Regiment.'

Sarah stared at him and ventured a small smile.

'You are?' she said.

'I am,' said Eddie. He thought how very pretty little Mrs Block was.

'And I'm to have my own batman, free lime-juice, half-a-bottle of whisky a day, and excellent pay,' he said, 'So, you see, Mrs Block, escorting you to Kampala, is child's play.'

'Yes,' said Sarah, 'I can see that,' and she closed her eyes.

All through the night, the train ground its way up the harsh gradients of the Great Rift Valley, and then it coasted its way down to Kisumu on the shores of Lake Victoria. It was unbearably hot and humid. The passengers bound for Kampala were shepherded across a tangle of railway tracks to the quayside; and by the time they had arrived there, they were drenched in sweat. A small steamer was moored alongside the quay; in its prow was a large machine gun.

When they landed in Entebbe, Eddie secured a rickshaw and handed Sarah into it. He shouldered the baby with professional aplomb, and gave directions to Kampala's Military Hospital. They made a quaint couple. Sarah, in her high-necked white blouse and her straight black skirt, looked little more than a girl. Eddie stood tall in his uniform, and his large sun helmet shadowed his face. Anyone seeing them would have thought them to be man and wife.

An overhead fan whirred from the ceiling of the room in the military hospital and the flies droned as they hurled themselves against its dirty windows. When her name was called, Sarah took the baby from Eddie and told him to remain behind.

She was relieved that she had done so.

'Unbutton your blouse, Mrs Block,' said Dr Cook after he had examined the baby.

Blushing scarlet, Sarah did as she was told. She looked away as the doctor ran his hands over her swollen breasts.

'Hmm. Nothing untoward there,' he said.

He turned back to the baby; she lay lifeless and glassy-eyed on the galvanized table.

'But that won't help this little lass,' he said.

He yanked a book off a shelf and flipped through it; then he snapped it decisively shut.

'Right,' he said, 'I'm putting her on a strict diet. Full cream cow's milk, pulped beetroot, pureed pumpkin and minced liver. My wife will show you how to prepare the food this evening. You and your husband will stay the night with us, and you can return to Nairobi in the morning.'

'He's not my husband,' said Sarah.

Dr Cook raised an eyebrow.

'My husband is in Dar es Salaam, fighting the war,' said Sarah, 'Eddie is…'

She faltered and blushed.

'Yes, well never mind what Eddie is, my dear,' said Dr Cook, 'I'm sure you'll sort it out for yourselves sooner or later.'

Back in Nairobi, Sarah was sure of one thing: Eddie was indispensible.

Only in Eddie's arms would Rita sleep, and only from Eddie would she take her food; she seemed to have no need of her mother at all. But Sarah didn't care, because Rita was recovering.

Gertrude Harrtz invited Sarah to remain with them in the Nairobi house. She prepared a bright room with blue and white gingham curtains. There was a cradle in one corner.

'The only thing is, my dear,' said Gertie, 'the baby's diet is all very well, but we are going to have to buy a cow.'

They took the pony and trap to a farm at the foot of the Ngong Hills where Michael Harrtz had a friend called Tom Bell[3] who was selling off his herd so that he might go into tea. He brought out a black and white cow with short curled horns and a ring through her nose.

'Best milker I have,' he said, 'and I will tell your husband so when I see him.'

'Will you see my husband?' said Sarah, confused.

'Bound to,' said Tom Bell, 'I'm off to Dar es Salaam to fight the Germans.'

CHAPTER 62

BACK HOME

A Hospital is no place to be sick.
–Samuel Goldwyn, Hollywood producer, (1882-1974)

ABRAHAM LAY ON THE DOCKSIDE in Mombasa and stared at the sky. Indian crows cawed amid the palm fronds. He was still lashed to his stretcher but nobody came near him. He wasn't surprised. He was soiled and he stank.

It was hot. He had a clawing, scouring pain in his bowels and he was desperate for water. But nobody came. Many hours passed and Abraham resigned himself to the fact that he was going to die where he lay.

'I think this one's had it, my lady.' The voice was British.

'No one has *had it*, as you put it, on my watch.' The voice was female and clipped.

A face appeared above him. It was framed in white cotton, and had a red cross on its brow.

'Take him into the shade and administer the usual treatment,' said the woman. She passed a cool hand over Abraham's brow.

'Immediately!' she said.

The porters hoisted Abraham's stretcher. He winced and closed his eyes.

'Buck up your ideas, man,' said the woman, 'I don't permit dying on my wards.'

Her pale beautiful face moved away.

Abraham was scrubbed, encased in striped pyjamas, and pinned to his bed with sheets so tightly tucked he couldn't move. Nurses in starched caps and long white aprons bustled up and down the ward. At one end, where the sun slanted down from a round window, sat the pale woman. She was writing at a desk, the light falling in bright shafts around her.

'Who is she?' said Abraham to the man in the bed to his right.

'Plum Duff,' said the man. His head was wrapped around with bandages and he looked like a mummy.

'Plum what?'

'Lady Duff of the Ladies' Volunteer Medical Corp,' said the man, 'woe betide you if she catches you doing anything other than what you're supposed to do.'

'What am I supposed to do?'

'Recover and free up the bed for another man,' said the soldier, mimicking Lady Duff's tones.

At six o'clock, Lady Duff did her rounds. Behind her trooped a platoon of nurses. One carried a bowl of water and a towel; another pushed a small, wheeled trolley that rattled with an assortment of brown bottles.

'Now, Mr Block,' said Lady Duff as the cavalcade halted at the end of his bed, 'how are we today?' She picked up a clipboard from the foot of his bed.

'Black water fever, malaria *and* dysentery' she said, 'dear me!'

Lady Duff pursed her pale mouth.

'Two teaspoons of rhubarb powder in water every hour,' she said to one of the nurses, 'it's Kill or Cure Burkitt's remedy, and if it works for him and the Carrier Corps, it will work for us.' She passed on down the line of beds.

It took time, but Lady Duff was determined, and Abraham recovered.

Looking up one day, he saw a familiar face. It was that of Michael London, one of the original band of six who had travelled with him from South Africa. Lady Duff did not permit talking on her wards so Michael only winked and said, 'I'll send word'.

The next day another face appeared.

'Don't have long,' said Tom Bell, 'Michael London said you were here and in a bad way. We'll get you shipped up to Nairobi on the train. Oh my God!'

'What?' said Abraham.

'She's coming,' said Tom Bell and disappeared.

'Well enough to chat are we, Mr Block?' said Lady Duff raising a delicate eyebrow. She stuck a thermometer in his mouth.

'Blanket bath, nurse!' she said, 'ice cold! Mr Block is leaving us for Dr Burkitt, so he'd best start as Dr Burkitt will mean to go on.'

Abraham had made many journeys on the Uganda Railway, but his trip from Mombasa to Nairobi on the Red Cross train was the worst of them all. Twelve stretchers were slotted into racks on the wall of each carriage. And twelve more were lined above them. Across the Taru Desert, the heat was such that it was all Abraham could do to watch the sweat gather into a droplet on the stretcher above, and wait for it to drop on his face.

Every so often, porters clad in khaki shorts and square-necked tunics, would sway through the stretchers with enamel buckets and ladles of water. On one of their rounds they stopped by the stretcher to Abraham's left and stared. White hands clawed at its rails. When the train stopped to take on water, the stretcher was removed.

Abraham wondered if the corpses were buried by the side of the track; and how long it would be before the hyenas arrived to dig them up.

As steadily as it had risen, the temperature dropped, and the cool air of the highlands replaced the clinging humidity of the coast. The train began to pant its way up through the green hills to the Athi Plains, and Abraham finally dared to believe that he might arrive in Nairobi.

When the train drew up on Nairobi Station there was an eerie silence. No rushing crowds, no shouting porters, just the patter of bare feet as the stretcher bearers ran down the train, and the jabber of Swahili as they struggled to pass the stretchers through the windows.

When his turn came to be manhandled through the window of the carriage Abraham slid down the stretcher and collapsed in a heap on the platform.

It was there that his wife, Sarah, found him.

CHAPTER 63

SON AND HEIR

Some regard private enterprise as if it were a predatory tiger to be shot.
Others look upon it as a cow that they can milk.
Only a handful see it for what it really is-the strong horse that pulls the whole cart.
—Winston Churchill (1874-1965)

W HETHER IT WAS THE DIET, or the cow's milk that persuaded Rita to resume the thread of her brief life, nobody knew. But a few months after Sarah had moved in to the Harrtz household, Rita's skin turned from parchment to rose and she began to put on weight. But the black-and-white cow produced more milk than even she could consume.

'We must bottle it, and sell it,' said Gertie Harrtz.

'Mayence Tate,' said Sarah.

'Will buy it?' said Gertie.

'Will provide the bottles,' said Sarah.

Over the next few weeks, Sarah and Gertie developed a milk round. The milk was poured into an odd collection of whisky, brandy and gin bottles, which had been purchased from Mayence Bent at the Stanley Hotel; and it was delivered by means of the pony and cart, which Samuel had given to Sarah. By the end of the first month, the demand for milk had far outstripped the black-and-white cow's ability to supply it. Using their profits, Gertie and Sarah bought another cow.

Arising early one morning to load the cart, Gertie found Sarah with her fingers hooked around the lip of the great stone sink in the dairy. Her arms were braced, she had her head down, and she was taking great gulps of air.

'How long have you known?' said Gertie.

'A few weeks,' said Sarah.

'It'll be a boy,' said Gertie, 'I'll take over the milk round; you supervise the milking and bottling.'

Over the period of the next six months, Sarah grew in size until it was all that she could do to walk to the milking sheds. She and Gertie had employed a group of Kikuyu women to milk the cows and their leader was known as Njeri. She had nut-brown eyes set in a wizened face topped by a shaved head, and she was known to be very wise. Njeri rested her hands briefly on Sarah's swollen stomach; she put her ear against it and listened, like a thrush for a worm, Sarah thought.

'Boy,' said Njeri, 'coming soon. Very soon, Mamma.'

It was not an easy birth. Granny Sheldon was persuaded to attend, but after seven hours she shook her head.

'Send for Dr Burkitt,' she said.

It was not Dr Burkitt who arrived; it was a tall, thin young man with a receding hairline of reddish gold hair and small gold-rimmed spectacles.

'There's an outbreak of Spanish 'flu,' he said, 'Dr Burkitt can't come, I'm Dr McElvoy.'

Sarah dragged herself up from her sodden pillows.

'He *must* come,' she said, 'you're too young!'

'Aye, and if you want to get much older, you'd best let me help you get this baby in to the world,' said Dr McElvoy, and he rolled up his sleeves.

Gertie and Njeri were correct; the baby was a boy. But unlike Rita, who had railed against her entry into the world, Jack Yaakov Block was immediately content with what he found there. He was serene and calm, and he had a certain knowingness of expression that gave the lie to his being a baby at all. When he was hungry he cried. When he was tired he slept; and in between Jack observed the life that went on around him with a slightly irritated detachment. As if he was counting the hours until he could participate in it.

'He's got a face like a little old man,' said Lily when she saw him.

'He looks like my father,' said Ettel, 'you should have called him Solomon.'

'I called him after my brother, the one who died when he was just four years old,' said Sarah.

'Hmm,' said Ettel.

'He's a very fine fellow,' said Samuel, 'well done, my dear.'

Freda, trailing ever resentfully in the wake of her mother, said nothing. She seemed also to be counting the hours until she could participate in life.

It was only when she had given birth to a boy that Sarah realized how restrained the reception had been to Rita's birth. At that time the attitude of Njeri and the Kikuyu women and been one of profound sympathy and commiseration. Now they were jubilant; they sang, they danced and they made honey cakes. They were not alone; everyone bought gifts, even Mr Marcus, who arrived with a large black perambulator with a folded leather hood, coiled springs, leather straps supporting its barouche-like body and a footbrake that could be applied to hold it in position. 'Came across it,' he said.

It was while the pram was being wheeled up and down the garden by a group of enchanted Kikuyu ladies, that Dr Burkitt arrived.

'Mrs Block,' he said as he walked up the garden path, 'I've news for you; its of your husband.' Sarah's eyes flew to his face.

'It's not bad news,' said Dr Burkitt, 'and it's not good news either; he contracted malaria in Dar es Salaam and it turned into black water fever. But he's lucky: he'll live.'

'Where is he?' said Sarah.

'Tom Bell saw him in the military hospital in Mombasa; he was under the care of Lady Duff and her girls. He was in a bad way, but we've managed to arrange for him to be transferred to Nairobi.'

'When?'

'In two week's time, on the Red Cross train.'

'Will they send him back to the war?' said Sarah.

Abraham Block with Jack in 1919

The Red Cross Train

'No. Not many survive black water fever and those that do are not fit for much. You must prepare yourself for a shock. He will look rough. I've arranged for him to recuperate at the Ol Donyo Sabuk Nursing Home.'

'Why can't I nurse him here?' said Sarah.

'When you see him, you'll understand,' said Dr Burkitt.

And he was right.

CHAPTER 64

OL DONYO SABUK

Life is God's novel. Let him write it.

–Isaac Bashevis Singer (1904-1991)

LOOKING DOWN AT HER HUSBAND as he lay slumped, gaunt and bearded on his stretcher, Sarah was shocked. She had expected Abraham to look ill but she had not expected him to look like a cadaver. She knelt on the platform beside him.

'Abraham,' she said, 'please open your eyes, Abraham.'

Slowly, as if returning from a far away place, Abraham Block opened his eyes and looked at his wife. He smiled but it was little more than a rictus.

'Good Lord, man,' said Dr Burkitt, 'you look ghastly.'

He bent and straightened Abraham's tumbled limbs.

'I've managed to get you into a convalescent home, but you're not fit to travel with the others that are going there; so I'll drive you to Ol Donyo Sabuk myself,' he said.

On the station frontage stood Dr Burkitt's car. It was a large green shooting brake with double doors at the rear. Like a hearse, thought Abraham as he was lifted through them. He wondered why they were going to Ol Donyo Sabuk. As he drifted off into his habitual semi-conscious state, a vision came into his mind of the mountain as he had last seen it: hunched beyond the shifting shadows of game that rolled across the plains at the back of Tommy Wood's butchery. It seemed a long time ago.

'Get in the front, my dear,' said Dr Burkitt. He turned to Gertie and Michael Harrtz, 'I'll bring her back this evening,' he said.

'Abraham has pushed his luck to the limit this time,' said Michael Harrtz as the doctor crashed through his gears and accelerated away.

'Yes dear,' said Gertie, 'but his luck stretches further than anyone else's.'

It was a winding road that led through the sisal plantations to Ol Donyo Sabuk. The fields were striped with long rows of blue-green tufts; they were dotted with swamps bordered by clumps of papyrus and in some of the swamps, hippos reared. Long bundles of papyrus were offered for sale; they were dried to a delicate gold colour and bound into roofing lengths.

The waters of the Athi River swirled broad, brown and flecked with dirty foam. A series of cataracts split the river into churning braids, and it plunged over a succession of small waterfalls amid spumes of khaki-coloured spray. Small boys leapt into its swirls holding their noses and splaying their feet.

'What is this place we are taking Abraham to?' said Sarah as the crouched hump of Ol Donyo Sabuk Mountain drew ever closer.

'It was the home of Northrup McMillan,' said Dr Burkitt, 'but he and his wife have turned it into a nursing home for the troops[1].'

'Who is Northrup McMillan?'

'He's an American millionaire from St Louis, Missouri. Arrived here around 1904. Came down the White Nile with some camels and a steamer. Mad as a hatter,' said Dr Burkitt.

Sarah glanced at him; he was fighting the bucking of the polished wooden steering wheel.

'But you can't help admiring the man,' said Burkitt, 'hugely rich, hugely generous. Made his money in Canada in fur, timber, railways and banking. Fell in love with this place, sent for his wife, Lucie, her maid; and his dog. Then he had a house sent out from England in sections. The present place is new and has to be seen to be believed; ballroom to hold two hundred, endless reception rooms and bedrooms, dairy, cheese factory, stabling for twenty-six horses, each with its own syce and ready to be ridden within five minutes. McMillan calls the house Juja after two idols he picked up somewhere along the Nile. Everyone has stayed there: Theodore Roosevelt, Winston Churchill and just about every beauty or title that has ever passed through Nairobi. He sends a fleet of cars into Nairobi every weekend just to collect them and bring them to his parties.'

'And what does he do? Apart from hold parties?' said Sarah.

'Like most rich men, his life is governed by a continuous succession of projects. Each is an all-consuming obsession; and none match up to his dreams. Dr Burkitt hit the horn and a herd of cows hauled itself to its feet and moved grudgingly to one side.

'He tried to make a go of farming,' he continued, 'like they all do. Whatever the fad of the moment, McMillan followed it: wheat, tea, ostriches, pigs, cattle, and sheep. But all the crops failed and all the livestock died of some disease or other. He built an abattoir and a bacon factory with a miniature railway to link the pig huts. That didn't work either. He's an idea's man not a farmer. And then, when the war came, of course he wanted to fight. He was one of the first to enlist and he turned up on the battle front at Kajiado. Though Lord only knows how they got him out there.'

'Why?' said Sarah.

'Absolutely colossal: a mountain of a man,' said Burkitt, 'over twenty stone, 54-inch waist. Had to have the side taken off the military staff car when it came to collect him at the station. They hacked the doors off on the spot I'm told. But when he climbed in it keeled over, so they had to balance him with four soldiers on the other side. But later, when McMillan got out, the car keeled over the other way.' Burkitt let out a bark of laughter. 'Even he could see it wasn't going to work, so he had to content himself with espionage. He planned the attacks and Meinertzhagen and Finch Hatton crept around in the bush as they chased von Lettow up hill and down dale. I hear McMillan made an excellent spy.'

Burkitt paused to ease the car through a rut.

'And I hear he is to be given a knighthood[2] for his work. But in the meantime he and Lucie have turned their house into a nursing home. And they don't come much grander, I can tell you that.'

In this statement, Burkitt was correct.

Turning off the main road, he guided the car along a sunken track, which wound around the base of Ol Donyo Sabuk Mountain. They drew up before a massive pair of scrolled gates flanked by a pair of emperor palms. Beyond the gates lay a mansion built from pale grey volcanic stone. Pulling to a halt in front of a pair of mighty wooden doors, Burkett honked his horn and climbed out of the car.

Sarah stared.

Above the gothic gable of the porch, was a carved scroll engraved with Latin script. There was a large cast-iron bell on a black chain, and to either side of the double doors were stone benches large enough to seat a giant. The pale grey walls were pierced by arched windows, and golden light poured out of them into the darkening day. The doors were fitted with twin lion heads with rings in their mouths, and they groaned as they were turned, and the doors swung open. A grey mastiff walked stiff-legged to stand beneath the portico. It had a spiked collar around its neck and its eyes flashed blood red in the light.

Sarah took a step backwards, her hands on the coachwork of the car.

'Now don't you mind Anubis,' said the small, rounded, African woman who emerged behind the dog. She wore a grey tailored dress with a starched white apron. 'He don't mean no harm,' she said. The woman walked to the car and looked in at Abraham prostrate in the back.

'This gentleman'll be for us, I guess?' she said, looking to Dr Burkett.

'Indeed, Miss Louise[3],' said Dr Burkett, 'this is Mr Abraham Block. And this,' he indicated Sarah, 'is his wife. We shall not linger, I know how busy you and Mrs McMillan must be.'

'Well now, you know you're always welcome, Dr Burkett,' said Miss Louisa in her soft American drawl, 'besides, we've a couple of fellas could do with a look over while you're here.'

Two barefoot African orderlies appeared and carried Abraham's stretcher into the great hall. Miss Louisa waived Sarah forward to follow them.

'Miss Louise is Mrs McMillan's maid,' whispered Dr Burkett, 'she's a virago but Mrs McMillan thinks the world of her.'

Inside the great stone hall, Sarah was dwarfed. From the vaulted ceiling hung a baronial candelabra the size of a cartwheel; it was lashed to the ceiling with a chain and it could be lowered and raised by means of a thick red velvet rope. The fireplace had twin inglenooks and a fire-basket the size of a barrel in which one gigantic log smouldered. The walls were hung with tapestries faded to a dull blue-green with age. To either side of the hall were rows of hospital beds, and men clad in striped pyjamas lay in them.

Through the arched windows Sarah could see lawns and terraces, flights of steps and urns. There were wickerwork basket chairs fitted with bicycle wheels, and men in dressing gowns lounged in them. Some read, some talked, some just stared out across the landscape.

When she turned back from the windows, Sarah found that Abraham had already been inserted between crisp white sheets. A nurse held his wrist, her eyes on the watch pinned to her apron.

Sarah stood silent.

'He'll need a lot of rest, Mrs Block,' said the nurse, 'but he'll recover, that I promise you. Come back and see him soon.'

'I just wanted to tell him—' said Sarah.

'Another time, my dear,' said the nurse.

'I just wanted to tell him,' Sarah insisted, 'that he has a new son, our first, born just two weeks ago.' She felt somehow embarrassed. The nurse smiled, 'make it quick,' she said.

Sarah looked down at Abraham. He looked like a marble effigy beneath the white sheets.

'I'm going now, Abraham,' she said, 'I will come back soon, but I wanted you to know that you have a son, he was born two weeks ago, I've called him Jack Yaakov.'

Abraham smiled weakly. He tried to bring his hand out from beneath the sheets, but he had not the strength to do so.

'Sarah,' he said, 'you are a magnificent woman, and I don't deserve you.'

Sarah kissed him goodbye and, as she did so, she wondered if she had finally replaced her sister, Rachel, in his heart. She knew that Abraham thought she did not know that it was Rachel he had fallen in love with. But she did. Of course she did: in fact it had been the first thing Rachel had told her.

Rachel had, of course, been listening at the door when Abraham's first proposal had been made.

For the first few weeks of his stay at Ol Donyo Sabuk, Abraham took little notice of his surroundings. He was mildly aware of the passage of time, and of the attentions that were given to his body. But he did not feel himself to be entirely present. That disembodied part of him, the part that thought, seemed to spend a great deal of time up on the ceiling of the great hall where the house martens made their nests; his spiritual presence seemed to prefer to remain there while his physical body lay far below.

But slowly, appetite, interest, even curiosity returned to him; and he began to venture out on to the lawn to sit in peaceable silence with his fellows. He chatted with the nurses and he watched the immense figure of Northrup McMillan as it laboured in the wake of his bustling wife, who was a fraction of his size.

One day a familiar face appeared above Abraham's chair on the lawn.

'Hallo Block,' said Denys Finch Hatton, 'I was visiting, and Lucie McMillan said you were here.'

Abraham made an attempt at a salute; Finch Hatton had been one of his commanding officers.

'I think we can forget all that now,' said Finch Hatton, 'your war's over. Mine too. Apparently it's only a matter of time before the Armistice is signed in Europe. But never mind that: I came to tell you that the McMillan's are holding a party: next week, and I thought you might like a lift up in my jalopy.'

'Up where?'

'Up the mountain: McMillan likes to hold his parties on its summit. The views of Nairobi are stunning, will you come?'

'Why not?' said Abraham, 'It's about time I saw Nairobi again.'

CHAPTER 65

ON THE MOUNTAIN OF THE BUFFALO

Time is money.

–Benjamin Franklin (1706-1790)

A CAVALCADE OF MULE CARTS AND ox-wagons, laden with round tables, golden chairs, wickerwork hampers and wooden crates, stood outside Juja House and, in the late afternoon, all those patients strong enough to attend the party were helped into a line of waiting cars. Denys Finch Hatton waved from a small, blue, Model T Ford.

Denys drove along the banks of the Athi River where the grey herons stood poised over the shallows. Lines of sisal tufts marched across the russet landscape as Ol Donyo Mountain swung in to view. It was a long slow climb up its flanks, which rose steeply from the flat plains. At first the flanks were bare and boulder strewn, then the trees closed in and the car passed through forests where black-and-white colobus monkeys leapt. The track grew ever steeper and the bends ever tighter until they emerged above the tree line; and then they arrived atop the baldpate of Ol Donyo Sabuk itself

Abraham got out of the car and smiled. He felt like a bird soaring, or a man finally released from darkness. Far away lay the sprawl of Nairobi, its tin shacks glinting in the dying sun. To the north, the long grey shoulder of Mount Kenya edged into a halo of cloud. To the west, the humps of the Aberdares lay across the horizon like an animal hide laid out to dry.

On the summit of the mountain tables and chairs had been laid out and encircled by burning flares. Behind a length of fluttering white damask, stood a row of chefs, each with his own silver-domed chaffing dish. Candles had been placed in brown paper bags filled with sand, and they flickered like Chinese lanterns. Waiters in long white robes wove through the crowds and bent stiffly from the waist to present trays laden with canapés and flutes of champagne.

Major Ringer moved through the knots of people, his eyes assessing those who were worth talking to and those who were not. He flitted from group to group; he made people laugh when he arrived; and when he left he contrived to put a jovial hand on the shoulders of the men, and to brush the arms of the women.

Charlie Bulpett[1] was there, Northrup McMillan's particular friend. Universally known as 'Uncle', Bulpett was handsome and witty. He had made his name in London by swimming across the Thames in a top hat and tails, and he claimed to have lost his fortune to a famous Parisian courtesan. He had journeyed down the Nile with McMillan, and rumour had it that he lived off him still. Abraham looked for Delamere but he was not there. Delamere, Abraham reflected, preferred to stand central to social storms of his own making. And most of those were more riotous than any that Northrup McMillan might stage.

The sun had set and the indigo arch of sky sparkled with stars when Fatty Garland, Abraham's old trading partner, strode over, pulled up a chair and sat down.

'They said you wouldn't make it,' he said, 'but I knew better.' From his inside pocket, he pulled out two cigars and offered one to Abraham. 'Time you got back to Nairobi,' he said proffering a lighted match in a cupped hand, 'there'll be a lot of money to be made once the Armistice is signed.'

'Mmm?' said Abraham, working the end of the cigar, 'but what about the post-war slump we are promised?'

'Oh, there's talk of austerity,' said Fatty, 'but to chaps like you, Block, that's a license to print money ain't it?'

'Chaps like me?'

'Chaps like you who can see into the future. Who know where the money can be made. And don't give me that old Jewish look, Block. You know exactly what I mean.'

Abraham blew out a cloud of smoke. He surveyed Fatty through its coils. Then he smiled.

'I do, Fatty,' he said.

'So where's your bet to be laid?' said Fatty.

'Cows.'

'Again?' said Fatty, disappointed, 'I thought we were done with cows.'

'Dairy cows,' said Abraham, 'you see that fellow over there talking to McMillan? His name is Destro[2]. He's Italian, and he went down the Nile with McMillan, he is his new business manager and I heard them talk of opening a dairy in Nairobi.'

'You always had good ears, Block,' said Fatty.

'Work with what you have, Fatty. Work with what you have,' said Abraham.

It was Sarah who had given Abraham the idea of going into the dairy business. She had told him of how she and Gertie Harrtz had built up a clientele for their milk. And how Mayence Tate had supplied the empty liquor bottles. 'How much did she charge you?' said Abraham.

'Two cents each.'

'And how much did you sell them for full?'

'Twenty cents.'

'Mmm.'

'We were the first Europeans to deliver milk to the doorstep in Nairobi,' said Sarah.

'You'll be the only Europeans to deliver milk to the doorstep,' said Abraham, 'the rest of them think it beneath them.'

'Have we done wrong?' said Sarah, alarmed.

'Not if it makes money,' said her husband, 'money is the great leveller, my love, as you will see.'

He looked again at the ledger of Sarah's figures.

'But to make a proper return,' he said, 'you will need more cows.'

'We don't have the space,' said Sarah.

'I've heard of a house with farming land for sale west of Parklands. It's going for a good price. I'll buy it and have Fatty look for a herd of dairy cows.'

'I'll need help, Abraham, I can't do it alone.'

'Of course you cannot. I will tell Dr Burkitt that I am ready to leave.'

'But are you?'

'Time is money,' said Abraham, 'I will have to be.'

A breakdown on the road

Travellers on the road, 1900

Northrup McMillan and Ewart Grogan

CHAPTER 66

SARAH BLOCK REACHES A DECISION

You must be the change you want to see in the world.
–Mahatma Gandhi (1869-1948)

ABRAHAM WORKED FROM HIS CHAIR on the lawns of Juja House. Within a month the land in Parklands had been purchased and Fatty Garland had been instructed to buy a herd of thirty dairy cows.

'Lily will have the house prepared for you and the children,' said Abraham to Sarah, 'I am to be discharged next week. We shall all go there together as a family.'

Sarah felt a sudden flash of resentment at Abraham's easy assumption of the role of the family man. She had never dared to think of Rita, Jack and herself as a family lest Abraham be killed in the war. And, while she had loved her sister-in-law, Lily, she had always felt alienated by Ettel and Freda. Nor did a day pass when Sarah did not think how different things might have been for her in Rishon Le Zion. There, she would have had the support of her mother and sisters in the raising of her children. There, she would have been part of a tight-knit community that was proud of its Jewish heritage; and there she would have had the social standing accorded to the beloved daughter of a highly respected Jewish scholar.

But in British East Africa, things were very different.

Unlike Abraham, Sarah had not experienced the anti-Semitic menace of the Russian pogroms, she had never been exposed to ethnic vilification, and she had been raised confidently Jewish in a proudly Zionist colony. But arriving in British East Africa, she had found her social status to be quite different; and she had learned, to her considerable astonishment, that the presence of Jews was not permitted in the Nairobi Club or in the newly opened Muthaiga Club, both of which were bastions of settler respectability.

This had shocked and shamed her.

Sarah's marriage had also fallen considerably short of her expectations. Abraham had been a good husband, and she was fond of him, but she had been encouraged to marry him on the basis of his being a wealthy man. And, as far as her own life with him had been concerned, Sarah had seen no evidence of this.

These things rankled, but Sarah Block did not permit them to ruffle the calm of her outward persona. She had never told her parents how far from the truth their idea of Abraham's financial standing had been, and she had never made any complaint about her own social standing in the colony of Kenya; but she guarded her pride jealously.

When Abraham clicked the horse to a halt outside the gaunt stone house that was to be their new home, Sarah made a decision: her time of humility and acceptance was over. Abraham had explained to her that wealth would buy them social standing, and she determined to do all that lay in her power to help him acquire it; but she also determined that British East Africa would take nothing more from her.

Few stood in the way of Sarah Block. Samuel Block, her father-in-law, adored her and regarded her slightest wish as his command. When she had been pregnant with Jack, Sarah had remarked, idly enough, that she had a desire for crystallized ginger. The next day Samuel had presented her with a box of it. Freda had been pained, Ettel disgusted, but Samuel had not even noticed.

Ettel Block hated to see her husband dancing attendance on his daughter-in-law when he seldom sought the company of his wife. Ettel was jealous of Sarah's looks and her assured presence; and she took it as a personal affront that Sarah had chosen to live, first with Lily and Simon Haller, and then with the Harrtz family rather than with herself.

'Am I not to see my grandchildren?' she said, 'after all that I have suffered? And all the years when I had no one, when I was left alone in Russia?'

'You were not alone, Mamma,' said Freda, 'you had me.'

Ettel rounded on her.

'You have not given me any grandchildren,' she said.

She glared at Sarah.

'But *she* has and she won't let me see them!'

Freda blushed peony red and fled from the room.

'We must find a husband for that girl,' said Samuel, 'she needs one.'

Ettel glowered at him, but made no reply. It had been on the tip of her tongue to say that she had need of a husband too. But her pride would not allow that.

Ettel was aged far beyond her sixty-four-years and she was discontented with her lot. She rarely moved from her chair, and from it she radiated disapproval of everyone and everything.

'You'll miss me when I'm gone,' she had taken to saying.

'You're not going yet,' said Abraham when he visited her.

But he was wrong.

One morning Ettel did not take possession of her chair in the kitchen. And when she was found in her bedroom she was staring unseeing out of the window. Still attired in her rusty black silk, Ettel Block had died as she had lived: stiff-backed, cold and with a look of immense disappointment on her face.

After Ettel had been buried in Nairobi's new Jewish cemetery, Samuel made an announcement.

'I'm going back to South Africa,' he said.

'I'm coming with you,' said Freda.

'No you are not,' said Samuel, 'it would not be suitable. You will go and live with your sister, Lily Haller, on the farm.'

Some months later, a letter was received. It was from Samuel Block. He had married a matron of Cape Dutch descent.

'How could he have found a wife so quickly?' said Lily.

'Perhaps he didn't,' said Abraham, who had long had his suspicions regarding his father's earlier life in South Africa.[1]

'But…' said Lily, 'that would mean…'

'Indeed,' said Abraham, 'best let sleeping dogs lie.'

CHAPTER 67

FREDA BLOCK

A woman knows the face of the man she loves as a sailor knows the open sea.
–Honore de Balzac, French novelist (1799-1850)

I N THE WAKE OF ETTEL Block's death, Freda Block's fortunes changed more than she had ever thought possible. She was twenty-six and her life up until that time had been dominated by the presence of her strong-minded mother. Nor had she had any real opportunity to experience the love of her father, because Samuel Block had left Russia when Freda was a baby and he had not reappeared in her life until she was nineteen.

Just seven years later, upon the death of Ettel, Samuel had walked out of Freda's life yet again, this time to marry a South African woman and set up home in Johannesburg. He had visited Kenya to introduce his new wife but the visit had not been a success. Lily and Freda had found it difficult to be anything other than civil to the new Mrs Block, and their coldness had been all too evident. For them, at least, the towering figure of Ettel Block could not be so easily replaced.

When Freda had first arrived on the Haller's farm, Lily had tried to find her an occupation; she had suggested that Freda might like to care for the three Haller children. There was Arthur Haller, born in 1914; Edith Haller, born in 1915; and the baby, Maurice, who had arrived in 1918. Freda was fond of the children, but they were fractious and cried in her care; and it soon became clear that they much preferred the cheerful chatter and easy presence of their African *ayahs*[1]. It was at this point that Lily suggested that Freda might like to help in caring for the wounded soldiers that Simon Haller had brought home with him from the war.

Simon Haller, once a strong, cheerful, bluff presence, had returned much changed by his war experiences. He was gloomy, silent, often empty-eyed, and given to disappearing on his motorcycle for long periods of time, or striding across the land with eyes on the far horizon.

A few months after his return from the war, Simon had asked Lily to help him care for some of his wounded comrades. Thinking that this might assist in healing some of Simon's own mental wounds, Lily had agreed; and they had taken in eight soldiers; two were amputees, four had shrapnel wounds, one was blinded and another had a head injury[2].

Freda made a good nurse; she was gentle and caring and, free of the domination of Ettel, lively and talkative. She was also shapely and possessed of a particularly expressive face and quantities of long dark hair, which fell continually free of its pins.

All of this did not go unnoticed by the wounded soldiers, who vied for Freda's attention, and the kiss of her dark hair on their skin. But one soldier was more captivated than the rest.

Morris Kirkel had a silver tongue and a story for every occasion. He was quick and amusing and Freda liked the timbre of his voice. But the fact was that she had never had the occasion to see his face. Morris had been shot in the head and such was the severity of his wound that it had necessitated his skull being tightly bandaged from crown to chin. He looked like a mummy: only his black eyes and his white teeth were visible.

One day Dr Burkitt decided that the time had come to remove Morris's bandages.

'I'll need your help,' he said to Freda, 'we must soak them before we can peel them off, and it's a delicate task.'

It took time to peel the long white bandages free of Morris's skull, but eventually they lay coiled in a bowl by Freda's side. And then she made a discovery: Morris Kirkel was an exceptionally handsome young man.

'Hello, Nurse Freda,' he said. He smiled, and a lock of dark hair fell across his brow. Freda brushed it back, and blushed. Two months later they were married, and Morris returned to his job as an accountant in Nairobi.

Towards the end of 1919, Freda gave birth to a daughter.

She called her Ettel Patricia.

In 1924 the news arrived in Nairobi that Samuel Block had died in South Africa.

CHAPTER 68

THE PARKLANDS HOUSE

A home is not a mere transient shelter:
its essence lies in the personalities of the people who live in it.
–H. L. Mencken, US editor (1880-1956)

T HE PARKLANDS HOUSE STOOD AMID rambling gardens. It was overshadowed by trees, which dripped a sticky white resin down on to anything that came within their orbit. There was a fishpond, but it was cracked and empty of water, and it was filled instead with the parchment blossoms of a bougainvillea whose winding coils were inexorably strangling the entire garden.

The house had a small verandah and a dark mahogany front door, which opened on to a gloomy hall. The floors were parquet, the corridors were long, and in the dining room the ceiling was supported by stone corbels, which gave it something of the air of a church. To the rear of the house there was a dank scullery with scrofulous walls, and a bleak kitchen. The house smelled of damp, there were stains on the ceiling where the roof had leaked, and it had no electricity. Sarah, who rather liked its air of faded grandeur determined to make changes.

'We shall need new curtains and new furniture,' she said, as she walked through the empty rooms.

'Can we not use the ones from the other house?' said Abraham.

'I would like to choose my own.'

'Very well, my dear, but...'

'But what, Abraham?'

'There is surely little point in buying what we don't need... is there?'

'No, there is not,' said Sarah decisively, 'but I shall be buying what we do need.'

Abraham could not stand unnecessary expenditure; money had always been hard earned in his life. But he knew that he and Sarah's marital life would run more smoothly if she were to be allowed to have her way. So Abraham looked determinedly the other way when Sarah purchased red velvet curtains and Turkish rugs. He applauded the arrival of the horsehair sofas and the rather ponderous armchairs, and he smiled when a dining table with ball-and-claw feet was wrestled through the door followed by six chairs and a matching sideboard.

But for every item that arrived in the house, Abraham calculated a corresponding credit in the balance sheet of his mind: he could not help himself.

Sometimes a particular domestic acquisition would be set off against the sale of a certain cow. Sometimes Abraham would cut his margins more ruthlessly than usual so as to 'pay' for Sarah's latest purchase. But for most of the time, Abraham simply worked harder and longer to finance Sarah's acquisition of gentility.

Abraham's pursuit of business deals took him constantly away from home, and Sarah used his absence to pursue her own ends. The gardens were landscaped, the fishpond acquired fish, and the dairy was renamed The Devonshire Dairy[1].

Sarah turned her hand to growing vegetables. She began in a small way growing peas, beans and cabbages, but then she diversified into lettuces, cucumbers and tomatoes. Within six months, Sarah Block was driving a cart of fresh vegetables into the Nairobi markets every week.

It was while Sarah was surveying her appearance, seated before her new kidney-shaped dressing table, which had triple mirrors and chintz flounces, that she decided that her own appearance must change along with that of the house. The next day she had her long black hair clipped fashionably short, and she began to touch her lips and cheeks with rouge. She dabbed her nose with powder from a gold-embossed compact, she purchased a long string of imitation pearls and a wristwatch; and she acquired a treadle sewing machine so that she might re-style her wardrobe to reflect the steadily rising hemlines and descending waistlines of post-war Europe.

Amongst the ladies of her, still limited, acquaintance Sarah had observed that white silk stockings were being worn with an entirely new style of shoes. These had a slight heel, a T-bar and a button fastening to the side. Sarah determined to obtain both the stockings and the shoes.

But they were not available in post-war Nairobi. So she decided to ask Eddie Ruben to obtain them for her.

CHAPTER 69

EDDIE RUBEN

People's fates are simplified by their names.
–Elias Canetti, Swiss author (1905-1994)

EDDIE RUBEN HAD RISEN TO the rank of captain in the Royal Lancashire Regiment; and he had enjoyed the batman, the fresh limejuice and the half-bottle of whisky that his rank had accorded him. But when the war ended he found himself at a loss. So he gravitated back to his old lodgings with the Harrtz family, and he asked Michael Harrtz for a job in his foundry.

'You can do better than that,' said Michael, 'did you manage to save anything from your army pay?'

'Nearly all of it,' said Eddie.

'So use it to buy out John Rifkin,' said Michael.

'Buy him out of what? I thought he was a blacksmith like you?'

'So he is, but he bought eight mules and a cart from a settler gone bust, and he wants to get rid of them.'

Eddie had spent much of his war dealing with mules, so he saw the hand of fate at play, and he seized it. With his elder brother, Charles, he raised the money to buy the mules, rent the stables and set up a simple sales office. They called the business Ruben Brothers Transport. It was later to become Express Transport[1], which was one of East Africa's most successful haulage companies.

Eddie was a gifted mule handler and he trained his team to such perfection that the daily harnessing of the Ruben mules became one of the sights of Nairobi. On a given signal, the long mule harness would be laid out in the street. The mules would line up alongside it and, as each one's name was called, it would step neatly into position.

Eddie had an honest face and he was an excellent salesman. His brother had an aptitude for figures, and their business flourished. They opened an office in Mombasa and began handling freight from overseas.

So Eddie Ruben was the ideal man to obtain Sarah's shoes and stockings from London.

'I'll need the size, Sarah,' said Eddie.

'You'll need more than that,' said Sarah, 'I've cut a picture from a British newspaper of the exact pair of shoes I want. I will have three pairs: cream, brown and black, and six pairs of cream stockings. Here is the address of the hosier.'

Eddie had made it his business to keep in touch with Sarah Block. He had no illusions as to the nature of her interest in him, but something about her square-jawed dark-eyed beauty enthralled him. And he liked her determined self-possession. She was, he supposed, his idea of the perfect wife. When he delivered the shoes, Sarah was enchanted. She extended her small foot and rotated it so that they might both admire the shoe.

'Now, Eddie,' said Sarah 'there's a new play on at the Theatre Royal and I'd like you to take me to see it. I want everyone to see these shoes, but I shall not be able to wear them for much longer.'

'Why won't you be able to wear them for much longer' said Eddie, mystified.

'I'm pregnant again,' said Sarah, 'can't you tell?'

A shy fellow, Eddie looked immediately away.

'Surely you didn't think I was always this fat?' said Sarah, 'did you, Eddie?'

'You always look lovely to me, Sarah,' said Eddie, 'when would you like to go to the theatre?'

Eddie became Sarah's regular companion, and this suited her. Where Abraham was short, Eddie was tall. With Abraham, Sarah was a wife; with Eddie she could be a girl. Eddie paid her compliments and Eddie's attention was always fixed on her, whereas Abraham's, more often than not, was trained on the next deal.

Eddie was happy to oblige Sarah in whatever she might want. Sometimes he would call to take her out to tea; sometimes they would push the large black pram along the rough red roads together. At one end of it would sit Rita, and at the other Jack.

Sarah's second son was born a few months before Christmas 1919. Abraham was present for the birth, but he left almost immediately afterwards. 'A land deal has come up in Nakuru,' he said, 'and Billy Judd needs a partner.'

'So who will register the birth?' said Sarah.

'Eddie can take you down there, can't he?' said Abraham.

Eddie, faithful as ever, arrived some hours later with some purchases that Sarah had asked him to make.

'Will you take me to Government House to register the birth of the baby?' she said.

'I'll go and do it for you,' said Eddie, 'you look tired.'

'Would you Eddie?' said Sarah, 'would you really?'

'Of course,' said Eddie.

Some hours later, he returned glum-faced.

'What happened?' said Sarah.

'I went there. I waited. They gave me a form. It was in English. And you know that my English is not so good, Sarah?' said Eddie.

'Yes. So?'

'So the man said he would fill in the form for me. We went through all the details together, your name, Abraham's name, the address; he wrote it all down.'

'Yes? And then?'

'And then he said, "name?"'

'And you said?'

'I said, Eddie Ruben.'

'So?'

'So your son is called Eddie Ruben Block'.

When Abraham returned, Sarah told him what had happened.

'Will people talk?' she said.

'People will always talk,' said Abraham, 'but if Eddie Ruben had been the father of this child, we're hardly likely to have put his name on the birth certificate.' He held out his arms for the baby, who was plump, pink and smiling. 'Tubby little chap aren't you, Eddie Ruben Block?' he said, 'a very tubby little Block indeed.'

He bounced the baby up and down and Sarah laughed; she sounded suddenly girlish. Abraham seized her and waltzed her around the room. The baby was sandwiched between them. As they whirled past the gilt mirror above the fireplace, Abraham and Sarah caught their image reflected there; they looked happy: times were changing for the better.

For some reason, perhaps because it reminded them of this happiness, the name 'Tubby' stuck.

Aboard the mule cart in 1908

CHAPTER 70

ALB BUILDS HIS EMPIRE

*Money is the seed of money, and the first guinea is sometimes more difficult
to acquire than the second million.*
–Jean-Jacques Rousseau, Philosopher, (1712-1778)

EVERY MORNING AT DAWN ABRAHAM rose and loaded the cart with liquor bottles full of milk. Genial and smiling, he was to be seen every day of the week, clicking his horses, flicking the reigns, and calling out greetings, as if the delivery of milk was his only mission in life.

But behind this façade, Abraham Block's meticulously ordered mind sifted and sought through all that he had learned. And every fragment, no matter how trivial, was slotted into the greater jigsaw of his mind.

When the milk round was over, Abraham would begin a second round of visits, but this time their purpose was more financially focused. From some Abraham would acquire information; to others he would impart it. From some he would buy; to some he would sell. No deal was beneath his notice, no commodity beyond his scope. No effort was too great; no wait too long. If money was to be made, ALB could smell it, and if a deal were to be had, he would forge it. But it was not until the end of the war, when the predicted post-war financial collapse arrived, that Abraham Block demonstrated his ability to make money when all around him were losing it.

And he did it by the simple expedient of always being in the right place at the right time.

The war had brought great change to British East Africa. Thousands of Africans had died for a cause that was not their own, but they had received neither recognition nor reward; and their perception of their colonial masters had changed radically. Before the war the white man had proclaimed himself to be omnipotent; but the war had shown him to be quite the opposite. Before the war, the African had been told that he was uncivilized; but after the war he knew that the white man was capable of behaving towards his fellow white man with no more grace than a barbarian. Before the war, the African had understood himself to be inferior to the white man; but after the war he knew that they had died side by side with equal amounts of bravery. All of these things shook the foundations of the black man's belief in the white man. And the white man fell from his pedestal.

When the soldiers, black and white, returned to Kenya, the settlers saw the light of a new understanding in the eyes of their former employees, so they put them hastily back to work, but the new dynamics were not so easily contained, and the British Government decided to redress the balance of power in the colony by doubling the numbers of white settlers.

In 1919 the Soldier Settler Scheme was announced and all those British soldiers who had fought the war were offered the chance of settling in Kenya where land was made available to them at minimal cost. But no such offer was made to the black soldiers whose land, arguably, it

One of Abraham Block's companies, the Boma Trading Company, Government Road, Nairobi, 1918

was. And herein lay the seeds of the final collapse of the British East African Empire.

By mid-1919, over two thousand would-be settlers had applied for land under the terms of the Soldier Settlement Scheme, but demand far outstripped supply. The Colonial Office seized the chance to refine the quality of the incoming settlers by declaring a lottery, but to participate in it every would-be settler was required to prove that he had five thousand pounds in capital and two hundred pounds a year in income. This effectively eliminated the lower ranks of the British Army from participation in the scheme, and ensured that the next wave of Kenyan settlers were staunchly middle class. When the 1,500 lottery winners were announced they were found to include 46 generals, 105 majors and 160 captains.

The flaws in the Soldier-Settler Scheme were many. In the first place, all 1,500 settlers arrived on the same ship, but only fifty beds were made available to them upon their arrival in Nairobi. Most were forced to buy tents, and the colonial administration stipulated that these should be sold to them at 'cost price', but nobody was quite sure of what that cost price should be; so money was made by all those in the right place at the right time.

Secondly, the actual allocation of land was chaotic: one settler found he owned a farm on the glaciers of Mount Kenya, another that his land lay in the bottom of a volcanic crater. There was a frenzy of land sales as the soldier-settlers sought to exchange their land; and the established settlers preyed upon their naivety to seize what they could. The soldier-settlers rushed to buy equipment, seeds, livestock, building materials and tools. But most were not farmers and they bought unwisely, planted badly, or found that their labour force had disappeared over night. They turned to the established settlers for help; and fortunes, once again, were made.

It was then that the British Government decided to replace the Indian Rupee, upon which the colony had been founded, with the Kenyan Shilling. It was a well-intentioned move and designed to boost trade; but it proved disastrous. The Shilling plummeted against the outgoing Rupee and impacted negatively on the mortgages and loans of the soldier-settlers. Plunged into negative equity, they became known as the victims of the Soldier Robber Scheme; and the value of land fell still further. Then the British Government declared that a number of imports into Britain were to be deemed illegal; and one of them was East African coffee.

As the prices of East African commodities collapsed, large swathes of the colonial farming community faced ruin. Relying as ever on the infallibility of his instincts, Abraham Block began to buy land. Following the advice of Lord Delamere, he bought four thousand acres on the shores of Lake Elementeita[1] and 11,000 acres of land on Lake Naivasha. Acting on a hint from Mr Marcus, who sat like a spider at the centre of all Nairobi intrigue, Abraham bought a number of Nairobi plots, and then he moved into the acquisition of residential property in Nairobi.

CHAPTER 71

A MAN OF PROPERTY

Labour diligently to increase your property.
–Horace (65-8 BC)

ABRAHAM BLOCK WAS NOW TRULY a man of wealth and property.

But he was not infallible.

He went into a deal with Billy Judd; they bought cattle in Ethiopia and Abraham was persuaded to ignore the quarantine regulations and drive them across anthrax-infected land. The repercussions of this decision were severe. Not only was Abraham Block responsible for the outbreak of an anthrax epidemic that blighted the entire colony, but he also destroyed his own herds. Within weeks every cow in The Devonshire Dairy herd was dead and all Abraham's farmland had been declared 'dirty'.

Disconsolate, Abraham made his way to the Long Bar of the Stanley, where he found that an impromptu reunion was being held for the ex-members of Bowker's Horse. Centre stage, stood the towering figure of Russell Bowker, his leopard skin hat on his head, his graying moustache stained yellow with nicotine and a shot of whisky in his meaty fist.

'Why the long face, Block?' said Bowker.

Abraham told him of his misfortunes; and he did not spare himself the blame.

'You don't deserve it,' said Bowker, 'but I have the solution to your problem.'

'I don't deserve it,' said Block, 'but what is it?'

'Thirty acres of prime land a few miles out of town with the foundations of a house on it in exchange for your Parklands house.'

'Your land?'

'My land, but my lady wife requires a house in Nairobi and she tells me that your Parklands house is just what she has in mind.'

Abraham Block sat silent for a few minutes as he ran the computations of the deal through his mind.

'Done,' he said.

It was with some trepidation that he broached the matter to Sarah, but she surprised him. 'Wonderful!' she said.

'Really?' said Abraham, 'I thought you might be displeased given all the time you have put into the house.'

'Not at all,' said Sarah, 'a while ago Mrs Bowker couldn't give me the time of day and now she wants my house.'

'But we shall have to build a new house,' said Abraham still unsure how far his luck would carry him.

'Yes,' said Sarah, 'and then we shall sell that for a profit too.'

Abraham regarded his wife with pride; the fragile girl that he had married had proved to be tougher than even he had thought possible.

'You can have whatever you want, Sarah,' he said.

Thereafter, Abraham encouraged Sarah to buy the best of everything, and to do things with all the style she could muster. The Blocks moved, and always to larger and more gracious properties. By the late 1920s, the Block property portfolio included some of Nairobi's most prestigious homes, while the Block's latest family home stood in Parklands, immediately adjacent to that of the Aga Khan[1].

Sarah was buying carpets in Nairobi's only general store. It went by the name of The Dustpan[2] due to the number of dustpans that lined its street frontage, and it was owned by Mr Sammy Jacobs, who had arrived from Eastern Europe at around the same time as Abraham Block. Mr Jacobs had done well, and he had recently expanded his store to include a second floor where an elegant selection of furniture and carpets were offered for sale. In the interests of pleasing his lady customers, Mr Jacob had engaged a number of young Jewish girls of good family to act as sales ladies, but the result of this innovation was not quite as he had intended.

'This shop is turning into a matchmaking agency,' he said to Sarah.

'Really, Mr Jacobs?'

'Young men everywhere,' he said gloomily, 'and they do nothing but make eyes at my girls. I'm too old for all of this.'

'Nonsense,' said Sarah, 'what would you do without it?'

'Plenty,' said Sammy, 'I have had all kinds of foreign companies approaching me; they all want me to act as their agent. I tell you, Mrs Block, I could make a fortune, but where am I? Stuck here protecting the virtue of my girls; and the worst thing is they're known as Sam's Floozies! It's not right, is it.'

'You need a manager,' said Sarah.

'I do,' said Sammy, 'a good Jewish boy with an eye for a deal, that's what I need?'

Sarah said nothing.

'Why don't you manage The Dustpan?' she said to Abraham later that evening.

'Why would I want to do that?'

'It would be ideal,' said Sarah, 'everyone would know where to find you, and you could go into partnership with Sammy Jacobs in his agency deals.'

Abraham regarded his wife carefully. She was, of course, absolutely correct.

'I'll go and see Sammy,' he said, 'but what about the Floozies, aren't you worried that I'll have an eye for them?'

'I'd be more worried if you didn't,' said Sarah. She had come to know that her husband liked a pretty face as well as the next man, and that he had an almost pathological dislike of unattractive people.

In his new role of Managing Director of The Dustpan, Abraham Block established himself as one of Nairobi's best-loved institutions. Every day, without fail, he was to be found on its front

The Dustpan, Government Road, Nairobi, 1918

steps sometimes puffing on his cigar, often with his hands behind his back, and a jaunty trilby hat knocked towards the back of his head.

And he played shamelessly to the gallery.

'Don't let Mrs Medicks buy that dustpan,' he would say, 'she can't afford it.'

'Good morning, Mrs Levy. My, my, we're looking younger today.'

Under his stewardship, The Dustpan flourished. Soon it had expanded to occupy an entire Nairobi block, it had attracted investors, and it had been renamed Rosenblum Bullows and Roy[3]. Now the company ceased trading in tin buckets and dustpans and began to amass an array of international trading agencies ranging from grain milling to tractor manufacturers.

In 1925 a fire swept down Government Road and consumed Rosenblum Bullows and Roy in its entirety. Sammy Jacobs surveyed the blackened remains and wrung his hands.

'What am I going to do with it?' he said.

'Sell it to me Sammy,' said Abraham.

'But all the stock's gone up in smoke.'

'Stock can be replaced,' said Abraham, 'reputation can't.'

The Prophet was correct. The international giant, Unilever, bought into the business, and Rosenblum Bullows and Roy grew to be East African Industries, one of the largest trading organizations in East Africa.

In 1922 British East Africa became The Kenya Crown Colony, but its financial circumstances remained troubled. There had been a drought, which had killed thousands of livestock. Hungry zebras grazed the lawns of Government House and prides of lions followed in their wake. Soon the announcement that there was a lion to be shot was a common occurrence, and Mr Hock, the German taxidermist couldn't stuff them fast enough.

In the wake of the drought came an outbreak of Spanish 'flu, which killed many thousands of Africans. In Nairobi the mayor, Tommy Wood, provided carts to tour the streets collecting corpses, and in the up-country town of Meru, where the local tribespeople held strong taboos against handling the dead, the hyenas began creeping into their huts to drag out the bodies. And when all the bodies were gone, the hyenas started to take bites out of the living.

In Nairobi, the settlers flocked to Dr Burkitt whose cold cure seemed to be the only thing that could bring down the soaring temperatures that characterized the influenza.

At first Dr Burkitt submerged his patients in tin baths of ice-cold water, but then he adopted more radical measures. Stripping his patients down to their underclothes, he would put them into the back of his car, which had an open top, and drive them around town at high speed. Then came the day when Russell Bowker contracted the 'flu. Dr Burkitt loaded the huge man into the back of his car and drove him furiously up and down Government Road, but to no effect; Bowker's temperature soared. Exasperated, Dr Burkitt pulled to a halt outside the Norfolk Hotel, stripped Bowker naked and drove on.

On the terrace, Lord Delamere was taking tea with Major Ringer.

'Is he mad?' demanded the Major.

'No, he's a genius,' said Delamere.

'How d'you make that out?' said the Major

'Last week he did the same thing with a young woman and her temperature immediately went down, but then she started to shiver, so Burkitt took off his jacket and put it around her. By the time they got back to his surgery he was naked and she was wearing his suit,' said Delamere.

'Did it work?' said the Major.

'No idea, but it made a damned good story.'

CHAPTER 72

AT THE NORFOLK HOTEL

All the world's a stage, and all the men and women merely players: they have their exits and their entrances; and one man in his time plays many parts, his acts being seven ages.

–As You Like It, William Shakespeare (1564-1616)

THE NORFOLK HOTEL HAD BECOME a legend. It had also acquired a reputation for wild behavior, and it was the chosen haunt of a clique that the famous settler, Ewart Grogan, liked to describe as, 'the maddest and baddest of a mad, bad lot'. More than one horse had been ridden up its front steps and into the bar; and more than one couple had been caught in disarray on its billiard table. But perhaps the best tale concerned Mr Goldfinch[1], who was the 'whipper-in' of the Nairobi hunt, and he was lassoed by a visiting cowboy called Buffalo Jones, who had been put up to the prank by Lord Delamere.

'One minute I was sitting by the window, reading the paper and smoking my pipe,' said Mr Goldfinch, 'and the next there was a whistling overhead and I was on my backside in the street.'

Lord Delamere spent long months on his ranch, where he rarely drank, and where his only entertainment was the daily playing of *All Aboard for Margate* on his wind-up gramophone. So when he came to town he liked to let his hair down; and even more so during Race Week, when he considered riotous behaviour to be the order of the day.

Delamere had his own chair on the Norfolk terrace and he liked to sit there in state. He would remove his large white sun helmet and pat the top of his bald head to call for drinks. Then word would spread that 'D' was in town, and people would rush for a ringside seat on the white picket fence, which divided the terrace from the road. It was Delamere's habit to ignore his street audience and play to the gallery of his acolytes, but one day he spotted a man wearing a bright red tie[2] leaning over the white picket fence. For some reason, this infuriated Delamere, and he halted the speech that he had been making about the need for self-governance in the colony.

'Why is that man wearing a red tie?' he said.

The bar fell silent.

'Why is that man wearing a red tie!' yelled Delamere, 'Is he a socialist?'

The wearer of the red tie began to back into the crowd, which parted to admit him.

'Get it OFF!' shouted Delamere, and he leapt from his throne and pointed a finger at the man's disappearing back. Immediately, one of his henchmen vaulted the fence, seized the man, removed his tie and presented it to Delamere with a flourish. But Delamere's attention, ever mercurial, had moved on. He gazed at the red tie as if he had never seen it before in his life, and waved it away. And then he pulled a large yellow silk handkerchief out of his cardigan pocket, knotted it at each corner, and placed it on his baldhead. Peering from beneath it, he winked.

'Shall we play rugby?' he said, 'or shall we wrestle naked?'

Of all the many schoolboy games that 'D' liked to play, his favourite was the organization

(PROPRIETOR: W. H. E. EDGLEY.)

Advertisement for the Norfolk Hotel, 1922

Rooms in the Norfolk Hotel's courtyard in 1922

of Rugby matches in confined spaces, such as that of the Norfolk's bar. He also liked to make everyone lie on top of each other on the floor. On a typical Delamere evening, his henchmen would begin to shoot out the Norfolk's electric lights; and Delamere would top this by shooting out the lights of the police station, which stood on the opposite side of the road.

At the outbreak of the First World War, Major Ringer had engaged a manager for the Norfolk Hotel; he was called Mr William Edgley[3], and he could not abide Delamere's bad behaviour.

On a certain night, when Delamere had begun shooting at the police station using the jail as a backstop, Mr Edgley could bear it no longer.

'If you don't desist, my Lord' he said, 'I shall have no option but to call the Chief of Police.'

'Don't be ridiculous, man,' said 'D', pointing to the man sitting next to him, 'who the hell do you think this is? He began to beat the top of his bald head.

'Bring more brandy!' he said.

'I fear the bar is now closed, Your Lordship,' said Mr Edgley.

Delamere stared at Mr Edgley, drew his brows together, and then looked away.

'Oh damn the man,' he said 'lock him up in the meat safe.'

Mr Edgley was carried off to the meat safe with his neatly laced shoes paddling the air.

'A bit strong wasn't it, 'D'?' said Major Ringer the following day, 'the meat safe was full of sheep carcasses.'

'Nothing else to be done,' said Delamere.

'But—'

'You'd have done it yourself if you'd been there.'

'You might at least have let him out before you went to bed,' said Major Ringer.

'Good Lord man, how could I?' said Delamere outraged, 'I'd forgotten all about the chap by then.'

In 1923 Major Ringer, who had bought out his erstwhile partner, Mr Aylmer Winearls, decided to sell the Norfolk. And Mr Edgley, who had run it for the past ten years, decided to buy it.

'Why didn't you put the hotel up for public sale?' said Abraham Block to the Major.

'Who else would have bought it?' said the Major.

'I would,' said Abraham Block.

'Oh come off it,' said the major. He placed a weighty arm across Abraham's shoulders and breathed sour cigar-breath into his face.

'I mean really, old chap,' he said, 'what would a man like you do with a hotel like this. It's hardly your sort of place, is it?'

Abraham Block made no reply.

CHAPTER 73

THE SUN SETS ON BUFFALO MOUNTAIN

A renowned genius once asked a student, "What are you watching when you sit on a hillside in
the late afternoon as the colors turn from yellow to orange and red and finally darkness?"
He answered, "You are watching the sunset."
The genius responded, "That is what is wrong with our age.
You know full well you are not watching the sunset. You are watching the world turn.
–Jeremy Kagan, *"The Jewish Self"*

IT WAS WHILST HE WAS standing on the steps of Rosenblum, Bullows and Roy smoking
his habitual cigar, that Abraham perceived a tall figure in a safari suit striding towards
him. It was rare for Denys Finch Hatton to be in town; he spent most of his time taking
his wealthy clients out on safari. And on the rare occasions when his time was not booked out,
he spent it with his paramour, the Baroness Karen Blixen[1] on her failing coffee farm at the foot
of the Ngong Hills.

'Morning, Block,' said Denys.

'Morning, Mr Finch Hatton,' said Abraham; he proffered one of his Cuban cigars.

'Will you join me?' he said

'Under any other circumstances I would,' said Denys Finch Hatton, 'but I have a serious
problem.' He walked Abraham away from the steps of Rosenblum, Bullows and Roy so that they
might not be overheard.

'Sir Northrup McMillan has been having trouble with his heart,' he said.

'I'm sorry to hear that,' said Abraham.

'A few weeks ago he went to a sanatorium in Nice,' continued Finch Hatton, 'and then he felt
better so he boarded a ship to come home.'

Abraham looked up at Denys Finch Hatton, who was considerably taller than him.

'And?' he said.

'And Lady McMillan has just heard that Sir William died while the ship was steaming out
of Marseille.'

'Was he alone?' said Abraham.

'Other than for his pet monkey, yes,' said Finch Hatton.

'Sad, but the problem is?' said Abraham.

'The body is packed in ice. It will arrive in Mombasa tonight, then it will go by train
to Thika.'

'And this is a serious problem?'

'My dear Block, of course it's not,' said Finch Hatton irritably, 'the problem is that, in his will,
Sir Northrup stipulated that he be buried on top of Ol Donyo Sabuk Mountain[2].'

'Ah.'

'And Lady Lucie is adamant that his wishes be respected.'

'So—'

'When was the last time you saw Sir Northrup McMillan, ALB?' said Finch Hatton.

'It's been a while.'

'Well the last time I saw him he weighed nearly thirty stone and had a sixty-inch girth.'

'So the problem is: how to get the coffin up the mountain?' said Abraham.

'And into the ground as soon as is humanly possible,' said Finch Hatton.

'Sooner,' said Block.

'Lucie has announced that the service will take place tomorrow on top of the mountain. It will be followed by the wake, which will also be held on top of the mountain. There will be at least two hundred guests, and they will have to be driven up the mountain, because it is alive with buffalo.'

'Mmm,' said Abraham, 'then the coffin must go up first.'

'Yes,' said Finch Hatton, 'but it is lead-lined, fearfully heavy, the track is treacherous, and it generally rains in the afternoon on the mountain.'

Abraham remained silent for some minutes.

'Skis,' he said.

'What?'

'Michael Harrtz and John Rifkin, the blacksmiths, will make a pair of iron skis. The coffin will be chained to them and dragged up behind a car. We can't put the coffin in the car because the sheer weight of it will cause it to sink up to its axles in mud,' said Abraham.

'Can they make the skis in time?'

'Leave it to me.'

Denys Finch Hatton gave Abraham his most penetrating stare.

Abraham returned it; his lips pressed together, his brows raised to his hairline.

Finch Hatton smiled.

'You are the only man I can leave it to, Abraham,' he said, 'the tragedy is that Northrup can't be there to see your solution in action: he adored theatre.'

'Just one request?'

'Anything. Cost, of course, is of no object.'

'May I bring my wife?'

'My dear fellow,' said Finch Hatton, 'if you can pull this off you can bring your entire family!'

And with that he was gone.

A few hours before dawn, Abraham Black loaded his cart with an enormous pair of iron skis and a series of chains and hooks. He loaded shovels, ropes, cans of axle-grease and two suitcases. Eddie Ruben had eight of his best mules in harness, and in his cart sat a team of his most trusted men.

As the morning sun rose, the cavalcade set off, Sarah sitting beside Abraham. It wound its way through the pineapple fields and down to the brown-swirling banks of the Athi River. But when it arrived at the foot of Ol Donyo Sabuk Mountain, instead of going to Juja House, it swung right and wound up the hill to the house of McMillan's manager, John Destro. It was an L-shaped house and in the central courtyard stood a large square coffin.

'Morning ALB,' said Denys Finch Hatton.

He doffed his hat to Sarah.

'Ravishing hat,' he said, and smiled at her.

It was said of Denys Finch Hatton that he could have any woman he wanted just by smiling at her. Under his penetrating gaze, Sarah blushed. Then she raised her square chin and smiled.

'You are very kind,' she said, her poise absolutely intact.

It took several hours to mount the great coffin on the skis, and to chain them to Sir Northrup McMillan's Rolls Royce, which had been strengthened to bear his enormous weight. When all was ready, the engine was started and the car eased forward until the chains were extended to their full length. For a moment nothing happened. Then the gears ground, the car lurched forward, the tyres skidded in the mud, and the great square coffin edged forward.

'The gradient gets much steeper half-way up,' said Denys, he looked apprehensively towards Abraham.

'We'll have the mule cart and men standing by,' said Abraham.

'There's a point where the ground levels and the trees clear. It was one of Sir Northrup's favourite lookout points, he buried his dog there, you'll see the gravestone. Have the mule cart and men wait there,' said Denys, 'I will go and get the cortege moving.'

'Might I have a room in which to change, Mr Destro?' said Sarah, her suitcase in her hand. She had opted for a deceptively simple ensemble. There was a black silk low-waisted dress, which fell in box pleats to just above her black-stockinged ankles. She wore a soft coat with an astrakhan collar that stood up to frame her face. Her black cloche hat had a veil that stopped short of her mouth. As she walked across the courtyard, she flicked a glance towards the men. The outfit was a success.

The sky was pink-streaked but the rain clouds were gathering as the cortege of fifty cars and as many horse-drawn vehicles drew to a halt outside John Destro's house. The coffin stood with its black velvet pall laced around with chains. Denys Finch Hatton strode up to Sarah.

'I hope you will not mind riding in the back of my little car with the Baroness Blixen?' he said and he opened the door for her.

'Karen, my dear,' he said, 'here's Mrs Sarah Block to keep you company.'

Seated in the back of the car was a slight figure with huge sunken black eyes and an almost hawk-like profile. Karen Blixen was not beautiful, but she was arresting.

'Mrs Block,' said the Baroness, 'do come and sit by me.' She had a curiously deep voice with precise Danish intonation. She drew Sarah to her side.

Denys Finch Hatton gave the signal and the Rolls lurched forward. The coffin slid in its wake, a wave of red mud cresting before it.

Progress was slow and all that could be heard was the grinding of the gears; but the cortege inched up the lower slopes of Ol Donyo Sabuk and into the dense tree cover. As the track steepened, so it narrowed, and soon there were only inches of clearance to either side of the car. Above its bonnet a heat wave shimmered and the smell of hot oil filled the air.

'Do you think it will make it, Denys?' said Baroness Blixen.

'If the gears don't burn out,' he said.

'And if they do?' said the Baroness.

'Abraham Block will have a plan,' said Denys Finch Hatton.

'Your husband commands high respect,' said the Baroness. Sarah smiled composedly.

'I believe he does,' she said.

Abraham and Eddie Ruben watched the progress of the cortege from their lookout point high above it. It had begun to rain.

'I don't like it,' said Eddie, 'the clutch is going to go.'

'Get the mules ready,' said Abraham.

The rain fell in sheets, hailstones bounced off the ground; and the wheels of the Rolls Royce began to loose their battle with the mud. For every inch that the coffin ground forward, it slipped back another two. The chauffeur shed his gauntlets and clung to the wheel until his knuckles gleamed white.

Abraham slithered down the track and edged his way along the bonnet of the car.

'Will the clutch hold?' he said.

'Not a chance, mate,' said the chauffeur, 'it's already burning out.' He pursed his lips and shook his head. 'Bloody madness,' he said.

'We'll hitch the mules to the car,' said Abraham.

'It still won't make it to the top,' said the chauffeur.

'I know,' said Abraham, 'but I have a plan.'

'Glad somebody does,' said the chauffeur.

Eddie Ruben hitched the mules to the chassis of the Rolls Royce and they strained to haul it forward. The engine laboured and clouds of black smoke puthered from its exhaust. The mules crested a rise, and Eddie waved them to a halt. Through a break in the forest a magnificent view opened up across the plains; it was as if a curtain had been drawn back. A pair of buzzards circled high above.

Abraham made his way back to Denys Finch Hatton's car.

'This is as far as we'll get,' he said, 'I propose you explain to Lady McMillan that we have to hold the service here.'

'The grave is already dug on the summit,' said Denys.

'We will hold the service here; you will lead the cortege to the summit for the wake. When you return the coffin will be in the ground; I have a team of diggers,' said Abraham.

'You knew this would happen?' said Denys Finch Hatton.

'No more than you did,' said Abraham Block.

The coffin stood in the clearing, its black velvet pall whipping in the wind. Lady McMillan stood by its side, her black veil blowing back from her face like a shroud, and her gloved hand in that of her maid, Louise. The mourners leaned against the sides of their cars straining to hear the words of the service, but most of these words were caught by the wind and tossed across the plains. When the service was over, the cortege struggled on up to the summit.

A reception had been laid out in Sir Northrup's favourite venue. The tables were shrouded in black crepe, and black-clad waiters stepped forward bearing silver salvers of champagne. At first subdued, the level of conversation rose and, hesitantly, the serious faces allowed themselves to relax; and the odd bark of laughter was heard.

Sir Northrup McMillan's last party had begun.

The sun had set when Denys Finch Hatton made his way across to where Sarah and Abraham stood. 'My congratulations ALB,' said Denys, 'it went off magnificently well. Largely thanks to you.'

When he had left, Sarah turned to her husband.

'Can you imagine?' she said, 'Denys has introduced me to everyone: Lord Delamere, Lady McMillan, Baron von Blixen, and Sir Edward Northey. Everyone!'

'Oh, its *Denys* now, is it?' said Abraham.

CHAPTER 74

FAMILY LIFE

Fathers should be neither seen nor heard. That is the only proper basis for family life.
—Oscar Wilde, dramatist (1854-1900)

TOWARDS THE END OF THAT year, Sarah announced that she was pregnant. It was 1926, and seven years had passed since the birth of her last child.

Rita, at twelve, was fast developing into a young woman. Her dark hair was fashionably bobbed. Her eyes were wide-set; and, with her mouth pursed into the fashionable rosebud shape of the day, she had something of the look of a Charlie Chaplin heroine.

Jack, at ten, was the serious little Whitehall mandarin that he had always been. His pockets displayed neat rows of pens, he read the daily newspaper, he watched the stock market, and he kept what he called his 'papers' in a leather briefcase. Tubby, at seven, was a plump, bustling, sunny-natured child whose guileless demeanor and shining innocence of expression was misleading. The boys were on easy terms with the African staff, who spoiled them. From Miuri, the head cowman, they learned how to make bows and arrows; and to spark fire in the traditional African way. From Jengo, the cook, they learned how to put pepper under the tails of chickens, salt on slugs, and to catapult birds out of the trees. But the notion of tying the cows' tails together came from entirely within their own heads. They fought constantly and took pride in their scabs. It was Tubby who had set fire to the green velvet curtains in the dining room, and Jack who had emptied a bottle of brandy over his brother's head and then danced around him with a box of matches.

'They're pyromaniacs,' said Eddie Ruben.

'They're spoilt,' said their Aunt Lily Haller.

'They're boys,' said their Uncle Simon Haller.

'They must go away to school,' said Sarah, who intended that they should have every advantage, and be raised as gentlemen.

'Where will you send them to school?' said Lily, horrified by the thought of such a waste of money.

'I had thought of Rishon Le Zion,' said Sarah.

Abraham raised his eyebrows.

'No, Sarah,' he said, 'if they are to prosper they must speak English, not Hebrew.'

'Where will they go, then?

'I shall write to Rabbi Sinson. He will recommend a good British school for them. And one for Rita as well,' said Abraham.

'Is *Rita* to go away to school?' asked Sarah; she had not foreseen this.

'She will have to, my love,' said Abraham, 'in a Kenyan school she may be made to suffer because she is Jewish, but at an English school she will be feted because she comes from Africa.'

The Block Family (Sarab with Ruth, Rita, Tubby, Jack and ALB) 1927

'No, Pops!' said Rita when she heard.

'Don't argue with your father,' said Sarah, 'he knows best.'

'But I don't *want* to go away to England,' wailed Rita.

'Want gets nothing,' said Sarah. She had already decided that if Rita were to make a good marriage she must be educated in England and finished in Rishon Le Zion.

As the time for the birth grew closer, Sarah reached another decision: Rita would be sent away to school before the baby arrived.

The Blocks had just moved into a new house; it smelled of wet plaster and paint and it was larger than any house they had lived in before. It spanned two wings and it stood high on a hill. Modern in design, 'the house on the hill' had metal-framed windows, terrazzo floors, high ceilings and unusually long passages. Every sound was magnified, and every shout echoed. It was neither warm nor welcoming, but it suited Sarah; and she arranged for tennis courts to be laid.

'We shall hold tennis parties,' she said.

'We know how to play tennis?' said Abraham.

'We shall learn, Abraham' said Sarah.

'And who will attend these parties?' said her husband.

'Everyone will,' said Sarah, 'why should they not…? Abraham!'

But Abraham was already walking away, hat on head, cigar in hand, bound for his office and the all-absorbing chess game of buying and selling, and winning and winning.

Rita (seated) Ruth, Jack (left) and Tubby c.1931

CHAPTER 75

THE END GAME

Everything comes to him who hustles while he waits.
–Thomas A. Edison, Inventor, (1847-1931)

IT WAS WHILST HE WAS engaged in negotiating the sale of a part of the land he had bought in Elementeita, for twice the price that he had paid for the whole, that Abraham Block received a hand-written note. It came from Mr William Edgley, the owner of the Norfolk Hotel. He requested a meeting and he suggested that it might take place at the Norfolk Hotel at three o'clock that afternoon.

Abraham had known Mr Edgley for thirteen years, but he did not know him well, so the invitation was unexpected. He crammed his hat on his head and flung his jacket around his shoulders while still wrestling his arms into it. He set off to the Stanley Hotel in search of news.

Luncheon was being served at the Stanley when Abraham arrived and, as was the custom on Wednesdays, it was goat stew. Down the years, Mayence Tate had gained a good reputation for many things, but her cuisine was not one of them. And of all the dishes on her menu, goat stew was the worst. Her clientele, however, was loyal and ate it without complaint; some even claimed to enjoy it. Abraham, who loathed it, waited until coffee had been served before joining the conversation in the dining room.

Anyone who knew him well would have observed that Abraham listened more closely than usual to the conversation that took place there. But it did him no good. All he learned was that the Norfolk was as popular as ever, that Mr Edgley's stewardship was as restrained as ever, and that plans for renovation were as distant as ever.

And all this he already knew.

Abraham arrived in the lobby of the Norfolk punctually at three o'clock. As he waited, he cast a glance around; the carpet was threadbare, the curtains were faded, the velvet was balding, and the springs of the chaise longue were spent. The differing shades of wallpaper also revealed where a number of pictures had been removed.

Mr Edgley emerged from his office as urbane as ever.

'Ah, Mr Block!' he said, 'thank you for coming. This way to my office.'

Abraham was shown into a spacious room with windows looking out over the central courtyard. When the pleasantries had been completed, Mr Edgley took a deep breath. He placed both hands palms down on his desk.

'I'll come straight to the point,' he said.

'Always best,' said Abraham.

'I need an injection of capital,' said Mr Edgley, 'I need to renovate, and I'm already receiving more complaints than I can handle.'

Abraham remained silent.

'And that's not all,' continued Mr Edgley, 'the foundations of Mr Ewart Grogan's new Torr's Hotel[1] have already been laid and he's already referring to it as The Carlton Hotel of East Africa. If I am not careful, he will take my clients.'

'Mmm,' said Abraham.

'I mentioned this to Major Ringer,' said Mr Edgley, 'and he suggested that you might be in a position to provide the capital required'. He cocked his head to one side, and looked enquiringly at Abraham.

'How much capital?' said Abraham.

When Mr Edgley told him, Abraham raised his eyebrows to his hairline.

'So little?' he said.

'I'm glad you think it so,' said Mr Edgley, 'I find it a very great deal indeed.'

'So little when there seems so much to be done,' said Abraham.

'I beg your pardon,' said Mr Edgley, bristling.

'You, of course, know better than I what is required, Mr Edgley,' said Abraham, 'but I had understood that the hotel no longer has the acceptable number of bathrooms in relation to its rooms, that the roof needs replacing, and that there is considerable termite damage to the woodwork. Though none of this is any of my business.'

'No, it is not, Mr Block,' said Mr Edgley. He put his hand to his brow.

'Although all that you say is true.' Mr Edgley sighed. 'But times are hard and there is only so much that I can accomplish, as I'm sure you appreciate…'

'I do,' said Abraham. He leaned back in his chair and gave Mr Edgley a long, calm, look.

'And that's why I am not going to offer you finance,' he said.

'You are not…?'

'No. I'm going to offer you land.'

'Land?' said Mr Edgley, blinking.

'How much would you say The Norfolk Hotel was worth? Roughly, Mr Edgley?' said Abraham. 'Do you have any idea?'

'I can tell you exactly, Mr Block,' said Mr Edgley bristling. He named a figure.

'And how much would you be willing to sell it for, good will and all?' said Abraham.

Mr Edgley slumped back in his chair and was silent for several moments. In the lobby the pendulum clock ticked, and the keys of a typewriter clacked. Eventually, Mr Edgley named another figure: it was slightly higher than the first.

'But I am not looking to sell,' he said.

'No. But as it happens, Mr Edgley,' said Abraham, 'I have a plot in central Nairobi, on Sixth Avenue. You may know it? It's the large one on the corner?'

Mr Edgley nodded, impatient.

'I had it valued last week,' Abraham continued, 'and at a conservative estimate, at auction, I believe it will sell for much the same value as the price you want for your hotel.'

'Indeed?' said Mr Edgley, 'then I congratulate you on your business acumen, but it is of little consequence to me since, as I said before, I do not wish to sell.'

'No,' said Abraham, 'but I also own a second plot. It is immediately behind the first, and will sell for a similar price.'

'I don't quite see where all this is leading,' said Mr Edgley.

'It is leading to the point where I offer you both of my plots in exchange for your hotel,' said Abraham, 'which means that I am offering you twice the value you have said you will sell it for.'

Mr Edgley's eyes narrowed as he took the figures in.

'But… how do I know that your plots will sell for the amounts you mention,' he said, and he licked his thin dry lips.

Abraham smiled.

'You don't,' he said, 'but you will make the necessary enquiries and if you discover that I am correct, we can strike a deal.' He sat back in his chair.

Mr Edgley stared at Abraham Block for some moments, then his gaze shifted slightly out of focus. Eventually he banged his palms down on the desk and stood up. He was smiling.

'What have I got to lose?' he said, 'I had not thought to sell. I admit it. But in the light of your offer which, if duly verified, is generous indeed, now that I do come to think of selling, I have to admit that I rather like the idea.'

'I am glad.' said Abraham. He handed Mr Edgley a small white visiting card. 'Here are the details of my solicitor,' he said, 'he will give you the necessary papers. Will forty-eight hours be sufficient time for you to verify my offer?'

Mr Edgley nodded. As he shook Abraham's hand he seemed slightly dazed.

As Abraham walked away, he heard the wheels of Mr Edgley's chair squeal, and the dull thud of its rounded wooden back hitting the wall[2].

Only when he had arrived back in his own office and sat down at his own desk, did Abraham allow himself to consider the advisability of his offer. It did not take long. As he had known at the time, the deal was a good one. He wanted the Norfolk Hotel; he wanted it very much. As for Mr Edgley, he clearly did not have the cash to keep it going and he was lured by the idea of getting twice his asking price for it.

For his own part, Abraham knew intuitively that his gamble would pay off. The hotel was dilapidated and not worth the price he had offered for it in terms of bricks and mortar. But in terms of cachet, charisma and potential, it was worth twice the amount he had offered.

But that was not all: as the owner of The Norfolk Hotel, Abraham Block would have achieved his goal. He would be somebody. And so would Sarah.

As he was reflecting upon this, the door opened and one of his girls put her head around it.

'Oh, Mr Block!' she said. 'I'm sorry for not knocking, but Dr Burkitt has just passed by. He couldn't stop! He said to tell you the baby is on its way and you're to come directly!'

Two days later, Abraham Block was the doting father of his second daughter, and the proud owner of his first hotel. When he had arrived at her bedside, Sarah had already gone into labour, but it was mercifully short. Yelling lustily, Ruth Block was born on the 12th of October 1927.

Some hours later, when Sarah had awakened and was staring down at her daughter, Abraham went to sit by their side.

'It's nowhere near as beautiful as Ruth,' he said, 'but I have something to give you.'

'What?' said Sarah. She did not look up. She was smiling down at the child.

'The Norfolk Hotel,' he said.

CHAPTER 76

THE OWNER OF A HOTEL

A good decision is based on knowledge and not on numbers.
–Plato (427-347 BC)

T HE ACQUISITION OF THE HOTEL was a lengthy business. Inventories had to be made; weighty documents with waxy-red self-importance had to be signed and sealed. But the day dawned when Mr Edgley found himself walking along the terrace of the Norfolk Hotel for the last time as its owner.

Its new owner, uncharacteristically superstitious, waited in the police station on the other side of the road.

'I don't want to walk into it until I know it's mine,' said Abraham Block to the Commissioner of Police, who had watched his nervous pacings up and down the white picket fence until he could stand it no longer.

'Do come in and have a cup of tea, ALB,' he had said, 'you're as jittery as a bridegroom.'

The Commissioner made numerous attempts to distract Abraham, but he would only stare fixedly out of the window at the object of his desire.

'Do you think you'll have any better luck in reigning in 'D' Delamere than he did?' said the Commissioner as Mr Edgley was seen to descend the steps of the hotel, throw his briefcase into his Model T Ford, and drive away without a backward glance.

For a long moment, ALB said nothing. Then he turned away from the window and picked up his hat. 'If it were not for Lord Delamere I would not be here,' he said, 'he can do whatever he likes in my hotel and I shall be grateful.' He stubbed out his cigar in the commissioner's ashtray, shook him by the hand, walked out of his office, across the road, and up the steps into his new hotel.

The acquisition of the Norfolk Hotel was a turning point in the life of Abraham Block, but it made no impression on the hotel itself. Abraham had retained the entire staff, at least six of whom were European, so there was no reason why the guests should sense a new hand at the helm. And even less reason to tell them of it. So the Norfolk Hotel sailed ahead with the serene composure of a dowager duchess at a minor coming out ball.

Abraham Block, nervous as a debutante, gingerly toured his purchase. There were only thirty rooms. Most were sparse, single and stood around a central quadrangle. A number of bathrooms opened off the creaking corridors, though there were nowhere near enough of them. All had black and white tiled floors, ponderous porcelain fittings, and large marbled lights, not unlike spittoons, which hung by thin chains from their flyblown ceilings. The plumbing was eccentric, and burly pipes gurgled along the corridors. The hot water erupted from the blunt nosed taps in explosive gulps, so hot as to scald, and so temperamental as to make filling a bath a devotion.

All this Abraham determined would have to change.

In the main building, which had evolved organically down the years, the wooden floors creaked and its many differing levels necessitated numerous short flights of stairs, which had balding carpets and brass stair-rods. The lobby was small and dissected by a high counter. Behind the counter were ranged rows of neat pigeonholes, and there was a small glass cubbyhole with an arched peephole.

In the cubby hole, raised on a patchwork cushion of her own making, sat a small mouse-like lady called Mrs Sexton. She prepared the bills, handled the cash, and enjoyed sole access to the heavy brass safe, which squatted like a pot-bellied stove in the corner of her room.

This too would have to change determined Abraham.

There was a cramped office where a typist clattered, and a heavy black telephone reclined in its cradle. Both the counter and the office were the domain of Yusuf, a Somali of regal bearing, impassive expression, and few words. He wore a long white robe, a crimson fez with a black tassel, and a pair of camel-skin slippers with turned-up toes.

Yusuf had served as the face of the Norfolk for as long as anyone could remember. His dark eyes were hooded and distant, like those of a hawk above the desert, and he was a master of the art of deferential distain.

A corridor led from the lobby to the Gentlemen's Bar, the Billiard Room and the Smoking Room, all of which were male preserves. Another corridor led to the Blue Room, the Reading Room, and the Card Room, which were not. The dining room, which doubled as the ballroom, lay at the end of the second corridor.

A pair of double doors stood between the Norfolk and the rest of the world. They were propped open with twin brass shell-casings and they remained so until the last guest was believed to have retired for the night. Then they were ceremonially closed and bolted by Yusuf, who handed the keys to his minion, Mr Rodriguez Pinto. A timorous walnut of a man, far too old for the silver-buttoned uniform and chin-strapped cap that he was compelled to wear, it was Mr Pinto's job to admit all latecomers.

The famous Norfolk Terrace was raised on polished timbers and edged by an elegant balustrade, and it featured numerous small round tables. At its far end stood the bar, which was known as The House of Lords. It was housed in a small, square, half-timbered bell tower, which gave the hotel its distinctive, mock-Tudor character. The bar also featured a curious lychgate, similar to those found outside English churches, which led to the road, and this was known to the bar's regulars as 'The Gallows'.

Abraham observed all of these attributes of his new hotel with minute attention, periodically nibbling his thumb. Then he emerged on to the terrace, where he found Major Ringer.

'Good morning, Major,' Abraham said, his expression bland.

'Morning, Block,' said the major, 'I've come to bid farewell to the old place.'

'Really, Major?' said Abraham, 'I do hope Nairobi is not to lose you?'

'Of course not,' said the Major testily. He sat down and shook out his newspaper.

'But I doubt the Norfolk will remain as it is for much longer,' he said. He pulled his spectacles from his pocket and affected to read.

'Why not?' said Abraham, who took a mild pleasure in provoking the Major.

'Oh damn it all, man,' said the Major, 'I've no doubt you'll attract your own sort of guests. Your own *type*, you know. And I wish you well of it, believe me. But I think you will find that

Caricature of Abraham Block by the artist, Mrs 'Sammy' Clayton

now *you* have taken over,' he stressed the word, 'the old guard will move on.'

The Major glanced up at Abraham. He was slightly red in the face and he knew that he was being offensive. 'No bad thing eh? Block?' he said, now faintly apologetic, 'move with the times and all that?'

'Oh I don't know about that, Major,' said Abraham, 'I plan to keep things exactly as they have always been.'

'Hmm, well, we shall see,' said the Major. He reopened his newspaper with deliberation.

'Indeed we shall,' said Abraham, 'good day to you, Major.'

CHAPTER 77

ALB AT THE HELM

You have to learn the rules of the game. And then you have to play better than anyone else.
–Albert Einstein (1879-1955)

THE MAJOR WAS WRONG IN his predictions. Lord Delamere[1] took up residence in his usual room for the remainder of Race Week, and the lobby of the Norfolk Hotel continued to seethe with its usual quota of titles, shooters, barons of industry, colonial faces and international names. Denys Finch Hatton took luncheon in the dining room with Baroness Blixen, and the room emitted its usual hum of polite conversation, clinking china and squeaking floors.

'Not changing anything are you, Block?' said Delamere.

'Certainly not, 'D',' said Abraham.

'Said you wouldn't,' said Delamere. He patted his head in the direction of his favourite waiter. 'Though you could usefully get rid of that blighter,' he said, 'I swear he makes it his business to look the other way when he knows perfectly well what I want. Come *on* man, I've got a bloody horse running at two.'

There were those who had voiced fears that Abraham Block might 'presume' upon his position as the owner of Kenya's most famous hotel; and there were others who feared he might 'push himself forward' and become what they liked to describe as 'over familiar'. But their fears, genuine or not, were ill founded.

Abraham Block took up station in his office and he remained there, the only clue to the change in its occupancy being the wreaths of cigar smoke that crept from beneath its door. Rarely did he venture into the dining room, and rarely into the lounge. And, on his infrequent trips down the terrace, it was clear from his demeanor that he regarded himself as no more than a member of the staff. Soon, all those who would have liked to have found the opportunity to snub Abraham Block were forced to accept that he comported himself well. And all those who wished him well relaxed.

And a number of subtle improvements came to the attention of all.

The plumbing became less vocal, the chipped china was replaced, the waiters' cuffs were no longer frayed, and it was no longer possible to put one's foot through the sheets. Relying on Sarah, who always ensured that her personal choices were endorsed by a select group of ladies, Abraham began to replace the faded curtains, and reupholster the tired chairs. Rolls of the finest Axminster carpet were to be seen marching down the platform of Nairobi Railway Station alongside bolts of Liberty chintz. Antique racing prints were ordered from London, gilt-framed oils from Paris, china from Limoges and feather pillows from Bavaria. And, as the hotel slowly cast off its mantle of blistered paint and bulging ceilings, it began to exude that particular aroma of expenditure and tradition that pervades all the best hotels.

And its owner began to emerge, tentative at first, into the light of his own creation.

Abraham developed a penchant for a particular chair in the Norfolk's lobby. It was small, scarlet and gold-tasseled, and it was strategically positioned immediately outside Mrs Sexton's office. When seated in this chair, Abraham Block would normally be obscured behind a newspaper, but those who knew him well were aware that he did not read it. Rather, they surmised, he used it as a screen from behind which he might observe the comings and goings of his guests; and he took an almost fatherly pride in these.

Occasionally, when a guest checked out, ALB might discreetly hold out a hand to Mrs Sexton who, opening her door a fraction, would hand him the bill she had prepared. Abraham would peruse it briefly and hand back to her. Not a word would be exchanged between them.

From time to time Abraham might allow himself the indulgence of wandering into the dining room, and there he would stand, discreetly out of sight, beaming on its diners. And out on the terrace, Abraham would observe with quiet indulgence as the mad, bad, lot vied to be the maddest and baddest of them all.

Unlike Major Ringer and Mr Edgley, both of whom had used the hotel as their own personal social arena, ALB never dined in the hotel's dining room. Instead, he either ate breakfast, luncheon and supper at home with Sarah, or he arrived with a metal chop-box of the type used on safaris: typically it contained a generous serving of homemade borsht.

As the Norfolk swirled her way through her usual calendar of social events, Abraham might permit himself a brief peep in on their sparkle and brilliance, but he did with it all the diffidence of a child creeping down from the nursery to peer over the bannisters at the party below.

In 1928, Ewart Grogan opened Torr's Hotel and the Long Bar of the Stanley instantly renamed it Tart's Hotel. It was an imposing redbrick structure, built to the exact design of Stockholm Town Hall, though nobody was quite sure why this should be. A slightly self-conscious edifice, it stood five grandiose floors high and dominated Nairobi's nascent skyline. On the ground floor, twenty-foot-high arched windows marched along the pavement until they met those of The Theatre Royale next door.

According to the advertisements, which were blazoned large in the papers, Torr's Hotel offered 'all the comforts of your home and the gaieties of a West End Hotel.'

The comforts were considerable. There was an area in which the guests might leave their cheetah cubs, or their pet mongooses. There were two lifts, the first of their kind in East Africa; there was a Pompeian Penthouse Suite, an Elizabethan Minstrels Gallery, and a Palm Court where tea dances were held. There was also a ballroom with crystal chandeliers so heavy that they had to be supported by iron girders set into the floor; and a dance band that had been imported from New York. There was also a temperamental French chef, and a cinema where a number of Hollywood starlets were able to applaud their own performances.

Despite all of this, Torr's Hotel was not the Norfolk Hotel, and it never would be. Nor would its bright flitting crowds ever quite escape the notion that they had somehow accepted second-best. Meanwhile, back at The Norfolk, the faces continued to flock, the safaris continued to go out, and the pearls continued to gleam with the conviction that only real pearls can.

CHAPTER 78

MAJOR RINGER REPENTS

Life is 10 percent what you make it, and 90 percent how you take it.
Irving Berlin, composer (1888-1989)

SINCE HIS PREDICTIONS REGARDING THE demise of the Norfolk, as he knew it, had proven incorrect, Major Ringer had no option but act as though he had never made them. Regular as clockwork, he arrived for his morning coffee, his perusal of the papers, his lunch, his evening 'peg' and his dinner. The Norfolk allowed a chosen few to hold accounts at the hotel, and the Major was a member of this group, but he had fallen on hard times. He had found that he could no longer afford to run his racing stables and nor could he meet the payroll on his farm out at Ol Donyo Sabuk.

Preferring to ignore this situation rather than to address it, the Major continued to treat the Norfolk Hotel as his second home; and his chits mounted up.

Mrs Sexton, the accountant, was frightened of Abraham Block, though neither of them knew quite why this should be; and she tried not to put herself in his way. But one morning she had no option.

'I'm sorry, Mr Block,' she said, 'but I have to bring something unpleasant to your notice.'

'What is that, Mrs Sexton,' said Abraham. He always made well-meaning attempts to engage her with his smile, but this frightened her even more.

'Major Ringer's account is running considerably in arrears, Mr Block,' said Mrs Sexton. She took a breath. 'And his last cheque has just been returned unpaid.'

'Bring me the accounts,' said Abraham, 'and think no more of it.'

Later that day, the Major arrived for his customary 'peg', and took up position in his favourite basket chair on the terrace.

'I wonder if I might trouble you to come to my office, Major?' said ALB. He stood deferentially to one side of the Major's table. The Major looked up at him. There was nothing in Abraham's demeanor to suggest that anything was other than as it should be, but the Major sniffed danger.

'What's all this, Block?' he said.

'Just a moment, in my office,' said Abraham. He bowed slightly and extended his arm in the direction of his office. When they were seated, Abraham placed the carefully annotated file of the Major's hotel account before him. On the top had been stapled the dishonoured cheque.

'Ah,' said the Major, 'now…'

Precisely, and deliberately, Abraham tore up the cheque.

He also tore up the folder marked Major Charles Harding Newman Ringer.

'Does that mean I'm black balled?' said the Major, whose fear of social bankruptcy was greater than his fear of the other kind.

'Only clubs black ball, Major,' said Abraham, 'all it means is that your account is terminated, and with it all the outstanding debts.'

The Major shuffled in his chair.

'I say. You're a good fellow, Block,' he said, 'and I think I owe you an apology. I spoke out of turn when you took over the hotel—'

'I have never heard you say anything that was out of turn, Major,' said Abraham, 'would you care for a cigar?'

The Major accepted the proffered cigar. As they puffed companionably together, an idea came to him. 'I say Block, old chap,' he said, 'you wouldn't have any interest in racehorses would you?'

CHAPTER 79

COLD WINDS BLOW

Therefore shall her plagues come in one day, death, and mourning, and famine;
and she shall be utterly burned with fire.
—The Bible

Rita Block was sent away. She was taken to the town of Hove, which stood on the Sussex coast of England. She was installed in the chilly dormitories of the select all-girls, all-Jewish school known as Mansfield College; and she hated it. As Abraham drove away down the long drive, beyond which lay the grim, grey oily-flat British sea, Rita screamed so long, so loud and so hysterically that the stiffly starched matron had no recourse but to slap her. But no matter how hard Rita screamed, it made not the slightest difference to her fate.

Two years later, the same fate befell the boys. First they were installed in a preparatory school in Brighton, and thereafter in the exclusive Loughborough College in Leicester[1], from whence they returned to Kenya so infrequently that Tubby was to complain in later life that he had not seen his mother for four years.

But Sarah Block knew that sending her children away was the price that must be paid to ensure that when they returned they would find every door open to them. But she did not extend this rule to include her youngest child. Elfin faced, pearly-toothed, cherub curled, and always meticulously attired in hand-smocked frocks with puffed sleeves and Peter Pan collars, Ruth Block was the darling of her father. And she did not need to be sent away to learn assurance, because she already knew she was a princess.

Precocious, beguiling and calmly confident, Ruth knew that she could do no wrong in the eyes of her father. Rita, Jack and Tubby had been forced to compete for Abraham's attention, and frequently been denied it; but Ruth could have it at will. Rita, Jack and Tubby's misdeeds had been punished, often harshly; but Ruth's were ignored. Rita, Jack and Tubby would not have dared to climb into their father's lap; but Ruth could do so whenever the whim took her.

Ruth's little hands could help her father pour his evening whisky, Ruth could help him clip his cigar, Ruth could play with his trilby, and Ruth could cling to his tie until it threatened to strangle him. She could even fall asleep in her father's arms as he listened to the large brown wireless that now took pride of place in the drawing room.

It was while he had his ear pressed to this wireless, which had a round hole pierced in the middle of its highly polished bulk, that Abraham heard something of a kind he had hoped he would never hear again. It was an interview with Adolf Hitler, the leader of the newly emerged Nazi Party, and the heir apparent to the position of the German Chancellorship.

'Once I really am in power,' Hitler had said, 'my first and foremost task will be the annihilation of the Jews. As soon as I have the power to do so, I will have gallows built in rows—at the Marienplatz in Munich, for example—as many as traffic allows. Then the Jews will be hanged indiscriminately, and they will remain hanging until they stink; they will hang there as long as the principles of hygiene permit. As soon as they have been untied, the next batch will be strung up, and so on down the line, until the last Jew in Munich has been exterminated. Other cities will follow suit, precisely in this fashion, until all Germany has been completely cleansed of Jews.'*

As the casual obscenity of these words hung in the air, Abraham turned the radio off. He looked down at Ruth, sleeping in his lap, and clenched his teeth. It was happening again, just as it had when he had been Ruth's age. But this time he determined that he would not be the victim of his own Jewishness. This time he would join with his fellow Jews to protect the persecuted.

When Abraham saw his sister Lily, he told her that she could count on his support in the building of Nairobi's first synagogue, and from that point on, he became one of its most loyal supporters.

The threat of another World War brought with it the threat of global financial collapse. In America, the Wall Street Crash heralded the first crack in the solidity of the post war economics. Gold accumulated in Paris and New York, and the stability of all the world's currencies was threatened. In the industrialized nations, commodity prices began to tumble, and unemployment figures began to soar. Then deflation began to squeeze the debtor nations until they burst. Germany announced that she could not afford to make any more post-war reparations payments; and the Austrian banking system collapsed. World credit teetered, tariff walls were erected, quotas and embargos were set.

In the Kenya Crown Colony, grain piled up in the silos, coffee was burned as locomotive fuel, and molasses was poured into the sea. In 1930, the price of Kenyan coffee dropped from £210 to £70 per ton. Maize, which had once sold for twelve shillings a bag now sold for only two, and the value of sisal halved in just one year. Soon Kenya's principal exports were selling for less than it cost to produce them.

Then, from the north, came great clouds of locusts. They swept through Sudan, Abyssinia, Somaliland, Nigeria and Sierra Leone leaving nothing but devastation in their wake. When they reached Kenya, the swarms of locusts were several miles long and so thick that they blacked out the sun. When they settled on branches, the trees collapsed; and when they settled on the fields a wheat harvest could be wiped out in an hour. They ate everything; crops, grass and gardens alike.

Kenya's farmers converged on Nairobi to demand help. They gathered on the terrace of the Norfolk to listen to Lord Delamere and Mayor Tommy Wood.

'An Anti-Locust Service will be set up,' said Tommy Wood.

'Vehicles will be mounted with flame guns,' said Delamere.

'My fields are heaving with them,' said one farmer, 'how will two flame guns make any difference?'

'We shall dig ditches and teams of volunteers will drive the locusts into them,' said Delamere, 'then we will douse them with flame.'

'The flames will take the crops,' said one man.

'The teams won't get there fast enough,' said another.

'Do you have a better idea?' said Tommy Wood.

* This is an actual transcript of Adolf Hitler's words, taken from a radio interview that he made.

Amid the headshaking, the settlers formed themselves into platoons. Michael Harrtz and John Rifkin constructed great black flame guns, which were lashed to the roofs of Model T Fords and trucks. It was a valiant effort, but it did not work.

By the end of 1931 the settlers had lost half their crops and the Kenyans had lost a fifth of theirs.

Then, just as mysteriously as they had arrived, the swarms of locusts departed.

And in their wake came famine.

CHAPTER 80

THE WINGS OF DEATH

Death is merely moving from one home to another. The wise man will spend his main efforts in
trying to make his future home the more beautiful one.

–Rabbi Menachem Mendel Morgenstern of Tomashov (the Kotzker Rebbe)

IT WAS AS THE KENYA Crown Colony struggled to withstand the blows of man and nature
that it was bereft of two of its most iconic figures.

First came the news that Denys Finch Hatton had crashed his plane in the hills just
outside Voi. His body, burnt beyond recognition, lay amid the wreckage in a halo of oranges,
which he had been flying back from the coast[1]. On the terrace of the Norfolk Hotel, the news
swept through the tables sparking and silencing conversations as it went. Denys Finch Hatton,
the wit, the character, the lover, the man so vitally, beautifully and insolently alive, was gone? It
did not seem feasible.

'Has Baroness Blixen been told?' said Sarah to Abraham.

'Lady McMillan is breaking the news to her now,' he said.

Later, it was learned that the Baroness was to organize Denys' funeral.

'He is to be buried near the foot of the Ngong Hills,' said Abraham, 'the cortege sets
out tomorrow.'

'Then we shall follow it,' said Sarah[2].

Karen Blixen's coffee farm stood several miles north of Nairobi and when Sarah and Abraham
arrived there, they found hundreds of mourners already standing hushed on the lawns of the
Baroness's small, grey house. Hundreds more streamed from all directions.

The coffin stood on an open-sided ox-cart. It had no pall and there were no wreaths, just
Denys Finch Hatton's hat and his gun. The Baroness, a slightly stooped figure, stood on the steps
of her house and greeted each of the mourners with a clasp of the hand, a murmured few words.
Behind her stood her Somali butler; he had a curved scimitar hooked into the scarlet sash that
bound his white robe. At the Baroness's feet lay her greying wolfhound with its ears laid quite flat
against its head, and its nose on its paws.

At a signal from the Baroness, a whip was cracked and the oxen set off. The cart swayed and
lurched, but the coffin, now secured with ropes, remained still. A muddy track led through the
coffee fields, beyond them, and up through all the small farms that clustered on the slopes of
the Ngong Hills. Clouds of yellow butterflies hovered over the puddles, and the air was scented
with the raw, red, rain-on-murram smell of Africa. Ragged children stood with their fists in their
mouths and their eyes wide as the cart laboured and the crack of the whip came more frequently.
As the track rose, the fields gave way to pine trees, and the creak of the cartwheels was deadened
by a carpet of needles. Breaks in the trees revealed glimpses of the blue-green haze of the plains
far below.

Baroness Blixen with her staff and her wolfhound on the steps of her Karen home

A plateau was reached, little more than a lip in the great knuckled imprint of the Ngong Hills. A grave gaped and high above it a pair of kites wheeled and keened, their talons catching and releasing as they fell through the air. It was a simple service, soon over and, as the mourners filed back down the track, the sound of earth being hurled down on to wood could be heard. And the quiet voice of Karen Blixen, who still read poetry as if Denys Finch Hatton still listened.

As evening fell, the mourners gathered on the terrace of the Norfolk Hotel. It was the natural centre of settler life; and they did not know where else to go.

'Where is Lord Delamere?' said Abraham as he surveyed the clusters of black-clad people.

'On his ranch at Elementeita,' said Fatty Garland, 'he is not well. Heart.'

A few weeks later, a Maasai warrior stalked down the road that led to the Norfolk Hotel. Hunched into his red cloak, he planted his spear beneath the eucalyptus trees, and he stood there completely still.

Abraham was talking with his manager, Tom Latham.

'What does he want?' he said, indicating the warrior.

'No idea,' said Tom, 'I'll go and find out.'

When he came back, his face was grave.

'I can't believe it,' he said simply.

'What?'

'Lord Delamere is dead, his warrior has come to lead us to the funeral.'[3]

Karen Blixen and her staff at the Karen house.

CHAPTER 81

THE LAST TRAIN TO MARGATE

Everything is only for a day, both that which remembers and that which is remembered.
–Marcus Aurelius Antoninus Augustus (121-180 BC)

THE DEATH OF LORD DELAMERE rocked the Crown Colony of Kenya. He had been its champion, its leader, its jester, and its prince. For seventy-five years Delamere had carved the character of the Colony from the face of its land. He had bred its cattle, imported its sheep, stocked its rivers, irrigated its badlands, and pioneered the crops that would make its fortune.

Delamere the fighter had battled for the rights of the settlers, and he had fought for the heritage of his beloved Maasai. Delamere the leader had harangued the Legislative Council, his letters had flooded into the Times of London, and he had championed the cause of British East Africa in the British Houses of Parliament.

Delamere had poured his entire fortune into the Colony. He had given his life to the land and his love to the continent. He was a character unrivalled and his death represented a great personal loss to the entire community. It also heralded the end of the ideals he had symbolized and the philosophies in which he had believed.

Ever the imperialist, Delamere had insisted on the supremacy of the white man and, even in the aftermath of the First World War, he had refused to relinquish this belief. Yet, of all the colonialists, Delamere's understanding of the African psyche had ranked supreme. He was one of the few settlers ever to conquer the language of the Maasai, and he indulged in a lifelong love affair with their culture.

Aristocratic and autocratic, Delamere had reigned supreme in his own culture. Irascible, wild, puckish of humour and irrepressible to the last, he had led both 'the mad bad lot' of the Norfolk and the louche coterie of the Muthaiga Club.

On the morning after the day of his death, Lord Delamere arrived on the shores of Lake Elementeita for the last time. Hundreds of mourners awaited him. Some came by train, others by car. Some came by cart, wagon or mule; hundreds came on foot. One old man came on the train from Mombasa carrying only a bunch of faded flowers. He had not had time, he said, to collect anything else. Others came straight off the land, dressed exactly as they were and carrying their tools in their hands.

Lying deep in the cleft of the Great Rift Valley, Lake Elementeita was ethereally lovely and utterly wild. Mirrored by shifting cloud patterns, it was enigmatic, shallow and bitterly alkaline; it was fringed by coral pink flamingoes and snow-white pelicans. Its shores were bare of structures, marked only by the bones of pink flamingoes bleached white by the sun.

To the north of the lake rose the rounded shoulder of Lake Nakuru, to the west the smoke-blue heights of the Mau Escarpment, and to the east the contorted folds of the Aberdares. To the south lay the blunted peaks of a volcano known to the Maasai as The Sleeping Warrior, and to the settler community as Delamere's Nose. At the tip of the lake, hot springs bubbled and the silhouettes of flamingoes and herons appeared like spectres out of the billowing steam of a ghostly oasis.

Delamere had chosen his own burial site; it was one of his favourite places for reflection. It stood atop a rocky knoll fringed with yellow grass and washed by white-crusted tides of mud. Below it, rocky islands rose from the placid waters of the lake, and they seethed with nesting pelicans. Around the knoll patrolled platoons of eland, zebra, buffalo and giraffe, and above it wheeled fish eagles, their screams echoing across the water.

A long procession snaked towards the knoll; it was led by twin columns of Maasai warriors, clad in their traditional scarlet cloaks and carrying their spears. They were followed by the Delamere family, their staff, and the ranks of Delamere's friends and acquaintances. Some were austerely elegant, some wildly bohemian. There were white-clad colonial officials, Kikuyu chiefs in full regalia, up-country cattle traders, simple farmers, and rippling lines of Maasai women.

Every sector of Kenyan society was present.

The words of the brief ceremony were not heard by most of the mourners. They were whipped away by the wind and carried over the lake. But this was as it should be.

When the funeral was over, and Sarah and Abraham had reached Nairobi, Abraham went directly to the Norfolk Terrace.

'Bring out His Lordship's chair,' he said.

'Where shall I put it?' said his manager, aghast.

'Where he liked it to be,' said Abraham.

As the chair was solemnly carried down the terrace, hats were removed, heads were bowed and silence fell. For a moment, as his chair was put in place, Delamere's presence was expected. People looked down the terrace. They almost expected him to come limping along it, sun helmet in hand, cronies at his heels; bellowing, blistering: the only character on the stage.

But he did not.

Hesitantly, the mourners began to recount their tales of his speeches and his crusades, his tirades and his capers, his irreverence and his sheer, towering refusal to accept any form of defeat.

'Well done, ALB,' said Fatty Garland, 'it's almost as if he's still here.'

'He always will be,' said Abraham, 'I'm going to rename this The Delamere Terrace.'

CHAPTER 82

RITA IS MARRIED

By all means, marry. If you get a good wife, you'll become happy;
if you get a bad one, you'll become a philosopher.
—Socrates (469-399 BC)

Since she had been the first child to be sent away to school in England, Rita was the first one to come home. Her education had changed her; she spoke with a precise British accent, her figure had rounded, and her face was that of a determined, if slightly challenging young woman.

Rita's horizons had broadened, but her conception of Nairobi's had shrunk.

In England, Rita had spent occasional weekends with the Sinson family in Leeds. They had taken her to a plethora of events, religious and social. They had introduced her to all manner of suitable young men; and many of the young men had shown flatteringly interest in her. She had been introduced to the brothers and cousins of her school friends and, as Abraham had predicted, the fact that she came from Africa had given her a certain gilded mystique.

Rita's charmed life ended when she arrived back in Nairobi, which she now saw for what it was: a colonial outpost. Then the home that she had missed and longed for turned into a prison.

'Why can't I go and work in one of the shops in town?' she said.

'Because it is not suitable,' said Sarah.

'It's suitable for Naomi Saltzer and Judith Abrahams.'

'Don't be impertinent, Rita,' said Sarah, 'and remember who you are.'

'Who am I?'

'You are the daughter of Abraham Block, the owner of the Norfolk Hotel; your relations in Rishon Le Zion are of impeccable Jewish breeding, you have been expensively educated in England, and you are *not* a shop girl.'

'What's the use of all that when I don't meet anyone?' Rita said.

It was a good question.

It also prompted Sarah to review the selection of suitable young men living in Kenya. They were pitifully few, and most were farmers' sons living up country.

'It's time Rita was married,' she said to Abraham.

'She's only just come home,' he said.

'Nevertheless, if we don't introduce her to some suitable young men, she will find an unsuitable young man.'

Abraham knew his wife well.

'So what have you decided, my love?' he said.

'I am going to take her to Rishon Le Zion. It is time I visited my family again, and it is time she spent time with her aunts and cousins.'

Rita with baby Ora

'As you wish,' said Abraham, 'but I cannot come with you; I've just taken a new warehouse with Markus, and it must be filled. There will be war, of that I am sure.'

'All the more reason for us to go immediately,' said Sarah.

Shortly afterwards, she, Ruth and Rita left for Rishon Le Zion, leaving Abraham to do what he did best: stockpile anything and everything that may prove useful were the Colony to go to war.

Six months later, a letter was received from Sarah. Her younger sisters, the twins, Hanah and Leah, had undertaken the chaperoning of Rita with a most satisfactory result. At a party in Rishon Le Zion, Rita had met a young man by the name of Jacob Hirshfeld[1], and Jacob had requested Rita's hand in marriage. His family, Sarah recounted, originated from the Ukraine, but had fled to Rishon in 1886 to escape the pogroms. Well-respected, and reasonably affluent, the Hirshfelds had planted vineyards and they grew almonds. The young man's father, Tzvi Hirshfeld, was dead, but he had been a man of considerable standing. His mother, Bracha, came from a staunchly religious Hassidic family, and had brought her son up to be both scholarly and respectful of his faith. She had also sent him to Tel Aviv's Mikve Israel Agricultural College, one of Eretz Israel's finest, where he had been so successful that he was currently managing the orange groves of one of his former lecturers, Professor Meir Vinik.

It was an excellent match, said Sarah. And she was ready to make plans for the marriage.

As he read the letter, Abraham smiled. He was pleased that Sarah's mission had been successful. And he looked forward to receiving his first son-in-law. But he was also delighted to find the missing piece for one of the many jigsaws that lay uncompleted on the worktable of his mind. As he had watched the inexorable approach of war, Abraham had formulated many plans. The most important concerned the laying of the foundations for an organization that would offer refuge for the persecuted Jews of Europe, and already a small group of these refugees were making their way to Kenya. That apart, Abraham was busy filling his warehouses with an astute collection of goods whose value he was certain would double with the arrival of war. Amongst these goods were all manner of tinned foodstuffs. But they were deficient in one area: tinned fruit.

Abraham wrote back to Sarah.

'Go ahead with the wedding plans,' he said, 'and do as you think fit; I will attend if I can[2], but in the meantime I am sending money for the purchase of a fruit orchard in Rishon Le Zion. I am also sending money for the building of a house for Rita and Jacob on the land. The boy must continue in his present employment, but he must also establish our own fruit orchards. I will pay him a salary, and he should prepare to ship fruit to Kenya as soon as possible.'

Sarah smiled. Her husband, she reflected, was a good man, but his mind would always be ruled by profit and loss, even when it came to his own family.

Then she thought again.

Her sons, Jack and Tubby, were coming home from their education in England, and she had great plans for them. Her boys were to mix with the very best of Nairobi society; and no door was to be closed to them. To move in such circles, they would require access to considerable wealth, so it was only right, she decided, that Abraham was devoting his time to creating it.

Ruth and Abraham with their grandsons, Tsvi, Eallan and Theo

CHAPTER 83

SONS AND DAUGHTERS

Sons have always a rebellious wish to be disillusioned by that which charmed their fathers.
–Aldous Huxley, English writer (1894-1963)

WHEN JACK AND TUBBY BLOCK arrived home from their many years away at school and in further education, Sarah could not believe what she saw. They were not the boys she had sent away to England; they had glossy slicked back hair, casually elegant suits, and almost matinee idol good looks.

'I say, Ma,' said Jack, 'what about a party for my twenty-first?'

'We'll see,' said Sarah.

'What about coming into the office, and seeing how the business is run?' said Abraham.

'Plenty of time for that, Pops,' said Jack, 'when we've done some travelling?'

'What travelling?' said Abraham, bemused.

'Everyone travels, Pops,' said Tubby, 'see the world and all that.'

'What happened to earning a living?' said Abraham.

'Leave them be,' said Sarah, 'they've only just come home.'

Ruth, now a teenager, regarded her handsome brothers with awe.

'Hello, little sis,' said Jack, absently, 'all grown up eh?'

Tubby ruffled her curls, 'if you're a good girl,' he said, 'I'll teach you how to play gin rummy.'

'You'll do no such thing,' said Sarah, 'and you won't play it yourselves either.'

'Oh come on, Ma,' said Jack, 'it's what chaps do; it was all the rage at school.'

'You're not at school now,' said Sarah.

'Beginning to wish we were,' said Jack to Tubby as they slouched off, hands in pockets, down the drive, 'let's get off down into town and find some cigarettes.'

'Or girls,' said Tubby.

'OK, or girls,' said Jack, 'but let's get the hell out of here.'

In the following months, Jack and Tubby established themselves as young men about town. They lounged on the counters of shops and stared soulfully into the eyes of the girls who worked there. They ambled into the Norfolk Hotel, where they were treated with the reverence due to young princes. They begged Sarah to buy them motorbikes, and then rode about on them with cigarettes in the corner of their mouths. And they spent long hours hanging around the racecourse laying bets on horses.

'Are they ever going to do any work?' said Abraham.

'There'll be time enough,' said Sarah, 'I thought we would hold Jack's twenty-first birthday party at our neighbours' house.'

'Which neighbour?'

'The Aga Khan; Ruth is friendly with the little princes and they've offered to host it.'

'What's wrong with The Norfolk?'

'The boys say it's stuffy,' said Sarah.

'Stuffy?' said Abraham, enraged, 'what is *stuffy*?'

'Old fashioned,' said Sarah, 'you know how they are.'

'I do, and I don't like it,' said Abraham.

A few weeks later, smoking his cigar on the garden terrace before the family supper, Abraham said, 'I've found Jack a job with Unilever.'

'In Nairobi?' said Sarah.

'Yes, but his first assignment will be to attend the World Trade Fair in New York. He wanted travelling, now he's got it'.

'What about Tubby?'

'I'm sending him down to Rosenblum Bullows and Roy in Mombasa; we have a shipping office there.'

'But that's not seeing the world, Abraham,' said Sarah.

'No. It's doing business with the world,' said Abraham, 'I don't understand the young men of today; they don't seem to appreciate that the world doesn't owe them a living. Money doesn't grow on trees: it must be earned!'

'I have had a letter from Rita in Rishon Le Zion,' said Sarah, changing the subject, 'she wants to come home to Kenya.'

'Alone?' said Abraham, his brows hitting his hairline.

'No, of course not! With our son-in-law, Jacob, and our grand-daughter, Ora.'

'So the boy is leaving his work already?' said Abraham, 'and he is leaving my orchards! Why?'

'Rita says he doesn't earn enough to support the family,'

'And this is my fault?'

'No of course not, Pops, but Rita wants a larger house, and she's finding it hard bringing up the child without help.'

'So why doesn't he work harder?' said Abraham, 'I did.'

'Rita is pregnant again,' said Sarah, and she wants to come here to have the baby. It won't be for ever, just until the baby is born.'

'As you wish my dear,' said Abraham, 'but Jacob is going to have to work when he gets here, I don't want to hear anymore talk of travelling.'

'Of course he'll work, Abraham. You will find him work.'

'And who found me work at his age?' said Abraham.

'Please, Abraham.'

'As you say, my dear,' said Abraham.

Then he brightened. He had just purchased a large coffee farm a few miles outside Nairobi. He had got it for an usually good price because the Swedish owners were anxious to return to Sweden before war broke out. There was a large house on the estate and it was fully furnished and ready to move into. If he were to put the young couple in this house, Abraham reasoned, surely everyone would be happy? And his son-in-law, Jacob Hirshfeld, could put all his book learning to proper use and make the farm prosper.

Later that year, after Jack had departed to America, and Tubby had been sent down to Mombasa, Rita and her husband, Jacob arrived. They brought with them Sarah and Abraham's first grandchild, Ora, a cheerfully exuberant four-year-old. Rita immediately and gratefully relinquished her into the care of Ruth's old *ayahs*.

'Why is she here?' said Ruth.

'She's your niece,' said Sarah.

'I meant my sister, Rita,' said Ruth.

'They're family, Ruth, please try and make them welcome,' said Sarah.

'How long for?' said Ruth, calmly practical.

'Until they go and run Pop's new coffee farm,' said Sarah.

'Oh. In that case I'll be nice to them,' said Ruth, 'since it's only for a short time.'

Several weeks later, Rita, Jacob and Ora departed for the new farm. Sarah was relieved, Ora was delightful but she was, in Sarah's opinion, over active: she ran up and down the stairs, she ran round and around the garden, she ran in and out of the kitchen, and she asked so many questions that the staff had christened her *Kwanini*, meaning 'Why?'

'She's just excited to be here.' said Rita, now heavily pregnant, it's a very different world for her.'

'It'll be an even more different world for her out on the farm,' said Sarah.

'For us too,' said Rita, 'Jacob has so many plans.'

'Your father will be delighted,' said Sarah.

Some months later, Abraham visited the coffee farm; he was looking forward to looking over the accounts. He had taken a liking to the confident young man his daughter had married. Unlike his own sons, Jacob seemed keen to work and was full of ideas as to how to make money.'

'I thought I produce vegetables and fruit' said Jacob as he was showing Abraham around the estate.

'Mmm,' said Abraham, 'let's concentrate on the coffee first.'

'Or I could quarry the stone, and build dams,' said Jacob.

'Let's see what you do with the coffee first, my son,' said Abraham.

If anything, he mused; the boy was too full of ideas. He had never thought he would live to see the day when a boy was *too* full of ideas; but he had to admit that it made a pleasant change.

Seated (left), Mrs Alfred E. Waterman, standing behind her Doris Waterman and Gladys Newman (Mayence's daughter). Seated (centre) Mayence Tate and Alfred E. Waterman, manager of the New Stanley Hotel

CHAPTER 84

ARE YOU MARRIED?
OR DO YOU LIVE IN KENYA?

Kenya, a community of English squires established on the Equator.
–Evelyn Waugh (1903-1966)

ABRAHAM HAD BEGUN TO BROADEN his horizons. The Norfolk did not require his fulltime stewardship and he had time on his hands. He had set up a new company called African Representatives, which was busy forging agency agreements with a wide range of industrial concerns. He had acquired the sole rights for the distribution of the Lever Brothers' products and, in 1931, he had acquired the agency for the Caterpillar Company of America, one of the largest heavy equipment manufacturers in the world.

All this was good; and all of it made money, but Abraham Block had discovered a new business; and he liked it. The idea had come from his sons, Jack and Tubby, who had alerted him to the arrival of the new craze: travelling for pleasure. And that had led him to the discovery of a new business: tourism; and Abraham sensed that it was going to be big.

In 1932 Imperial Airways flew their first flight from London to Cape Town and Abraham realized that it would only be a matter of time before air travel replaced sea travel. When this happened, he reasoned, Africa would be accessible, and the safari business would take off: like never before. But Abraham Block, the Prophet, saw much more than this; he saw that the safari business itself must change and that in the wake of the millionaires and the aristocracy would come the middle classes; and that they would require hotels. So Abraham set about acquiring them; and on the top of his list was the Stanley Hotel. But Mayence and Fred Tate were not willing to sell.

'When I leave here,' Mayence said, 'it'll be feet first in a box.'

'No doubt, Mayence,' said Abraham, 'but if you ever decide to sell, will you give me the first refusal?'

'Depend upon it,' said Mayence, 'and what's all this about a Gold Rush in western Kenya?'

'A mirage, I think,' said Abraham.

'I hear Dan Noble has found a nugget the size of an egg,' said Mayence.

Dan Noble irritated Mayence. Once the postmaster of Nairobi, Dan had purchased the original Stanley Hotel when she and Fred Tate had built their new one. Mayence did not begrudge Dan the old hotel, but she did begrudge him its name, and this Mr Noble had refused to relinquish. Because of this, Mayence and Fred had been forced to call their hotel the New Stanley; and Mayence did not feel it had anything like the same ring to it. This rankled with her and she could see no good reason why Dan Noble should have been fortunate enough to dig up a nugget of gold the size of an egg.

'He has called it The Elbon,' said Abraham, 'it's a play on his name.'

'Such delusions of grandeur,' said Mayence, 'you'd think it was the Koh-in-Nor. He can talk of nothing else. According to him, we should all be rushing off to Western Kenya to dig for gold. What do you think, Abraham? Is there easy money to be had up there?'

'There's no such thing as easy money, Mayence,' said Abraham, 'and gold rushes… are just that'

As usual, Abraham was correct.

Gold was discovered in Western Kenya in 1898, but in such small quantities that its existence was largely ignored. But when the British Colonial Office found itself to be more pressed for cash than usual, an eminent geologist, Sir Albert Kitson, was sent out to investigate the possibility of Kenyan gold. Sir Kitson's investigations confirmed what everyone already knew: which was that Kakamega's gold was minimal and hard to extract, but unfortunately, Sir Kitson was persuaded to write an article for the British magazine, *The Spectator*, and in it he drew an unhappy comparison between 'the road to Kakamega' and 'the road to Klondike', which had been the scene of Canada's famous Klondike Gold Rush of 1897. The reference was taken out of all context and blown out of all proportion, and the gold diggers of the world rushed to Kakamega, which was a small rural town not too far distant from the shores of Lake Victoria. Predictably they were disappointed and, predictably, they rushed elsewhere shortly afterwards, but by that time the damage had been done and Kenya had established a reputation as an equatorial Eldorado. People spoke of it as the new Shangri La, a sunny wonderland where the streets were paved with gold, titles were two-a-penny, land was cheap, lifestyles were lavish, and morals had gone out of the window. Around the cocktail parties of London a new phrase was coined: 'Are you married or do you live in Kenya?'

A wave of dilettantes dashed to drown in the decadence of the Crown Colony of Kenya; and when they arrived they spent money. They spent it on building Surrey Tudor mansions in the style of Lutyens; they spent it on limousines, they spent it on travel and they spent it on luxury hotels. They also followed slavishly in the wake of an exceptionally wealth group of young socialites known as The Happy Valley Set, whose wealth the newcomers could never hope to replicate.

The Happy Valley Set lived in the Wanjohi Valley of the Aberdares where they had built beautiful houses and pursued lives of frenetic gaiety fuelled by cocaine and cocktails. Their parties were legendary. There were pink gins at breakfast, gin fizzes with tea and champagne at any other time. They danced naked in the gardens; they tossed feathers in the air to decide who would sleep with whom; and everyone slept with their leader, Countess Alice de Janze, whose bed was known as The Battleground.

Alice was beautiful, American, and an heiress of fabulous wealth. She had a leopard cub on a silver chain and it was her habit to receive her guests while lying in an onyx and gold bathtub wearing only her pearls. All her male guests were handsome and witty; and they all wore brightly coloured silk shirts, rakish felt hats and long Somali scarves. All her female guests were beautiful; and they all wore tailored shorts and pearls.

The Happy Valley Set liked to drive into Nairobi, deposit their lion cubs at Tart's Hotel, drink White Lady Cocktails, and dance there until dawn. Afterwards, they liked to move on to the Muthaiga Club where there would be pink gins with a full English breakfast, and where the men of their party would 'hang from the rafters like apes' or push lines of chairs around making woo-woo train noises.

The original settler community observed the behaviour of The Happy Valley Set, and their less affluent clones, with horror.

'Third-class travelling first,' said Freddy Ward.

'Building equatorial Ealing,' said Galbraith Cole, Delamere's brother-in-law.

'Obsessed by the cult of urban snobbery,' said Ewart Grogan.

'Shady people looking for a place in the sun,' said Fatty Garland.

But, to Abraham Block, the new arrivals served only to confirm his view that Kenya was poised to take off as the fashionable place to be. And, when he heard that Imperial Airways were to land 'flying boats' on Lake Naivasha, and that the passengers were to be ferried to Nairobi in limousines, he was convinced.

Kenya was to become the aspirational venue of choice, but before it could establish itself in this role, the Second World War intervened.

CHAPTER 85

WORLD AT WAR

There was never a good war or a bad peace.
–Benjamin Franklin (1706-1790)

I N 1933, ADOLF HITLER WAS proclaimed Chancellor of Germany and his promised persecution of the Jews began. News began to filter back of Jews being snatched off the streets of Vilnius and shot in the forests of Lithuania; of Polish Jews being herded on to cattle trains and secreted in detention centres from whence they never returned; of German Jews being hurried into concentration camps and herded into gas ovens. It seemed that Hitler's 'Final Solution' to the Jewish Question was being enacted and, as thousands of Jews fled Eastern Europe, many of the Western democracies began to deny them visas.

In Nairobi, Abraham Block, now the President of the Kenya Zionist Organization[1], devoted himself to the task of providing a sanctuary for the refugees in Kenya. When the first boatload of Polish refugees docked in Mombasa, Abraham and his friends were there to meet them and, as the hunched figures shuffled off the ship, Abraham was reminded of his own arrival in Hull. He stepped forward to embrace the refugees; he greeted them in Yiddish, he ensured that they were given food and clothes; and he arranged that they be escorted to Mombasa Railway Station. And in doing all of this, he felt he was, in some small way, repaying a debt long-owed.

When the refugees arrived in Nairobi, they were welcomed into Jewish homes, the Jewish Board of Deputies was set up to take care of their welfare, and Eddie Ruben's Express Transport Company was on hand to ferry them out to those farms that had agreed to offer them employment. The Plough Association was established to teach the refugees how to farm, and a monthly fee was paid to any Kenyan farmer willing to accept refugee workers. At first, the Kenyan settlers were alarmed by the idea of having penniless Jewish refugees foisted upon them.

'What have you got to lose?' said Abraham, 'it's free labour isn't it?

'They won't know what to do,' said Tom Deacon.

'We've trained them,' said Abraham.

'We can't afford to keep them,' said Russell Bowker.

'You're being paid to take them,' said Abraham, 'all you have to do is provide them with bed and board.'

'They don't speak the language, they're aliens,' said Freddy Ward

'They'll learn the language,' said Abraham, 'and they're no more alien than I am.'

'It's not the same, and you know it,' said Max Nightingale

'You never know, you might get to like them,' said Abraham.

As usual, Abraham was correct; and the Norfolk Terrace began to buzz with refugee success stories.

'I was nearly sick with apprehension when I got the wire saying that my refugees were coming,' said one farmer, 'and I was horrified when they arrived; a man and his daughter. They were skeletons. They ate like starving dogs. They cowered away from the Africans, and they cowered away from me! The next day I showed them what had to be done and they set to work. And now? Well, now I don't know what I'd do without them. They've turned the farm around; my machinery works like never before, my yields are up, my livestock is healthy, my house is spotless and I've never eaten so well in my life.'

The euphoria was not to last. When Britain declared war on Germany the command went out from Government House that all German refugees were to be rounded up and put into internment camps. The conditions in the camps were appalling and the refugees began to die of malaria and black water fever.

Abraham was incensed.

'They're not Germans, they're Jews!' he said, 'they are the ones the Germans are putting into concentration camps and killing; they're not soldiers or spies.'

'Makes no difference,' said the British official, 'technically they're Germans.'

'No,' said Abraham, 'I will not allow this to happen,' and he called in every favour that he had ever amassed down the years, and every contact that he had ever made with the Administration, to campaign for the release of the refugees back to their farms. Eventually, he was successful and, as the settlers were called up for military service, the refugees repaid their faith in them.

It was a triumph for Jewish relations. The refugees ran the farms as if they were their own, and many a farmer returned to find his farm more prosperous than when he had left it.

'The committee of Muthaiga Club has agreed to lift the ban on Jewish membership,' reported Eddie Ruben in triumph.

'It won't happen,' said Abraham.

Two days later, Eddie returned long faced.

'The members of Muthaiga Club have burnt the grand piano in protest at the lifting of the ban on Jewish membership,' he said.

'Let's sell them a new Bechstein, then' said Abraham.

A few weeks later, Ruth came home from school in tears.

'What has happened?' said Sarah.

'I went for my tennis coaching at Muthaiga Club,' she said.

'Yes?'

'And, afterwards, the coach invited us on to the terrace for a cool drink.'

'And?' said Sarah, knowing what was to come.

'My tennis coach was told not to invite me again; because I'm Jewish,' said Ruth.

When Sarah told Abraham what had happened, he sighed.

'I warned you not to enroll her there,' he said.

'But they accepted the money for the fees,' said Sarah.

'They always do,' said Abraham.

CHAPTER 86

THE FAMILY AT WAR

Somali, Somali, we're here for your sake
But what the hell difference does the NFD* make
Mussolini can have it with a great rousing cheer
Moyale, Mandera, El Wak and Wajir.

They say that the eyeties are ready for war
They want Abyssinia, but God knows what for.
But if they want somewhere why not NFD
They can have every acre its OK by me
–The song of the Wajir station 1935-36

*Northern Frontier District

IN 1937, JAPAN WENT TO war with China and the world divided along its battle lines. On one side stood the Allies, on the other the Axis. In 1939 Germany invaded Poland; and France, Britain and the Commonwealth declared war on Germany. Thereafter began the greatest war the world had ever seen.

In the Crown Colony of Kenya preparations were made. Italy's fascist leader, Benito Mussolini, had massed his troops in Abyssinia and it was expected that he would declare war on the Allies and invade Kenya at any moment.

'What have we got to face him with?' said Jack Block, just returned from America.

'Six battalions of the King's African Rifles and one mounted Indian battery with about 7,000 men,' said Tubby Block. He had been called back from Mombasa and had made it his business to find out everything he could about the imminent involvement of East Africa in the War.

'What's Mussolini got?' said Jack.

'Three hundred thousand men, well equipped and with powerful air and artillery support,' said Tubby.

'Phew,' said Jack, 'we better enlist.'

'I already have,' said Tubby.

'You might have waited,' said Jack.

'Wanted to get on the staff of General Dickinson the senior officer in the East Africa Command, or on that of his staff officer, General 'Dimmy'.'

'Dimmy?' said Jack, '*Dimmy*?'

'Dimoline,' said Tubby, reddening. 'That's what all the chaps call him.'

'My, my,' said Jack, 'you do know your stuff. Race you to the first medal.'

The next day, Jack enlisted and was posted to the First East African Infantry Brigade. Tubby

Jack and Doria during their wedding celebrations

had already been sent to join the First East African Light Battery under Commander Wavell.

'What will be their role?' said Sarah as calmly as she could.

'Tubby has been put in command of the 53rd East African Light Battery,' said Abraham, 'they have large guns called Howitzers.'

And Jack?

'The Infantry are being sent to defend the coast.'

Sarah intertwined her fingers and clenched them. Her knuckles cracked.

'They've done well to enlist, Sarah,' said Abraham, 'it's what is expected of them. Out of the entire white male population of this colony, three thousand men have volunteered and three thousand have been gazetted into the reserve occupations that are vital to the war effort. And 50,000 Kenyans have also volunteered. Jack and Tubby have done as they should. We must be proud.'

Sarah said nothing.

In June 1940, Mussolini declared war on the Allies. In East Africa, he moved straight into the offensive and captured the outposts of Moyale and El Wak on Kenya's northeastern borders. The towns were largely undefended and after a bloody clash at Moyale between the Italians and the King's African Rifles, General Dickinson ordered an immediate withdrawal of troops from the border country of Kenya's Northern Frontier District. As the Kenyan troops formed a defensive line further south, the Italians advanced and Kenya braced for invasion.

'Where are the boys?' said Sarah.

'Tubby is on the southern front with Commander Wavell,' said Abraham, 'and from what I understand Wavell is planning a three-pronged invasion into Abyssinia. Our troops will come in from the east through British Somaliland, from the north through Sudan, and from the south through Kenya; and that's where our boys will be.'

'Have the reinforcements arrived?' said Sarah who was watching the war effort with hawk-like precision.

'They are just about to. Several thousand are moving up from South Africa and Rhodesia, more are coming from Nigeria and the Gold Coast. The South Africans are passing through Nairobi in the next few weeks, and I have offered them hospitality at the hotel.'

A few weeks later, Abraham came home with news.

'There are about forty Jewish soldiers within the South African reinforcements,' he said, 'I have invited them back to the house to celebrate Rosh Hashanah[1],' he said, 'it's the least we can do.'

'I will make the preparations,' said Sarah.

CHAPTER 87

LOVE IN THE TIME OF WAR

There is no avoiding war; it can only be postponed to the advantage of others.
–Niccolo Machiavelli (1469-1527)

THE SOUTH AFRICAN SOLDIERS ARRIVED at The House on the Hill in the late afternoon of the eve of Rosh Hashanah. The celebration of the Jewish New Year would begin at sundown.

A traditional feast had been laid out in the dining room. In pride of place was a whole fish surrounded by black-eyed peas, stuffed vegetables, spinach, and leek fritters. There were piles of round *challah* bread, and tiny *mansanada* pumpkin tartlets. There were apples glazed in honey, baskets of dates and even some pomegranates that Eddie Ruben had somehow managed to produce.

Sarah and Abraham Block stood at the door to welcome the young men, and they had invited a large group of family and friends to celebrate with them. It was a warm evening and the crowds drifted out on to the terrace overlooking the gardens.

Ruth Block was fourteen. She had a new dress for the occasion and was acutely conscious of it. It was red and had a full skirt and a tight-fitted bodice rising to a neat collar. Ruth had wanted a lower neckline, but Sarah had forbidden it. The shoes were a compromise; they had just the slightest suggestion of a heel. They were slightly too large and Ruth had spent all afternoon practicing walking in them. She had reddened her lips with cochineal begged from the cook.

'You're a picture, Ruth,' said her father.

'Wipe your lips at once,' said her mother.

'But its only cochineal,' said Ruth.

'I don't care what it is: it is not suitable,' said Sarah.

'Nothing ever is,' said Ruth, 'why must you spoil everything for me?'

'Ruth—,'

'Let her be,' said Abraham, 'it's her first party and she's never had so many young men staring at her.'

'They're hardly staring, Abraham' said Sarah, 'they're wonderfully polite, and so handsome in their uniforms.'

'One is staring,' said Abraham, 'I can see it from here.'

Ruth fled from her parents, heading for the stairs and the privacy of her room. As she reached the banisters she tripped and a hand came out to steady her[1].

'Allow me,' said a soft voice with the slightest South African lilt.

Looking up, Ruth saw the most handsome young man she had ever beheld. She knew that in an instant. He was not tall, but he had shoulders so broad that the uniform looked better on him than it did on any other soldier in the room. Something about it, and him, made Ruth's

337

stomach flutter. The soldier had thick, wavy hair, coaxed into shining waves. He had brilliant blue eyes and an impossibly wide smile. It stretched literally, she thought, from ear to ear. The soldier bent down and retrieved her shoe.

'Lean on me while you put it back on,' he said. He placed the shoe where she might slip her foot in to it. Into her mind came the thought of Cinderella and she giggled.

'That's better,' said the young man, 'shame to waste that smile. I'm Sol Rabb[2], who are you?'

He had the very slightest lisp and it was attractive. His smile was utterly guileless. It was as though he was delighted just to look at her. Such a thing had never happened to Ruth Block before. Restored to her shoe, she looked up at him.

His smile remained, his interest focused.

'Ruth Block,' she said, 'would you like to share a pomegranate?'

The East African Campaign of World War II was over remarkably quickly. First came the news that the Italians had invaded and occupied British Somaliland. This was followed by the news that the combined colonial forces from Kenya, Rhodesia, Nigeria and the Gold Coast were advancing into British Somaliland under the command of General Cunningham. Weeks later came the news that the capital of British Somaliland, Kismayu, had fallen to the Allies without a fight. Now the Allied troops headed into Abyssinia, and a month later the capital, Addis Ababa, had fallen to them, and that the Emperor Haile Selassie had been returned to his throne from exile. The Allies headed into Eritrea, where they captured its capital, Asmara, and forced the Italians into retreat

'Does that mean we've won?' said Sarah

'The East African Campaign? Yes,' said Abraham, 'but not the war'.

'So what will happen to Jack and Tubby?'

'The East African regiments will be sent elsewhere.'

'Where?'

'Rumour has it that some of them will be sent to Madagascar.'

A few months later as the family huddled around the wireless, the news came in that the Japanese had joined the war and were fighting against the Allies in Hong Kong, Malaya and Burma.

A letter arrived. It was from Jack.

'He's been posted to Madagascar,' said Abraham, reading the letter.

'What about Tubby?' said Sarah.

'He's been sent to Burma with the 11th East African Division of the King's African Rifles,' said Abraham, 'Jack says it's madness, the KAR have never fought outside Africa; but the War Office has decided that they are more suited to Burma than any of the other troops.'

'Why?'

'According to Jack it's because they think the Africans are more resistant to malaria and know how to fight in jungles.'

'Is that true?'

'No. Most of them have already got malaria. And the jungles of Burma are nothing like those of Kenya.'

'Doesn't the War Office know that?'

'It seems not.'

A few weeks later another letter arrived. It was from Jack.

'The fighting is over in Madagascar,' read Abraham, 'he's been posted to Burma.'

'And Tubby?'

'No news but Jack has heard that the African troops have been forced to make a number of retreats.'

In Jack's next letter he said that while his brigade had been waiting to be shipped to Burma, the news had come through of another retreat. As a consequence, Jack was not going to Burma and had been granted sick leave. He was, he said, much weakened by malaria.

CHAPTER 88

COMING HOME

There is no subject on which more dangerous nonsense is talked and thought than marriage.
–George Bernard Shaw, English writer (1856-1950)

IT WAS NOT UNTIL 1945 that Abraham and Sarah's sons were returned to them. Both had attained the rank of Major. Tubby returned from Burma with a Military Cross[1], one of the few to be awarded to Kenya's troops.

Jack returned with a bride.

Doria Beiles[2] had been born in Nairobi; she and Ruth Block had played together as children. Doria had then gone with her sister, Valerie, to live in New York when her parents had emigrated there.

It was while he was working for Unilever and attending the World Trade Fair in New York that Jack Block met Harry Beiles. They met first in a shipping office, where Jack had chanced to notice that Mr Beiles was booking a ticket to Nairobi. The two men had exchanged pleasantries and parted. Some hours later, Mr Beiles got on the same train as Jack and, in the laughter that ensued, invited him for dinner. After dinner, Jack noticed the photographs of Mr and Mrs Beiles' two beautiful daughters, which stood in pride of place on the mantle-piece. Joking, he said he would come back to meet them when he was next in New York.

In 1944, Jack was given sick leave from the War and passed through New York, so he looked up the Beiles.

Even Jack was surprised by the Beiles sisters. Doria and Valerie Beiles were beautiful, intelligent, charming and possessed of more domestic attributes that even the most exacting of Jewish mothers could desire. But they had something else; they knew Africa. They understood what Jack meant when he spoke of the smell of new rain on African soil; they could envisage the mango-pink of the sun as it sank; and they too loved the haunting call of the rain bird as it trilled out its insistent, 'it-will-rain, it-will-rain.'

The Beiles sisters came from his world; they were almost family.

Doria, the elder sister, had the polish and style of a Hollywood starlet, and the determination of a woman who knew exactly what she wanted out of life. And since what Doria wanted out of life was Jack, they were perfectly suited.

Jack and Doria were married in Johannesburg and some months later they returned to Nairobi. A few years later, Valerie, now grown up, paid a visit to her sister, Doria.

Valerie had all the attributes of her sister, but a quite different character. Where Doria had poise; Valerie had calm. Where Doria had charisma; Valerie had gentleness. Where Doria had wit; Valerie had a quiet self-possession.

'She'll be perfect for Tubby,' said Jack.

'Just so long as she doesn't realize we're matchmaking,' said Doria.

'Why?' said Jack.

'She'd be horrified, then she'd be embarrassed, and then she wouldn't be herself …and then it wouldn't work,' said Doria.

'So what do we do?'

'Nothing,' said Doria.

'You're sure?'

'Just watch,' said Doria.

Before the War many had supposed the Block brothers to be twins. Two years apart in age they shared the same good looks, they had the same easy charm, and they took the same delight in the irreverent and the ridiculous. They were both clever and ambitious and both had inherited their father's startling business acumen and remarkable nose for a deal.

But his time in the War had changed Tubby.

Before the War, Tubby had been the wild one, the instigator of pranks; the one who laughed loudest and longest. But when he returned from it, Tubby was reserved, reflective and much less sure of life. His faith in humanity had been badly shaken and he needed healing. So when Valerie's gentle gaze met his, and her slightly diffident smile lit up her eyes, Tubby knew that he had to marry her.

'Rita and Jack married; Tubby soon to be married,' said Sarah, 'only Ruth left.'

'Well, there's no hurry is there?' said Abraham, 'she's only eighteen.'

'I was not much older than that when I married you,' said Sarah.

'It was different then,' said Abraham.

And so it had been. In those days, daughters had remained at home until they were married; and they most certainly had not gone out to work. But Ruth Block was of a new generation, and she had other ideas. Sarah and Abraham had decided to move from the Nairobi suburbs to a house on a coffee estate, which Abraham had bought in partnership with a Palestinian called Israel Massader[3].

'What am I going to do out there?' said Ruth.

Sarah and Abraham exchanged glances.

'It's all very well for you, Dad,' said Ruth, 'you can do your deals just as easily out there as you can in town, but what about me? I'll be marooned in the middle of nowhere.'

'Limuru is hardly the middle of nowhere,' said Sarah, 'its only fifteen miles out of Nairobi.'

'Might just as well be one hundred and fifteen, though,' said Ruth. She could sense her advantage. 'Why can't I get a job in Nairobi and go and live in one of the cottages in the grounds of the Norfolk? Like Jack and Doria?' she said.

'Jack and Doria are married and they're only staying in the cottages until their house is ready.' Sarah said.

'What chance will I ever have of marriage if I'm stuck out in Limuru?' said Ruth

'Don't exaggerate, darling,' said Sarah

'But what harm can come to me if I stay in a cottage in the grounds of my own father's hotel?'

Jack (top) and Tubby Block 1960s

said Ruth.

'Ruth! I've said—'

'She's right,' said Abraham, 'but there's a condition.'

'What Dad?' said Ruth, 'What!'

'That you work on the front desk at the Norfolk Hotel.' Abraham said.

'Done,' said his daughter.

Thereafter, while Abraham Block was to be found on the front steps of his hotel, his slim, elfin-faced daughter was to be found behind the front desk and, more often than not, his handsome sons were to be found in the management offices.

'And that's exactly how it should be,' said Abraham, happy at last.

Jack bounded up the steps to the Norfolk Hotel.

'Dad, I've got something to discuss,' he said.

'So have I,' said his father, 'it's time you boys took over the running of this hotel. I'm over sixty, it needs young blood.'

'Plenty of time for that,' said Jack breezily, 'anyway I've decided to go and work with Ker and Downey Safaris.'[4]

'What?' said Abraham.

'Donald Ker and Syd Downey; Donald learned to hunt with your friend Denys Finch-Hatton and Syd Downey was a safari outfitter. We all met up at the fall of Addis in 1941. Donald and Syd said they were going to set up the best safari company the world had ever known if they ever made it back to Nairobi, and now that they have, they've asked me to join them in their business.'

'What about the family business?' said Abraham.

'There isn't room for you, me and Tubby in the family business,' said Jack, 'got to go, catch you later.'

'There might not be room for Dad and I in the same company,' said Tubby when Jack recounted the conversation.

'Then make room,' said Jack.

'And don't think I don't know why you want to work with Ker and Downey,' said Tubby.

'Really?' said Jack, 'So why's that, then?'

'Hollywood is coming to town and Ker and Downey have been signed up for the filming of *The Macomber Affair* in the Masai Mara,' said Tubby, 'And it stars Gregory Peck, your hero.'

'True, but the director, Zoltan Korda, is also one of Hollywood's finest. It's going to be quite a show. Can you believe we're hiring every spare tent in Kenya and most of the vehicles too?'

Tubby sighed.

'I can. And I guess you and Doria will be going along for the ride?'

'Wouldn't miss it for the world,' said Jack, 'besides, Stewart Granger and Deborah Kerr will be out next to film Metro Goldwyn Mayer's *King Solomon's Mines*.'

'Will they by staying at The Norfolk?' said Tubby.

'Of course,' said Jack, 'doesn't everybody?'

CHAPTER 89

THE NEW STANLEY HOTEL

Whatever may happen to you was prepared for you from all eternity.
–Marcus Aurelius Antoninus Augustus (121-180 BC)

T HE NORFOLK HOTEL WAS ABRAHAM Block's great love; but the Stanley Hotel was his first love, and he never got over it.

The original structure had burned down in 1905, when Mayence Bent, or so legend had it, had tossed her best enamel chamber-pots down into the street to save them from the flames. She had then moved everything else into a half-finished building further down the street, hurled a tarpaulin over its rafters, and carried on as before. In later years, she had been persuaded by her new husband, Fred Tate, into buying a plot of land in the centre of town. And there, together, they had built a new hotel that was larger, grander and taller than the old hotel had ever had any hope of being.

The New Stanley Hotel rose to two floors, it had a red-tiled roof, it was white-painted and it was extensive. Yet for all its chintz, it still retained something of the air of a Wild West saloon. There was a Long Bar down which shot glasses could be skimmed. There was a barman in shirtsleeves, a black waistcoat, and a long white apron who acted as mediator, broker and bouncer alike. And there was a buzz of commerce and business in the air that caused The Long Bar to change its name to The Exchange Bar. And thereafter, in the absence of any other, the bar of the New Stanley became the official Nairobi Stock Exchange.

The New Stanley had established its rather rough, ready and gritty reputation during the First World War, when it was the preferred haunt of officers and men. And, such had been its profitability, that Mayence and Fred Tate had been able to retire to London, where they purchased an elegant flat and lived a life of leisure. This had suited Fred, but it had not suited Mayence, who could not grasp the concept of leisure. In 1933, the couple returned to Kenya to manage the hotel, but this was too much for Fred Tate, who died in 1937 leaving a desolate Mayence to run the hotel alone. She did so until the end of the Second World War; but then she made an announcement. 'It's not the same without my Fred,' she said, 'I'm going back to London where we were happy.'

'And the hotel?' said Mr Waterstone, her General Manager.

'I promised Abraham Block he could have first refusal on the hotel,' said Mayence, 'so that's what I will give him.' Mayence had installed telephones in the Stanley, but she didn't 'hold' with them, so she pinned on her hat, grasped her handbag, and set off by rickshaw to call on Abraham Block.

'Mr Block is away,' she was told.

'Away where?' said Mayence, irritated.

'In Cape Town, Madam.'

Kenyatta Avenue (New Stanley Hotel on left) in 1950

'Cape Town! What does he want with Cape Town?' said Mayence, ' 'Oh, never mind! When he gets back, tell him I have news for him.' She cast an all-seeing glance around the prints, curtains, wing chairs and light fittings, and swept out of the hotel.

Abraham had left for Cape Town in a hurry; and this did not suit him. He hated to be hurried and he disliked leaving the Norfolk Hotel. He knew that it did not need him but the fact remained that he liked to be in it. He liked to stand on the steps and smoke a cigar, and he liked to wander into the management offices to look over people's shoulders, open ledgers and finger invoices. And every time he did so, he was amazed by what he found. He learned that it was the fashion for suppliers to send gifts to his managers. What profligacy? He learned that they left samples of wine, cigars, crystal and fine china for his managers. Why? Worse still, he learned that these gifts lay around unclaimed for months on end. What a waste!

He couldn't stand it.

'I'll just take this,' he would say, picking up a bottle of port.

'You won't mind if I take this?' he would murmur, whilst pocketing a crystal ashtray.

'No sense in wasting these!' he would say with studied distain, and he would walk off with a box of crystalized fruits, which he most certainly did not want. But then, he didn't want any of the things he appropriated: but he could not resist the idea of getting something for nothing any more than he had been able to resist the bent nails of his early life.

When he wasn't prowling the management offices, Abraham liked to check the bills.

He never found fault with them, but he could not permit himself to leave the hotel without a brief inspection. 'You never know…' he would say, 'got to keep the back doors shut, and watch the front doors, eh?'

'What does that saying of yours actually mean, Pops,' said Tubby, who had heard it a thousand times.

'It means you have to know what's coming in and going out,' said Abraham, exasperated.

'But we've got people to do that,' said Tubby.

'People!' said Abraham, 'People! What is all this PEOPLE? You've got to do it *yourself*, my boy! Money doesn't grow on trees!'

'Okay, Dad,' said Tubby. He was well aware that to argue would merely provoke his parent into producing further maxims. But Abraham, once launched down a promising financial trail, was difficult to halt. 'How much did we pay for this?' he would say, holding up whichever item came first to hand.

'Miss Baines, how much did we pay for this?' Tubby would say and some time later the answer would be returned by the shapely Miss Baines, whose tight skirt Tubby hoped might distract his father from his mission, but it never did.

'You paid WHAT?' Abraham would say, his eyebrows flying up, 'if you had gone down to the Indian Bazaar, you could have got it for HALF that!'

'The Indian Bazaar was burned down years ago, Dad, after the fifth outbreak of bubonic plague,' Tubby would say, 'it's called Biashara Street now.'

The New Stanley Hotel in 1923

'What does it matter what it's called?' Abraham would say.

His shoulders would hunch and his hands would extend as if holding an invisible football. 'Never mind what it's *called*, you could have got this cheaper there!'

Mayence Tate and her daughter, Gladys

The Block grandchildren (Nicholas, Jeremy, Geraldine, Lyn, Jeremy and Leigh) planting the first acacia tree in the courtyard of the New Stanley Hotel in 1961

CHAPTER 90

AN UNSUITABLE SUITOR?

If you press me to say why I loved him, I can say no more than because he was he, and I was I.
–Michel de Montaigne, French philosopher, (1533-1592)

W HEN SARAH ANNOUNCED THAT SHE was taking Ruth to Cape Town and that she wanted Abraham to go with them, Abraham had resisted.

'I've already bought the tickets,' said Sarah.

'How much did you pay for the—'

'It doesn't matter how much, I paid for them, Abraham,' said his wife.

'So where did you—'

'Or where I got them from. The point is, that we have to go immediately,' said Sarah.

'Why?' said Abraham.

'Because Ruth is becoming too friendly with that friend of Tubby's.'

'What friend of Tubby's?'

'The *war hero* from Burma…'

'War hero from Burma?' echoed Abraham, 'and this is a reason that I should go to Cape Town. A war hero from Burma?' His eyebrows shot up.

'Yes, Abraham it is. He's too old, and he's unsuitable.'

'But—'

'And he's not Jewish, Abraham.'

'I—'

'When we get back the man will have gone,' said Sarah.

Abraham squinted at her, and nibbled nervously at his index finger.

Sarah ignored this tactic, picked up her gloves, snapped shut her handbag, rose to her feet and smoothed down her skirts. And something in the way she carried out these movements told Abraham all that he needed to know.

'As you wish, my dear,' he said.

It was as the Blocks were checking into the Queen's Hotel in Cape Town that Abraham became aware of the fact that a man was looking expectantly at him. As if he wished to be recognized. But Abraham did not recognize him.

'Mr Block?' the man said, approaching him.

'It is Mr Block isn't it?' he said, 'you might not remember me. My name is David Solomon[1]; I came to your house in Nairobi for New Year in 1940. My platoon was passing through Nairobi from South Africa.'

'Of course!' said Abraham. He beamed. He didn't remember the fellow in the slightest, but he was always delighted to meet new people.

'I was there with the Rabb twins, Sol and Chaim,' continued David Solomon.

'Of course you were, David, and how good it is to see you again!' said Abraham. He had perfected the art of the genial handclasp and the slightly American pat on the back.

'Why don't you all join us for a drink this evening?' he said, 'I'm sure my wife and daughter would be delighted to meet you again.'

'You're very kind, Sir,' said David Solomon, 'I should like that very much, and I'll let the Rabb twins know.'

'You do that,' said Abraham, 'yes, you do that: shall we say six o'clock in the bar?'

By the time Sarah and Ruth were dressed to their satisfaction, six o'clock had come and gone and the Block family entered the bar to find the three young men already seated around one of the low glass-topped tables. Ruth recognized her soldier immediately.

He had not changed.

She hoped that she had.

Sol Rabb was seated next to another young man who looked exactly like him: twins! Ruth was enchanted. Introductions were made, the War was discussed and, as the hour for dinner approached, Sol Rabb politely enquired of Sarah how well the family knew Cape Town.

Abraham lived here for a while,' said Sarah, 'but Ruth and I don't know it at all.'

'Then might my brother and I have the pleasure of taking you both for a stroll around the sights, Mrs Block,' said Sol Rabb. As he bent deferentially towards her to ask this question, Sarah reflected on what an exceptionally charming and good-looking young man Sol Rabb was. As was his brother: just the antidote for the war hero, she thought.

'What a splendid idea,' she said, 'should we say tomorrow morning? At eleven?'

The next morning at breakfast Sarah told Ruth that Abraham needed the company of his wife around town. 'You'll have to go sightseeing without me,' she said.

'Is that entirely proper, Mum?' said Ruth innocently pouring milk on her cereal.

'It wouldn't be proper with one young man,' said her mother, 'but with two brothers, to whom you have been properly introduced, it will be quite proper.'

She glanced suspiciously at her daughter but could detect no irony in her expression.

As she walked along the beach, her toes curling into the wet sand, her sandals swinging from one hand, and her full skirt flattened against her bare legs, Ruth reflected that there could not be many girls so lucky as she. She had two identically handsome young men, both vying for her attention, and both making her laugh. This was novel. Most of the young men she had

Ruth and Sol Rabb at the Norfolk Hotel, 1948

met in Nairobi were tongue-tied, inept and clumsy. And most seemed incapable of holding a conversation, other than for Tubby's friend from the war, of course, but he didn't seem quite so immediate anymore.

Above the sweep of the bay, Table Mountain rose like a Hollywood film set. The glass-green waves were whipped by white-flecked crests, and shiny-black seals bobbed just yards from the shore. It's utterly perfect, thought Ruth, except for one thing.

'I'm cold,' she said. 'I should have brought my cardigan.' And she wrapped her bare arms around the thin cotton of her dress.

'Have this,' said Sol Rabb and he wrapped his jacket around her shoulders.

'But then you'll be cold too,' said Ruth, laughing.

'It's a privilege,' said Sol. He was in his shirtsleeves with his hair blowing in the wind and he looked exceptionally handsome.

'Good old Sol. Always the ladies' man,' said his brother as he ran into the wavelets with his trousers rolled up.

Walking back along the beach, hugging Sol's jacket to her, Ruth inhaled the smell of him. When she handed it back to him, she felt an infinitesimal flip in her stomach. She had felt it before.

'May I write to you when you get back to Nairobi?' said Sol, his smile as boyishly guileless as ever. As if the question meant really nothing at all.

'If you wish,' said Ruth, and she hoped that it meant anything and everything.

Princess Elizabeth visits the New Stanley Hotel in 1952 (Tubby is standing on the left)

CHAPTER 91

SONS OF THE FATHERS

Each player must accept the cards life deals him. But once they are in hand,
he alone must decide how to play the cards in order to win the game.
–Voltaire, French author (1694-1778)

WHEN ABRAHAM RETURNED FROM CAPE Town, he found Jack lolling in his chair.

'Welcome back, Pops', he said, 'How was Cape Town?'

'How's business?' replied Abraham, who hadn't thought about anything else since he had left.

'All under control, no need to worry,'

'I'm not worrying. But how is business? And where's your brother?'

'Looking over the New Stanley Hotel.'

'The New Stanley Hotel! And for what?' said Abraham, who lost his English when irritable.

'Mrs Tate called while you were away. She has decided to sell, she said you wanted first refusal. So we made her an offer and she's accepted. So Tubby's gone to look it over.'

There was a moment of silence as Abraham surveyed his eldest son, and then the barrage began.

'You made … an offer!'

'We had to Dad, other people were interested.'

And,' Abraham screwed up his eyes. 'How much was that offer?'

Jack told him.

'What?'

'It's a good deal, Dad.'

'A good deal? Don't tell me what a good deal is.'

'But—'

'And you agreed to *that* deal?

'Dad—'

'You? My sons! You both agreed to *that* deal?'

'We had to, Dad, she had other offers.'

'Other offers! Ha! You tell me about other *offers*?'

'I'm trying to tell you, Da—'

'What have I always told you? Why did you not bargain?'

'There was no bargaining to be done, Dad, it was take it or leave it.'

'Take it or leave it? Take it or—' Abraham clapped his fist to his forehead. 'And you didn't think even to call me? Your father?'

'Come on, Dad, there wasn't time.'

'Time! Time. There is always time to make a good deal!' said Abraham.

Ruth Block and Sol Rabb's wedding 1948 (l to r) Chaim Rabinowitz (Sol's twin brother), Naomi Abramowitz, Yakov Hirshfeld, Doria Block, Lynn (Doria and Jack's daughter), Ora, Jack Block, Abraham Block, Tubby Block, bride and groom, Sarah Block. L. Kaplan, Arthur Haller, Rita Hirshfeld, Judith Abramowitz, Nehemia Abramowitz. In front (l to r) Eallan, Theo and Henry (Tzvi) Hirshfeld.

'What have I done to deserve such sons? For this I sent you away to an expensive school?'

Abraham flung himself up and down the room for some minutes, his brow furrowed, his hands behind his back, his nose down to the floor like a bloodhound on a scent. Every now and again his eyes would fly up to his son's face then drop down again to the carpet. Eventually, he stopped pacing.

'So when do we take it over?' he said, as if all that had gone before were as nothing.

'Tomorrow.'

'Tomorrow?' Abraham stared at his son in disbelief. 'Then why are you wasting my time like this?' he said. 'Why are we not supervising the inventory?' He wrung his hands. 'This is the crucial time! If trickery is to be done, trickery will be done now!' Abraham seized his hat and crammed it on his head. From his inside pocket he took a cigar, it was half-smoked and carefully rolled in a square of newspaper. He lit it. 'Come my boy,' he said, 'let's go and find Tubby immediately. You should have said that he was there alone. Why did you not tell me this *sooner*?'

It took many hours before Abraham Block was satisfied that he had seen all that there was to be seen at the New Stanley Hotel.

And it took many more hours before he was willing to agree to the inventories that were put before him, but then the piles of green accounts ledgers were put away, and the clusters of keys and padlocks were returned to their hooks.

Later, Abraham Block was to be found puffing on his cigar on the front steps of the New Stanley Hotel. From time to time he would wave at a passing acquaintance, or raise his hat to a lady. That he stood on the steps of the New Stanley at all was a seemingly small gesture, but it said so much. It indicated that Abraham Block now owned the New Stanley Hotel; and everybody knew it.

'It's going to need a lot of money spent on it, Dad,' said Tubby.

'Money? What money?' said his father.

'We need to expand, build more floors, build more bathrooms, make it more like the Norfolk.'

'Tubby, my boy,' said Abraham, 'it will never be like the Norfolk. I don't want it to be like the Norfolk. It is not the Norfolk.'

'But Dad—'

'But,' said his father, 'I agree that the times are changing and that, perhaps, Abraham Block is not moving with them. I agree that this new tourism idea is the modern thing. And I agree that you young ones understand it better than I do. This is why I sent you to England; this is why I invested in your expensive education. And besides, I am not getting any younger, and it is about time that I slowed down and spent more time with your mother.' He beamed on his sons, who stood on the lower steps looking up at him.

'So, my sons,' he said, 'I will leave it to you to make all the decisions from now on.'

'Really?' said Jack.

'Of course,' said Abraham Block, 'but I shall be watching.' And he turned and walked up the steps into the hotel leaving a ghostly trail of cigar smoke in his wake.

Abraham Lazarus Block 1883-1965

CHAPTER 92

CLOUDS

I have found the most perfect spot, come!
–Myra Wheeler to Colonel E.S. Percy-Smith, 1935

'We seem to be having trouble with our children,' said Sarah.

'We do?' said Abraham.

'Ruth wants to go and work for Imperial Airways.'

'What's wrong with her job at The Norfolk and her cottage in the grounds?' said Abraham.

'She likes the uniform, she likes the idea of going out to the airport and meeting people and escorting them back to Nairobi. It's what they call being an air hostess these days; it's glamorous.'

'And The Norfolk Hotel is not glamorous?'

'Don't be difficult, dear,' said Sarah.

'That girl should be married,' said Abraham.

'Yes dear, and I am confident that she will be soon. Sol Rabb is writing to her.'

'*Writing* to her?' said Abraham, 'don't young men know how to do things anymore?'

'And that's not all,' Sarah said.

Abraham surveyed his wife: he braced himself

'Tubby and Valerie want to build a house.'

'And?'

'And they want to stay with us while they do so and—'

'I can imagine what all the other "ands" are,' said Abraham. 'Let them come; I'll talk to Tubby about the money. And Jack and Doria? Has Jack agreed to leave Ker and Downey? Are he and Doria going to run the Norfolk as I asked?'

'Yes, dear, but…'

'But?'

'But Jack says he wants to work on two more films before he leaves Ker and Downey. He and Doria met Stewart Granger and Deborah Kerr and Gregory Peck and Susan Heyward. Ava Gardner is coming out soon and Doria thinks she might bring her fiancée, Frank Sinatra.'

'Who *are* all these people?'

'Hollywood stars, dear.'

'Hollywood stars! Jack would do better to get down to business than chase stars.'

'They're young, Abraham. They're happy, they're enjoying themselves, and they're invited everywhere,' said Sarah. 'They have so many invitations on their mantelpieces they're putting them in piles of order of preference.'

'And all this matters more than business?' said Abraham.

But beneath the bluster he was proud.

His children had done well.

Abraham Block had come a long way. Into his mind came a picture of the grey streets of Leyland, his time as a grease monkey, and his days picking wool off fences.

'Invitations don't turn a profit,' was all he said.

It was as a result of an invitation that the next Block Hotel was purchased.

Tubby and Valerie Block made a handsome couple; and they were in great social demand. Parties had become fashionable in Kenya; and Tubby and Valerie were invited to them all. Many were up-country house parties, and the hosts required their guests to stay one night, sometimes two. It made practical sense. Distances were long and the roads were rough. There was also a sense of unrest in the country as the calls for independence grew.

'We've been invited to a house party up-country,' said Tubby.

'Who's invited us?' said Valerie. She pouted to apply bright red lipstick and clasped a set of pearls around her neck.

'It's not clear. I'm not sure it's from anyone in particular. I think they want to sell the place and this is just a clever ploy to get us all up there.'

'Up where?'

'Up Mount Kenya: the house is on its slopes. It's called *Mawingo*[1], 'Clouds', you know? I hear it's quite something.'

'Then do let's accept, Darling' said Valerie.

The road to Mount Kenya was long. It wound out of Nairobi through the sisal fields of Thika and past the hunched bulk of Ol Donyo Sabuk. It passed through coffee country, tea country and wheat country until the massive grey shoulder of Mount Kenya dominated the entire scene. Beyond the small town of Nanyuki, Tubby turned the car off the main road and followed a track up the mountain. It was rough and rutted and snaked through small villages and farms. There were goats in the road, children in knitted woollen hats, old men in wellington boots and balaclavas. The houses were timber-built, laced in moss and every door, painted blue, faced the mountain so as to keep the god, *Ngai*, who lived amid its peaks, always in sight.

The forests closed in suddenly and the car entered a silent world of half-light where ferns grew thick and the camphor trees were festooned with white star orchids. The podo trees grew straight, grey, gaunt and tall, and the turacos swooped between them with a sudden flash of their scarlet flight feathers. The road passed over mountain streams and laboured around steep bends. It was a world of cool and green and moss scented air; and then a clearing was reached and the road swept up a drive to where a large white house stood.

Above and around the house there was an immensity of sky and it was filled with fast-moving tufts of soft white cloud. Above the house rose the flanks of the mountain thick-clothed in forest on its lower slopes, then purple-yellow with heath and, finally, silver grey and bare. Then came the rocky spires of the peaks, Lenana, Nelion and Batian, dusted with snow so white that they shone like fractured sugar cones.

Tubby stopped the car and gazed at the house called Clouds.

'Now that's a house,' said Tubby.

'More than a house,' said Valerie, 'a dream: Camelot.'

And Camelot it was. A waiter stood by the double doors bearing a silver salver loaded with chilled champagne. There was a linen-fold panelled vestibule with a black-and-white chequer-board floor and a crystal chandelier. Beyond it was an orangery full of light, and a central Persian garden. A white marble spiral staircase with a delicate wrought iron balustrade led to the floor above.

'That's the Rhoda Lewisohn Suite, ' said Ronnie Deverick. He was the house agent and he had joined them on the lawn around the lily pond.

'Rhoda built the house,' he said, 'it took a year and cost seventeen thousand pounds, like to see around it?

Tubby nodded and he and Valerie followed Ronnie through a string of suites. Each was exquisitely presented with floor to ceiling windows looking out on to the mountain. In one of the bathrooms a brass line ran along the floor and down the centre of the marble bath.

'Equator,' said Ronnie, 'Rhoda liked to stand naked with one foot on each side.

Ronnie considered this for a moment. He was languid and pale with a receding chin and a prominent Adam's apple.

'Or so I hear tell,' he said, carelessly.

Descending to the ground floor, Ronnie led them through an immense circular drawing room, with French doors leading to a magnificent terrace. There was a mirrored cocktail bar with a black marble fireplace, there was a stone-built dining room hung with antlers and glass-eyed game trophies. There was a ballroom with a minstrel's gallery, and a central courtyard with fountains. Here, where their fellow guests were clustered into little knots of conversation, a jazz band played.

'It's the Syd Zeigler band from Torr's Hotel,' said Valerie.

'It would be,' said Tubby.

They walked down the terrace and saw where the formal gardens merged into the dark embrace of the forests.

'Rare orchid garden,' said Ronnie. He waved languidly in one direction

'Rose garden, tennis courts, boating lake, bridle paths into the forest.' He waved in another. 'There's also the original house, where the first owner, an American heiress lived. Care to see?'

'Do let's, Tubby,' said Valerie, catching hold of his hand.

In a clearing edged by trellised tumbles of Old English pink roses, stood a pair of simple stone rondavels, each with a high thatched roof and a half-glassed door with a round brass knob.

'Bathroom, kitchen and guest bedroom,' said Ronnie, 'It seems Mrs Myra Wheeler and her fiancée, a Colonel Smith-Perkins lived in a rose-pink silk tent with gold-plated tent poles, Persian carpets, crystal chandeliers and a solid silver samovar that was once owned by the Tsar. They liked it to be filled with champagne.'

Tubby stared at Ronnie unseeing.

He had fallen under the *Mawingo* spell.

That evening Valerie was left to chat with her fellow guests. The light had faded and the peacocks shrieked. Miniature fountains tinkled in the lily pond, tall church candles had been placed around it and their flickering flames were reflected in the water and the glass panes of the many windows.

'I've bought it.' Tubby said when he returned.

'But it's far too big for us,' said his wife.

'I haven't bought it for us,' said Tubby, 'I've bought it to turn it into a hotel.'

CHAPTER 93

THE MOUNT KENYA INN

In the facades we put on for others we demonstrate our potential;
through our children we reveal our reality.
–Lawrence Kelemen, orthodox rabbi and author of *Permission to Believe*

A
BRAHAM AND SARAH RETURNED FROM a holiday in Rishon Le Zion where the family had been celebrating the establishment of the State of Israel. As soon as he could find the opportunity, Tubby told Abraham that he had bought *Mawingo*.

'How much did you pay for it?' said Abraham.

'Fifty-thousand pounds,' said Tubby waiting for the eruption. It did not come.

'And what are you proposing to do with it?' said Abraham, dangerously quiet.

'I'm going to make it into an exclusive hotel.'

'It's too small for a hotel.'

'An inn then.'

Abraham said nothing.

'Are you sure anyone will bother to drive all the way up there?' said his brother, Jack, 'it's not exactly around the corner, is it.'

'That's the whole point,' said Tubby, 'people want to get out of town, experience the wilderness. The days of the safari are over—'

'The days of the safari are *over*?' said Abraham. 'What nonsense is this?'

'Okay, not *over*, Dad,' said Tubby, 'but there's a new kind of safari emerging. Ordinary people can't afford the cost of the old safaris. And they can't afford to take off into the bush for three months at a time. They have jobs.'

'So do you,' said Abraham, 'but all you ever seem to do is buy hotels.' He turned and walked out of Tubby's office.

'Is that it?' said Tubby, 'is that all he's going to say?'

'Seems you got away lightly, little brother' said Jack, 'but *Mawingo* had better pay, because if it doesn't he's going to have a lot more to say, I can promise you that.'

'Then help me make it into a success,' said Tubby, 'send some of your Hollywood people up there.'

Jack clapped his brother on the shoulder.

'You know what?' he said, 'that's not a bad idea. But we'd better turn it into a hotel first.'

Mawingo did not adapt well to being turned into a hotel. Once all its paintings and furnishings had been removed it seemed petulant and cruelly bare. Without its guests and its risqué parties it seemed bleak. The forest swallowed it and the mountain outshone it. Tubby and Jack built a safari bar in the grounds, but it's supposed rustic charm rang false. They built a golf course, but nobody played on it.

Mount Kenya Safari Club

The staff say the house is jinxed,' said Tubby. 'Every one who has ever owned it has met with tragedy. The first owner's lover died in a drunken brawl, the second owner died in a plane crash.'

'Oh come on,' said Jack, 'you don't believe all that, do you?'

'They say there was an ancient fig tree in a clearing that the local Kikuyu worshipped. Rhoda Lewisohn cut it down. They say witch doctors came and cursed the house and everyone who lived there.'

'It's hardly the valley of the bloody kings, Tubby.'

'Seriously, Jack.'

'I am serious,' said Jack, 'but the whole curse thing gives me an idea. MGM are about to shoot a new film here in Kenya, it's called *King Solomon's Mines*. It's about the curse of some long lost treasure or other and it will be shot mostly on location in the bush, but it needs studio time.'

'So?'

'So the stars are Stewart Granger and Deborah Kerr. They'll want luxury. Stewart Granger takes his stardom very seriously.'

'So?'

'So we'll turn the *Mawingo* stables into a studio. Even the best Hollywood studios are little more than barns. MGM will love it. And if they love it, all Hollywood will love it; and we'll be made.'

'And if they don't love it?'

'Then they'll love staying in the house, and you'll throw some marvelous parties there. And they'll love that instead.'

Jack was correct. *King Solomon's Mines* was a box office success and blazed the trail for a whole raft of swashbuckling films set in Kenya. Gregory Peck, Susan Heyward and Ava Gardner starred in *The Snows of Kilimanjaro*; Clark Gable and Grace Kelly starred in *Mogambo*; Ava Gardner brought her jealous fiancée, Frank Sinatra, along to glower and throw punches. And everyone partied with the glamorous young Blocks up at Mawingo.

But it still didn't pay as a hotel.

In 1959, the American film star, William Holden, organized a safari for two of his friends, a Texan oil millionaire and a Swiss banker. They stayed at *Mawingo* and, like everyone else; they fell under its spell. And William Holden shot part of the film *The Lion* in the studios that Tubby had built in the stables.

When William Holden first called to ask Tubby Block if he would sell *Mawingo*, Tubby was on the golf course. He sent a message to say he'd call back when he had finished his round. This naturally made Holden even more determined to buy, and he called again.

'I'll make a generous offer,' said Holden when Tubby eventually came to the phone.

'Such as?' said Tubby.

William Holden told him.

'Double it and *Mawingo* is yours,' said Tubby.

'Done,' said Mr Holden.

It was one of the few deals made by his sons of which Abraham Block ever approved.

Abraham and Sarah Block at the opening of the New Stanley

CHAPTER 94

FAMILY MATTERS

And make ye marriages with us; give your daughters unto us, and take our daughters unto you.
–Genesis 34:9

RUTH BLOCK LIVED IN ONE of the small cottages that stood in the gardens of the Norfolk Hotel. It had originally been one of the hotel's few married quarters, but it was cramped and dark with blue chintz curtains and a matching blue candlewick bedspread. There was only one window, a bed, a dressing table and chair, and a door leading to a small, dank, green-tiled bathroom. And Ruth was enchanted by it.

It was while she was living in the cottage, working on the front desk of the hotel, that she received word that her interview for a position as a hostess with Imperial Airways had been successful.

'Well of course it was, dear,' said her mother 'how could it have been otherwise?'

A parcel arrived at the Norfolk Hotel. It contained a tailored white blouse, a sky-blue jacket with padded shoulders and silver wings on the pocket, a straight skirt with kick-pleats, white stiletto heels, white gloves and a jaunty little hat. Ripping the items out of their brown paper packaging, Ruth put them on.

The dressing table mirror was small, and she had to stand on the chair to see the bottom half of her figure. She had never worn heels, she despised hats, and she had never been allowed to wear a suit so tight and so explicitly tailored. She examined her reflection from all angles. She was slim, her legs were good and, set on the side of her dark curls, the hat made her look like someone she didn't know: someone hard, mature, brittle and sophisticated.

Ruth reached to the back of the dressing table drawer and extracted the bright red Max Factor lipstick that her sister-in-law, Doria, had brought her from New York. She pulled her mouth into the shape she had seen her mother pull, and she applied the lipstick as she had seen her mother do. It felt odd and it smelt odd, but she pressed her lips together and blotted them on a tissue, and the effect was startling: she loved it.

Nairobi airport was little more than a field with a hastily erected control tower. Ruth's job required her to wait in the control tower until the long silver planes had come in to land, then she would be driven out to them and wait while the steps were put in place. She would mount these with self-conscious care, hand on hat, and position herself by the door. As each passenger emerged, she would extend a gloved hand, bestow a scarlet smile and say, 'welcome to Nairobi.'

When all of her passengers were assembled, Ruth would usher them into a fleet of cars and escort them in to Nairobi. Then she would check them in to either The Norfolk or The New Stanley.

'Nothing like keeping it in the family,' said Jack.

'I love that uniform,' said Doria.

Jack, Doria, Tubby, Jeremy and Aino Block

'You have lipstick on your teeth,' said her mother.

'What was wrong with the front desk at The Norfolk?' said her father.

When the first letter had arrived from Sol Rabb, Ruth had seized it and retired into a corner to read it. Light-hearted in style, it was warm, friendly and informative. But it was not a love letter. And nor were any of the letters that followed, but they came every week.

After six months, a different letter arrived, and it stated, quite simply and without any particular preamble, that Sol Rabb wished to marry her. He had, he said, always wanted to marry her, but he had not wished to rush things.

Sitting down as abruptly as the sky-blue skirt allowed, Ruth held the letter tightly in her hand; she stared straight ahead. She had not seen Sol Rabb since the time he had put his jacket around her shoulders on the beach in Cape Town. Nor had she spoken to him. But she had come to know him through his letters, and now he seemed to be a part of her life.

But, did she want to marry him?

Ruth put her white-gloved hand flat on the lapels of her pale blue jacket and took in a deep breath. She held it for a couple of seconds, and then exhaled.

Of course she did.

'Are you sure?' said Sarah, when Ruth told her, 'you spent no time with him, you know. And you don't *know* him.'

'I do know him,' said Ruth, 'and it feels completely right.'

'There's no need to rush in to it,' said Sarah.

'I can't wait to rush in to it,' said Ruth.

'Very well, darling, but we'll have to ask your father what he has to say about it.'

Abraham Block had only one thing to say about it: 'You will get married at the Norfolk?' he said.

'Where else?' said Ruth.

It was 1948, the war was recently over, and nothing was in abundance.

'Where on earth will we find a dress?' said Sarah.

'Leave it to me,' said Doria, 'we don't have all these Hollywood connections for nothing.'

'Plain, high-neck, well-tailored,' said Sarah, 'she'd look ridiculous in frills.'

'I think lilac, full-length and picture hats for the bridesmaids, though,' said Doria, 'don't you?'

'What's a picture hat?' said Ruth.

'Oh really, Ruth,' said Doria, 'you have no idea. Just leave it to me.'

CHAPTER 95

THE WIND OF CHANGE

'The wind of change is blowing through this continent.
Whether we like it or not, this growth of national consciousness is a political fact.'
–Harold Macmillan, British Prime Minister, South Africa, 1960

Beyond Kenya's borders, the political sands were shifting. Britain was bankrupt, India had gained her independence, and the British Government was beginning to question the viability of Imperialism.

The first demands for Kenyan independence came at the end of the First World War when the Kenya African Union was established with a largely Kikuyu membership. Its demands were ignored and, by the end of the Second World War, another movement had been established, this time by the radical youth of the Kikuyu; and it was known as the Mau Mau.

The members of the Mau Mau were angry: wages were low, food prices were high, jobs were hard to get, they faced an uncertain future, and they believed that their ancestral lands had been stolen from them by the settlers. More than this, they were disillusioned with colonial rule, enraged by its racial prejudices, and out of all patience with their own leaders, who they saw as being old, hide-bound and in league with the British for reasons of their own. Young, disaffected, idealistic and inspired, the Mau Mau decided that the time for asking for independence was past, and that the time to fight for it had arrived.

At first, the settler community did not take the threat of the Mau Mau seriously. They dismissed it as an outbreak of mass hysteria amongst the Kikuyu; they scoffed at the lurid tales of anti-Christian oaths, sexual rituals, and the bonding of blood brothers. But then the settlers heard how the Mau Mau treated their fellow Kenyans, even their fellow Kikuyus, and their attitude towards them changed. They heard of how those who refused to espouse the Mau Mau cause had their children slashed to death before their eyes, of how pregnant women were ripped open, and of how elderly men and women were burned to death in their huts. If the Mau Mau could treat their own people like this, reasoned the settlers, how would they treat any colonialists that fell in to their hands?

Within months, the Mau Mau had begun to attack the settlers' farms, where they murdered the African workers, killed livestock, burned crops and sabotaged dams and roads. Then they began to attack the settlers themselves; and the settlers called upon the Colonial Administration to protect them and all those Kenyans who refused to join the Mau Mau.

In 1950, the Mau Mau was banned, but the ban was ignored. Next the British Government sent out their strong man, Sir Evelyn Baring, who took over as Kenya's Governor in 1951. Sir Evelyn's approach was simple; he declared an immediate State of Emergency and placed all the leaders of the Kenya African Union, including their charismatic spokesman, Jomo Kenyatta, on trial. Then began a bitter guerilla war with the Mau Mau themselves, who took to the forests of Mount Kenya and the caves of the Aberdares, from whence they launched their increasingly violent attacks.

Jack, Tubby, Rita and Lily Haller met at the Norfolk Hotel to discuss the situation.

'Mum and Dad cannot remain out in Limuru surrounded by hundreds of Kikuyu workers,' said Jack, 'and nor can you, Aunt Lily.'

'I'm not afraid,' said Lily, 'I speak Kikuyu, I've taught their children, I treat their sicknesses. They are as much my family as my own children are.'

'That may be true,' said Tubby, 'but your Kikuyu workers cannot protect you from the Mau Mau, and its them that you have to fear.'

'If the Mau Mau want to come and kill me, let them,' said Lily, 'but I'm not moving.'

'What about you and Jacob, Rita?' said Jack, 'your farm is isolated and you also have a Kikuyu workforce.'

'Jacob has a reputation for treating his workers well,' said Rita, 'they call him *Kihoro*, "the good man", he has built stone houses for them, and looked after their welfare, we won't be attacked.'

'But all that is no guarantee,' said Tubby, 'it's not your workers that are the threat, its the guerillas of the Mau Mau, and they will simply murder your workers if they don't support them; and then they'll murder you.'

'So, are you and Valerie going to move out of your nice new house and into that cramped cottage at the Norfolk?' said Rita, her arms akimbo and her chin tilted.

'Valerie is pregnant,' said Tubby, 'so yes, I think we must.'

'And what about you, Jack?' said Rita, 'are you and Doria moving into the Norfolk cottages? And what about Ruth and Sol? Are they?'

'We spend most of our time at the Norfolk anyway,' said Jack, 'and Ruth and Sol have a house in town.'

'Have you told Mum and Dad that they have to move into a cottage?' said Rita.

'You can't tell Mum and Dad anything,' said Tubby, 'but I'm trying to persuade them. Pops is nearly seventy, he says he won't retire until he's seventy-five; and he says he won't move back into Nairobi until he has retired. But according to Mum he has not been well; he's got arthritis, his breathing is bad, and he's soon going to need medical care.'

A few weeks later, Tubby walked into his office at the Norfolk Hotel to find his father already sitting there. For a moment, Abraham did not look up. He seemed to be gazing into the distance and, for the first time in his life, Tubby realized the frailty of his father.

Abraham rose stiffly to his feet and embraced his son.

'How's business?' he said.

'Doing better than ever, Pops,' said Tubby, 'all the publicity surrounding Princess Elizabeth's luncheon at The New Stanley, and her accession to the British throne the very next day, has brought visitors flocking to us; we can't build the new rooms fast enough.'

'You haven't shown me the plans for the renovation of the Stanley,' said Abraham, 'I hope you're not going to make too many changes to the old place?'

'None that you won't approve of,' said Tubby mentally crossing his fingers.

But the truth of the matter was quite different; he and Jack had decided to completely re-build the Stanley. It was to re-open with 284 beds, it would rise to nine floors, occupy an entire block, and it would cost half-a-million pounds of Block money. But, by tacit agreement, neither Jack nor Tubby had told Abraham about this.

'Good,' said Abraham, 'there's no need for change, the New Stanley got where it is today by offering value for money; and that's still what people want. Those that want more can go to the Norfolk.'

'Yes, Pops,' said his son, 'so will you be having a look around the Stanley while you're here?'

'No. I've come to tell you that your mother and I have decided to move into one of the Norfolk's cottages. Just until all this Mau Mau business blows over.'

'I thought you were dead against the idea?'

'I was, but I overheard a discussion between two of our coffee-pickers the other day; they didn't realize that I speak Kikuyu.'

'And?'

'They said they'd had word from that General of theirs, Dedan Kimathi. He wants oaths of allegiance out of them and if they refuse they will be punished. They said they would obey, and I don't blame them; they risk being killed. But I can't risk your mother's safety.'

'I'm relieved, Pops,' said Tubby, 'only yesterday I heard how that harmless old couple, the Bruxnor-Randalls, were slashed to death in their Limuru cottage; and they lived just half a mile down the road from Eddie Ruben.'

'It will all blow over soon,' said Abraham.

CHAPTER 96

MAU MAU

'If I had revenged as I had been ordered by Kimathi, I would have put your house on fire, but I
spared it in order to prove to you that we are not so destructive as you might think.
All we want is freedom to form an African Government which will ban all discriminatory bars
and extend individual freedom in movement, press and speech, give better pay and conditions
and, most important, eliminate European's selfishness and pride. We do not hate the white man's
colour, but we cannot tolerate seeing a foreign settler with 50,000 acres of land, most of which
only wild game enjoy, while thousands of Africans are starving of hunger in their own country.
Nor can we accept the white man to remain as a master and the African as a servant.'
–Brigadier General Karari Njama to Major Owen Jeoffreys, September 1954

I T TOOK FOUR YEARS FOR the Mau Mau uprising to be suppressed. It was a dirty war and a bitter one. 25,000 Mau Mau fighters waged a guerilla war against a few thousand well-armed and well-trained '*wa Johnny*', or British troops. And the British were supported by 25,000 African troops.

The Mau Mau, outmanned and out-gunned, took to the forests of Mount Kenya where they believed the British would not find them. But the British became skilled in tracking them down and eventually 85,000 Kikuyu men were captured and placed in detention camps where the treatment they received was so harsh as to prompt protest even in Britain. But by 1954 'Operation Anvil' had eradicated the Mau Mau from Nairobi leaving only 15,000 guerilla fighters in the forests of Mount Kenya and the Aberdares. A year later, only 1,500 Mau Mau remained there under the leadership of General Dedan Kimathi.

In 1956, a manhunt was sent out to capture Dedan Kimathi, but succeeded only in capturing his last thirteen supporters. Kimathi fled; he covered eighty miles in one day before collapsing on the fringes of the forests, where he was captured. He was taken to hospital, sentenced and hanged.

With the death of Dedan Kimathi, the Mau Mau insurgency ended. But the damage to British Colonial rule had been done. In 1960 the State of Emergency was ended and the British Prime Minister, Harold Macmillan, delivered his 'Wind of Change' speech, which signaled the end of British Colonial rule in Africa. At first Kenya's settler community refused to believe that Macmillan would abandon them. But in 1960 the Lancaster House Conference made the first step towards handing majority rule back to the Kenyans and a date was set for elections the following year. Black majority rule was now inevitable. In 1961 Jomo Kenyatta and his fellow detainees were released from their seven-year imprisonment and, on the 12th of December 1963, the Union Jack was hauled down and replaced with the flag of the Republic of Kenya.

The transfer of power was peaceful and devoid of animosity.

'Whatever we may feel or say about the European settlers in colonial times,' said President

Kenya's first president, Mzee Jomo Kenyatta at State House (Jack Block 2nd from the right), 1971

Mzee Jomo Kenyatta with Jack Block (far right)

Jomo Kenyatta, 'it's entirely thanks to them that Kenya is so far ahead of her neighbours and will stay so.'

He went on to reassure the settler community.

'I think some of you may be worried,' he said, 'about what will happen if Kenyatta comes to be the head of government? He has been in prison, maybe he has given trouble. What is he going to do? Let me set you at rest. That Kenyatta has no intention whatever to look backwards… I am a farmer like you.. I believe the most disturbing point among us is fear…created by not knowing what the other side is thinking. If we must live together, if we must work together, we must talk together, exchange views… we must also learn to forgive one another. Whether we are white, brown or black; we are not angels; we are human beings. And all of us can work together to make this country great… This is what I beg you to believe is the policy of your government.'

For the settlers there remained a straightforward choice: whether to embrace life in the new Kenya or to leave. Of the 61,000 Europeans resident in the colony in 1959, 20,000 elected to leave, but it was not so easy for the 125,000-strong Asian community. In 1967 they were issued with an ultimatum: take out Kenyan citizenship as a sign of their loyalty and commitment to the new Kenya, or leave. The exodus was so great that Whitehall was forced to remove all Kenyan-Asian rights to British citizenship.

Abraham Lazarus Block, 1883-1965

CHAPTER 97

THE END TIME

Why would I want to leave? In this country I am somebody;
in England I would only be a number on a door.
–Abraham Block 1886-1965

THE COTTAGE IN THE GROUNDS of the Norfolk Hotel was small, but Abraham Block had never been a man who could be defined by where he lived, or how he lived.

When Sarah and Abraham had first taken up residency in the cottage, they had declared that they would stay there only until the Mau Mau insurgency was ended, but then they came to a realization that surprised them. They had thought that living in a one-roomed cottage would limit them; but they discovered that it set them free. They had thought that it might shrink their horizons; but they found that it drew on a much larger human canvas. They had thought that they would miss the harsh dictates of agriculture and business, but they found that life in the hotel lifted the mantle of responsibility from their shoulders. They had thought that they would be lonely, but they found that they sat at the centre of the family universe, and that the family orbited around them as calmly as the moon orbits the earth. And they grew to live by an entirely different round of rhythms and seasons.

In the early mornings, there would be the soft tread of porters as they padded along the dew-wet paths, the hushed hefting of suitcases; the wafts of bacon, and the steadily growing hum of the hotel awakening to its day. As night fell, there would be a steady closing of doors, a whisking of curtains, a dying fall of voices, and an extinguishing of lights. And yet the hotel was never absolutely still or perfectly silent.

And they were never totally alone; because the heartbeat of the hotel was steady; and the pulse of their family was strong.

In 1958 Abraham announced that he would retire on his seventy-fifth birthday and hand over the mechanisms of control of his empire to his sons. The empire was large: in 1950, Block Hotels had become a public company and a new company, Block Estates had been formed to handle the Block's property and business portfolio, which was extensive.

There were those, his sons among them, who were surprised when Abraham Block made this announcement, but not his wife, Sarah, because she had watched him age during their six years in the cottage; she had seen that his arthritis grew ever more painful; she knew that his heart was weakening; and she saw that his body, once so strong, was now moving inexorably into decline.

Nobody expected Abraham Block to relinquish his grasp on his empire easily; and he did not. The older he became, the more he refused to accept change, and the more he reverted to the parsimonious ways of the past.

New curtains were hung in the dining room of the Norfolk Hotel.

'We don't need them,' said Abraham.

The bar was extended and a roof built so that the guests would not be caught in the rain.

'Waste!' said Abraham waving his stick at the rafters, 'these boys of mine don't know what life is! Life is making money not spending it! And why did they not tell me what they were doing?'

The following week, Tubby told his father that the poultry farm on the shores of Lake Naivasha was to have a new galvanized iron roof.

'Why an iron roof? Why don't they thatch it with the papyrus that grows on the lake shore?' said Abraham, 'it was good enough for us in the past, why isn't it good enough for you now?'

Gradually, Jack and Tubby decided that it was best to spare their father the anger and distress that change and expenditure so obviously caused him. But there was one change that they could not hope to keep hidden from him: and that was the New Stanley Hotel.

Jack and Tubby had arranged for Sarah and Abraham to visit Richon LeZion while the destruction of the old hotel had taken place, but the new hotel had risen from the dust a nine-storey colossus of change, and a beacon of expenditure that spanned two entire blocks. It dominated the Nairobi skyline, it monopolized the city centre, it had more beds than any hotel in East Africa, and its sheer mammoth splendour caused people to stop and stare in the street. Then, two weeks before its Grand Opening Ceremony, the New Stanley, was given several coats of white paint, and now it stood as gleaming and massive as Mount Kilimanjaro.

'What are we going to tell Pops?' said Tubby.

'Do we have to tell him anything?' said Jack.

'He's going to hear about it.'

'Not necessarily,' said Jack, ever the optimist.

'Come on, Jack,' said Tubby, 'he might be getting on, but his brain is every bit as sharp as before; and his hearing isn't bad either. He's going to find out.'

A week later, their worst fears were realized.

Making his way painfully on to the terrace, leaning heavily on his stick, Abraham called for his manager, Brian Burrows.

'I'd like a car, Brian, please,' he said.

'Right away,' said Brian, for whom Abraham Block could do no wrong, 'err, where shall I say you are going?'

'To the New Stanley Hotel, Brian' said Abraham, and walked purposefully down the terrace. As the car pulled away from the curb, Brian Burrows sprinted up the steps of the Norfolk Hotel and into his office. He called the New Stanley and asked for Jack or Tubby; but they were not there.

'Well, who is there?' he said.

'Mrs Doria Block,' he was told.

'Oh Lord,' said Brian, 'then please tell her that Mr Abraham Block is on his way.'

When she received this message, Doria's beautifully painted red mouth elongated into a grimace of horror and she hurried out on to the front steps of the hotel. On the opposite pavement a car had stopped. Abraham Block got out of it. Painfully, he walked to the corner of the street, from whence he could get an uninterrupted view of the New Stanley Hotel. And there he stood, leaning on his stick and gazing at the hotel. Doria could not make out his expression.

Dodging cars and rickshaws, Doria wove her way across the dusty street in her high white stiletto heels, her hand on her beautifully coiffed hair. Arriving in front of her father-in-law, she

Jack and Doria on the roof of the New Stanley Hotel in 1961

smiled brightly, removed her sunglasses, and opened her mouth to speak.

Abraham held up his hand to indicate silence, and continued to gaze at the hotel. His expression was bleak, his breath laboured.

'Look at that great white elephant my sons have built for me,' he said.

'We thought it would be best if –', began Doria.

But Abraham had already turned away. He signaled for the driver to bring the car to the curbside where he stood. He winced as he climbed in to it. He gave Doria a dismissive wave of farewell, but he said nothing.

The car drew away leaving Doria marooned on the pavement, a slight figure in a white dress with large red poppies blossoming across it, and a skirt so full it was supported by three layers of net petticoats. She looked, like the hotel, completely if gorgeously, out of place.

Some hours later, Jack and Tubby arrived at the Norfolk Hotel and sought out their father. To their surprise, he did not appear to be angry.

'When is this Grand Opening that I hear is planned?' was all he said.

'The week after next, Pops,' said Jack.

'There is only one thing that I ask,' said Abraham, and he looked into the distance.

'Of course, Pops, what is that?' said Tubby.

'That Mayence Tate be invited to it, and that all her travel and accommodation be paid for.'

'It will be done,' said Jack.

Later, when the brothers were alone, Tubby swirled his whisky in his glass.

'Do you think that means he likes it?' he said.

'I don't know,' said Jack, 'I really don't know. But you heard what Doria said about the white elephant?'

'I did. But what is a white elephant?' said Tubby.

'I looked it up in the dictionary.'

'And?'

'I can't recall the exact words,' said Jack, 'but it said that a white elephant is a possession that is useless or troublesome, expensive to maintain and difficult to get rid of. It also said that the term originated from a story about the kings of Siam who insisted that all the white elephants born in their country were given to the courtiers that they particularly disliked. It was a subtle way of ruining them due to the huge expense of keeping the animal while not daring to offend the king.'

'He's still as sharp as ever, then,' said Tubby.

'Sharper,' said Jack.

For all his sharpness, Abraham Block could not stave off the march of time, and he grew steadily more infirm until, eventually, it became impossible for him to leave his bed without help. Two nurses were engaged to give him constant care. Sarah moved in to the cottage next door to him, and a wheel chair was purchased.

In 1964, as the new Kenyan Republic was declared, a party was held for Sarah and Abraham's Golden Wedding Anniversary. It was a particularly grand affair to which all their family and

The 'great white elephant' on completion in 1960

Jack, Tubby and Doria Block at the New Stanley Hotel in 1961

friends were invited. The Norfolk Hotel rose to the occasion with her usual style, wreathed in billows of gold tulle and adorned with thousands of yellow roses.

After the dinner, when all the speeches had been made, and all the glasses had been raised, Abraham surveyed the ballroom with satisfaction writ large upon his face. Then he smiled at his wife and asked his daughter, Ruth, to wheel him back to the cottage in the grounds.

'I want to smoke a cigar before I sleep,' he said.

Ruth wheeled Abraham's chair back to the cottage and knelt beside it, her lavish skirts belling around her. It was a warm night laced by the delicate scent of frangipani; the nightjars were calling, and the strains of the dance band floated across the ghostly-grey lawns. Above the hotel, the deep blue dome of the night sky was spangled with stars.

'You go back to the party,' Abraham said, 'I will sit here and look at the stars.'

Ruth kissed her father and walked away. Just before she disappeared into the warm yellow glow of the hotel, she turned and waved.

Abraham lit one of his fine Cuban cigars, and out of the gloom a waiter stepped forward with an ashtray extended.

Mrs Van de Loren was making her way back to her room when she saw the bent figure of an old man in a wheel chair. The chair was parked in the centre of the lawn and a waiter, clad entirely in white, stood still and silent by its side. The waiter was holding an ashtray, and he and the old man were staring up at the stars.

As Mrs Van de Loren approached, the old man withdrew his gaze from the heavens and watched her walk past. She was a large woman and she was wearing a pair of white Capri pants, and there was something about the sway of her hips that reminded Abraham Block of a white cow with a velvet dewlap that fell like a fall of lace to her knees. He could see the cow in his mind, she had come from very far back in time, and she wanted him to follow her.

Slowly, Abraham raised one hand and gave Mrs Van de Loren a regal wave, then he blew a perfect smoke ring, and returned to his contemplation of the stars.

'Well really!' said Mrs Van de Loren to her husband, 'just look at that! What is a strange old man like that doing in a place like this? And who on earth does he think he is?'

'I don't know, dear,' said her husband, 'you'd think he owned the place.'

EPILOGUE

Abraham Lazarus Block died 18th April 1965 and was buried in the Jewish cemetery in Forest Road, Nairobi. His own memoirs are included on page 390.

Sarah Block (nèe Tulipman)
Sarah Block continued to live in the cottage in the grounds of the Norfolk Hotel until her death on Christmas Eve, 1980. She was buried alongside her husband in the Jewish cemetery in Forest Road, Nairobi.

Samuel Block
Samuel Block was born in Kirkel (also spelt Kirkl), Kovno in 1849. He moved to Vilnius in 1871 and married Ettel Soltz in 1878 whereupon they moved to a farmhouse in Gilwan, Kovno. Samuel Block fled Lithuania in 1892 and went to South Africa where he had a furniture business. In 1905 he was joined by his daughter, Lily. In 1908 Lily and Samuel were brought from South Africa to Kenya by Abraham, who settled them on his farm. When Ettel Block died in 1918, Samuel returned to South Africa where he married a Cape Dutch matron. He returned to visit Kenya with his new wife but his daughters did not accept the new Mrs Block. Samuel died in South Africa in 1924 and is buried there.

Ettel Block (nèe Soltz)
Ettel (also spelt Ethel) was born in Birzai in 1854. She married Samuel in 1878 and had four children, Annie, Abraham, Lily and Freda. She moved to Salcininkai in 1893 to live with the Sinson family. In 1907 Ettel went to England with Freda and lodged briefly with the Sinson family in Leeds. She then travelled to Kenya as described. Ettel died in Nairobi in 1918.

Fanny Sinson (nèe Soltz)
Fanny was the elder sister of Ettel, she married Rabbi Sinson and the couple had four children. Mary, the eldest daughter, travelled to South Africa with Lily when she left England. Mary, however, returned to England. The Sinsons lived in Salcininkai where, according to Lily, they had a large house. Fanny left for England with the family in 1895 and lived thereafter in Leeds.

Annie Harris (nèe Block)
Annie, the eldest Block child, was born in 1879 in Gilwan. In 1895 she left for England with the Sinsons and in 1898 she married Nathan Harris in Leeds; they had two children: Elsie Harris and Charles Lewis Harris. Nathan died in 1936 and Annie in 1939. For a brief period of time they lived in Nairobi and ran a second-hand clothes shop in the centre of town, but when Nathan died in Kenya, Elsie took her mother back to Leeds.

Lily Haller (nèe Block)
Lily was born in 1888 in Gilwan. She left for England in 1901 and arrived in Capetown in 1902. She arrived in Nairobi in 1905 with Samuel and ran Abraham's farm. She married her neighbour, Simon Haller, in 1913. The couple had four children; Arthur Abraham, (1914-

1970), Edith (1915-1986), Maurice (1918-1934) and Bertie (1920-1964). Simon Haller died in 1942. Lily took care of Sarah when she arrived in Kenya and helped her with the birth of Rita as described. In later life she not only managed the Block farms but also many of her own. Lily was known as 'Mother of the Kikuyu'. Never at any time did she lock the doors of her home and her charitable deeds and hospitality to Jewish refugees and Italian POWs in both World Wars was renowned. She died in 1963 after 57 years of residence in East Africa. Lily's memoir is included on page 396.

Freda Kirkel (née Block)
Freda was born in 1891 in Gilwan. She came to Kenya in 1908. She married Morris Kirkel whom she nursed while he was convalescing at Lily and Simon Haller's a convalescent at the farm. The couple had two children, Ethel Patricia, born in 1919; and Jean, born in 1922. Morris died in 1945 and Freda in 1966, she is buried in the Forest Road Cemetery in Nairobi.

Rita Hirshfeld (née Block)
Rita was born in 1915 in Nairobi, schooled in England and, later, sent to Rishon Le Zion where she met Jacob (Yakov) Hirshfeld (1911-1991) under the chaperonage of her aunts, Leah and Hannah. She married him in 1937 in Rishon Le Zion. Rita and Jacob arrived in Kenya in 1939 and farmed (primarily coffee but also fruit, sisal, dairy, ranching and poultry. They sold their farm in 1973 and moved to Israel. Rita died in 2008 in Israel. Rita and Jacob were survived by Ora, born in 1934, Tzvi Samuel (1939-1992), Theodor Benjamin, born in 1942, and Eallan, born in 1944.

Ora Hirshfeld married Avshalom Leshem (1921-1999), an Israeli lawyer, in 1954. The couple had a daughter, Adah, born in 1956; Ora and Avshalom were were divorced in 1958. Ora later married Milton Perlman and they live in Tel Aviv. Theo Block lives in Buffalo, Wyoming and is married to Dawn Wilson. He works in real estate as a ranch appraiser. Eallan, a qualified accountant, married Esther Teacher, and the couple live in Raanana, Israel. Ora's book on her family, Spring in Eternity was published in 2006 and the extract pertaining to the Block family is given (with her kind permission) on page 403. She was also kind enough to supply a number of old photographs of the Block family.

Jack Block
Jack (Jacob/Yaakov) Block was born in 1916 and was schooled at Parklands School and Kenton College in Nairobi. Later he attended Loughborough College in England. Jack returned to Kenya in 1933 and began his working career with Unilever. Jack served in the 2nd/4th Battalion of the Kenya African Rifles during the 2nd World War and it was whilst he was on sick leave in 1944, that he hitched a lift to South Africa where he met Doria Beiles. Major Jack Block and Doria were married in 1945 in Johannesburg. The couple had two children: Lynda (Lyn) in 1946 and Jonathan David in 1949. Elizabeth Hannah Ruben, born in 1946, was adopted by Jack and Doria. Jack died in a fishing accident in Chile in 1983. Doria died in Nairobi in 2010. Lyn Block married Albert Fuss (1935-2012), Jonathan Block is married to Henrietta Kirkpatrick, and Elizabeth Block is married to David Hopkins.

Eddie Ruben (Tubby) Block

Tubby Block was born in 1919 and went to Parklands School before attending preparatory school in Brighton and Loughborough College in 1929. The story regarding his name in drawn from family lore. Tubby married Valerie Beiles, Doria's younger sister. Valerie died in 1955 whilst carrying the couple's second child, who also died. Their first child, Jeremy, married Maria Adriana Abolos and the couple had one daughter, Valerie. They later divorced and Jeremy married Caroline Fox. Tubby married for the second time, Aino Niiranen, in 1957, and they had two sons, Simon (1961-1964) and Anthony born in 1962. Anthony lives in San Diego, USA.

Tubby served in the 1st East African Light Battery under Commander Wavell and was in command of the 53rd East African Light Battery (on the southern front). Kenya African Rifles (Northern Brigade and Southern) during the 2nd World War and was posted to Burma as described. He was decorated with the Military Cross. Tubby Block died in 1996 and was buried in the Forest Road Jewish cemetery.

Ruth Rabinowitz (nèe Block)

Ruth was born in 1927 in Nairobi where she grew up and was schooled. She married Solomon Rabb (born Rabinowitz), in 1948. The couple had three children; Leigh, born in 1950, Geraldine born in 1951, and Nicholas born in 1955. Sol, a chartered accountant, was the Chief Accountant for Block Hotels until 1970; he died in 2009. Ruth lives in the Fairseat Retirement Home in Nairobi. Leigh is a paediatrician, he married Celia Meecham and they live in the Midlands of the United Kingdom. Geraldine married Martin Dunford and they have a restaurant and tourism business in Nairobi. Nicholas is unmarried and lives in Nairobi.

The Block Empire

Block Hotels became a public company in 1950 and by 1975 its portfolio included **The Norfolk Hotel** (purchased in 1927 and sold to Lonrho Hotels Kenya in 1989. The hotel was acquired by Fairmont Hotels and Resorts in 2004); **The New Stanley Hotel** (purchased in 1947 and sold to the Sarova Group in 1978), **The Nyali Beach Hotel**, Mombasa (management contract acquired in 1972), **The Lake Baringo Hotel** (management contract acquired in 1978), **The Lake Naivasha Country Club** (management contract acquired in 1980), **Keekorok Lodge**, Masai Mara and Samburu Lodge (leases acquired by Block Hotels in 1965/66), **the Outspan** and **Treetops** (acquired by Block Hotels in 1966 and sold in 1978 to Aberdare Hotels Ltd), and the Simbad Hotel in Malindi (management contract acquired in 1980). Block Hotels also managed three hotels in Leshotho: Sehlabathebe, Molimu Nthuse and Quacha's Nek. **Block Estates** (formed in 1950) owned farms in and around Nairobi and the Rift Valley, dairies, a bacon factory and a Nairobi housing estate. African Representatives, a small company initially involved with the distribution of Lever Brothers products; later became **East African Industries**, one of the largest manufacturing companies in Kenya. **The Kulia Group/Kulia Investments** later took over ownership of Block Hotels, Farmer's Choice and a number of representative agencies including Afro-Swiss Engineering, and Business Machines Ltd.

The Hirshfelds in 1951 left to right Theo, Rita, Eallan, Jacob and Tsvi and Ora standing)

Jeremy (left), Jonathan, Leigh (rear) and Nicholas Block

ABRAHAM'S NARRATIVE

Transcription of an interview carried out by Doria Block with Abraham Lazarus Block. Actual date of interview unknown but thought to be around 1950/55.
Edited by Jane Barsby

1903 heralded a great change in my life. In March of that year I attended a lecture in Cape Town given by the late Joseph Chamberlain, the British Colonial Secretary. He spoke of a new discovery in the British Empire; a colony where a treaty had been signed with many of the elders that allowed for European settlement in a new land called British East Africa (BEA). Chamberlain stressed in his lecture that a single-track railway had been built by the British, which ran from the coastal town of Mombasa right through into the African interior on the shores of Lake Victoria. This lecture made a great impression upon me. I was a young man full of adventure, and I decided immediately to set out for a new start in British East Africa.

A few days later I read in the press that a proposal had been put forward by the late Sir Harry Jones, and endorsed by Joseph Chamberlain. It suggested that a settlement might be established in BEA for the oppressed Jews of Europe and that this might prove beneficial to the ongoing settlement efforts that the British Colonial Office was making in relation to BEA. After I had learned this, my interest in BEA grew even stronger. I wanted to be part and parcel of the pioneers of BEA. I had no capital, but I had plenty of the spirit of adventure; and I wasted no time in getting in touch with a few friends of mine. Seven of us made up our minds to make our way to BEA.

We began by making enquires as to what shipping lines ran up the coast from South Africa to Mombasa. We discovered that an Austrian boat called the *Feldmarshall* was trading between Europe and South Africa, and that it stopped at all the small ports between Trieste and Mombasa. There was only one problem as far as I was concerned,

and this was how I might obtain enough money to pay for my passage and that of my two treasured Basuto white ponies.

Eventually I managed to raise enough money to pay for my passage and for the freight of my ponies. As a farmer's son, I also considered it advisable to take some South African seed stock with me. I took a bag of 'Early Rose' potatoes, a bag of beans, a bag of linseed and a bag of peas – and this was my stock in trade as I started out for British East Africa. I also had twenty-three pounds in cash, but most of this was expended on paying for my freight and excess baggage.

It took me three days or so to collect my ponies, then we travelled together by train to Delagoa Bay, which was where the boat docked. We left at the end of June, 1903. I travelled Third Class at a cost of 10 Rupees (about fourteen shillings), and the journey took 21 days stopping off at each and every African port.

We reached Mombasa at around 6am on a sunny morning and my first impressions of it were tremendous. There was no port, we landed from rowing boats and were carried ashore on the backs of Swahili porters.

My first task on arrival was to discover if there were any Jews already settled in Mombasa. To my surprise there were two Austrian Jews: one was a man by the name of Markus, who is still living at the coast, and the other was his partner, a Mr Loy. They were partners in a trading concern. Mr Markus was also the Acting Consul for the Austrian Government and the agent for a number of shipping lines. Mr Markus gave me a hearty handshake and asked if there were more of us coming to East Africa, and whether we proposed to take up trading or farming. I replied 'there are seven of us arrived on this boat! And we are ALL contemplating farming!'

I discovered that there was another trading company in Mombasa, which was called Smith MacKenzie. It was run by a man by the name of Mcjohn, who also ran a bar with a couple of lodging rooms. There was another hotel called the Africa Hotel, which stood close to where the present Mombasa Club stands, but it's gone now. At that time all the land that surrounded the Africa Hotel was owned by Indians with a just a sprinkling of German traders.

I embarked for Nairobi on the train, a journey that took 36 hours. Meals were taken in the railway sidings where there were *Dak* bungalows catered by a Goanese called Mr Nazareth. I recall that the cost of dinner and lunch was 1 Rupee; breakfast cost 75 Annas.

My friends decided to go immediately to visit the District Commissioner of Nairobi, Mr Ainsworth (after whom Ainsworth Bridge was named). He too extended a warm welcome to us all and gave us full information about the land sales, which he said fell under the responsibility of the Government. He referred us to the Land Office and they referred us to the High Commissioner, Sir Charles Eliot, a pioneer who had done much to encourage European settlement. Sir Charles Eliot supplied us with maps of the land available, some of which had already been surveyed. My friends immediately set off on *safari* to choose their land.

When I arrived, I found the settlement of Nairobi to be much less impressive than Mombasa. And whenever the rains came, which was often because it stood in the lee of the Aberdare Mountains, it became just one huge muddy puddle. Mr Ainsworth had set up a free campsite for the use of all new arrivals (it was in what is today known as Duke Street), but I had no tent, so I decided to look for a bed and a place to put my ponies.

I found a small hotel, which belonged to a man called Mr Wood. It was a small wood and iron structure, which consisted of a butcher's shop, a grocery and three or four lodging rooms. Each contained a bed, a paraffin box, a basin, a jug and a chair. There was a dining room too, with seating for twelve. The charge for a bed, three meals and tea was 3 Rupees a day (four shillings).

Mr Wood, who had an assistant by the name of Mr King, generally occupied himself in straightening out nails and grumbling at every customer who entered his shop. It was Mr Wood who had imported some cats to keep the population of rats in check. And when he told me this I remembered that we had put up with the continuous wailing of these same cats on board the *Feldmarshall.*

It was Mr Jevanjee who gave me a place for my ponies alongside two that he had of his own. He had built all the houses for the permanent staff of the colony, and he had also been contracted by the railway. At that time he owned practically the whole of Nairobi.

My six friends had now applied for land (they had three hundred pounds each, which at that time was considered enough to start farming) and they were granted plots in Molo and Ruiri and Kiambu. The next morning I asked Mr Wood, and also Mr Jeevanjee, if they might be aware of any land for sale in the colony. But they did not know of any, so I remained in Nairobi for another three months. During that time I went to see a man called Mr Ward about the possibility of work (he was a big landowner who had come from India) but he had no job for me. He did, however, offer me free accommodation.

In 1904 a European settler was killed in the Londiani area by a group of Nandi warriors and, for a while, this had a negative impact on the flow of incoming settlers. Then, in 1905, a group of settlers arrived from South Africa with their oxen, mules and horses and this encouraged us all because it meant that there were many more European settlers in the colony as a whole. It was around this time that our High Commission, Sir Charles Eliot, fell out with the Colonial Office in London and he left the Colony. A new High Commissioner was appointed but he was, in my opinion, the wrong man for the job. Since the colony was a protectorate and since all direction came from London, however, none of us had any say in the matter. In that same year there was an uprising in Nandi country. Under the able command of the Commander of the Kenya African Rifles (KAR), however, this was quickly quelled. Indeed the leader of the rebellion, Arab Koitalel, was shot and killed by Richard Meinertzhagen.

From the start of the colony, the colonial office gave no encouragement to the settlement, nor did they help the settlers in any way. Indeed from 1913 the colonial administration lived off the subsidies they received from London, but there was nothing for we settlers. Even at this time there was also unrest between the local population and the settlers – this due to the very weak administration from Mombasa and Kisumu. If there had been wisdom of any form from the colonial office in London encouraging settlement in the colony, the numbers would have risen to at least a thousand settlers by 1913. Life, even during that period, for those who had no money was a very hard struggle. Some of the DCs in administration were sympathetic to the plight of those early pioneers, but still others were against the whole idea of settlement.

An example of how difficult it was – one could hardly earn 2 Rupees for a 90kg bag of Irish potatoes. I still remember coming into Nairobi with a load of beautiful cucumbers, cabbages, lettuces and garden peas after trekking for two days with my ox wagon and I was offered 10 Rupees for the whole lot. Guarantees were not available. There were no restrictions on movement up to Fort Hall, but thereafter one had to get permission to enter the districts at ones own risk for trading purposes as the locals were rather hostile.

About that time a Mrs Tate with the help of Mr De Souza, a Goanese merchant, had started building a hotel four blocks from T.A. Wood's place on the present Victoria Street and called it the 'Old Stanley'. It was made of corrugated iron sheets. She had tables and chairs made by local Indian carpenters. She had imported the iron beds but had no mattresses. Having as served as an upholsterer and a mattress-maker among my many occupations, I offered my services if material could be purchased. Mr De Souza had ticking in stock so I gave him a sketch and his tailor produced a sample to my measurements. The greatest problem, however, was to obtain mattress needles. Luckily a metal smith by the name of Bennett whom I knew from South Africa managed to make me two needles out of bicycle spokes. The next trouble was to obtain material to stuff the mattress and while riding about

I had noticed great amounts of grass, which had been cut by the railways, so I immediately went to the superintendent of the railway and asked if I could use it. He offered it free of charge and gave me boys to gather it and have it properly dried. I was able to complete the job within three weeks and proudly delivered the mattresses to the hotel. They looked well but were not very comfortable so I advised Mrs Tate to put a thick blanket over each one so as to prevent her customers from being severely pricked. I was paid handsomely at the rate of 10 rupees a mattress (10 shillings) for my labour and so ended my first job in Nairobi.

Having thus earned a few more shillings, I decided to look out for a small farm, which I could buy on easy terms. I met a Doctor Hoffman, a German, and a Mr Lauterbach who were anxious to get rid of their farm of 640 acres freehold for 1500 Rupees (100 pounds); repayment was to be made within five years. I immediately concluded the deal by giving them a 100-Rupee deposit and we made an appointment to visit the solicitors, Mr C.M.N. Harrison and B.G. Allen, to draw up an agreement.

Mr Allen saw me before the others arrived and suggested that as he had 100 pounds lying idle he would pay for the farm and take transfer in my name holding the titles as security for the loan, which I found more to my liking and within a week I had taken possession of the farm which had a mud hut already built, a gunny bag as a door, and another for a window. There was a bed made from wooden sticks, and a couple of sacks for a mattress; a few pots and pans, and a few paraffin boxes for seating. This was to be my future home for the next five years. I also had a few chickens and pigeons, which were killed within my first week because the stupid *toto* forgot to lock them up one night and they were devoured by a mongoose.

I had my two ponies and my seeds but I did not have a plough or oxen so the first heart-breaking thing I did was to sell my two ponies to a man by the name of Lashington for the large sum of 1000 rupees and considered myself very wealthy.

I walked into Nairobi 17 miles on foot and Mr Marcus sold me a double furrow and Rudsek plough made in Germany. Six oxen were purchased from a Mr Dickens who had a farm where the present Mathari hospital now stands. I had great difficulty carting the plough to the farm, as I had to walk back and engage native women at 10 cents per load and dismantle the plough and had them carrying it in pieces to the farm. The next few days I was busy assembling the plough and making furrows. I spanned my oxen and then to my next disappointment I found six oxen were unable to pull a two-furrow plough so this made my task more difficult.

After struggling like this for six months my labour was rewarded by one crop of potatoes and oats, which I sold. The crops were harvested by Kikuyu *bibis* (married ladies)– and I sold the oats and hay to Mr Marcus for a handsome profit and was able to retain seeds to plant a further two acres and some with potatoes. But as a young man I could not exist on a diet of sweet potatoes and meali-meal and bananas. So I walked into town feeling rather gloomy and met Lord Delamere in Mr Marcus's office. He wanted to know why I looked so dejected and I told him I had made up my mind to go back to South Africa. He replied that he could ill afford to let young men go and asked what I wanted. 'A few oxen to draw a double furrow plough and more money to improve my living conditions,' I said. He spoke to Mr Marcus and dictated a letter to his manager at the Njoro office with instructions that they should send back to Limuru railway station 12 of his best oxen and a couple of dairy cows. He also asked Mr Marcus to give me every month 100 Rupees and debit his account – these words were a great comfort and within a few days the oxen and four cows arrived and also Mr Marcus gave me 100 Rupees. I immediately got to work and within 6 months I had 40 to 50 acres cleared and ploughed and as soon as the rains came I planted peas, oats, beans and potatoes. I was the first farmer to plant flax, which proved very successful. Having harvested my crops by hand, with the resulting income, I started rebuilding my house with the help of a few boys. It was still made from mud and wattle, which were stronger, and instead of a grass roof

I utilized flax for thatching. That was the middle of **1904**.

The situation in the colony had changed considerably as more settlers had arrived; most were farmers from South Africa, and there were a few businessmen from England. My colleagues had, by then, taken over occupation of their farms and had started working the land.

More land was opened for settlement with my neighbour having taken up several farms from the government – with two Scandinavian and three South Africans. The native population was very small at the time and most labour came from the Fort Hall Nyeri district – wages were low – around 8 Rupees including food. During the later part of 1904, when I had finished planting, I took a job at a neighbouring farm at the rate of 90 Rupees a month plus lunch. I used to return home around 6pm and in the morning I would organize my own labour before leaving for my daily job. This job continued until **1907** at the same wage, and thereafter I left to attend to my own personal farming business.

I had started paying off my debts to Delamere and, by **1906**; I had paid for all my oxen and cows. It was a very satisfactory existence by this time; I could speak Kikuyu very well and I was at peace knowing that what I had I owned – I was totally motivated. I had also been able to pay off Mr Allen the one hundred pounds that he had leant me to buy my first farm. At last I was free of debts and I held the title deeds to my farm.

In **1908** I sold my farm to a man called Hoddinot for the great sum of one pound an acre thus realizing a profit of 640 pounds. I decided to halve the money and go on a trip to Europe. I was then aged 24. Before leaving I bought another farm of 1000 acres freehold from Mr Ross and Mr Van de Bragh. My excursion lasted four months and on my return I was totally re-motivated and I began working on my new farm. At this time I was offered yet another adjoining farm for 400 pounds, of which I took possession. I borrowed money from Capt. M. Cowie the father of Mervyn Cowie, who went on to become the Director of Kenya's National Parks.

Having two farms and a few Rupees in the bank I started trading cattle from the Masai who lived close to Limuru station, and I had no difficulty selling these cattle to the new settlers coming to the colony. I had an ox wagon and spare cattle for myself, so I carried on until **1913**.

In **1908** I was approached by two old friends who asked me to join them on a venture to go to Uganda to buy some cattle in the Ankole country. They were to supply the capital and for a one-third share I was to bring the cattle back by road from Uganda. I accepted these conditions and the three of us went to Ankole country first by boat from Kisumu to Port Bell, then by safari (journey) to Ankole country. It did not take us long to purchase 200 head of cattle with all the cash we had available in rupees.

I started my trek back with the cattle and had no trouble, but the journey took many weeks and I arrived in the Rongai Valley not even knowing the date. I camped near the Rongai River and after two days a Somali arrived on a mule with a letter from Lady Delamere. 'My boy has informed me that a European is camping on the Rongai River and as it is Christmas Eve, we would like to know if you would like to come and have dinner with us and celebrate Christmas?'

Well, after being on the road for weeks and in dirty clothes I did not feel I could accept such generosity and replied to this effect. In two hours Lady Delamere arrived herself in a buggy and insisted that I join them. She pointed out that most of the guests would be either dressed in pyjamas or khaki like myself. The dinner party went off most successfully and was the first decent food I'd eaten in months. The spirit of hospitality was definitely overwhelming and as long as I live I shall never forget this hospitality and kindness. I progressed on my journey, camping enroute and in due course I met up with my business partners and we finalized our agreement. My share of the profits worked out at 3,000 Rupees. By now I had quite a large bank balance and decided to start trading on a bigger scale so as to be more profitable.

Now considering myself a wealthy man, at my young age in **1911**, I took on what was a highly paid job in those days. I escorted safaris as an assistant 'white hunter'. Unfortunately most of those people I accompanied are long forgotten by me, but I was still going strong in 1913.

Unfortunately, **1913** was a disastrous year owing to an invasion of locusts, which destroyed all that lay in their path. Being far-sighted, I managed with the help of my labourers to cut the bush and chase the locusts on to the reserve close by, thus happily saving most of my crop of mealies and experimental wheat.

Having the funds available to trade on a large scale, I was able to accumulate sufficient funds to visit Europe again. My first inclination was to see the Holy Land and I arrive there in November **1913** (this was the first time I saw an aeroplane, piloted by a French man). From here I booked a passage on a tramp steamer to Constantinople, which was at that time called the 'land of dogs'. It was truly filthy and the people used the dogs to scavenge. I then went to Europe and visited Austria and Romania. I loved Budapest on the beautiful Danube but even in those days, although the beauty of Europe appealed, I always felt the pull of Africa. After three months in Europe, which in those days one could do very cheaply, I decided to go back to Africa via Palestine. I had to get a visa on my passport in Turkey to enter Jaffa.

It was mid-winter when I met my wife-to-be in the colony of Richon Le Zion where I was visiting acquaintances. She was the second daughter of Alexander Tulipman a well-known farmer. I proposed marriage and, to my surprise, she accepted and we returned together landing in Mombasa on 26th July **1914**.

There was already talk of war in Europe and, by 3rd August 1914, it had been declared. As a young man I volunteered and joined the East African Mounted Rifles. My wife I left with my parents on the farm that I had bought for them in Limuru (having brought them up from South Africa in 1909).

We had our first encounter with the Germans in Longido; on the border with Tanganyika and being repulsed we withdrew to Namanga. Many young soldiers fell to German bullets but it was at this time that some South African and Indian troops came to join us. Most of our mounts fell to horse sickness so we became foot soldiers until transport was organized and then we were dispatched to the front.

The First World War was fought, by us, in Kenya, on several fronts. The South Africans were mainly in the Taita/Taveta theatre of war, which extended down to Moshi and was commanded by Van Deventer and Jan Smuts. The Germans, however, fought with well-trained African soldiers, modern arms and strong leadership, and they put up a very strong resistance and had to be pursued well into Southern Africa. They also continued to fight until well after the war had been officially ended, and only surrendered arms having been formally advised as to the armistice. General Von Lettow was acknowledged as a truly great warrior by the victors and decorated for his greatness.

In **1915** my first child, a daughter, was born. I was present for the birth having received permission from my colonel to take compassionate leave. I rode my original pony (which I still had) and, armed with my official permit, I arrived in Nairobi with just three days to spare. I spent the next six weeks with my wife and baby daughter. I applied for a discharge from the army, but in vain. Instead, I was re-posted to that dreadful place, Dar es Salaam. Here I was unfortunate enough to contract malaria, the symptoms of which I still carry with me. After malaria I was again bedridden with black water fever, and it was only as a result of my strong will to live that I managed to pull through. I was transferred by ship to Mombasa and arrived there to find such disorganization that I was left lying on a stretcher for two hours before being transferred to Mombasa Hospital. Here I contracted dysentery. I survived only as a result of the generosity of Lady Duff and her nursing staff. I returned to Nairobi on a Red Cross train and was discharged after three weeks in Nairobi Hospital. It took many months of convalescence until I was back to my old self.

1919 brought new hope to the Colony. In the post-war years Sir Edward Northey was appointed the new Governor of the Colony of Kenya and he was sympathetic to the plight of European settlement. Our numbers were also gradually increased by the settlement of ex-soldiers by means of a lottery. I joined my wife and child, who were then living with my parents. In the meanwhile I planned to open a dairy near Nairobi in an area known as Upper Parklands Estate.

The responsibility of a family meant that I needed a healthy income so I invested in large dairy herd, which I purchased from Lumbwa. Starting on 14 acres (plus a small home) this cost 900 pounds. Our labour comprised a few locals.

Towards the end of **1916** my son was born, and my first year of business had proved successful with milk being delivered to customers in old whisky bottles (bought at 2 cents each empty bottle from Indian bars and dukas). We were the first Europeans to supply fresh milk to the door at 20 cts a bottle. The third year of operation was marred by my losing most of my herd to East Coast Fever and Anthrax. Since this resulted in the land we occupied being infected by disease, we bought more land in a different district (from a Mr Barker/Bowker) on 30 acres and began again.

Ends

LILY'S NARRATIVE

A transcription from Lily Haller's memoirs by kind permission of her granddaughter, Iris Haller. Edited by Jane Barsby

I arrived in British East Africa in 1906 young, eager and ready to grasp the future with both hands and mould it to my liking. I soon found that to fight against nature brought one little besides heartache and disappointments. So I gradually learned to fight with nature. The lesson has been a long one and the method a hard one; but, as an old women, wiser and more temperate than the girl I once was, I am proud to belong to that little band of pioneers who helped to create the Kenya of today from the raw bush of yesterday.

I was born in Russia in 1888 and lived with my brother and sisters on the family estate at Gilwan, Kovno. My earliest impressions, for they are too nebulous to be called memories, are happy ones. We were a happy family in those days and I can still hear the scamper of our feet as we rushed to meet Father when he came in from the fields. I can still hear his jolly laugh echoing through the house; and I can still feel the warmth of Mother's smile as she watched us play.

One evening, late in 1892, I was awakened by the sound of sobs. A strangely grave Father had come to our nursery late in the night to bid us all goodbye. When he leant over my cot I clung to him in fright and would not let him go. Gently he calmed me and laid me down to sleep. Then, after a quiet goodbye to the elder children, he closed the nursery door. It was to be 13 years until I saw him again. We learned later that Father had been forced to flee from Russia because he had refused to supply fresh horses from his stable to a party of Russian officers in pursuit of a band of Polish insurgents. To avoid imprisonment and possible death, he had decided to leave Russia the same night.

The days following Father's departure brought terror and distress to us all. In recognition of his loyal services, the Tsar had conferred on my grandfather the concession of Posts and Transport throughout the length and breadth of Russia, and my father, in his turn, had retained the concession. Now, however, by his refusal to aid in the hunting of a human quarry, Father had lost his right to this concession; and Mother was given a month's notice to leave our home and estate. We were even told to leave the town of Gilwan and move out of the district. Until we did so a police watch was put on our house.

At first, we children did not realise what was wrong and every day became a holiday for us. Mother was forced to leave us to our own devices. She was too busy to scold us even when we got into mischief. But, as the novelty wore off, we began to feel the change in our daily life. We missed Father's cheerful presence about the house and the games we had been used to play with him; we were frightened too by mother's regular fits of weeping. Our servants were dismissed and there were no more chocolates and sweet dishes for dessert, no more drives in our carriage. No longer did the people of society call on our parents or invite us to play with their children. The house and its inhabitants felt forlorn and neglected and our hearts were heavy. We were quite alone, for father did not have any near relatives and mother was too proud to appeal to hers for help.

When mother had fallen in love with and married a farmer her aristocratic family had turned away in disgust and had had little to do with her since. Although Father came from good stock, he was not on the same social level as the Soltz family; for they were the only Jews in Russia to have been granted special rights and privileges. The universities were open to them and they could hold positions of high rank in the army. Unlike other Jews in Russia, they were allowed to live where they wished and could carry on any trade or profession they were interested in. The Soltzs were well known for the intellect of their men and the beauty of their women, so their surprise and disdain when mother became the wife of a country farmer can well be imagined. There was one member of the Soltz family who still cared for us, however, and when we were lonely and deserted mothers' only sister, our dear Aunt Sinson, came to our rescue. She arrived suddenly one morning, in a splendid carriage and spent hours closeted with mother while we waited out in the garden agog with excitement. Just as we had reached boiling point, mother came and told us we were to pack at once for we were all to go back with her to Selznick. There, she added, we should learn to do useful things and cease to run about like wild goats as we were doing now. At midnight, several days later, we arrived at Uncle Sinson's house to find our young cousins still waiting up for us. They were shy and viewed us with suspicion, wanting to know what presents we had brought them from distant towns. But friendship was all we could offer them for we had little else.

Aunt Sinson arranged that we would share our cousins' lessons with their private tutors and she gave us a house to live in not far away. Mother unpacked our silver and glass and various ornaments and object d'art she had brought with her. Then she produced the linen cloths the peasant women of Gilwan had embroidered and spread on our beds fine linen sheets woven by father's own peasants from flax grown on his farm. We began to feel at home. We soon made friends with our cousins and had grand times together after lessons.

Our schooling was a painful process, particularly for a little girl like me who was over fond of talking. How strict those tutors were. I shall never forget their throwing books at me for the slightest mistake or sign of inattentiveness. Yet, try as they might, they never broke me of my habit of talking to everybody around me. As we grew older, life became most interesting, for we met many important people at my uncle's house. Loved and respected by all who met him Rabbi Sinson was indeed the spiritual leader of our community. At his home we were introduced to all as members of the Soltz family and, as such, we were treated with the respect due to so aristocratic a name. But I always felt that Uncle's grand visitors saw through this verbal disguise and that they really regarded us as 'those poor children of Ethel Block', who had married beneath her station. My cousins, four of whom were boys, were a little older than us, so when Aunt Sinson realized they would soon be called up to serve in the Russian army, she persuaded my uncle to leave Russia and

settle in England. Once again we were to be parted from those we loved.

The Sinsons packed up and left for England taking my elder sister with them. As soon as my brother reached the age of thirteen, he too was sent to England. So, at the turn of the century only my mother, my little sister, Frieda, and me were left living in Seleznic; and the rest of our family lived thousands of miles away.

My mother was a very proud woman and believed it was her duty to continue living in the manner to which we had been accustomed when Father was with us. Now there was no greater crime in mother's eyes than that of allowing our friends to learn of, or even suspect, our poverty. Once father had been established in South Africa, he had been able to send money at intervals; and Aunt Sinson had helped us as unobtrusively and tactfully as she could. But now we were alone in Russia and the Boer War was taking place in South Africa, so mother had to fall back on her own resources. To work or to borrow were both out of the question for her, so she fell back on selling our valuables, as so many others were to do in the years to come. We had often noticed that a vase or a plate, or perhaps a picture had disappeared from the house before, but had thought little of it. Now, however, things began to disappear more rapidly. As the house become more empty, mother's stratagems increased. Our best clothes were carefully cleaned and mended and we were only allowed to wear them when out visiting. Although our meals at home usually consisted of black bread, soup and vegetables, we were not allowed to accept food in our rich friends' houses lest they should think we were hungry, which of course we often were. Today mother would be called a snob, but I have only admiration for a human being who so believed in the maintenance of a certain standard of social behaviour that she was prepared to make both herself and her children miserable to maintain it. To watch her conduct a meal of black bread and soup with the utmost propriety and elegance, dressed in an outmoded yet well-preserved, velvet gown was to witness a small triumph of mind over matter. It was not until some months after the end of the Boer War, when father was able to get some money to us, that she was able to relax. Then we were gay and happy and could say with genuine regret, 'no I thank you, but I really couldn't eat even a small apple,' and smile and shake our heads.

It was now the beginning of the twentieth century and the old world order was changing. People were no longer able to resist the new ideas that were spreading across Europe, and they could no longer silence the new voices clamouring to be heard. Even as a young girl living quietly at home in the country, I could not remain unaware of the mounting despair of the peasants; and of their ever-growing desire for freedom. Like the peasants who lived on my friends' estates, I too had a great desire to study and to learn, yet my ambition was even greater than theirs; for they only wished to learn to read and write, whereas I had already received a good education from my cousins' tutors. The quality of our desire, however, was the same. Since I knew that my dream of going to university would come to nought, I sought an outlet for my intellectual emotions and I interested myself in the activities of the peasants. I understood their terrors and humiliations, for throughout my childhood I had come into contact with the peasants daily. I had often watched the village children gazing in wonder at the carriages of the rich landlords as they drove through the village. And I had watched the children run in terror from the hunting dogs of the nobility, which made no distinction between deer and serf.

Generations of peasants had been exploited by the Russian upper classes. The army took their sons as soon as they were old enough to fight, the greedy landlords demanded their labour and paid a miserable wage in return. And if these poor people managed to save any money from the sale of butter and eggs, the tax collectors and the clergy would demand their due. Nor had they any redress, for refusal to comply would result in their loss of land and home. These were often a one-room shack housing three families, a number of scraggy hens and sundry livestock. Their diet, meanwhile, would be only bread, beetroot and potatoes; and should they manage to produce milk, eggs or bacon these would be taken immediately to market – for the

need of money to pay taxes was more pressing than the need of food, much though there were near starving.

After the Russo-Japanese War the situation in Russia became critical. Thousands of conscripts had been sent penniless to their villages, many crippled and sick, all disillusioned and shocked by the defeat of the mighty Russian fleet by the little yellow foreigners. And when they found themselves still despised by the landlords, still regarded as slaves and still expected to work under the same conditions as had prevailed before the war, their discontent became widespread and they provided a fermenting ground for the growth of the seeds of revolution. Eager as the peasants were to follow the teachings of Lenin and Trotsky, however, they were handicapped by their ignorance and poverty. Many upper class idealists joined the campaign to educate the masses; and many wealthy people gave up their riches to aid the peasants. Most, however, found that their reward was persecution by the police and exile to Siberia where the life of political prisoner was no safer than it is today.

I had met a teacher who was a social democrat and it was through him that I first learnt of the secret meetings being held in dense forests and underground cellars; of the literature being smuggled into Russia from Lenin and his associates; of the people listening to revolutionary speeches at the risk of their lives. And I used to contrast the doctrines of the church and the socialists: the former offering the peasants a wonderful life after death, while ignoring the sufferings of their present life; and the latter offering them, nay promising them, complete freedom of thought and action in this life and, in addition, enough bread to fill their shrunken bellies. History has shown which doctrine appealed most to these practical people.

As my enthusiasm grew, I persuaded mother to give me a room in our large house so that we could open a school for the local peasants. We soon had enough pupils to keep two teachers busy, and I spent most of my time in the schoolroom helping the poor people to learn to read and write. Every pupil's ambition was the same - to be able to communicate with their children, all of whom were either in the army or in the cities working as servants and labourers. We used to read extracts from newspapers smuggled in from abroad to our pupils, but always made sure that we kept ordinary school books to hand in case the police should suddenly decide to inspect the class. Although our school was private, we still came under strict government supervision; and every movement was watched by the police. At that time all letters and parcels from outside Russia were opened by the secret police and searches and arrests were a daily occurrence. One day the police found a bundle of foreign magazines in a writing desk; though neither my mother nor I knew anything about it. It was only mother's name and the influence of her family and friends, which saved me from severe punishment; possibly death.

My experience with the secret police convinced me that we should all leave Russia. The unrest was getting worse, bitterness and hatred were everywhere, and much of it had been directed at my own people, for we heard dreadful stories of pogroms in other parts of the country. I wrote to father and asked him to send us the money to help us leave. After months of anxious waiting, he replied that we should all join him in South Africa, which was returning to normal after the Boer War. He urged us to come out to land where freedom and justice flourished.

When I showed the letter to mother she was much moved at the thought of seeing father again, but after some thought she declared that she could not bring herself to leave her home and journey to a foreign country where she was unknown and would be a stranger. Nor, she said, could she bring herself to master a new language at her age. I think she felt that by refusing to leave she would eventually persuade Father to return home to her beloved Russia. Loathe as I was to leave my mother and little sister alone in Russia, I felt I could not agree with her and I decided to make my own arrangements to join father. It was not an easy decision for I was only sixteen and had no money at all. Neither had I a passport and to cross the border without one would be a dangerous undertaking.

Once again it was the Sinson family who came to my aid. Uncle Sinson sent money to his colleague in Lida with a request that he should help me leave Russia and join the Sinsons in Leeds, England where he was a rabbi. My first task was to leave Seleznic without mother's knowledge and get to Lida where my uncle's friends awaited me. Surreptitiously I packed a few things in a bag and wearing as many clothes as possible I quietly left our house for the ten-mile walk to the station. It was just before Christmas 1904 and the roads were blocked with ice and snow and the temperature below zero. My feelings were mixed on the walk, and my companion, a teacher in the school and my avowed admirer, was constantly forced to reassure me that I was doing the right thing. At one step I was eager to be gone, eager to start a new life abroad and make a new home with my father. And at the next I was assailed by doubts and fears – how would mother and Frieda fend for themselves? Would they be question by the police about my departure? What would happen to them if they were?

When we reached the station I said goodbye to my young companion, the only person in Seleznic who knew of my intentions, and I bade him return to my home and tell my mother that I had gone away. As soon as the train had drawn out of the station he returned to my home but, in spite of my enjoinder that he should not to tell mother where I had gone, he found himself blurting out the whole story. As I had expected Mother was furious and the next day she left in pursuit of her headstrong daughter. She found me in Lida at the home of Uncle Sinsons friend and we argued for hours. I was on the point of giving in, convinced that my duty lay with my family in Russia, when my new friends intervened and begged mother to allow me to go to South Africa. She had seen how strong was my purpose and, when they pointed out that probably I should be able to persuade Father to return to Russia, she relented. Soon she was content that I should leave and interested herself in my plans for escape.

In spite of mothers influence and the help of uncle's good friends, I was unable to obtain a passport and was forced to put myself in the hands of a notorious band of agents who guaranteed to help me escape across the border. They promised safe conduct across the border and a comfortable passage to the country of their choice. Their fees, however, were exorbitant and all too often their transactions ended in capture or death for the unhappy people on the run. The guards at the frontier were loyal and devoted servants of the Tsar, trained to believe they had been especially chosen by God to protect the Tsar and Russia against her enemies both abroad and at home. They were firm in their belief and there was little hope that they would show mercy to those wishing to escape their beloved Russia. Unlike the government officials, their moral code was high and few of them could be bribed to hold their fire when an escapee was spotted.

The agents had defined escape routes and I was taken to a public bath a few miles from the German border where I found a number of other people waiting. We were all examined by a German doctor and four prospective emigrants were pronounced unfit to travel. I shall never forget the looks of despair and misery on their faces as they learned of this – effectively a death sentence. Only one other woman passed the medical examination and at midnight we were taken outside and pushed into the back of an open cart to start the last stage of our journey to the border.

It was a nightmare journey, for added to our fear of discovery and the discomfort of driving over rough cart tracks, was the unexpected conduct of our guide. Every half mile or so he would stop the cart and demand more money before he would continue. We had to accede for we were terrified that he would leave us stranded in the dark forest. By the end of the drive we had very little left other than our steamer tickets and the clothes we stood up in. Our guide led us as near to the border trench as he dared and bade us lie down in the snow in the shadows until he gave us the word to go. Seized by terror I lay face down in the hard snow, my reflexes deadened until I thought I would never have the courage to get up again. After an eternity of waiting, our nerves tensed and our bodies numbed, watching with despair the white expanse ahead of us, we realised that the word would never come. The agent had left us.

We now had no alternative but to go forward alone, for we could not remain where we lay because we would have been frozen to death by morning; and we could never have found our way back through the forest to the town. So we crawled on our stomachs across the hard shining snow; straining every nerve for the sound of boots crunching the crystal surface, or the faint click of a rifle being cocked. Our progress was slow for my companion was old and, as dawn drew near, she lost hope and lay down gasping that she could go no further and would rather freeze to death than die in agony from a bullet wound. Her weakness inspired me with the strength of a man and I dragged her unwilling body off the ground and forced her to continue. Hand in hand we walked in the direction of hope; and we turned our backs on Russia forever. We stumbled in a daze, certain that we were walking to our deaths. Here and there a dark shape would loom out of the grey light and we would start, certain that it was a Russian solider. Then, peering ahead, we would see that it was only a tree and so we would carry on our way. Amazement began to take hold of me as I thought of myself only a week ago. Then I was a girl happy amongst her friends and brimming over with plans for the future; now I was merely a numbed body propelled by fear; its only aim to cover a few hundred yards of snow. And yet I was convinced that it was utterly possible to cross the border to safety.

And so we came to the frontier trench. For a moment I stared at it vacantly, wondering what to do, then we heard running footsteps and several shots rang out. Fear came to our aid and we scrambled across the trench, sure that the frontier guards had discovered us. But we were lucky: it was some other unfortunate party that had been discovered and, in the diversion they caused, we were able to cross the frontier easily. Trembling and with heavy hearts as we thought of the price of our escape, we made our way into Germany. As we walked slowly to the border I thanked God that He had seen fit to let me live and I prayed that in return I might be able to do some good in the world and for the family. I can't remember what happened after this, but I think I must have fainted because the next thing I remember is an old man urging me to get up and move out of the range of the Russian riles. My elderly companion had vanished.

The old man led me along the road and tried to explain in German that he was taking me to friends. While he was talking I searched for my purse containing what little money I had left and, most important of all, my steamer ticket. They were gone – I began to weep. I was ashamed that the old man should see my tears, but then I remembered I had sewn the ticket into the lining of my coat.

The haven that the old man took me to was a beer house and he left me there saying that I must wait until morning before going into the town. There were one or two men sitting there who eyed me with such curiosity that I shut myself in the lavatory to avoid their stares. I huddled myself in a corner desperately cold and longing for a hot drink; then I waited for sunrise watching the sky through a small iron grille in the wall, too tired to move and frightened to come out. A repeated knocking awoke me from an uneasy doze and I saw daylight shining through the grille. I opened the door to find a servant girl who cast one look at my dishevelled figure and ran away crying in German that she had found a ghost. Reason prevailed and she soon arrived with a large tin mug filled with hot coffee. I had not moved from the doorway but waited there peeling off the chipped green paint with my fingernail and wondering what these strange people would do with me. When I was revived by the coffee I told the girl my plight and she immediately took me to the shipping office where my passage to Leeds, England was booked.

The shipping clerk, after expressing his initial surprise that I had actually arrived, took little interest in me beyond telling me the name of the boat I was to take. After some enquires I found the so-called 'luxurious ship' that was to take me to Hull was a cattle boat filled with refuges and cattle in equal quantities. There was no food on the boat and, after a day at sea, we were all ravenous; for none of us had eaten in the days before. I forced half-cooked potatoes down my throat because I could not wait for them to finish cooking. It was

heart breaking to watch the little children growing weaker each day through lack of food.

Dirty and cold we slept on beds made of planks. One night I awoke to find a sailor going through the pockets of my only coat. I screamed and tried to grab him but he disappeared into the shadows. Our whole voyage was a struggle for existence, even the boat herself had to fight against the heaving waves. But the necessity of having to fight for my daily needs was my salvation, for I had no time for idle speculation or morbid thoughts about my family: I was too busy trying to live.

On the last day we were told that we would reach Hull at seven that evening and had to be off the boat by seven thirty. I wondered where I would go, for I had no money left to telegraph my uncle in Leeds to tell him of my arrival, nor could I ask anyone for help, as I could not speak English. We arrived in Hull in drizzling rain and crowded down the gangway like a flock of lost sheep. I darted from one docker to the next gabbling questions at them in Russian German, Hebrew and Yiddish, but not one word did they understand. The other refugees had wandered off together and, thinking that they had found somewhere to sleep, I followed them. At least we found an empty waiting room and huddled together on a wooden bench trying to keep warm. The roof leaked and there was no fire but at least it was shelter and we decided to wait there until morning. Although we had attained our gaol we were too taken up with your physical miseries to realise that at last we were free and safe. Imagine my relief when two men came into the waiting room and spoke to us in Russian – they had come to offer help and knew my uncle. They offered to take me to their home and though I was hesitant at first remembering the stories I had heard of girls accepting invitations from strangers – I overcame my fears. They took me in a car for a long drive through the brightly lit streets of Hull then into the country until we reached a large house and I was met in the hall by an elderly lady who spoke to me in Yiddish and assured me that I could say with her as long as I wished. I was given dinner and a warm bed and she listened to my stories of the suffering of the people of Russia.

The next day I was put on the train for Leeds well stocked with fruit and papers for the journey. Fifty years later I am still grateful for the kindness shown to me by these good people. It was in the train that I was overcome by the feeling that I was truly in a strange land. Looking at the newspapers they had given me I could not understand one word and even the pictures conveyed little meaning. I was overcome by self-pity – but I arrived and the sight of my uncle and cousins on the station cheered me up. The next six months while I stayed with them were to be the happiest since my childhood. My uncle Rabbi Sinson was a great scholar and at his house I was privileged to meet many famous men. I was happy and immediately began to learn English; and whenever my uncle could spare the time he would help me. In the evening we used to listen to him discussing the problems of the day with his friends, many of them were brilliant men such as Raskin, the poet, and Dr Lokolev, the philosopher. Just as in Seleznic men of learning were attracted to Rabbi Sinson's house and so they came to visit him in Leeds. Tolerant and kind he would listen with intelligence to other men's ideas and talk until the early hours of the morning. During the day he was busy visiting his congregation, the majority of whom were poor and ignorant. Always ready to listen to their troubles and to help them whenever possible he was loved and honoured by the entire Jewish community of Leeds.

But although my uncle was loved and respected by all who came into contact with him it was my aunt who held first place in the hearts of the poor people around her. Her kitchen door was always open to those in need and she was always ready to help. Uncle's stipend was very small one, barely enough to feed and clothe his own family, but somehow or other my aunt always managed to save a few pence to give away. I never saw her idle or heard her complain and yet her life was totally different from that which it had been in Russia. There she had a large house, beautiful gardens and plenty of servants. Now she had to do her own housework, sew for her children and spend most of her time devising ways in which she might save money in order to give it away to those less fortunate.

I spent six months learning to live in a free country and learning the language. As soon as I could understand it reasonably well my greatest delight was to listen to the street corner orators as they ran down the government or anything else they happened to dislike. I could never get over my amazement that these people could air their views in public without fear of arrest, and while I listened to them I was constantly glancing over my shoulder to see if the secret police were anywhere around. The kindness and politeness of the officials of the city, whether they were policemen, bus conductors, park attendants or postmen, warmed my heart.

The time had now come for me to leave England and continue my journey to South Africa. Refreshed by my stay, I was eager to set forth on the last stage of my travels and, in order to keep me company, my uncle allowed his daughter Mary to come with me. We left England with mixed feelings for we had both grown to love the country and its people; but we were young and the unknown land across the sea had a stronger call. And I was keen to see my dear father and sister and family.

Ends

ORA'S NARRATIVE

Selected extracts from the book *Spring in Eternity, A Family Saga*, by Ora Hirshfeld

The story of my grandfather Abraham Lazarus Block (known by everyone as ALB) really begins with that of my great-grandfather, Samuel Block, married to Ettel, daughter of the aristocratic Soltz family, the only Jewish family in Russia upon whom various rights and privileges had been conferred. Samuel was a farmer as well as a cabinetmaker; he and Ettel had four children: Annie, Abraham, Lily and Freda. The family lived in relative luxury on the family estate outside Vilna, Lithuania. In 1891, when Abraham was eight years old, Samuel left Russia for South Africa, where he had heard the Jewish immigrants there were flourishing. There are conflicting reports as to why he left. Some think it was just to seek a better life, leaving behind the pogroms against the Jews, which were rampant at that time. He intended to establish himself in South Africa and then send for his wife and family. Many years later, his daughter, Lily claimed her father was wanted by the secret police and was forced to flee – but no evidence has come forth to substantiate this version. Whichever was true, the fact remains that Ettel and her children were left alone. After a short time, Ettel's sister, Fanny (Sinson), who was married to a rabbi, came and took all the family and arranged a house for them near to her own. Ettel's children participated in the cousins' lessons with private tutors.

However after a few years when the Sinsons' sons were approaching army age, the family upped and emigrated to Leeds in England, taking the Blocks' eldest daughter, Annie, with them. In those days Jewish families did everything they could to avoid their sons having to serve in the Russian army. A few years later, Abraham too was smuggled out of Lithuania in a cart covered with straw, and went to join rabbi Sinson and his family in Leeds. His journey must have been nerve-wracking. We are not sure of his age, but he was probably around twelve or thirteen, only speaking Yiddish and maybe Russian and Lithuanian. No doubt he was escorted across Europe by paid couriers to a port, possibly Hamburg or Danzig (today Gdansk) where he was put on a ship bound for England.

Abraham was not happy there; the family tried to further his education and then even get him a job, but he was a restless young man, and he decided to go and join his father in South Africa. Of course, he did not have enough money to buy a ticket, but managed to work his passage on a boat leaving from the English port of Hull to Cape Town, South Africa. He knew his father was in Johannesburg, so spent the next few months working his way to join up with his father. According to family legend, Samuel was working as a cabinetmaker and although Abraham joined him, we don't know if he helped him with his work or worked on his own.

Abraham was very worldly young man and made it his business to know what was happening on both the local and global scene. Thus, in March 1903, he attended a life-changing lecture given by the British Colonial Secretary, Joseph Chamberlain.

From this point, Ora's version mirrors Abraham's own. We take up her story at the point when Abraham had made his fortune and decided to travel.

Family lore has it that when Abraham was setting out on his journey, as he was about to get on the boat at Mombasa, he happened to meet three young men speaking Hebrew or Yiddish, who were disembarking, Abraham fell into conversation with them, and told them of his plans to visit Europe. "Why don't you go to Palestine?" said the three young men, and it seems they persuaded him to do so, gave him the addresses of their families in Rishon le Zion, and hastily wrote letters for him to deliver ... One of these young men was David Tulipman. The voyage took Abraham through the newly constructed Suez Canal. Disembarking at Port Said (Egypt), he took a train across the northern Sinai desert via Gaza, until he reached Rechovot, where he left the train and continued his journey by local transport – probably a horse-drawn carriage (known as a diligence).

Thus after a few weeks, Abraham arrived in Rishon on a Friday afternoon, and soon found the Tulipman family home, right next door to the main synagogue. On hearing his story, Alexander and Batsheva Tulipman invited him to stay for Shabbat. The Tulipmans had five daughters and one son, David. One daughter was already married, and the family story goes that the next daughter Sarah opened the door for him, but his eye fell on a younger daughter, Rachel. Father Tulipman told him in no uncertain terms, that Sarah was the next one to be married. So Abraham had no choice but to court Sarah, and eventually proposed marriage to her. He continued on his European trip, telling the family he would return to claim his bride. They were not sure whether he would, but return he did, and he and Sarah were married. There is a family story that he had been 'betrothed' to a young lady in Leeds, and he obviously had to deal with this if he wanted to marry Sarah. He went to England and the matter was settled amicably, even though we were told that on future occasions when he visited the United Kingdom he always visited his 'Rosie'.

While he was in Rishon, Abraham went to the Great Synagogue there, and because he spoke only Yiddish and English (not Hebrew) he was directed to sit next to Tzvi Hirshfeld – who spoke perfect English. Little did they know that many years later, their children would marry each other!

The young couple arrived in Kenya, and what a culture shock it must have been for Sarah! Not that Rishon was so modern, but compared to Kenya! Sarah came with a trousseau – she was a wonderful seamstress, she knitted and crocheted. One can only imagine the 'home' Abraham brought her to – probably some sort of structure with a corrugated iron roof – and the floor – maybe cement, but possibly mud...

Being well-to-do Abraham did what he could to make her life more comfortable but there is no doubt she was unhappy at the beginning, particularly because she was extremely fastidious and house proud, and – if there were such a thing – would have taken the first plane home! Soon after their arrival, the First World War was declared, and

Abraham left his new bride on the dairy farm with his parents in Limuru, while he signed up with the East African Mounted Rifles. He saw quite a lot of action during the war. Sarah was already pregnant when he left, and in June 1915, Abraham requested compassionate leave to be with his wife when their first child was born; this was granted, and my mother, Rita, the second Jewish child born in East Africa came into the world.

Abraham tried to extend his compassionate leave, but failed, and had to return to the war. He joined his unit in – as he describes it – "that dreadful place Dar es Salaam." From there his unit advanced to Morogoro, where he contracted malaria and black water fever. Not many people survive black water fever and only through "... the will power to live, I came through it." He was transferred by the Red Cross to the hospital at Mombasa, where he lay for a month, before being transferred to a hospital in Nairobi, where he spent another three weeks. Eventually he was discharged from the army as an invalid, and it still took him months to recover.

At first he joined Sarah and little Rita on the farm at Limuru; once he was well enough, he had to re-start his life. The family expanded with the birth of two sons, Jack in 1916 (named after a brother of my grandmother who had died in infancy) and Eddie (Tubby) in 1919. An amusing story surrounds the registration of Tubby's birth. Apparently my grandfather was not around and my grandmother sent a Ukrainian friend called Eddie Rubin to register the birth for her. Eddie did not understand English very well, and when the clerk asked him for the name (meaning the name of the newborn baby) Eddie replied with his own name. Thus my uncle's name in all official records is Eddie Rubin Block. But he was always known by his nickname, Tubby – because as a child he was – tubby! Eventually, when my mother was twelve, another daughter, Ruth, was born.

Abraham decided to start a dairy farm near Nairobi, and to start off, purchased a large herd of cows from Lumbuwa and a fourteen-acre farm, which included a small house, for the sum of 900 pounds. This was in the area of Parklands, which today is part of the city of Nairobi. The dairy farm was called 'Devonshire Dairy'.

Block's first year was very successful, the milk being supplied to individuals in old whiskey bottles! Deliveries took place with a mule and cart, and Grandfather was the first European "to supply fresh milk to the door at 20 cents a bottle." According to my Aunt Ruth, my grandmother helped with the deliveries, driving the cart!

Life was very hard for my grandmother; my grandfather was often away doing other business deals, leaving her alone with the children. As well as the dairy farm, they had a plot of land where they grew vegetables, which my grandmother supervised, growing the produce and selling it at the market in Nairobi. She worked extremely hard and everyone in the family knew about it!

My mother was a sickly child, which added to the travails of my grandmother, who had no one of her own family to help her. The farm prospered for two years until an epidemic broke out amongst the cows, and most were lost with East Coast fever and anthrax. Abraham decided that the whole farm was probably infected, moved and bought another farm and house in a 'clean district'.

Because the education system was not yet developed in Kenya, once they reached a certain age, the three older children were all sent to boarding schools in England. When she was 12 years old, Rita was taken by her father to England to attend Mansfield College in Hove, Sussex. This was the only school for Jewish girls, and was attended by girls from England and many parts of the world. My mother always spoke very favourable of the director, Mrs. Hart, with whom she stayed during the school holidays. The school closed down during the Second World War. A couple of years after Rita went to England, Grandpa took Jack and Tubby there to attend Loughborough College in Leicester. Nowadays this is a college of higher learning and not a boarding school. Travel not being what it is today the children did not return home till their schooling ended. I remember my Uncle Tubby in his later years bemoaning the fact that he did

not see his mother for four years and that he did not even have a barmitzvah. When their formal schooling ended the children returned to Nairobi. Only my Aunt Ruth completed her education in Kenya, by which time there were schools of a high standard in the Colony.

After some years, my grandfather looked beyond dairy farms and agriculture. He became manager of Bullows and Roy, the department store in Nairobi, and eventually owned it. He also became the agent of various large companies in England, such as Lever Brothers, to import necessary merchandise before Kenya started producing its own. He owned a plot of land on what was called Sixth Avenue which, we are told, in 1927 he 'exchanged' for ownership of the already established Norfolk Hotel.

In the 1930's as Hitler's influence spread across Europe, many Jewish 'refugees' found a haven in British East Africa, and the established community set up committees and organizations to assist them – both for housing and employment. My grandfather was also involved in this charitable work. Abraham Block personally financed and guaranteed many of these new 'refugees'. He was also one of the nucleus of the new pioneers that set up the Jewish community and organized the building of the synagogue. He was an active and charitable congregant. Every year, till he passed away he was called upon to read the 'neila' service, which closes the Yom Kippur fast. At that time, when the refugees were coming, most of the available work in Kenya was in agriculture, whereas most of the newcomers were professionals or artisans. Most of them had to adapt themselves and were sent to work on farms.

Soon the winds of war were blowing. Jack had been on a journey to the Far East and had returned home from China just a few days before the Second World War started. Both young men immediately volunteered for military service, and became high-ranking officers in their regiments. Tubby served in Asia and fought in Burma. He was awarded the Military Cross for bravery and, at the end of the war, went to Buckingham Palace, London to receive it from King George V1.

It was only after World War II that the country experienced an economic boom and those refugees who elected to stay in the country could develop in their own professions and trades. Abraham Block also took advantage of the post-war boom, especially when he realized Kenya could become a popular tourist destination. In 1947 he purchased the New Stanley Hotel, which had replaced the original one – the very place for which he had sewn the mattresses all those years ago! By now, his two sons were in the business as well, and assisted him in building up the Block Hotel industry and the Block Estates. He had bought several farms and land over the years and these were all developed and managed by his sons.

My uncles Jack and Tubby married two sisters Doria and Valerie Beiles from Johannesburg, South Africa. They made their homes and raised their families in Nairobi. Jack and Doria had two children, Lyn and Jonathan, who both live in the United Kingdom today. Some years later, Jack and Doria adopted Elizabeth Ruben who had been orphaned. Lynn is married to Al Fuss and they have one daughter, Justine, married to Jason Alderwick. Jonathan is married to Henrietta Kirkpatrick. They have two children, Jack and Sarah. Elizabeth Ruben Block married David Hopkins; they made their home in Kenya and the United Kingdom, and have three sons – Mark, Jeremy and Samuel.

Valerie, Tubby's wife, died suddenly in 1955 when their son Jeremy was still an infant. Tubby married again some time later to Aino and they had two sons – Simon, who unfortunately died in infancy, and Anthony, who lives in San Diego, and has one son, Andrew. Jeremy, Tubby and Valerie's eldest son, still lives in Kenya. He is married to Caroline Fox, and they have one daughter, Valerie. Jeremy is also in farming and business in Kenya.

My Uncle Jack died in a fishing accident whilst on holiday in Chile in 1983 and Tubby passed away in 1996. Both are buried in Kenya.

Both my uncles were astute businessmen and followed in their father's footsteps developing the businesses, and they worked tirelessly during their lifetimes for many charities and non-governmental organizations. They were both influential in helping the newly elected government to function once Kenya obtained independence in 1961. I believe that Jack took it upon himself personally to ask the president to grant permission for Israel to land her planes in Nairobi during the Entebbe episode in 1976. They are still well known and spoken about in superlatives in Kenya.

Ruth married Sol Rabb from Cape Town in 1948. Whilst serving in the army during World War 11, Sol's regiment passed through Nairobi, and like many other young soldiers he was entertained by the Blocks. The visit was obviously a memorable one and once the war was over contact was remade and a romance blossomed. Their wedding at the Norfolk Hotel is one of my vivid childhood memories. Sol and Ruth still live in Kenya, spending some months of the year in the United Kingdom. Sol is a chartered accountant, and in later years worked in the Block business. They have three children – Leigh, Geraldine and Nicolas.

Leigh is a pediatrician in the Midlands in the United Kingdom. He is married to Celia Meeham; they have seven children: Matthew, Rosanna, Benjamin, Nicolas, Miriam, James and Harriet, and another child Daisy died while still a baby. Geraldine and Nicolas both still live in Nairobi.

Geraldine is married to Martin Dunford, who is in the restaurant and tourist business in Kenya. They have three sons; Robert, Jason and David. Jason and David are champion swimmers and represent Kenya in world championships. I have eight first cousins on my mother's side of the family. Abraham died in his Norfolk Hotel in 1965, his widow, Sarah fifteen years later.

BIBLIOGRAPHY

Block, Doria, *Notes Taken from Abraham Lazarus Block*.

Cocker, Mark *Richard Meinertzhagan* (Mandarin, London, 1990)

Fox, James, *White Mischief* (Penguin Books 1982)

Haller, Lily Block, *Memoirs* (unpublished typescript written in the 1040s and partially serialized in the East African Standard kindly provided by Lily's daughter-in-law, Iris Haller.

Hemsing, Jan *Then and Now Nairobi's Norfolk Hotel* (Sealpoint Publicity Nairobi, 1982)

Hirshfeld, Ora *Spring in Eternity* A family Saga (Docostory, Israel, 2006)

Huxley, Elspeth, *White Man's Country* (Chatto and Windus, London, 1935) and *Nine Faces of Kenya* (HarperCollins, London 1991)

Markus, Otto, *Unpublished Memoirs* supplied by Markus's granddaughter, Eve Pollecoff.

Meinertzhagen, Richard, *Kenya Diary (1902-1906)* (Eland Books, London, 1957)

Miller, Charles, *The Lunatic Express* (Macmillan, New York, 1971; Ballantine ed., 1973)

Paice, Edward, *Lost Lion of Empire* (HarperCollins, London, 2001)

Salvadori, Cynthia *Glimpses of the Jews of Kenya 1904-2004* The Nairobi Congregation 2004

Trzebinski, Errol, *The Kenya Pioneers* (Heinemann, London, 1985)

Under His Wings

1 The Kaddish is the Jewish mourner's prayer.

Chapter 1

1 Shtetles were small towns (typically around 1,000 people) usually centered on a synagogue and marketplace, within the Pale of Jewish Settlement.

Chapter 3

1 Kovno (Yid., Kovne or Kovna; Pol., Kowno; Rus., Kovno; Ger., Kovne).
Now known as Kaunas, this is the 2nd largest city in Lithuania. Jewish merchants visited Kaunas in the fifteenth century and some settled there, notably Daniel of Troki in the 1500s. The succeeding centuries were marked by intense competition between Christian and Jewish merchants and were punctuated by periodic expulsions. In 1761, there were violent attacks on Jews and their property, and Jews were once again expelled from the town. Rabbi, Mosheh Soloveichik, responded by suing the municipality before the royal court. From 1864 to 1896, Yitsak Elanan Spektor was rabbi of the community. His enormous erudition was complemented by his leadership skills not only for the community but also for Russian Jewry as a whole. By 1897, 40% of the population of Kovno was Jewish.

2 The word 'pogrom' became linked to anti-Semitic violence after the outbreak of three great waves of anti-Jewish rioting in the Russian Empire in 1881-82, 1903-06, and 1919-21. The violence usually consisted of looting, assault, arson, rape, and murder.

3 *Haskalah* (Hebrew) or Jewish Enlightenment, was a movement among European Jews in the 18th–19th centuries that advocated adopting enlightenment values, pressing for better integration into European society, and increasing education in secular studies, Hebrew language, and Jewish history. *Haskalah* in this sense marked the beginning of the wider engagement of European Jews with the secular world, ultimately resulting in the first Jewish political movements and the struggle for Jewish emancipation.

4 The Peasant Reform of 1861 (also known as the Emancipation Reform) was the first and most important of liberal reforms effected during the reign of Alexander II of Russia and caused 23 million Russian serfs to be granted their liberty.

Chapter 4

1 Vilnius (also known as Vilna and Wilna) is the present capital of Lithuania and is located in the south east of the country. Known as the 'Jerusalem of the North' it was the seat of the Grand dukes of Lithuania and has a venerable Jewish heritage. Its statues, gates, icons and churches are as described.

Chapter 5

1 Birzai: Biržai [Lith], Birzh [Yid], Birzhi [Rus]. Birzai is located 94 km east of Siauliai in NE Lithuania at the confluence of the Apascia and Agluona rivers and along the banks of Lake Siruinis. According to local legend the 20-meter-deep sinkhole known as Karves Ola (Cow's Hole) was discovered by a farmer after his cow disappeared. The local community of Lithuanian Jews, which settled in the Duchy of Biržai at the end of the 16th century, was influential, establishing an interest-free loan society, two major flourmills, and an international linen export business.

2 The name 'Lazarus' is a fiction based on the fact that Ettel called her son Abraham Lazarus. The first names of Mr and Mrs Soltz are not known.

Chapter 7

1 Gilwan was a small Jewish town in the Kovno region not far from Vilnius.

Chapter 10

1 See Lily's Narrative on page 396.

Chapter 11

1 Šalčininkai is a city in Vilnius County, Lithuania; it is situated near the border with Belarus.

Chapter 12

1 Yehuda Lev is a fictitious name since we do not know the name of Lily's so-called admirer, but

his part in her story is given in her narrative on page 396.

Chapter 16

1 There is no evidence to suggest that the Sinson family lived in Leylands but this seems more than probable since it was the Jewish quarter of Leeds and the place to which all immigrants gravitated on arrival as is illustrated by the true story drawn from the West Yorkshire Archives regarding Mr Louis Teeman. He wrote, 'My father left his town, Mariempol, Russia (now in Lithuania, the birthplace of most of the Jews who came to Leeds), to escape conscription. They were taking boys aged 15 and 16 - he was reaching that age and they had to get him away - for the period of army service was as long as 25 years. He and many others crossed the frontier into Prussia at night and made their way to Hamburg. They took the boat to England. The journey was several days - they slept on deck in all sorts of terrible weather, as they didn't have the money to go below - and eventually they reached Hull. At Hull, they were assembled and interrogated. He went on to Leeds, he had been told to as there were Jewish slipper makers there and he might find a job - Leeds was the only word of English he knew. If he found a job then he would make enough money to send for his parents. When the train drew into Leeds, the porters shouted 'Leeds, Leeds!' and of course the doors were thrown open, and a man with a handcart seized the passengers' bundles of belongings. His name was Jimmy Gilmour and he was a fighting Irishman who when drunk used to fight lampposts with his bare fists. He would pile all these bundles on the handcart and take them along Boar Lane to point out the sights. Jimmy was very proud of his knowledge of Yiddish which he'd picked up in Leylands. It was a Sunday and the churchgoers would eye this group of men following a handcart, dressed in Russian peaked caps, long thigh boots and long overcoats to their ankles, very bedraggled after the journey. All of them were unhappy, miserable, and homesick; they would reach Kirkgate and pass the open market and then they were in the Leylands. At last they

recognized something - the smells of fried fish, chicken feathers burning - and Jimmy Gilmour would shout out loud in Yiddish 'mir zanen do' (we are here)! And the doors and windows would fly open; men, women and children would rush out and scan the faces to see if they recognized relatives and friends. My father got a job as a slipper maker, which was his trade. They couldn't find him accommodation so, like many others, he slept under his bench, beneath the treadle machines. People typically lived in tiny houses; many of the rooms were no more than 12 or 14 feet square. They crowded in as many people as possible. They not only let out rooms, they let corners of rooms and in some rooms there were four couples each with a blanket spread over the corner.'

2 Abraham Block did not work for Montague Burton who actually arrived in England at around the same time as he did. However, Burton's Concord Mills dominated the Jewish district of Leylands in Leeds, which was almost certainly where the Sinson family would have lived. Moshe Osinsky was born in Lithuania in 1885, arrived in England in 1900, and built up an empire of 400 shops and factories around Leeds and Sheffield.

Chapter 18

1 Abraham Block worked for Rakusen's, a kosher food manufacturing company that was established in 1900 in Leeds. It was founded by a watchmaker, Lloyd Rakusen, who started baking *matzos* (Passover biscuits) in his own kitchen.

2 Annie, the eldest Block child, was born in 1879 in Gilwan. In 1895 she left for England with the Sinsons and in 1898 she married Nathan Harris in Leeds; they had two children: Elsie Harris and Charles Lewis Harris. Nathan died in 1936 and Annie in 1939. For a brief period of time they lived in Nairobi and ran a second-hand clothes shop in the centre of town, but when Nathan died in Kenya, Elsie took her mother back to Leeds. The story that Annie worked at Rakusen's and that Abraham met Rosie at her house is a fiction.

Chapter 19

1 Abraham Block fell in love with a girl called
Rosie (second name not known) while he was
working for Rakusen's in Leeds. He returned
to Leeds around 1913 to ask her to marry him
and was refused on the grounds that she did
not want to live in Africa. She married a dentist
called Peers (Piers) and Abraham used to visit
her when he went to England, send her flowers
and chocolates. He referred to her as 'my Rosie'.

Chapter 22

1 Eli Mieikus is a fictitious character though Lily
did go to Lida as outlined in her narrative on
page 396.

Chapter 23

1 Abraham is actually believed to have served in a
British commando unit in the Boer War, but no
further information is available.

Chapter 25

1 There is no evidence that Abraham met Ewart
Grogan in South Africa, though both men where
there at around this time. Colonel Ewart Grogan
('Cape to Cairo Grogan') was a gentleman
adventurer famed through the British Empire as
one of the most brilliant and controversial figures
of African colonial history. For the story of his
life read *Lost Lion of Empire* by Edward Paice.

2 This description of the meeting between father
and son is a fiction since no records exist as
to exactly where and when they met in South
Africa. Samuel did, however, have a carpentry/
cabinet-making business and Abraham refers to
schmussing in his own narrative on page 390.

3 Eli Levy is a fictitious character invented to
make the story flow.

4 The Rt. Hon. Joseph Chamberlain (1836-1914)
was the British Colonial Secretary between
1895 and 1903. He made a tour of British East
Africa in early 1903 and suggested on his return
that Theodor Herzl, who was the leader of the
Zionist movement, use an apparently vacant part
of 'Masailand', (the Uasin Gishu Plateau), as a
temporary homeland or 'stepping stone to the
Promised Land' for persecuted Russian Jewry.
The proposal came to be known as the Uganda

Plan (even though the territory in question
was in Kenya). The Zionist Organization, after
some deliberations, rejected the proposal, as
did the British settlers in East Africa. Although
one of the prime movers in the Boer War,
Chamberlain was keen on promoting Anglo-
Afrikaner conciliation and on speeding South
Africa's absorption into the Empire. A passionate
imperialist, Chamberlain believed in the creation
of a federation of Anglo-Saxon nations, which
would be headed by Britain. Convinced that
there was no limit to the extent to which the
British Empire could be extended he was quoted
as having said, 'I believe that the British race is
the greatest of the governing races that the world
has ever seen... It is not enough to occupy great
spaces of the world's surface unless you can make
the best of them. It is the duty of a landlord
to develop his estate.' Chamberlain, known as
Joseph *Africanus*, made two visits to South Africa
and spoke at over 60 gatherings in support of
colonial settlement.

Chapter 27

1 Delagoa Bay is now in Mozambique. Then it
was known as Port Matolla and linked to the
railhead at Lourenco Marques (now Maputo) by
a six-mile private railway.

2 Abraham Block, Isaac Hotz, M.J. London,
Simon Medicks (sometimes spelt Meddicks),
E.N. Moskow and Wolf Sulsky came from South
Africa together on the *Feldmarschall* and landed
in Mombasa in July 1903 – all had heard of the
'Uganda Plan' and came from central European
farming backgrounds. They were granted land
in Molo, Ruiru and Kiambu. London gave up
farming in Rongai to open a grocery shop in
Hardinge Street, Nairobi. Simon Medicks was
born in Poland in 1875 and established the
Machine Metal Works of Nairobi. In 1907 he
set up the E.A. Tank and Metal Works with
Michael Harrtz. Simon Medicks also built the
Theatre Royal, which was listed in 1919 as one
of only two theatres in Nairobi.

3 McJohn was an Armenian Jew who was the
manager of Smith Mackenzie, a major European
trading company. He ran a small bar with a
couple of rooms near the Cecil Hotel.

Chapter 28

1 There were only three hotels in Mombasa, the Grand Hotel in MacDonald Terrace, the Cecil, almost next door, and The Africa, which was in Vasco da Gama Street. The Grand Hotel was built in 1899 and run by Mr G. Anderson, his Belgian wife and their German friend, Rudolf Mayer, as described.

2 Otto Markus arrived with his friend Rudly Lowy (anglicised to Rudolph Loy) in 1903 and their history is as stated. Loy walked to the West Coast of Africa and back. The journey took 24 months. Messrs Loy and Markus established the East Africa Trading Company in Mombasa in 1903 and had branches in Entebbe and Uganda. They dealt in ivory, hides, skins, rubber and oil seeds. In 1914 Markus, as Austrian Consul, was repatriated to Vienna and Loy was sent to internment camp in India. Their company was taken over by its English employees who later changed its name. Markus and Loy returned to East Africa in 1922/23 and re-founded the company, which was now named The Old East Africa Trading Company.

Chapter 29

1 Henry Du Pré Labouchère (1831-1912) was an English politician, writer and publisher whose journal *The Truth* was severely critical of colonialism in general and the Uganda Railway in particular.

2 The Uganda Railway (also known as the 'Lunatic Line' and the Kenya Railway) left Mombasa twice weekly at noon and the 327-mile journey to Nairobi took anything from twenty-four to thirty-six hours. The roofs of the coaches, which carried four passengers (bed linen not provided), were prone to leakage; the carriages shook to such an extent that all were advised to remove their false teeth for the journey; and sparks from the engine and red dust from the surrounding countryside poured in through the windows and doors. A lady called Daisy Pitt is recorded as throwing her dusty clothes out of the window of the train in 1910 - see *The Kenya Pioneers* by Errol Trzebinski. The train stopped for meals at corrugated iron *dak* bungalows operated by a Goan contractor, Mr J.A. Nazareth, where 'revolting meals' of soup, stringy goat and tinned beef or salmon would be served accompanied by tepid beer. Markus and Loy were on a train when its boiler was punctured by a charging rhino. Sam Pike, one of the engine drivers used to halt between stations and walk back along the line and demand a whisky. Unusual pets were common – monkeys young gazelle, mongooses, tame baby leopards or young lions. The railway carried domestic livestock exotic trophies, rhino horns and elephants' feet and all manner of skins.

Chapter 30

1 T.A. 'Tommy Wood' came from Sheffield, a steel-town in Yorkshire, Britain. He spent eleven years in South Africa before coming to Nairobi in 1900. He became the undisputed leader of the commercial sector, founded the Colonists' Association and was Nairobi's first Mayor. Abraham Block stayed with him on arrival and became his friend. The Victoria Hotel stood on Victoria Street and is described by Abraham in his narrative on page 390. It was a flimsy structure of corrugated iron and wood on stilts with nothing but cloth for its internal partitions while its sanitation system consisted of 'a bucket and the great outdoors'. Dinner usually consisted of tins of pickled herring. Tommy Wood was enterprising and liked to sit on committees, he ran the first post office and his safe, in the early years, was the only bank in town. Tommy Wood quarrelled with Mayence Bent causing her to set up the Stanley Hotel. By 1903 Wood's Hotel (as it was known) had four rooms a butcher's shop and a tailor's; the dining room seated twelve. From its back veranda the mountain Ol Donyo Sabuk could be seen and tame gazelles came to be fed. Tommy Wood was known as *Wataka Nini* (meaning 'what do you want?') for the reasons stated. Tommy acted as auctioneer and when the first land sales were held the whole of central Nairobi could have been bought for five hundred pounds, yet not a single plot was sold because everyone believed that a more favourable location would be chosen for the capital. Tommy did hang out a sign reading 'East Africa may be Jewed but you will not if you deal with T.A.

Wood'. Protest meetings were held at his hotel and he did indeed say, 'the British taxpayers want people to settle who will give a return on the money invested. How can they expect this if they located possibly the lowest class of white men in the heart of the country?'

2 Indian rupees were the principal medium of exchange in British East Africa. In 1921 the East African shilling replaced the East African florin. The EA shilling was used until September 1966 when it was replaced by the Kenya shilling.

3 Mayence Woodbury/Tate/Bent. Mayence Woodbury is thought to have been born in 1872 and has been variously described as being Belgian American and British. She was actually the daughter of Walter Bentley Woodbury (1834-1885), an inventor and pioneering English photographer who worked in Australia and the Dutch East Indies. His two youngest children were called Fayence and Mayence. She is thought to have been the common-law wife of W.S. Bent, a railway engineer, and arrived with him from Nigeria in 1900 (some accounts say 1898). She married Fred Tate in 1909. Mayence Bent ran the millinery department of Tommy Wood's shop but quarrelled with him and set up the Hotel Stanley. In 1905 when fire broke out she was seen dropping her new enamel chamber pots one by one into the street rather than give them up the fire.

Chapter 31

1 A.M. Jeevanjee was a wealthy ship-owner (as described by Tommy Wood) who headed a firm of contactors and general merchants. A member of Nairobi's Bhora community (a Shi'ite sect of western India retaining some Hindu beliefs) he cut a graceful eastern figure with his grey beard and golden turban and was always clad in immaculate white. A keen racing enthusiast, his was the first horse to win at Nairobi Racecourse in 1903. His family set up Jeevanjee Market in 1906 and he presented Nairobi with Jeevanjee Gardens complete with a statue of Queen Victoria. He and his fellow members of the Indian community (such as Messrs Suleman, Virjee and Alibhai Sharif) built many of the Parklands villas, all of which featured

balustrades, columns and ornate plasterwork; and many of which were painted in fondant colours 'like heavily iced cakes'.

2 Hugh Cholmondeley, Third Baron Delamere, (1870-1931) reached the future Kenya in 1897 after a two-year trek from Berbera in Somalia. Six years later he returned to become the country's boldest and most influential rancher, and the political leader of the white settlers. In 1904 he was living on Equator ranch which is described as 'grass huts surrounded by a corrugated iron *boma* into which cattle were driven every night. There were no proper doors or windows to the grass huts so that at night the cows were liable to poke their heads through the apertures and breathe heavily in your face. He built a little wooden hut for Lady Delamere. Inside the floors were made of earth uncovered and largely unlevelled. Some good furniture had been imported from England and fine mahogany sideboards and valuable oak tallboys stood at drunken angles on the uneven floor around the walls of the huts.' Delamere was never without an enormous sun helmet, the biggest ever seen in East Africa, which practically obscured his face and dwarfed his slight figure. He wore his ginger hair unusually long to protect against the sun on his neck and allowed it to hang down almost to is shoulders. He generally dressed in an old pair of khaki breeches and a woolly cardigan. His theory of agriculture was that ploughing should be done in the cold of the early morning before sunrise so he got up at 4am, breakfasted on gazelle chops by the light of a hurricane lamp to the accompaniment of his favourite tune played constantly on the gramophone 'All Aboard for Margate'. His raffish guise caused many a new arrival in the Protectorate to mistake him for a tramp. But never for long: he exuded a natural authority which was backed up by a very quick and often violent temper, a propensity to alternate unpredictably between exquisite charm and biting sarcasm and a pair of piercing blue eyes. He was known as 'D'. For full details on his life *White Man's Country, Lord Delamere and the Making of Kenya* by Elspeth Huxley.

Chapter 32

1 Ali Khan was a Pathan horse-dealer who ran the Nairobi horse-drawn taxi service. He sported a huge whip, breaches and gaiters and rode around wearing blue glasses. *'Mr Aly Khan whose mule buggies used to meet all the trains rested the animals outside the white picket fence of the Norfolk and became himself very much part of the Norfolk picture. His Livery Stables were in Market Street and he was always clad in riding breeches and gaiters and brandishing an immense riding whip.'* (Jan Hemsing).

2 Tom Deacon owned land near Donyo Sabuk, which he acquired through settlement of a gambling debt. He raised pigs but they died of swine fever, he experimented with wheat but it failed; he planted coffee but it did not produce a yield until five years later. Ultimately his farm became one of the finest plantations in the country and, after Independence, became the property of the late President Kenyatta.

3 Frank Greswold Williams was an Englishman who had lost an eye in an accident caused by a defective gun. He had a thousand head of cattle on a farm called Knightwyck and was a racing enthusiast. He was one of the Happy Valley crowd and supplied them with the fashionable drugs of the day, cocaine and morphine, which he obtained from Port Said and plied openly at the Muthaiga Club in the 1940s.

4 Herbert Binks was a chemist who came to East Africa when his proposal of marriage was rejected. He was a farmer, prospector, hunter, contractor, astronomer and photographer (and a builder of planes and tin windmills). It was Binks who arrived at Nairobi Station and asked 'How far is the town?' and was told 'This is the town.'

Chapter 33

1 Reginald Barton Wright was employed as a surveyor on the Uganda Railway (Lunatic Express/Kenya Railway). He became Acting Land Officer in 1903 and Official Land Officer in 1906. His red three-wheeler car was one of the first to arrive in Nairobi.

2 John Ainsworth (known as Johnny Gumtree) was one of Her Majesty's Vice-Consuls before he was made Sub-Commission of Ukamba, Machakos. He came to Nairobi in 1889 and built an office by the Nairobi River (a tin shack with a flag pole with a Union Jack that was lowered at sunset as described). He built Ainsworth's Bridge in 1900 and it was washed away twice. The Secretary of the Agricultural Society he had a garden of exotic shrubs that attracted thousands of butterflies and he planted blue gums (imported from Australia) all over Nairobi.

Chapter 34

1 Sir Charles Norton Edgecumbe Eliot (1862-1931) was a British knight diplomat, colonial administrator and botanist. He served as Commissioner of British East Africa in 1900-1904. He encouraged European immigration into BEA by the wholesale award of land concessions to European settlers. By 1903 he was encountering opposition from the Colonial Office, which felt he was proceeding too rapidly. In 1904, after being criticized for granting a concession on land previously reserved for the indigenous Maasai people, he resigned his position. He was dubbed 'the Great Sea Slug' by Ewart Grogan. He spoke 24 languages, read Chinese verse in the evenings and was the world's leading authority on the sea slug (Nudibranchiates). He was succeeded by Sir Donald Stewart who was known as a hard drinker with little interest in BEA.

2 This speech actually derives from a statement made by Abraham Block in later life. He said: 'What will maintain the prosperity and dignity of this Colony? Nothing. The prosperity is false; it is based on false economy. And nothing but the feeling of adventure had enabled this colony to weather many a crisis. If you don't have that feeling of personal risk and the joy of adventure, but have a moneymaking philosophy then this colony will be a flop. If a man comes here with a cheque of 20,000 pounds and expects a safe return he is a dangerous man to the country. If a man comes with 2,000 and the determination that nothing on God's green earth is going to drive him out of Kenya, than that's the man we want. We want the plugger, the sticker. They're

the men who made Kenya.'

3 The East Africa Land Order Council was set up in 1901 and allocated land as indicated. Charles Harries walked 400 miles before applying for land at Thika and Naivasha. A.C. Hoey covered a thousand miles before applying for land on the Loita Plains.

4 A man called Ortlipp, who worked for the Land Office, was drowned while crossing the Morendat River and his papers were taken by a python – the accident caused severe delays in the Land Office.

Chapter 35

1 E.W. Kreiger was an American missionary who raised pigs and cured pork for bacon at Kiambu; Abraham Block bought a butchery from him.

2 William Northrup McMillan was born in St Louis, USA and first came to Africa in 1901. He travelled down the Nile by steamer, by camel and on foot with Charles Bulpett and John Destro.

In 1904 he decided to settle in Kenya. He served as a major in the East African Campaign and made his Nairobi house and his upcountry estate into convalescent homes in the First World War. He was knighted in recognition of his war efforts in January 1918. He died and was buried as described. Alongside his grave are those of Louise Decker, (Lady Lucie McMillan's maid) and McMillan's dog. He weighed over twenty stone and had to have special cars made for him.

Chapter 36

1 W.S. Bent (William Stanley) was born in Lancashire in 1858 and was employed on the Nigeria Railway. Mayence Bent was his common-law wife. He was Chief Clerk in the Locomotive Department of the Uganda Railway and President of the 'Railway Strike Committee' in Nairobi in 1900. He won a prize from Lord Delamere for a political essay he wrote. He was recorded as living at Fort Smith with his 'wife' and daughter Gladys (born 1897). According to the EA Handbook he died in 1918.

2 James Ignacious Marcus. Mr J. Marcus, as he was known, was a Rumanian Jew, the first Jew to arrive in British East Africa (from India) in

1901. He supplied the early East African farmers with their requirements and exported local produce, mostly potatoes, trading as Marcus Tate and Co. His business premises were situated in Government Road. His advert in the paper read: 'J. Marcus, Produce Merchant. Importer of all well known makes of agricultural implements and machinery, spring waggons, light traps and transport waggons. Commissions of all kinds undertaken locally and abroad. Ostrich feathers bought and sold.' He eventually became an estate agent and auctioneer. Mr Marcus sold Abraham Block his first plough and gave him a monthly allowance of 100 Rupees from Lord Delamere. This meeting is described in Abraham Block's own narrative on page 390.

Chapter 37

1 Richard Meinertzhagen arrived in British East Africa in 1902 and was a Lieutenant with the First Battalion of the Royal Fusiliers. He wrote in his diary, 'I met Mr Block this morning recently arrived from South Africa and exploring the possibilities of making his fortune in this country. Being a Jew I think it more than likely he will succeed, as he seems full of ideas. He asked my advice and I told him I though that most money could be made from land speculation, to this he replied that he had little cash - twenty pounds, a pony and a sack of potations. I advised him to borrow from the bank and apply for land. I liked him, for he was full of enthusiasm. (Meinertzhagen's diary 1957). Meinertzhagen also said, 'Tate tells me there is a plan on foot to offer the Jews a home on the Uasin Gishu Plateau. I hope they refuse it, for it is just asking for trouble. In the first place, the Jew's home is in Palestine, not in Africa. The scheme would only add to political confusion, and God knows there will be enough trouble here in 50 years when the natives get educated. (Meinertzhagen's *Kenya Diary* (1902-1906)).

2 Dr Ufferman and Mr Lauterbach alerted Block to the fact that a man called Corran (also spelt Corren) had put the disposal of the 640-acre farm, 'Njuna', in their hands and left the country. See Abraham Block's narrative page

390. Half of Njuna was sold in 1908 for one pound per acre and divided into three farms. Later it was developed and renamed Kamundu Estate. In 1911 Abraham formed the Kamunyo Syndicate (comprising Captain Montague, Mr Price Williams and The Forbes Brothers) and the syndicate purchased the Kamunyo Estate (the remaining half of Njuna) calling it 'Kathpat'; they then developed it into one of Kenya's first coffee farms. (The first coffee originated from Kohn Patterson at Kibwezi whose first crop fetched ninety shillings per hundredweight in Europe in 1896). The land was later sold to Azama Ltd in 1921 and taken over by the Krags in 1960.

3 Abraham sold his ponies to 'Bano' Niverson (his narrative reads 'Mr Lashington' but this is probably how the name sounded to Doria Block during the interview) for a thousand rupees – almost as much as 'Njuna' had cost, the equivalent of 75 pounds at the time.

Chapter 38

1 According to Errol Trzebinski in *The Kenya Pioneers* such anti-Zionist meetings did take place, the comments described were made, and the advertisement was placed outside Tommy Wood's hotel as described.

Chapter 39

1 W.J. King was the first agent for the first crop of potatoes that were dispatched to South Africa; they rotted enroute due to having been placed too close to the boiler and were unsaleable.

2 The letter from Rosie is a fiction though Rosie and Abraham undoubtedly kept in touch since he later returned to Leeds eleven years after he had left with the sole intention of asking her to marry him. The story of Rosie marrying Mr Rakusen is a fiction invented to account for the eleven years that elapsed between Abraham leaving and returning to Leeds.

Chapter 40

1 The opening of the Jeevanjee Gardens took place in March 1906 as described (including the cloaking of the Maasai warrior with the tablecloth).

2 *Duka* is the Swahili word for 'shop'.

3 Dr Rosendo Ayres Ribeiro arrived in Nairobi in 1900 and was the infant town's first private medical practitioner. He came from Goa, wore a Stetson, was very plump, and rode a tame zebra.

4 Gailey and Roberts was founded in 1904 by J.H. Gailey and D.O. Roberts both surveyors on the railway. By 1925 it had expanded rapidly to establish five branches across the country and was appointed the Caterpillar Dealer for East Africa. Abraham Block purchased the company in 1930. It was sold to the United Africa Company (part of the Unilever Group) in 1937.

5 A.B. McDonnell was the first man to plant tea in Limuru. He employed young boys to push and pull him as described and often dismantled his bicycle and swam it across rivers as described.

6 Randall Swift and Ernest Rutherfoord reduced the exertion of 46-mile walk from Kamuyu to Nairobi by sharing a bicycle in the manner described. Rutherfoord was known to the Africans as 'Kiama' meaning 'very young' because he took his physical condition seriously and used to carry a bag of maize on his back and one under each arm to improve his stamina.

Chapter 41

1 A considerable liberty has been taken with the name of Major Ringer, who actually left British East Africa in 1910 and drowned in Bournemouth in 1912. Major Charles Harding Newman was born in England in 1860 and arrived in British East Africa in 1903. Ringer and his partner R. Aylmer Winearls opened the Norfolk Hotel on Christmas Day 1904 (and an elephant was shot during the laying of the foundation stone). It was Winearls who nailed up the door of the widow of the Indian civil servant. Major Ringer had a farm 30 miles from Nairobi at the foothills of Ol Donyo Sabuk where he kept a string of prize racehorses. Prior to his arrival in Kenya he had fought in Nigeria and told 'bloodthirsty stories. He also (according to Jan Hemsing in her book, *Then and Now Nairobi's Norfolk Hotel,*) had a small ivory fetish called a Juju that he had taken from a witch doctor. Major Ringer called his farm Juju and Northrup McMillan, his neighbour,

called his farm Juja for the reasons described. Major Ringer sold the Norfolk Hotel to the East Africa and Uganda Corporation in 1910 and left British East Africa. He drowned in a yachting accident in Bournemouth in 1912.

2 Dr John Gilks kept a tame leopard, which he took with him on his visits. It was called Starpit – dubbed by the Africans who heard Dr Gilks saying, 'Stop it, stop it' to it. One patient claims she was cured by sheer fright when the leopard came in behind the doctor and leapt straight on top of her in bed.

Chapter 43

1 Abraham is actually believed to have sold Samuel's gold watch in order to put down a deposit on his first farm.

Chapter 44

1 Fred Tate worked at the Railway Institute in Nairobi. He married Mayence Bent in 1909 in Zanzibar. The announcement published in The Leader read 'The marriage of Miss Mayence Woodbury with Mr Fred Tate was celebrated.' suggesting that she was not married to W.S. Bent. Fred bid for two plots at public action in 1912 as described. Fred died in 1937.

1 Ben 'Fatty' Garland was an experimental maize farmer while Fred Raper founded Nairobi's best saddlers, Raper and Pringle. Garland and Raper, both friends of Abraham Block, financed the purchase of the Ugandan cattle, which took place roughly as described. Block also met up with them in Nakuru to share the profits. Fatty Garland weighed over twenty stone and was a heavy drinker. The Africans called him *Tumbo* (the stomach). Block and Garland went into partnership and were caught and jailed for breaking East Coast Fever quarantine regulations. Garland also farmed in the Nakuru area.

3 The Lady Abambara is a fiction, as is this entire chapter. Abraham Block did, however, journey to Uganda to purchase Ankole cattle as described in his memoirs.

Chapter 45

1 The Nakuru Hotel was actually called The

Railway, and was later bought by Abraham Block. He later exchanged it as part of a property deal (the Railway Hotel and the sum of two thousand pounds in exchange for the coffee estate known as Samuru).

Chapter 47

1 Simon Haller arrived in Nairobi from Poltava in the Ukraine in 1903 (some accounts suggest 1906) via South Africa (where he humped carcasses like Abraham Block) and bought a farm in Ruiru. Lily Block married Simon Haller in 1913 and they bought a farm of 560- acres in Kiambu. Prior to this time he was engaged to marry Miss Rosenblum. Simon's nephews Chaim, Eddie, Aaron and David Ruben (the sons of his sister) came from the Ukraine to join him in 1912. Simon was conscripted into the army in 1916. He also had a workshop in Nairobi and made the first tin bath and water tanks.

2 John Rifkin was a Jewish refugee from Russia who arrived around the same time as Abraham and his friends. He worked with Michael Harrtz and was a farrier and a tinsmith. It was from John Rifkin that Eddie Ruben bought his first mules.

Chapter 48

1 Ostrich farming was widely practised in 1907 by all the people mentioned and with all the results indicated.

2 Victor Newland and Leslie Tarlton were settlers from Australia who founded a safari outfitting and land agency business in 1904. Lionel Tarlton, Leslie's son, was killed in the East Africa campaign of the First World War.

3 David Tulipman was the brother of Sarah Tulipman and he worked as an accountant for Newland and Tarlton, the safari outfitters. He married Shifra Singer in Cairo and they had three children. He was murdered in his orange grove in 1936.

4 William Judd was a hunter with Newland and Tarlton who also conducted a private safari for William Northrup McMillan as described. Garland and Block used Billy Judd's farm as a staging post for their cattle trading.

Chapter 49

1 The Hon. Denys George Finch Hatton (1887–1931) arrived in BEA in 1910 and bought land in the Great Rift Valley but spent most of his time hunting. He met Baroness Blixen in 1918 and had a close relationship with her. In 1925 he moved into her house in Karen and began leading safaris for wealthy sportsmen. He was killed in a flying accident over Voi in 1931. There is no record of Abraham Block ever having worked for Denys Finch Hatton. However, Abraham's own memoirs state that he was employed as an assistant to many 'white hunters' between the years of 1911 and 1913 and during this time Newland and Tarlton were the largest and most famous safari outfitters in Nairobi. They also listed Denys Finch Hatton as one of their hunters; while David Tulipman, Abraham's friend and (later) brother-in-law was employed as an accountant by them. Denys Finch Hatton was also a friend of Delamere's and traded regularly in cattle.

Chapter 50

1 Eddie, Archie, Charlie and David Ruben joined their Uncle, Simon Haller, at Kiambu in 1912 just after he became engaged to Lily Block. They came from the Ukraine and helped him on the farm.

Chapter 51

1 Abraham did not actually meet David Tulipman in Constantinople, though it was in this city that he decided to go to Palestine. See Ora Hirshfeld's narrative on page 403.

Chapter 52

1 Alexander and Batsheva Tulipman lived in Rishon Le Zion as described. They had five daughters (Rivka, Sarah, Rachel, Hannah and Leah) and one son, David (Jack, after whom Jack Block was named, died at the age of 4). The story of Abraham's desire to marry Rachel rather Sarah is drawn from Block family lore.

Chapter 56

1 According to Errol Trzebinski, 'the settlers not knowing where to go upon the outbreak of War rushed to the Norfolk but reconvened immediately at Nairobi House, which was the main recruiting office.'

2 According to Errol Trzebinski Abraham joined the Legion of Frontier's Men though his own narrative mentions the East African Mounted Rifles.

3 The phrase the 'Ice Cream War' was drawn, by William Boyd in his book, *An Ice-Cream War*, from the letters of Francis Harold Burgess, East African Railway Volunteer Force to his sister, Mrs Arthur Lamont in October, 1914. Mr Burgess said, 'Lt Col. Stordy says the war here will only last two months. It is far too hot for sustained fighting, he says, we will all melt like ice-cream in the sun!'

4 Paul Emil von Lettow-Vorbeck (1870 –1964) was a general in the Imperial German Army and the commander of its forces in the German East Africa campaign. For four years, with a force that never exceeded about 14,000 (3,000 Germans and 11,000 Africans), he held in check a much larger force of 300,000 British, Belgian, and Portuguese troops. Essentially undefeated in the field, von Lettow-Vorbeck was the only German commander to successfully invade imperial British soil during World War I. His exploits in the campaign have come down 'as the greatest single guerrilla operation in history, and the most successful.'

Chapter 59

1 *Bwana* means 'Sir' in Swahili and *'Memsahib'*, Madam.

2 Granny Shelton was the midwife who delivered Rita, Jack and Tubby. She was also a teacher and later the Head Teacher at the Little Parklands School, which they attended.

3 Dr Roland Wilks Burkitt, known as 'kill or cure Burkitt' was an Irish doctor who had a surgery in Nairobi in 1911 and delivered all of Sarah Block's children. He was a friend of Denys Finch Hatton and it was thanks to Dr Burkitt that Abraham Block was moved from Mombasa to Nairobi at the end of the war. He was famous for his 'cold cure' and his black water fever cure; and the stories/descriptions regarding him are drawn from *Nine Faces of Kenya* by Elspeth Huxley and

The Kenya Pioneers by Errol Trzebinski.

Chapter 61

1 It was not actually Eddie Ruben who escorted Sarah to Kampala to visit Dr Cook but Jack Katzler, who was one of Eddie's friends.
2 Michael Harrtz arrived in Nairobi in 1901 from Russia. He was the second Jew to arrive after Mr J. Marcus. He established a tinsmith business in Hardinge Street; it was later known as Haartz and Bell. He married Gertie, who died in Nairobi in 1925. Gertie Harrtz and Sarah Block were close friends and ran a small dairy business during the war years.
3 Tom Bell worked for Michael Harrtz and it is thanks to he and Dr Burkitt that Abraham was moved up-country in 1917.

Chapter 64

1 The McMillans did turn both their Nairobi house and their Ol Donyo Sabuk house into convalescent homes during the War – but we have no evidence that Abraham Block went to either of them to convalesce. The military hospital in Nairobi, however, was hopelessly oversubscribed, under canvas and the tents pitched on the outer slopes of Nairobi cemetery – so it is not beyond the bounds of possibility that Dr Burkitt would have sent Abraham to convalesce at McMillan's Ol Donyo Sabuk House.
2 William Northrup McMillan was knighted in January 1918, so throughout the War years he did not have a title.
3 Louise Decker was Lucie McMillan's maid and came with her from America. She was the daughter of an African slave. She is buried alongside McMillan on Ol Donyo Sabuk. According to Errol Trzebinski, she was of German nationality.

Chapter 65

1 Charles Bulpett lived with the McMillans and was known as 'Uncle'. Something of a colourful figure, he claimed that a famous courtesan 'La Bell Otero' had ruined him. He was also famous for having swum across the Thames at Greenwich in a top hat.

2 John Destro came from Venice; he travelled down the Nile with Northrup McMillan and became his farm manager. He went into partnership with Abraham Block in the Villa Franca dairy in Nairobi.

Chapter 66

1 Samuel Block did return to South Africa and marry a Cape Dutch matron but there is no evidence to suggest that he had any relationship with her or anyone else prior to Ettel's arrival. He was, however, without his wife from 1892, when he left Russia, until 1908 when Ettel arrived in Kenya.

Chapter 67

1 An *ayah* is a nursemaid or a nanny in Swahili.
2 Simon and Lily Haller did run a convalescent home on one of their farms and it was here that Freda met Morris Kirkel (1895-1945). History suggests, however, that he had small pox and that Freda also caught it; both however recovered and then married.

Chapter 68

1 Around 1919, The Block family lived (for around three years) in the Kabete area of Nairobi where they ran the Devonshire Dairy with the help of two labourers to care for the cows. Abraham delivered milk around Nairobi in old whisky bottles for which he had paid 2 cents each. He delivered milk from door to door, using his mule-cart, and charged 20 cents a bottle. Sarah often accompanied him on his rounds, as did the children.

Chapter 69

1 Edward Abraham Ruben arrived in Kenya 1912. He was born in Poltava, Ukraine in 1896 and served through both world wars. He lied about his age to join up in the First World War. In the 2nd World War he was a Major with the RASC (Royal Army Service Corps). Eddie worked with oxen and mules in the War. When it ended he bought a couple of mules and carts and founded Express Transport in 1918. Later eight mules were acquired at a local auction and the town blacksmith John Rifkin produced some mule

carts. In 1919 Jack Katzler joined the Ruben Brothers and they added & Co to their name. The story of the mules being harnessed is true. The name Express Transport came into being in 1921. Eddie Ruben kept in touch with Ruth Block throughout the war years and according to family lore – the reason for Tubby being officially called Eddie Ruben Block is as stated.

Chapter 70

1 Abraham later sold 4,000 acres of his Elmenteita holdings to Mr 'Black' Harries for one pound an acre.

Chapter 71

1 The Blocks lived next door to the Aga Khan's property in Nairobi for many years. Ruth played with the little princes and Jack had his 21st birthday party at this house.

2 Sammy Jacobs and his wife Gertie arrived in 1906 from South Africa (where he had been employed by the East African Standard) and took up farming near Thika. Later they opened a general store - the famous 'Dustpan' emporium in Nairobi (S. Jacobs Ltd), which traded in 'carpets linos, upstairs furniture and mattresses, drapery haberdashery'. Later branches were opened in Eldoret, Mombasa and Nakuru; and the wives and daughters of Jewish families worked in his shops. Part of his Nairobi shop was a butchery, which was run by Abraham Block. Later, Abraham bought out Sammy Jacobs.

3 Abraham Block purchased the company Rosenblum Bullows and Roy from Fred Roy and Frank Bullows in 1928. Hitherto it had been known as Bullows and Roy but he changed the name to include that of Rosenblum. Rosenblum was a hardware store set up for Africans in 1907. Later it was managed by Abraham Block and finally bought out by him when, in 1925, it perished in a Nairobi fire. In the slump of the early 1930s, Block sold Rosenblum Bullows and Roy to the United Africa Company, but remained with them as its manager. It was whilst he was managing the company that he purchased Gailey and Roberts on United Africa's behalf and the transaction was so successful that

in 1930 it also garnered the Caterpillar franchise for the company. At this point, Abraham formed African Representatives Ltd, a small firm that originally distributed Lever Brothers products in Africa and went on to become the giant East African Industries. S. Rosenblum arrived in Nairobi in 1906 and went into partnership with Abraham Block on his first farm. His sister, Bertha, was a friend of Lily Block and went to live with Samuel and Lily on their farm in Kiambu. It was to Bertha that Simon Haller was engaged before he met Lily, at which point the engagement was broken off.

Chapter 72

1 G.H Goldfinch was a whipper-in with the Masara Hounds (which hunted pigs and other game outside Nairobi) and this story is recounted in *The Kenyan Pioneers* by Errol Trzebinski.

2 This event actually took place in Nakuru and is recounted in *Nine Faces of Kenya* by Elspeth Huxley.

3 Mr W.J.E. Edgley bought the Norfolk hotel in 1923 for the sum of 150,000 Rupees. He had previously managed it for around ten years for the East Africa and Uganda Corporation, who took it over from Major Ringer. Mr Edgley was a speculator and a pioneer of East African Breweries. He was described as, 'a vehement, pugnacious man, who always believed that right was on his side.' It was he who was shut in the meat safe by Lord Delamere.

Chapter 73

1 Karen Blixen arrived in British East Africa from Denmark in 1914 and went bankrupt in 1931 after spending 17 years trying to grow coffee.

2 Sir William Northrup McMillan was in the habit of holding parties on the summit of Ol Donyo Sabuk and he was buried there as described. The presence of Denys Finch Hatton, Baroness Blixen, Abraham Block and Eddie Ruben and his mules, however, are all additions that may or may not be true.

Chapter 75

1 Ewart Grogan opened the Torr's Hotel in

1928. It was known as 'Tart's Hotel' and had five stories and towered over the Theatre Royal next door. Grogan determined to make it the 'Carlton of East Africa' and imported a five-man jazz band from London. It was the first hotel in Africa to offer dancing every night.

2 Abraham Block bought the Norfolk Hotel from Mr Edgley in 1927 for 28,000 pounds and a plot on Delamere Avenue (now Kenyatta Avenue).

Chapter 77

1 According to Errol Trzebinski, 'Once Muthaiga Club opened in January 1914 both Denys Finch Hatton and Delamere based themselves there and not at the Norfolk any longer.

Chapter 79

1 Jack (Jacob) Block was born in 1916 and was schooled at Parklands School, Hospital Hill School and Kenton College in Nairobi. Later he attended Loughborough College in England. Tubby Block was born in 1919 and went to Parklands School and Hospital Hill School before attending preparatory school in Brighton and Loughborough College in 1929.

Chapter 80

1 Denys Finch Hatton died when his Gypsy Moth crashed in the Mwakangale Hills at Voi on 14th May 1931.

2 There is no record that Sarah and Abraham did or did not attend the funeral of Denys Finch Hatton who was buried as described.

3 Lord Delamere died on November 13th 1931 and he was buried on his Soysambu Estate (on a rocky knoll above Lake Elmenteita). His funeral was attended by a great diversity of people as described.

Chapter 81

1 Lord Delamere did have his own chair on the terrace, but it was the restaurant and the bar that were actually named after him.

Chapter 82

1 Yakov (Jacob) Block (1911-1991) was the son of Tzvi Hirshfeld and Bracha Krichevsky, Tzvi

originated in Lithuania, Bracha was of a Hassidic Jewish family (originally from Smolensk in today's Belarus) living in Rishon Le Zion. Yakov was brought up in Rishon and educated at the Mikve Israel Agricultural College. He met Rita at a party in Rishon and the two were married in Rishon Le Zion in 1937.

2 According to Ruth Rabb, Abraham did attend the marriage of Rita and Jacob in Rishon Le Zion.

Chapter 85

1 The Plough Settlement Association was formed by Abraham Block in London in 1938. Selected refugees were sent on agricultural courses in Europe. European farmers in Kenya were paid ten pounds a month for every male refugee they employed as a trainee. 1938 the Kenya Jewish Relief Committee was formed to deal with refugee settlers and Abraham Block sat on the committee.

Chapter 86

1 Rosh Hashanah is the Jewish New Year and is a two-day celebration that typically begins on the evening before. Rosh Hashanah meals usually include apples, honey, whole fish, pomegranates, dates, black-eyed peas, pumpkin pastries leek fritters, challah bread and stuffed vegetables.

Chapter 87

1 The story of Ruth and Sol's meeting is a complete fiction since Ruth herself can hardly remember the exact details of the events (though she did mention that there was no shoe involved and that the house in question did not have any stairs). They did, however, meet on the occasion of Rosh Hashanah as recounted.

2 Sol Rabb was born Solomon Rabinowitz in 1920 in South Africa. Haim (Chaim) and Solomon Rabinowitz (twins) came with the South African forces and enjoyed dinner on Rosh Hashanah in 1940 with the Blocks as described. Sol married Ruth in 1948. The couple had three children; Leigh, born in 1950, Geraldine born in 1951, and Nicholas born in 1955. Sol, a chartered accountant, was the Chief Accountant for Block Hotels for many years; he died in 2009.

Ruth lives in the Fairseat Retirement Home in Nairobi. Leigh is a paediatrician, he married Celia Meecham and they live in the Midlands of the United Kingdom. Geraldine married Martin Dunford and they have a restaurant and tourism business in Nairobi. Nicholas is unmarried and lives in Nairobi.

Chapter 88

1 Tubby served in the 1st East African Light Battery under Commander Wavell and was in command of the 53rd East African Light Battery (on the southern front). Kenya African Rifles (Northern Brigade and Southern) during the 2nd World War and was posted to Burma as described. He was decorated with the Military Cross. The citation reads: Major Eddie Reuben Block. During the period under review from 16th May to 15th August, 1945, this officer commanded his Battery of the East African Field Regiment with outstanding zeal and efficiency. From August to December 1944 during active operations, his Battery was continuously supporting the leading infantry. In order to support the attack by 22 KAR on 25th October, 1944 on KAY RU595962 Major Block crawled to within 20 yards of an enemy bunker and in spite of extreme danger from the fire of the enemy and from rounds of his own guns, ranged his Regiment and coordinated the fire plan with such effect that the attack was a compete success. On the night of 3/4th December, 1944, he crossed the Chindwin with the assault Battalion 34 KAR. On the following days the attack was at first held up by enemy positions on the bare and precipitous hill features surrounding the bridgehead. It was impossibly to observe without exposing himself to the enemy with complete disregard for his own personal safety he carried out numerous shoots. His control of his FOOs and his planning of the fire support for each successive attack made it possible for the infantry to maintain their positions and eventually complete the capture of the bridgehead. These are examples of the unfailing courage, leadership and determination which he has shown at all times whilst serving in this Battery for five years including the campaigns in

Somaliland, Abyssinia and Burma.

2 Mr and Mrs Beiles lived in Crooked Lane, Nairobi until Harry Beiles, who was a chemist, took the family to live in New York in 1938. The couple had two daughters, Doria, born in 1924 and Valerie born in 1932. Harry met Jack Block in the Robins Steamship Line office in New York and again on the subway and invited him to dinner the following day. Jack met Doria in 1944 in Capetown, they were married in 1945. Valerie, Doria's younger sister came out to Kenya several years later.

3 Raoul Israel Massader allegedly came from Rishon Le Zion and was known to have had a 'chocolate and tobacco empire' in the London West End before arriving in British East Africa. According to a 1978 interview with Brian Burrows (one time manager of the Norfolk) Massader was a millionaire and he and Abraham bought a large plot of land now known as Kitisuru and the farm known as Kipipiri together. The partners also bought a coffee estate in the 1950s that they 'split it up into plots now the Bernard and Lavington Estates. Massader, described by Ora Hirshfeld as a 'shady character', fell into debt and nearly bankrupted Abraham, who was forced to cover Massader's debts.

4 Jack never 'worked for' Ker and Downey though he was closely associated with them and later served as Chairman of the company. Donald Ker and Syd Downey founded a safari company in 1945 on their return from the war. Their first office was in the New Stanley Hotel and they acted as safari consultants to some of the most famous films of the time. They included; Metro Goldwyn Mayer's *King Solomon's Mines*, filmed on location in Kenya in 1949, and starring Stewart Granger and Deborah Kerr; Gaumont's *Where no Vultures Fly*, filmed in 1950, and starring Anthony Steele and Dinah Sheridan; Twentieth Century Fox's *The Snows of Kilimanjaro*, filmed in 1951, and starring Gregory Peck, Susan Heyward and Ava Gardner; Metro Goldwyn Mayer's *Mogambo*, filmed on location in Uganda and Tanzania in 1952, and starring Clark Gable, Donald Sinden and Grace Kelly; Gaumont's *The Lion*, filmed in

1960 and starring William Holden and Trevor Howard; Paramount Malabar's *Hatari*, filmed in 1962 on location in Tsavo and Lake Manyara, and starring John Wayne and Elsa Martinelli; Gaumont's *Call me Bwana*, filmed in 1962 and starring Bob Hope and Anita Ekberg; *Sammy Going South*, filmed in 1962 on location in Tanzania, and starring Fergus McLelland, Edward G. Robinson, Constance Cummings and Harry H. Corbett; Mr Moses, filmed in 1964, and starring Robert Mitchum, Carroll Baker and Ian Bannen; *Cowboy in Africa*, shot in 1967, and starring John Mills; *Gilligan's Last Elephant*, filmed in Amboseli in 1968, and starring Stewart Granger; and the multi-award winning *Out of Africa*, filmed in 1985, and starring Robert Redford and Meryl Streep.

Chapter 90

1 David Solomon is a fictitious character but the rest of the story is as recounted by Ruth Rabb.

Chapter 92

1 Tubby Block organized the purchase of Mawingo (for the sum of fifty thousand pounds) in 1949. The Block Family extended the house to become a hotel called The Mount Kenya Inn. In 1959 the film star, William Holden, stayed there with his friends Ray Ryan and Carl Hirshmann and all three men fell in love with the place. They bought the property (the negotiations taking place as described) and turned it into one of the most exclusive clubs in the world, the Mount Kenya Safari Club.